Becoming a Christian

Becoming a Christian

Combining Prior Belief, Evidence, and Will

OLA HÖSSJER

Foreword by J. P. Moreland

WIPF & STOCK · Eugene, Oregon

BECOMING A CHRISTIAN
Combining Prior Belief, Evidence, and Will

Copyright © 2018 Ola Hössjer. All rights reserved. Except for brief quotations in critical publications or reviews, no part of this book may be reproduced in any manner without prior written permission from the publisher. Write: Permissions, Wipf and Stock Publishers, 199 W. 8th Ave., Suite 3, Eugene, OR 97401.

Wipf & Stock
An Imprint of Wipf and Stock Publishers
199 W. 8th Ave., Suite 3
Eugene, OR 97401

www.wipfandstock.com

PAPERBACK ISBN: 978-1-5326-1977-9
HARDCOVER ISBN: 978-1-4982-4633-0
EBOOK ISBN: 978-1-4982-4632-3

Manufactured in the U.S.A.   MARCH 20, 2020

Bible quotations are from the New International Version,® copyright © 2011 by Biblica, Inc.™ Used by permission. All rights reserved worldwide.

To Evelina and Linnea

The heart has its reasons which reason does not know.
—Blaise Pascal

Contents

List of Illustrations | ix
List of Tables | xii
Foreword by J. P. Moreland | xiii
Preface | xv

Part I: Modeling the Decision to Become a Christian

    1   Introduction | 3
    2   The Two Alternatives | 20
    3   The Decision | 28
    4   The Aposteriori Wager | 33
    5   Prior Belief | 59
    6   Adding Evidence | 71
    7   Willingness Assignment | 76
    8   Justifying Christian Belief | 92

Part II: Penetrating the Evidence

    9   Historical and Cultural Evidence | 103
    10   Evidence from Reason, Consciousness, and Morality | 125
    11   Scientific Evidence | 136
    12   Theological Evidence | 183
    13   Personal Evidence | 226

Part III: Crossing the Line

    14   Changed Life Situation | 235
    15   Conclusions | 245

Appendices

Appendix A: Bayesian Decision Theory | 251
Appendix B: Reward Table and Strength of Will | 253
Appendix C: The Bayesian Decision Rule | 255
Appendix D: Many Alternatives | 258
Appendix E: Accumulation of Evidence | 261
Appendix F: A Numerical Example | 265
Appendix G: Approaches Other than Bayesian Decision Theory | 268

Bibliography | 271
Name Index | 285
Subject Index | 293
Scripture Index | 307

List of Illustrations

Figure 1.1   Two possible alternatives for the decision to have a leg surgery or not | 9

Figure 1.2   Two alternatives for a job offer | 9

Figure 1.3   Decision between two alternatives N and C | 11

Figure 1.4   A reward assignment of a person that chooses between Christianity and Non-Christianity | 13

Figure 1.5   Thomas Bayes, a British Presbyterian minister and mathematician | 16

Figure 4.1   Illustration of how the strength and centrality of our beliefs jointly affect our tendency to act in accordance with them | 35

Figure 4.2   Illustration of Strength of Rational Belief | 40

Figure 4.3   Illustration of Strength of Will | 42

Figure 4.4   Illustration of a neutral willingness table for the decision between Christianity (C) and Non-Christianity (N) | 43

Figure 4.5   Illustration of which combinations of Strength of Rational Belief and Strength of Will lead to conversion | 44

Figure 4.6   Christian interpretation of the Aposteriori Wager for the decision to become a Christian | 45

Figure 4.7   Naturalistic interpretation of the Aposteriori Wager for the decision to become a Christian | 46

Figure 4.8   A possible interpretation of the human heart | 49

x   LIST OF ILLUSTRATIONS

Figure 5.1   A model with four components of prior belief | 66
Figure 6.1   Illustration of how the evidence of figure 4.6 is divided into various units | 73
Figure 6.2   Illustration of how different types of evidence are pieced together for four persons | 74
Figure 7.1   Illustration of Pascal's willingness table for the decision between Christianity (C) and Non-Christianity (N) | 77
Figure 7.2   A possible willingness assignment for a person with a nothing-to-lose attitude towards Christianity (C) and Non-Christianity (N) | 79
Figure 7.3   A possible willingness table when the reward of becoming a Christian is smaller than the reward of Non-Christianity, regardless of truth | 85
Figure 7.4   A possible willingness table for a person who is hostile towards God in his choice between Christianity (C) and Non-Christianity (N) | 91
Figure 9.1   Approximate timing of some major events in the history of Israel based on a literal chronological interpretation of the Bible from Abraham and onwards | 116
Figure 11.1 Categorization of a stated conflict between an interpretation of the Bible and a scientific theory | 141
Figure 11.2 Hempel's model of scientific explanations | 143
Figure 11.3 Illustration of time and space for a cosmological model with a first start | 154
Figure 11.4 Models of human (left) and chimpanzee (right) ancestry according to common descent (a) and uncommon descent (b) hypotheses | 167
Figure 11.5 William Paley, an English apologist from the late eighteenth and early nineteenth century | 169
Figure 11.6 A Mandelbrot set, whose boundary repeats itself when magnified (so-called self-similarity) | 178
Figure 11.7 Illustration of the golden ratio | 179
Figure 11.8 Kurt Gödel, who is most famous for having proved that mathematics is incomplete | 181
Figure 12.1 Who was Jesus? | 222

Figure 14.1   Our understanding of God and how it evolves over time | 237

Figure 14.2   Illustration of how a changed life situation may lead a person to Christian faith or not | 239

Figure F.1   *Illustration of where Adam and Ben are located in a plot of Strength of Will versus Strength of Rational Belief* | 267

List of Tables

Table 1.1   Overall structure of the book | 18

Table 1.2   Common arguments for and objections against Christianity or theism | 19

Table 4.1   Engel's scale of spiritual decision | 48

Table B.1. Reward table for decision between Christianity and Non-Christianity | 253

Table C.1. Standardized reward table for decision between Christianity and Non-Christianity | 257

Table F.1. Expected rewards for Adam and Ben | 266

Foreword

EVER SINCE PASCAL'S WAGER was first formulated in the seventeenth century, it has been an object of fascination for many, many people from all walks of life. And the argument has brought comfort to Christian believers and represented a challenge to unbelievers regarding the rationality, or at least the prudential wisdom, in placing belief in the Christian God. Of course, the argument has had its critics over the centuries, and in the last few decades there has been a renewed interest in the Wager.

One of the interesting features of the argument is its association with approaches to making decisions and probability theory. And that is what makes this book so important, relevant, and unique. For one thing, it is written by Ola Hössjer. Hössjer—well known to Europeans but not to North Americans—received a PhD in Mathematical Statistics from Uppsala University, Sweden, in 1991. Appointed Professor of Mathematical Statistics at Lund University in 2000, he has held the same position at Stockholm University since 2002. His research focuses on developing statistical theory and probability theory for various applications, in particular population genetics, epidemiology, and insurance mathematics. In 2009 he was awarded the Gustafsson Prize in Mathematics.

It is evident that professor Hössjer is beyond well qualified to work on Pascal's Wager, and he applies his considerable tools to clarifying and defending the argument in the pages to follow. But there's more good news. Hössjer has the skills needed to take a very complicated topic and bring it down to a general, educated audience, and those skills are evident throughout what follows. He uses Bayes' Theorem to interpret what he calls the *aposteriori probabilities* in the argument, and he focuses on the rewards aspect of the

Wager in terms of an act of will, e.g., our willingness to become a Christian in accordance with different degrees of evidence for the decision.

In *Becoming a Christian*, Hössjer limits—and appropriately so—the alternatives for decision to naturalism or Christianity, and he presents a very nice summary of each, along with what the decision looks like from the vantage point of each worldview. Following this, Hössjer further clarifies what he takes to be the precise nature of the Wager, the issue of prior belief before considering the Wager, and the role of volition or willingness in making a decision relative to different assessments of the evidential situation. Finally, Hössjer treats the reader to a very nice précis of a unique, general case for the Christian God that many will be exposed to for the first time.

I must mention one more thing before closing this foreword. Perhaps the real value of this book lies in its impact on doing evangelism. We live in an increasingly secular culture, and if we are to present a thoughtful gospel to others, we must be able to clarify for people the nature of the decision they are about to make, along with the implications of different choices and the evidence for choosing Christianity. This book does just that. Consequently, it should be used in college-age or adult evangelism classes.

I can't thank Ola Hössjer enough for writing this book and using his training, passion, and talents for the kingdom of God in this way. I highly recommend this book for all those who want to learn more about Pascal's Wager and how to use it effectively in discipleship and evangelism. Study and enjoy!

J. P. Moreland
Distinguished Professor of Philosophy
Talbot School of Theology, Biola University, La Mirada, CA

Preface

THIS BOOK IS MY attempt to describe the decision to become a Christian or not from a mathematical and theological point of view. As a mathematician and statistician I have been interested in decision theory for a long time, and in 2008 I started to work on a model where the decision to become a Christian is described mathematically. About a year later Pastor Kjell-Axel Johansson contacted me. He wanted to start a Christian think tank, and at our first meeting I mentioned my ideas. Kjell-Axel immediately commented that my thoughts seemed to generalize Pascal's Wager, which I was unaware of at the time. I knew about Blaise Pascal as a prominent mathematician, physicist, and inventor, but not as a theologian and philosopher. This made me even more interested and focused on carrying on the project I had just started, the outcome of which is this book.

I soon found out that not only the Wager, but also Pascal's writing about Christian faith and human nature in general, is extremely relevant. His posthumously published *Pensées* touches upon a number of central issues such as the relative importance of faith and evidence, the hiddenness of God, our desire to live a happy life, and man's split condition in terms of greatness and wickedness. Pascal is no doubt one of the leading Christian apologists of the last centuries. He urges us to wake up and think about the meaning of life. Although his thoughts were important among his seventeenth-century contemporaries, they are even more significant in our secularized Western society. In this context I would recommend Douglas Groothuis's book *On Pascal* for a comprehensive account of Pascal's life, and Thomas Morris's *Making Sense of It All: Pascal and the Meaning of Life*, which puts Pascal's Christian apologetics into a modern perspective.

Pascal' Wager is part of the *Pensées*. Its main argument—that it is rational to start believing in God even with incomplete evidence—has been controversial and much debated. But in recent years there has been a renewed interest in his model for the decision to become a Christian. Accounts of the Wager literature can be found in Jeff Jordan's *Pascal's Wager: Pragmatic Arguments and Belief in God* and Michael Rota's *Taking Pascal's Wager: Faith, Evidence, and the Abundant Life*. Both of these authors defend Pascal's argument as rational, and in this book I do the same.

This book project of mine took a long time to complete. Before I started I realized that it was a high wall to climb. But the best thing I could do was to throw my hat over the wall to get myself going. My original mathematical model was much more complicated than the one you will find in this book, involving something called Markovian decision theory. I soon found out that I preferred a simpler model, which I hope captures the essential elements of the decision to become a Christian in favor of a more complicated model. The reason for this was not only to increase the number of potential readers, but I also applied a general principle of model selection called Occam's razor or the law of parsimony: When choosing between two models, go for the simpler, unless the more complicated one summarizes your ideas a lot better. I urge you as a reader to judge whether I have succeeded or not. Indeed, sometimes one fails to explain matters in a simple way because of an inability to understand them on a deeper level.

A summary of my model has already been published in the peer-reviewed apologetic journal *Theofilos*.[1] In this book I present the arguments in more detail and you can read it at several levels. First of all, it extends Pascal's Wager model so that the decision to become a Christian has three main ingredients: prior belief, interpretation of evidence, and an active response of will. Second, the Wager model is interpreted from Christian and naturalistic points of view. Third, the book provides apologetic arguments for Christian faith.

To some extent I have used an analytic approach based on logic, which I sometimes backed up with mathematics. The more technical parts are put into appendices and the main text has a more narrative form. This reflects a view of mine that formal logic and mathematics should only be a tool, not a purpose of its own. The American philosopher Eleonore Stump has similarly suggested that analytical philosophy would benefit by drawing more attention to literature and storytelling.[2]

---

1. Hössjer, "Aposteriori Wager."
2. Stump, "Problem of Evil."

Writing a book about the conversion is at the heart of Christianity. Christians may have varying viewpoints on what causes a conversion. A decision is an act of will, and it has a slightly different interpretation in Calvinist theology (willingly approving planned actions of God) compared to in Arminist theology (having genuine free will). My own point of view is close to Molinism—that these two interpretations of a decision need not be contradictory. I believe God can move outside our notion of time and knows what *would* have happened if we had chosen to act in some other way.

Perhaps you are curious about my theological position. I grew up in a Christian environment in the Swedish Lutheran (former) state church. I am very grateful to my parents, who brought me to Sunday school and later inspired me to go through Lutheran Confirmation, where adolescents learn more about Christian faith. During these years I developed an intellectual understanding of Christianity. But I was more than twenty years old when I received a personal relationship with God through belief in Jesus Christ. Although I cannot pinpoint the exact moment when this happened, at the age of twenty-six I decided to be baptized as an adult. Based on my own experience, I have thought a lot about what it means to become a Christian. I am currently a member of a Swedish charismatic Pentecostal church and a big friend of ecumenics. I have studied some theology, but I am neither a theologian nor a philosopher by training, although these topics interest me a lot. My hope is to bring complementary points of view to theology and apologetics. Since I cover a number or areas where I have no professional expertise, I invite you to read my arguments critically.

I am indebted to many people without whose generous comments and help this project would never have been finished. In particular I want to thank Kjell-Axel Johansson and his wife, Vivi Ann, for great encouragement and support. A number of other people have contributed with many insightful ideas, important references, and helpful criticism, either while reading earlier drafts of the book or through conversations. Among them I want to mention Patrik Adlarsson, Günter Bechly, Greg Carson, William Craig, Lars Dahle, Allan Emrén, Per Ewert, Andreas Forslund, Richard Gurton, Stefan Gustavsson, Marcus Högås, Peter Imming, Lars Jägerskog, Timo Koski, Per Landgren, Peter Loose, Dan Mattsson, Andy McIntosh, Stephen Meyer, Lennart Möller, J. P. Moreland, Jan Nylund, Jacob Rudenstrand, Rüdiger Sens, Scott Smith, Christer Sturmark, Richard Swinburne, Stefan Swärd, Peter S. Williams, Martin Wärnelid, and Andreas Östling in particular. I am also very grateful to the organizers and volunteers of the European Leadership Forum, which I attended four times in 2010-2013. This gave me unique opportunities to network, and to access a number of valuable books and other resources. During the preparation of the manuscript I received lots of help from Brian Palmer, Matthew Wimer, Nathan Rhoads, and Kyle Lundburg at Wipf and Stock. Lastly—and above all—I want to thank God for guiding me through this work every step on the way. Without his help I would not have had the courage or endurance to carry on a project like this.

If you are not a Christian, I hope you will not find the statements provocative, but that the text increases your curiosity and intensifies your thinking about a decision that I believe is the most important one has to make in life. My hope is to convince you that no matter what life situation you may have becoming a Christian is easy, although the consequences are dramatic. I suggest you have a Bible at hand while reading to look up the various passages referred to.

Ola Hössjer
December 4, 2017 (first printing) and March 19, 2020 (second printing)
Stockholm

PART I

Modeling the Decision to Become a Christian

1

Introduction

1.1 DECISIONS IN LIFE

LIFE IS FULL OF small decisions that we make each day, like how to dress, what to choose for breakfast, and which route to take to work. Some decisions are of intermediate importance, like choice of hobby, and these we make less often. Some of them are big, like choice of education, job, and which person to marry. Typically we only make one or a few of them during our lifetime.

The biggest decisions of all are those that relate to our very existence; such as the meaning, purpose, and destiny of life. They are so big that we actively make them perhaps only once in life. But very often we don't even know what to decide. The American philosopher Thomas Morris (1952–) writes:

> Looking around, it seems that your are equipped for a journey of some kind, but you realize to your utter astonishment that you have no idea where you came from, how you got here, where in the world you are, or where you're going. You have no map or compass. And your surroundings seem, in various ways, very strange, even dangerous. If someone else were to appear on the scene who seemed to understand your situation and to have answers for all your questions, you'd listen. At least if I were in such a position, I certainly would.[1]

Christians among many others want to offer such a map, and this book is all about describing the map and how to respond to the offer. This boils down to a decision for or against Christianity. Later on we will formalize it, using ideas from a branch of mathematics called decision theory.

---

1. Morris, *Making Sense of It All*, 1.

Even though we all face the same decision regarding Christianity, our routes to it differ a lot. Was it good or bad evidence from childhood that formed our decision? Or was it a testimony of a Christian friend? Maybe misconduct of some Christian influenced us negatively. Did university studies have a big impact on our decision? Was it a life crisis that made us question the meaning or purpose of life and urged us to start reading the Bible? Perhaps we only know some elusive parts of the Christian map, not enough to make an active decision. In any case, there are few things that interest us as much as the life stories of others, and to hear about the map they decided to use and what compass they followed. We tend to identify ourselves with what they tell and hope it will help us on our own journey through life.

Indeed, the history of the church is full of testimonies of people whose lives changed after their conversion to Christianity. For some people this conversion was very radical. In the book of Acts in the New Testament we read about Saul. He was a Pharisee and a persecutor of the early Christian church when he suddenly experienced an extraordinary event:

> Meanwhile, Saul was still breathing out murderous threats against the Lord's disciples. He went to the high priest and asked him for letters to the synagogues in Damascus, so that if he found any there who belonged to the Way, whether men or women, he might take them as prisoners to Jerusalem. As he neared Damascus on his journey, suddenly a light from heaven flashed around him. He fell to the ground and heard a voice say to him, "Saul, Saul, why do you persecute me?" "Who are you, Lord?" Saul asked. "I am Jesus, whom you are persecuting," he replied. "Now get up and go into the city, and you will be told what you must do." The men traveling with Saul stood there speechless; they heard the sound but did not see anyone. Saul got up from the ground, but when he opened his eyes he could see nothing. So they led him by the hand into Damascus. For three days he was blind, and did not eat or drink anything.[2]

After three days Saul regained his sight, got baptized, and was renamed Paul by God, with a special mission to spread the gospel to Gentiles in present Turkey, Greece, and Italy. Today he is often regarded as the most important Christian missionary of all time.

Blaise Pascal (1623–62) was a scientist, writer, and inventor, born in the French provincial capital city of Clermont.[3] Already at the age of three he lost his mother, and after this tragic event his father, a lawyer and ama-

---

2. Acts 9:1–19.
3. Groothuis, *On Pascal*.

teur mathematician, decided to leave his job and move to Paris with Blaise and his two sisters. He wanted to give the children cultural stimulation and proper education, and started to home school them. The family engaged in the social life of Paris, meeting many of the most influential people of the day. It was soon discovered that Blaise was a prodigy with a very broad range of talents. He is perhaps most famous for having constructed the first mechanical calculator, and in mathematics he made profound contributions to projective geometry, combinatorics, probability theory, and philosophy of mathematics. In physics his work in hydrodynamics is especially well known. Although Pascal grew up in a Catholic environment he was mostly occupied with science, and not very interested in religion. In the 1640s things changed gradually. When Blaise's health started to impair he was recommended by doctors to decrease the intensity of his scientific work. As a substitute he engaged socially. This did not seem to increase his happiness though, and at this time the whole Pascal family was influenced by the very sincere Christian faith of two brothers and bonesetters that helped the father after an accident. They were both followers of Jansenism, a seventeenth-century movement within the Catholic Church that emphasized original sin, human depravity, and divine grace. Blaise became interested in the new and theologically controversial ideas, and one of his two sisters became a nun. Blaise even wrote *Provincial Letters* in defense of Jansenism, printed in secret and widely spread. But he had still no peace in his heart, and the death of his father in 1651 made him even more restless and increasingly weary with the world. In 1654 things changed radically after a strong experience of God in a dream, usually referred to as his second conversion. His seems to have written down the vision instantaneously as a poem—"The Memorial." It was found after his death, sown into the inner lining of his jacket. Pascal probably transferred the poem to every new jacket he wore without telling anyone. Its last verse reads:

> Let me not be cut off from him for ever!
> "And this is life eternal, that they might know thee, the only
> true God, and Jesus Christ whom thou has sent"
> Jesus Christ.
> Jesus Christ.
> I have cut myself off from him, shunned him, denied him,
> crucified him.
> Let me never be cut off from him!
> He can only be kept by the ways taught in the Gospel.
> Sweet and total renunciation.

Total submission to Jesus Christ and my director.
Everlasting joy in return for one day's effort on earth.
I will not forget thy word. Amen.[4]

After this experience Pascal changed his priorities in life. He did not abandon natural science, but theology and philosophy became his main fields of interest. Pascal's most influential theological work, *Pensées* (*Thoughts*), was published posthumously after he died.[5] It is an apologetic work (a defense of Christian faith) organized into notes, based on the scraps of paper he left behind.[6] Apart from his great achievements as a scientist, he is still regarded as a prominent Christian philosopher and apologist.

John Newton (1725–1807) was a slave trader in the eighteenth century. At the age of 23 his ship encountered a severe storm and it almost sank. He woke up in the middle of the night and called out to God. The ship and John's life were saved from the storm, and he became a Christian and later an Anglican priest, abolitionist, and Christian hymn writer. Even to this day "Amazing Grace" is one of the most well known psalms of all time.

Friedrich Nietzsche (1844–1900) was the son of a Lutheran pastor. When Friedrich was only five years old his father died, and the next year his younger brother died as well. After these tragic events he moved with his mother and younger sister to live with relatives. Nietzsche was devoutly religious in his childhood. He entered studies in theology and philology at the University of Bonn at the age of 20. In the following years he gradually lost his faith. In his most well-known book, *Twilight of the Idols*, he declared that any truth claim was an idol, and in particular that God was dead. Shortly after the book was published in 1889 he went insane, and he died about ten years later.[7]

C. S. Lewis (1898–1963) was an Oxford academic, novelist, and poet. During adolescence he fell away from the faith of his childhood and at the age of 15 he became an atheist, thinking that religion was more of a duty than joy. But J. R. R. Tolkien (1892–1973) and some of his other Oxford Christian literary friends had a big impact on his life. Gradually he changed his mind, and first he became a theist in 1929 and then a Christian in 1931. He later said that he was brought into Christianity like a prodigal, "kicking, struggling, resentful, and darting his eyes in every direction for a chance to

---

4. Pascal, *Pensées*, 285–86.
5. Pascal, *Pensées*.
6. For recent treatments of Pascal's Wager model, see Groothuis, *On Pascal*; Jordan, *Pascal's Wager*; Hájek, "Pasal's Wager" and "Blaise and Bayes"; Craig, *Reasonable Faith*, chapter 2; Rota, *Taking Pascal's Wager*, and references therein.
7. Cowan and Guinness, *Invitation to the Classics*, 299–302.

escape." But in the end he surrendered to Christ, believing that Jesus is the Son of God.[8] He became one of the most successful Christian apologists and fantasy novelists of the twentieth century, and today his books are still sold in great numbers.

Bertrand Russell (1872–1970) was a British philosopher, mathematician, and historian. He is regarded as one of the founders of analytical philosophy, and together with Alfred North Whitehead (1861–1947) he attempted to build mathematics on axioms and rules of logic.[9] He was also a social critic and pacifist, arguing for nuclear disarmament. At 15 years old he started to think about the validity of Christian dogma and three years later he finally decided to discard Christianity. Unlike Lewis, he never returned to the faith of his childhood but remained an atheist for the rest of his life.

Kim Il-Sung (1912–94) was the first leader of communist North Korea. During his childhood many Christian missionaries lived in North Korea, and Pyongyang was often referred to as Jerusalem of the East. Both of Kim's parents were devout Christians and the family fled to Manchuria in 1920 because of the Japanese invasion. Six years later, when Kim was only 14 years old, his father died. This severe loss seems to have influenced Kim a lot. He soon entered the Chinese communist party and joined various guerrilla groups, hoping to liberate North Korea from Japanese occupation. Not only did he abandon the Christian faith of his childhood, but he also became increasingly negative towards Christianity. After being installed as the first North Korean leader in 1945 this soon escalated into severe persecution of Christians and eventually he introduced a personal cult of himself.[10]

Being surrounded by all these witnesses of people who made an active decision for or against Christianity, we are triggered to think about our own decision. But the crucial question is: Do we take the time for that? Perhaps not, since lack of time is an intrinsic part of a modern, materialistic society. We are often so busy that we tend to forget about the big questions in life. Or, because of their importance, we easily postpone or suppress them. Pascal was very much aware of this and wrote:

> The immortality of the soul is something of such vital importance to us, affecting us so deeply, that one must have lost all feeling not to care about knowing the facts of the matter. All our actions and thoughts must follow such different paths, according to whether there is hope of eternal blessing or not,

---

8. See for instance Lewis, *Surprised by Joy* and Sayer, *Life of C.S. Lewis*.
9. Whitehead and Russell, *Principia Mathematica*.
10. Martin and Bach, *Back to the Jerusalem of the East*.

> that the only possible way of acting with sense and judgement is to decide our course in the light of this point, which ought to be our ultimate objective. Thus our chief interest and chief duty is to seek enlightenment on this subject, on which all our conduct depends. And that is why, amongst those who are not convinced, I make an absolute distinction between those who strive with all their might to learn, and those who live without troubling themselves to think about it.[11]

Pascal distinguishes between two types of persons. Some of us are indifferent and don't care. Others are ignorant and feel they haven't learned enough about the map yet. In the latter case, it may be wise to suspend the decision for a while in order to gather more background information. But sometimes we use this as an excuse for suppressing the decision. In this way we easily cheat ourselves, since not making an active choice is a decision, and we don't know how long we will live. For this reason, it is my genuine wish that you will have the time to read this book closely and think about its contents. If so, I hope you will find the efforts rewarding.

1.2 FORMALIZING THE DECISION PROCESS

We will start by formalizing what it means to make a decision, using concepts from *decision theory*. Decision making is relevant for a part of philosophy called epistemology, which deals with the theory of knowledge, and the decision maker is also referred to as an epistemic agent.

We first have to compare the *alternatives* or propositions to choose between. In the simplest case there is complete information available, so that the consequence of each alternative is known. For instance, think of a medical doctor that makes a diagnosis of a patient having certain problems with his legs (see figure 1.1). Based on this diagnosis he may suggest surgery or no surgery. Of these two options, no surgery leads to a high degree of mobility with much pain, whereas surgery leads to a low degree of mobility with no pain.

---

11. Pascal, *Pensées*, note 427. This Penguin edition of the *Pensées* uses the Lafuma enumeration of Pascal's fragments, referred to as notes.

                    Decision= No surgery   Decision=Surgery

Consequence | Lots of pain | | No pain |
                | High degree of mobility | | Low degree of mobility |

Figure 1.1: Two possible alternatives for the decision to have a leg surgery or not. The consequence of each alternative is known. Each alternative is given a single reward.

Before a decision can be made, we have to order the consequences in some way based on the *rewards* (or *utilities*) that we assign to each one of them. When this has been done the patient chooses the treatment with the highest reward—his decision.[12] Although this sounds simple, it may be very difficult to assign rewards. Do we prefer high mobility and much pain, or low mobility and no pain? It is clear that the reward assignment will be influenced by the goal of the decision maker. If the overall goal is to minimize pain, then surgery is decided. But if the goal is to maximize physical fitness, then no surgery is decided. For other decisions the goal might be to maximize profit or overall happiness in life. But very often it is hard to define the goal explicitly.

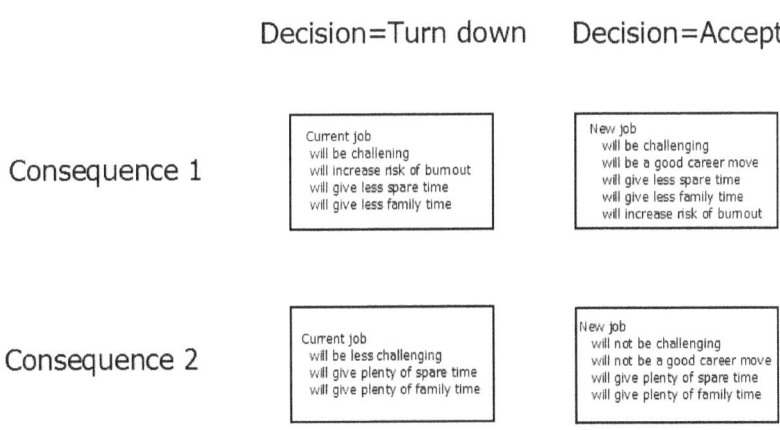

Figure 1.2: Two alternatives for a job offer. Each alternative has two possible consequences, and a reward is assigned to all four consequences.

---

12. Often the chosen alternative is referred to as *action*. But we will rather refer to action as the act of will concerned with "making the decision" or "finalizing the decision."

For most decisions there is only incomplete knowledge available, with each alternative having several possible consequences. This is illustrated in figure 1.2 for choice of job. As in the leg surgery example, we need to assign rewards to all of the listed consequences. However, this is not enough. Because of the incomplete information we also have to give each consequence our credence based on how likely we think it is. For instance, when deciding whether we should accept a job offer or not, we usually have much more information about the current job than the new one, and therefore it is harder to estimate the consequences of switching jobs. When finally we make a decision and act, we tend to choose the alternative whose most likely consequence has the highest reward. Whether a consequence is regarded as likely or not depends our *prior conceptions* as well how we evaluate the *evidence* we have so far. In case we are very uncertain about the consequences, we usually want to postpone the decision, if possible, in order to gather more evidence or analyze more closely the evidence we have already, thereby making the decision more *informed*.

You may object, saying that although a job may be selected in this manner very few people decide for marriage in such a rational way. However, the process I described above can in fact be more or less subconscious, involving the intellect, emotions, and most importantly love. In addition, by reward we don't necessarily mean degree of benefit or striving for happiness. The reward of a consequence is defined much more generally as our *willingness to act* according to it, perhaps without being able to formulate any goal explicitly. Indeed, feelings of fear, insecurity, passionate love, willingness to take risks, and striving for changed life priorities may all be part of the reward, making it highly *subjective* and dependent on our personality, previous experience, and life situation. Of course, it is not only our reward calculation that is subjective but also the way in which we evaluate evidence, and the two cannot be totally separated.[13]

Suppose you believe in one of the two alternatives as being *right* and the other one as *wrong*. For instance, you may think you are *meant* to have a certain job or marry the person you are currently dating. Then you have adopted a meaning of *truth* that is not simply *what will happen*, but a more abstract concept rooted outside your everyday life, either because you believe in destiny or you are religious and think of one alternative to be in line with God's will.[14] This makes the decision process slightly different, since truth

13. Things that are difficult to formulate explicitly but nevertheless affect the decision are usually referred to as *tacit assumptions*.

14. Here we use the correspondence theory of truth, where a statement is believed to be true if it corresponds to a more abstract idea behind the statement. The alternative coherence theory of truth asserts that a statement is true if it does not contradict

and falseness are the most fundamental consequences of each alternative, completely out of our control. However, you may still be uncertain about which alternative is true and get the options of figure 1.3. There are four possible ways to combine decision and truth, and a decision is considered right if true and wrong if false.

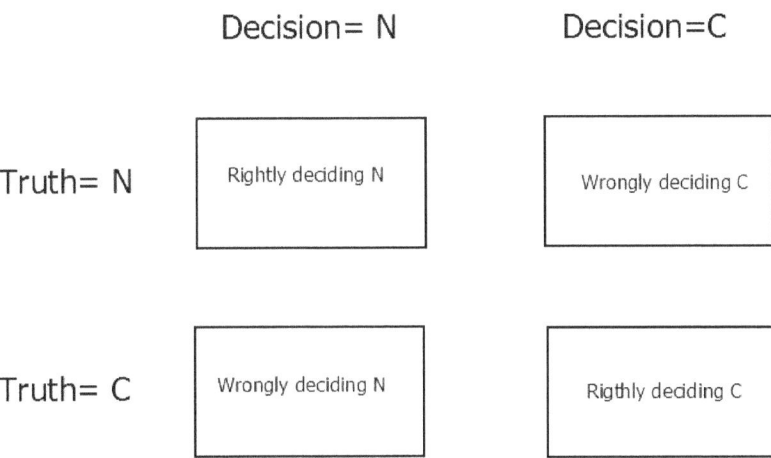

Figure 1.3: Decision between two alternatives N and C. Each alternative has two possible consequences, of which one is true and the other one is false, although one does not know for sure which. A reward is assigned to all four consequences, that is, to all four combinations of truth and decision. When applied to the decision to become a Christian, C means that Christianity is true and N that it is not.

1.3 PASCAL'S WAGER

The decision about Christianity can be viewed as having a table as in figure 1.3, with the two alternatives

N: Christianity is not true,
C: Christianity is true

to choose between. Since the Bible makes several claims, which logically are either true or false, it is indeed very natural to bring truth into the decision

---

other true statements. It requires less of a true statement, since it avoids the need of an abstract idea behind the statement. Moreland and Craig, *Philosophical Foundations*, chapter 6; and Jonsson, *Med tanke på Gud*.

process.[15] This is the starting point of the Wager, which Pascal introduced as a way of gambling with truth:

> Let us then examine this point, and say, "God is, or He is not." But to which side shall we incline? Reason can decide nothing here. There is an infinite chaos which separated us. A game is being played at the extremity of this infinite distance where heads or tails will turn up. What will you wager? According to reason, you can do neither the one thing nor the other; according to reason, you can defend neither of the propositions.[16]

Pascal concluded that we are into this game whether we like it or not, and therefore we have to bet. In doing so we have to wager the benefits of either choosing Christianity or not. As for the job example, this boils down to a more or less subconscious and very subjective assignment of rewards to all consequences. In the Wager these consequences are the four ways to combine truth and decision.

It may surprise you that a utilitarian reward concept is applied to the decision to become a Christian. Recall, however, that we interpret reward very widely as our willingness to act, given the information and knowledge we have. In figure 1.4 we have exemplified a reward assignment. For each of the four alternatives, the larger the reward number is the more inclined we are to act according to this alternative. A reward of zero means we are neutral, a negative reward that we consider this alternative to be costly, and a positive reward that the benefits (interpreted in a very wide sense) outweigh the costs. If Christianity is true we give it a large reward (5), because of the biblical promises of a relationship with God in this life and then for eternity, whereas Non-Christianity gets a negative (-5) reward, because of the prospect of being separated from God after death. On the other hand, if Christianity is false we may think of the Non-Christianity option as rightly deciding for atheism and basically carrying on with life as before, giving it a neutral reward of zero, whereas we value a decision for Christianity negatively (-1) since we don't want to live on a myth. A person with such a reward assignment favors Christianity a bit. But he still wants to live according to the truth, always giving a higher reward to a true alternative than to a false one.

---

15. As in footnote 14, we implicitly assume the correspondence theory of truth. Since Christianity requires the correspondence theory of truth, we can rephrase the two alternatives as C: The correspondence theory of truth holds and Christianity is true, against N: C does not hold.

16. Pascal, *Pensées* (ebook), 53–54.

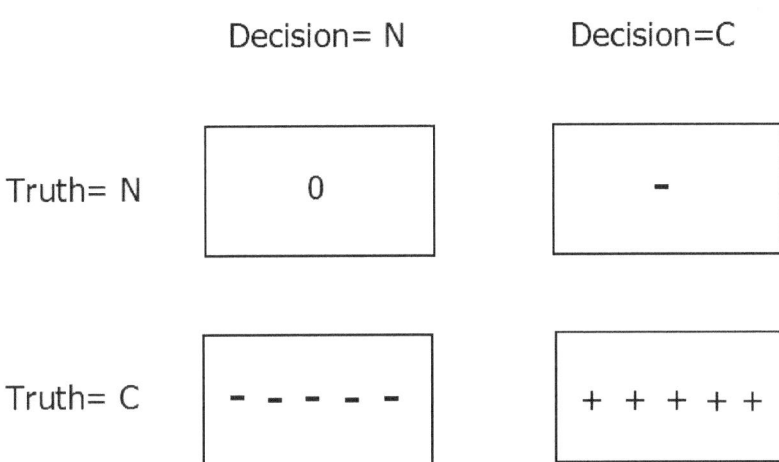

Figure 1.4: A reward assignment of a person that chooses between Christianity and Non-Christianity. Christianity (C) gets a reward 5 if true and -1 if false, whereas Non-Christianity (N) gets a reward of zero if true and -5 if false. This person wants to live according to the truth, always giving higher reward to the true alternative of each row. But overall, Christianity is favored somewhat over Non-Christianity.

It is not only the reward assignment that is subjective, but also our belief in which alternative is true. In order to quantify strength of belief in Christianity and Non-Christianity, Pascal introduced probabilities. This was no coincidence since Pascal had earlier in 1654 (in fact, the year of his dramatic spiritual experience), together with the French lawyer and amateur mathematician Pierre de Fermat (1601–65), derived important rules for how to calculate probabilities. The concept of probability is nowadays very much used in philosophy of religion.[17] It is a bit subtle since there are several versions of it.[18] In the Wager argument Pascal used *subjective probabilities*. The subjective probability of a statement C is a number between zero (being certain that C is false) and 1 (being certain that C is true) that quantifies our strength of belief in C. If the subjective probability is 0.5, we think it is equally likely that C or N (that is, not C) is true. Since we are

---

17. Since the first edition of Swinburne, *Existence of God* was published in 1979, probability theory has been used a lot within philosophy. See for instance Chandler and Harrison, *Probability in the Philosophy of Religion*.

18. Section 4.2 provides a more detailed discussion of different kinds of probabilities. For a historical account of the development of the concept of probability, see Hacking, *Emergence of Probability*. This development was also influenced by social science, as described in Courgeau, *Probability and Social Science*.

mainly interested in subjective probabilities in this book, we will often omit the word "subjective" and simply write "probability."

People are often more used to think in terms of odds than probabilities, although both ways of assessing degrees of belief are equivalent. Since the Wager can be phrased as a bet against the truth, it is perhaps more natural to quantify uncertainties in terms of odds. For instance, if your (subjective) odds of Christianity versus Non-Christianity are 1 to 1, you assign the same probability 0.5 to both alternatives. On the other hand, if your odds in favor of Non-Christianity are 19 to 1, you assign a probability 0.95 to Non-Christianity, which is 19 times as large as the probability 0.05 for Christianity.

But how do we finalize the decision of the Wager, once rewards have been assigned to all combinations of truth and decision, and probabilities to the Christian and non-Christian alternatives? Pascal actually had three versions of his Wager argument, and two of them employed the *expectation rule* in order to select between Christianity and Non-Christianity.[19] This means that we calculate the expected (or average) reward of choosing Christianity by weighting the two rewards of the right column of figure 1.4 according to their probabilities, with the most likely alternative given the highest weight. In the same way, we calculate the expected reward of not choosing Christianity by weighting together the rewards in the left column of figure 1.4. Finally, we decide the alternative with the highest expected reward. For instance, if Christianity and Non-Christianity are given equal odds of 1 to 1, Christianity gets a higher expected reward and is decided for, whereas we decide for Non-Christianity if it is favored by odds of 19 to 1 (see appendix F for details).

Pascal had several versions of the reward assignment. For the most radical and well known, Christianity is assigned an infinite reward if true. Based on this he argued that although the message of the gospel could not be proved in a strict logical sense a rational person should still take at least the first steps to believe in God since one has everything to gain and nothing to loose by living a Christian life. The Wager was in this way groundbreaking, not only by formalizing decision theory with rewards and probabilities, but also as an apologetic argument for Christian faith.

19. See Hacking, "Logic of Pascal's Wager" and Hájek, "Blaise and Bayes" for an account of the three different versions of Pascal's Wager. The Expectation rule is one of many possible rules to govern the decision between the two alternatives (C and N) under uncertainty, and it results in the Canonical Wager. Other versions of the Wager are obtained if some other rule (some of which don't require subjective probabilities) is used, such as the (Weak or Strong) Dominance rule, the Satisfactory Act rule, the Maximin rule, the Maximax rule, the Next Best Thing rule, and the Risk-Weighted Expectation rule. More details are provided in Jordan, *Pacal's Wager and Pragmatic Arguments*, chapter 1; and Buchak, "Rationality and Evidence Gathering."

1.4 METHODOLOGY, OUTLINE, AND PERSPECTIVE

Before carrying on we will first give a brief outline of the book. In chapter 2 we simplify and assume that Christianity and naturalism are the two alternatives to choose between, and define each one of them in some detail. Then we interpret the decision from a Christian and naturalistic point of view in chapter 3, so that the meaning of the four possible outcomes of the table in figure 1.3 is clarified.

In chapter 4 we address the first (and methodologically most important) goal of the book: to apply something called Bayesian decision theory[20] to the Wager. This is a mathematical treatment of decisions named after Thomas Bayes (c. 1701–61), an English mathematician and Presbyterian priest, who is depicted in figure 1.5. Pascal was not very detailed about how to calculate probabilities and Bayes devised a formula (often called Bayes' Rule or Bayes' Theorem) for modifying degrees of belief, or *apriori* probabilities, into *aposteriori* probabilities when new evidence is accumulated.[21] In our context the aposteriori probability of Christianity depends both on our religious disposition from birth (the apriori part) and all the evidence we encounter in life. Usually it is only the apriori part that is regarded as subjective. But we will argue that for the decision to become a Christian it is rather the interpretation of evidence that is subjective, since siblings or other persons with very similar life experience may reach very different

---

20. For decision theory as a theory of rational behavior, see Neumann and Morgenstern, *Theory of Games*, and for Bayesian decision theory, see Berger, *Statistical Decision Theory*. Statisticians tend to formulate Bayesian decision theory by minimizing an average or expected loss rather than maximizing an average reward. However, the two approaches are equivalent since a negative loss can be interpreted as a reward.

21. For an account of the development of statistics before 1900, see Stigler, *History of Statistics*. Thomas Bayes' work was posthumously published by his friend Richard Price in Bayes, "Solving a Problem in the Doctrine of Chance." This line of thought was later developed into a theory of inductive reasoning by the French mathematician Laplace in *Philosophical Essays on Probabilities*. It remained predominant during the nineteenth century but it was then criticized because of its need to introduce probabilities in a subjective way. In an attempt to circumvent this, a frequentist school of decision theory was developed based on hypothesis testing. At first it seems to depend on accumulated evidence only; see for instance Neyman, "Frequentist Probability." It should be noted though that hypothesis testing also requires assumptions—not about apriori probabilities, but rather on which models to use. In recent years the Bayesian school of thought has experienced an upswing, as summarized by Savage, *Foundations of Statistics*; Albert, "Bayesian Rationality"; Huber and Schmidt-Petri, *Degrees of Belief*; and Chen et al., *Frontiers of Statistical Decision Making*. For an overview of decision theory from a Bayesian point of view, see Berger, *Statistical Decision Theory*. Bayesian reasoning has also been used in informal logic and argumentation theory, where the complicated part of decision making due to debates and other types of social interaction is acknowledged; see Korb, "Bayesian Informal Logic."

conclusions. We extend Pascal's Wager by treating probabilities as aposteriori, based on evidence and prior belief, and refer to it as the *Aposteriori Wager*. The decision for or against Christianity then consists of three main ingredients: prior belief, evidence, and willingness to become a Christian, which we argue are combined in a highly personal way. Then we give an equivalent graphical interpretation of the Wager with the strength of our rational belief (which includes prior belief and evidence) in Christianity on one axis and our willingness to become a Christian on the other. A diagonal line of conversion separates the decisions for and against Christianity, and it is faith that makes us act and cross this line. In order to make the book more accessible we have avoided mathematical details in the main text and put them in the appendices. There we also discuss other approaches and their relation to Bayesian decision theory.[22]

Figure 1.5: Thomas Bayes, a British Presbyterian minister and mathematician.[23] He is most well known for having proposed a formula (Bayes' Rule or Bayes' Theorem) that is most helpful for assessing how likely a statement is in terms of an aposteriori probability that combines prior conceptions and evidence. The Aposteriori Wager of chapter 4 combines Pascal's Wager with Bayes' Rule.

22. See appendix G for details.
23. Image is in the public domain and taken from https://en.wikipedia.org/wiki/Thomas_Bayes#/media/File:Thomas_Bayes.gif.

A work related to ours is that of British physicist Stephen Unwin, who used Bayes' Rule in order to estimate the probability that God exists. He combined this with the Wager, using Pascal's most radical reward assignment with an infinitely positive reward for Christianity if it is true. But Unwin abandoned this version of the Wager since it leads to a decision to become a Christian even when one has only a small degree of belief in Christianity before the decision is made. Instead he used a faith math approach.[24]

A second goal of the book is to *interpret* the decision to become a Christian, both from a Christian and naturalistic perspective. We argue in section 4.4 that the Aposteriori Wager is equally valid for both of these worldviews, as illustrated by causal diagrams.[25] We spend quite some time defining rational belief before the decision and belief by heart after the decision, two concepts that Pascal distinguished as well. This part of the book is very important, since the Wager has often been criticized (and misunderstood) for suggesting that one may become a Christian without believing that Christianity is true. These and other objections against the Wager model are discussed in section 4.5.

In the next four chapters we explain the Aposteriori Wager in more detail, mainly from a Christian point of view. We give a Christian interpretation of prior belief in chapter 5, and how to interpret and combine various types of evidence in chapter 6. Several reward assignments are presented in chapter 7, of which Pascal's *nothing to lose* assignment is one. In this chapter we show that our attitudes towards Christianity divide us into three main groups: those who take a step in faith and become Christians even with a small amount of evidence before the decision, those who want more evidence in order to know the truth before they take this step, and those who do not become Christians—regardless of evidence. Then in chapter 8 we discuss more formally whether a Christian's belief can be justified or not.

The third major goal of the book is to present apologetic arguments for Christianity from a classical Christian point of view.[26] In chapters 9–13 we penetrate various types of evidence that people tend to interpret in favor of or against Christianity. In chapter 14 we describe how people may become Christians after a changed life situation by modifying their reward assignment, interpretation of evidence, or both. Finally in chapter 15 we summarize and make some conclusions.

---

24. Unwin, *Probability of God*.

25. For an introduction to the mathematical theory of causality, see for instance Pearl, *Causality*.

26. In section 2.1 we will explain in more detail what we mean by Classical Christianity.

Table 1.1: Overall structure of the book		
Part	Theme	Chapters
I	Modeling the decision to become a Christian	2–8
II	Penetrating the evidence	9–13
III	Crossing the line	14–15
Appendices	Mathematical details	A–G

The overall structure of the book is summarized in table 1.1. In order to give you a more detailed overview of its apologetics, table 1.2 sums up where some well-known arguments for and against Christianity appear in the text. We do not give a full apologetic treatment, and instead we provide a number of references.[27]

---

27. See for instance Craig, *Reasonable Faith* for more on offensive and defensive apologetics arguments.

Table 1.2: Common arguments for and objections against Christianity or theism.
For each argument it is shown where it appears in the book, with Ch=Chapter, and Unit referring to either of S=Section, PB=Prior Belief, Ev=Evidence, or WA=Willingness Attitude.

Argument for Christianity	Ch	Unit	Criticism	Ch	Unit
Life without God	3	S 3.3	Burden of proof	4	S 4.5.1
	7	WA 1	Counter cosmological	11	Ev 13
Will to believe	4	S 4.5.1	Inconsistent revelations	9	Ev 1
Ontological	5	PB 1	Problem of evil	9	Ev 2
Cosmological	5	PB 2		12	Ev 17
	11	Ev 13			Ev 20
Simplicity	5	S 5.1	Universalism	9	Ev 1
		PB 2	Religious wars	9	Ev 2
Democracy and human rights	9	Ev 3	Misconduct of Christians	9	Ev 3
Impact on culture	9	Ev 4	Age of universe	11	Ev 12
Jewish history	9	Ev 5	Evolutionary theory	11	Ev 14
Church history	9	Ev 6	Parsimony	11	Ev 15
Argument from reason	10	Ev 7	Poor design	11	Ev 15
	11	Ev 10	Problem of free will	12	Ev 17
Argument from consciousness	10	Ev 7			Ev 19
Morality	10	Ev 8–9			Ev 21
Transcendental	11	Ev 10	God of the Old Testament	12	Ev 18
Teleological/design	11	Ev 14–15	No reason argument	12	Ev 17
Effectiveness of mathematics	11	Ev 16	Argument from unbelief	12	Ev 17
Miracles	11	Ev 11	Destiny of unevangelized	12	Ev 19
	13	Ev 24	Hiddenness of God	12	Ev 19
Archeology/Old Testament	12	Ev 22	Fall of man	12	Ev 20
DNA of Jewish population	12	Ev 22	Problem of hell	12	Ev 21
Resurrection of Jesus	12	Ev 22			
Old Testament prophecies	12	Ev 22			
Biblical portraits of humans	12	Ev 22			
Apocalyptic	12	Ev 22			
Testimony	13	Ev 23			

2

The Two Alternatives

WE FIRST NEED TO define more closely the two alternatives to choose between. The only requirement is that either the Christianity or the Non-Christianity option is true. In the next two chapters I will simplify though and assume that the alternative to Christianity is naturalism, the most common worldview for atheists. Then the two alternatives Christianity and naturalism are in a sense opposite, and the meaning of the decision is clarified. It is true though that most people hold on to some kind of belief other than naturalism,[1] be it a religion, belief in destiny, or not taking a stand (agnosticism). Later in the book we will actually consider scenarios where some worldview other than Christianity or naturalism might be true.[2] While this will slightly change the reward assignment, interpretation of prior belief, and evidence if Christianity is false—the top row of figure 1.3—it does not change the meaning and consequences of the decision if Christianity is true. And the overall principles of the Wager are the same.

2.1 CHRISTIANITY

Christianity grew out of Judaism when Jesus of Nazareth started a public ministry in Palestine around A.D. 30, claiming that he was the Messiah foretold in sacred Jewish scriptures—the Old Testament. He gathered a number of disciples and gave them a ministry to spread his teaching after his death.

---

1. For instance, there is a worldwide Ipsos poll from 2010 where more than 18,000 citizens responded to the question whether or not they believed in one or many god(s)/supreme being(s). Less than 1/5 were sure they did not believe. Ipsos Global @dvisor, "Questions on Supreme Being."
2. See section 4.5.3 and evidence 1.

His preaching was opposed, for instance, by a majority of the leading Jewish authorities, and after three years of ministry he was crucified at Calvary outside of Jerusalem by the Roman occupying power. His followers then claimed that after three days Jesus resurrected from death and appeared to many of them before ascending to heaven. After that they followed Jesus' missionary command and started to spread the Christian message. Most of the first Christians were Jewish, but the majority of Jews did not accept Jesus as Messiah. Within a few decades Christianity was recognized as a separate religion. It spread quickly throughout the Roman Empire, with Peter (one of Jesus' 12 disciples) and Paul the two most well-known missionaries among the first generation of Christians. Today Christianity has penetrated many cultures and countries, and it is the largest world religion.

The sacred scripture of Christianity is the Bible, in which the New Testament has been added to the Old Testament. Most books of the New Testament were written down during the first three decades of the Christian church, with eyewitness reports of Jesus' public ministry (the four gospels), the first history of the early church in the book of Acts, and the letters of Paul, Peter, and others with further teaching of Christian dogmas. The last book, Revelation, was authored by the apostle John and usually it is dated around A.D. 95. Most parts of the New Testament were quite soon agreed upon by the early church, but the formal canon was finally settled during the councils of Hippo and Carthage in 393 and 410.[3]

The goal of systematic theology is to give a coherent account of Christianity. In this book I take a classical Christian point of view. By this I mean that the Bible is the reliable Word of God, written down by humans that were inspired by the Holy Spirit.[4] This is in contrast to a more liberal interpretation where humans are thought to have written down their conceptions of God. If the Bible is true, this classical view is the faith that the apostles hold on to. It also agrees with the teaching of the early church, as summarized for instance in the Nicene Creed from 325. The assumption that the Bible is the Word of God, inspired by him, does not mean that all Christians have the same interpretation of all its details. But they agree upon the main dogmas, which are summarized below.[5] For brevity we will most of the time write "Christianity" and suppress the word "classical."

First of all, Christianity holds that the universe is not all there is. It is an open system created by God, who exists in three distinct persons in perfect harmony: the Father, the Son (Jesus Christ), and the Holy Spirit—the

---

3. Geisler, *Systematic Theology*, chapter 28.
4. Mark 7:5–14; 2 Tim 3:16–17; 2 Pet 1:20–21.
5. This is further discussed in evidence 10.

Trinity.[6] Apart from the visible world God also created angels, spiritual creatures without bodies but with moral judgment and high intelligence, whose purpose is to guard and protect us and to glorify God.[7] All three persons of the Trinity took part in creation of the visible and invisible world.[8] God not only created the world, he also maintains it and reveals himself either directly or through the Bible.

Second, absolute moral values exist, in particular good and evil. God himself has personal characteristics and all that is good in creation originates from him. He is almighty, truthful, holy, loving, and has always existed. And God's creation originally was good:

> God saw all that he had made, and it was very good. And there was evening, and there was morning—the sixth day.[9]

But evil came into creation. The Bible is very clear that the spiritual world is divided into a good and evil part. The devil is the leader of the evil part, and his main goal is to destroy all activities of God. Scripture is somewhat less detailed about the origin of the evil part, but passages in the Old and New Testaments mention a rebellion among the angels.[10]

Third, creation of mankind was God's final purpose with our world. Adam and Eve were given the responsibility to administer it and were created in the image of God. However, suffering entered the world through the fall of man[11] when the first two humans were tempted by the devil and disobeyed God's command not to eat fruit from the tree of knowledge that was placed in the midst of the garden of Eden. The human image of God was then distorted and the connection to him broken. To understand the consequences of the fall, it is important to know something about the classical Christian view of the nature of man. According to the *trichotomy* view, man

---

6. Gen 1:1–2; John 1:1–4.

7. The angels are most of the time invisible to us, and they often protect us (Ps 34:8). But sometimes God gives us a special ability to see them, as when Gabriel announced to Maria that she would give birth to Jesus Christ (Luke 1:26–38) or when the shepherds were told of his birth (Luke 2:13). Similar encounters have been reported in modern time; see for instance Strand, *Angels at My Door*.

8. Col 1:16.

9. Gen 1:31.

10. Two Bible passages that clearly refer to a rebellion among the angels are 2 Pet 2:4 and Jude 6. There are less details about the devil or Satan as a fallen angle and a leader of this rebellion, but Isa 14:12–15; Ezek 28:12–17; and Rev 12:7–10 are often interpreted in this way. In any case, the devil is mentioned both in the Old Testament (Gen 3:1; Deut 32:16–17; Job 1:7—2:7; 1 Chr 21:1; Zech 3:1; Ps 106:35–37) and at numerous places throughout the New Testament.

11. Gen 3:1–7.

consist of three parts: body, soul, and spirit. The body is the physical part of our being and the soul distinguishes our personality in a unique way, with a mind, emotions, and the ability to make choices.[12] The spirit is our source of life—the part of man that connects to the spiritual world. It should be noted though that a majority of theologians hold on to a *dichotomy* view, by which man consists of two parts: body and soul. Regardless of whether one prefers a dichotomy or trichotomy view of man, the Bible emphasizes that we are created by God as a unity, and none of its parts should be devalued. Although we use a trichotomy perspective in this book, it can as well be read from a dichotomy point of view. The spirit is then that part of the soul which most directly relates to the spiritual world.[13]

God's intention for us was to have a full relation with him in perfect harmony, affecting not only our spirit, but also our body and soul. But the connection to God through the spirit was more or less cut off after the fall of man. This had a profound effect on the way we act, since our soul—the decision maker—is influenced by the flesh,[14] the outside visible world, and the spirit. As long as the spirit remains disconnected to God we lack the necessary resources for following his will, although we try our best to live a decent life.[15] The Bible refers to this as sin and makes it clear that no one is free of it.[16] Since God is holy he cannot tolerate sin, and therefore death came into the world after the fall. At the moment we die, the soul and spirit leave the body and we are separated from God.

Fourth, although our situation seems hopeless, there is a way out. Sin can be paid for or redeemed, but the Redeemer has to be free of sin himself. As planned already before creation, and then gradually revealed through the Old Testament and the four New Testament gospels, God the Father sent Jesus Christ to our world as a Redeemer in our place, the perfect sacrifice for humanity.[17] Though free of sin, he was sentenced to death on Calvary

---

12. Evidence 7 elaborates more on the connection between body and soul.

13. Bible passages that indicate a trichotomy view are 1 Thess 5:23; Heb 4:12; 1 Cor 2:14—3:4; and 1 Cor 14:14. In particular, the first two of these suggest that the spirit and soul are different entities. However, a dichotomist would argue, based on these and other parts of Scripture, that the Bible uses "soul" and "spirit" synonymously. In any case, many Bible verses (for instance Mark 12:30 and Matt 22:37) stress that we should honor God with all our being. More arguments for a dichotomy view are found in Grudem, *Systematic Theology*, chapter 23.

14. The flesh refers to our tendency, after the fall of man, to live in a self-centered way not in line with God's plan for us, and in particular not allowing him to control our lives (Rom 7:14, 21; 8:3; Gal 5:17–21; and Matt 5:38–48).

15. Acts 8.

16. Rom 3:9–10; 5:12–14.

17. Eph 1:3–12; Col 1:26–27; 1 Pet 1:20; Gen 3:14–15; Deut 18:15; 2 Sam 7:8–16; Isa

to pay for our trespasses and resurrected on the third day—the good news of the gospel! We become Christians when we truly believe that Jesus is the Son of God who died on Calvary to cleanse us from sins before being raised from death by God, confess our sins, repent (ask Jesus for forgiveness), and commit ourselves to follow Jesus as the Lord of our lives. We are then *justified* by God (made free of guilt) and get a restored connection to him. This happens instantaneously the moment we surrender to Christ and our spirit gets renewed by the Holy Spirit. Our decision has eternal consequences in that the soul and spirit are *saved*, and we are promised as a free gift to spend eternity *together with God*.

Finally, the Bible tells that Jesus will return as king a second time to complete judgment of the world and create a new heaven and Earth.[18] But as a Christian you are already justified, and you will obtain a new heavenly resurrected body that is completely restored into the image of God,[19] so that the destructive influence of the fall finally disappears.[20]

2.2 NATURALISM

Naturalism is a philosophy of life. It is based on the idea that only natural laws and forces ever operated in the universe, without any supernatural or spiritual influences. It is often used synonymously with atheism, the belief that there is no God or gods, but the two concepts are not identical. Although the roots of naturalism can be traced back to ancient Greeks (in particular Stoicism and Epicureanism), the predominant Western worldview has still been Christian—at least since the Middle Ages. Christianity emphasized that mankind was dependent on reason *and* revelation for individual and collective well-being. But the Renaissance then spurred new interest in ancient literature and philosophy, and the scientific revolution of the seventeenth century as well as the Enlightenment of the late eighteenth century increased credence to human reason, with profound effects on literature and social, political, and economic theories. Up to this point only a minority of philosophers, writers, and scientists had been naturalists. But in the nineteenth century a number of atheistic theories were developed,

---

53; and Matt 16:21; 17:22–23; 20:17–19.

18. Matt 25:31–46.

19. 1 Cor 15:35–58; 2 Cor 5:1–5.

20. The Bible tells that the soul and spirit of Christians who die before the second coming of Christ will spend an intermediate period together with God in paradise (Luke 23:43; 2 Cor 5:8; Phil 1:22–24; Heb 12:23). The near-death experiences of many people seem to confirm this. See evidence 7 of this book; Springer, *Within Heaven's Gates*; and McCormack, *Glimpse of Eternity*.

for instance in politics (communism), psychology (psychoanalysis), and Friedrich Nietzsche's philosophy of the worthlessness of life and God as an idol. Other theories were not purely atheistic, but they nevertheless fueled interest in naturalistic thinking. This includes existentialism and Charles Darwin's (1809–82) theory of evolution based on natural selection.

A modern version of naturalism is humanism. It is rooted in the belief that mankind is capable of creating a better world by itself, much in line with Enlightenment thinking. Its main dogmas can be found for instance in Human Manifesto III, published in 2003 by the American Humanist Association, or the Amsterdam Declaration of 2002, published by the International and Ethical Humanist Union. Postmodernism, on the other hand, is not genuinely naturalistic, since it emphasizes freedom to generate our own belief systems up to the point that absolute truths are denied. But it often leads to a worldview similar to naturalism, since an objective existence of God is denied. In recent years New Atheism has entered the public scene. It is well known for its criticism of religion in general and Christianity in particular. Proponents of this line of thought are Richard Dawkins (1941–), Daniel Dennett (1942–), Sam Harris (1967–), and Christopher Hitchens (1949–2011).[21]

In more detail, by naturalism we mean a worldview usually referred to as *metaphysical naturalism*.[22] According to this theory, reality only consists of natural phenomena (matter and energy) that can be studied empirically through natural science. Although mental properties like abstract objects, ideas, reasoning, emotions, and moral values exist, they are either direct products of matter, energy, and random events (physicalism) or at least causal consequences of them (pluralism or property dualism).[23] In any case, our mind is fully dependent on physical properties of the brain and there is no soul or spirit with independent existence. The observable world is a closed system with no outward influence and in particular there is no God that actively interferes with it. As a consequence, man only consists of or is totally dependent on the body, and there is no life after death. On the

---

21. Dawkins, *God Delusion*; Dennett, *Darwin's Dangerous Idea*; Harris, *Letter to a Christian Nation*; Hitchens, *God Is Not Great*.

22. This should not be confused with *methodological naturalism* (see evidence 10), whereby knowledge can only be attained through empirical studies of nature. Although this rules out the possibility of divine revelation within the framework of objects studied by natural science, it does not exclude the existence of a deity per se.

23. This is one of many points of view regarding the *body-mind problem*, i.e., whether a separate soul exists and if so whether it exists by itself or is a causal effect of the physical body. See for instance Moreland and Craig, *Philosophical Foundations* and evidence 7 for more details.

collective level life on Earth will cease at some future time point, and then the history of mankind will be forgotten.

Our universe may be believed to be all there is, and existence then started uncaused through the Big Bang.[24] Alternatively, one opens up for the existence of other universes and an infinite past through a multiverse theory. In any case, everything in nature is thought to be governed solely by natural laws that are formulated with mathematical equations. Life arose from inorganic compounds under the guidance of these laws, and since then they have evolved through blind mechanisms, with mutations, random genetic drift, and natural selection as the driving forces of change.[25]

Naturalism often leads to great admiration and reverence of nature, sometimes to a proportion close to pantheism[26] or deism, with the laws of nature replacing a god that first created the universe. It is believed that societies and moral values evolved through social and cultural evolution, blindly governed by natural laws and without external control by any god. Ethics is derived from human needs and interests, but no objective moral laws exist outside the realms of nature, and man is not accountable to any god. Since no divine revelations or sacred scriptures may teach us right and wrong, it is up to mankind to define or interpret moral values. There is no good or evil. When there is violence, war, hatred, and jealousy, it rather reflects deficiencies of our society, caused by our own lack of knowledge, prejudice, and religious beliefs. Within humanism in particular, it is still believed that mankind is capable of developing our society in a positive way, using science and technology as major tools. Individual happiness and fulfillment of life is maximized when we take part in this process.[27]

---

24. However, the Big Bang doesn't necessarily contradict Christianity. On the contrary many argue that the Big Bang theory and other cosmologies based on a first singularity event are *more* in line with a Christian (or theistic) worldview than a naturalistic one. See evidence 12, 13, and 15.

25. The alternative to blind evolution is either theistic evolution or a design/creationist theory; see evidence 14 and 15.

26. The philosophical theory that combines religious elements with naturalism is called *religious naturalism*. For a Christian, nature is created by God and therefore most valuable, and mankind is responsible for preserving it (Gen 1:28–30). But nature itself should not be worshiped, only God.

27. The Christian view is rather that a society that abandons God will develop morally in a negative, self-destructive way (evidence 18) even if some of the guiding principles of that society include Christian virtues. This is ultimately a consequence of the fall of man. Christians also believe in work to improve society, guided by a mandate from God to administer the world and to follow the golden rule (Matt 7:12). But it is also clear from the Bible that we cannot follow this rule consistently by our own efforts alone (see evidence 8).

Religious beliefs are regarded as superstitious, a remnant of older civilizations when science had not developed so far. Sometimes the positive individual effects of religious practice are acknowledged, but this is still regarded as a psychological phenomenon—a kind of delusion that gives people a false hope of eternal life after death. On the collective level religion is regarded as something that divides rather than unites people.[28] Although religious freedom is usually advocated, from time to time religion is thought of as something that should be kept in the private sphere.[29]

---

28. This view is essentially shared by Christians, but for a totally different reason: Religious doctrines often do separate people, but the deeper underlying cause is the fall of man. Only a relation with God through belief in Jesus Christ can unite people in a profound way (see evidence 2 and 3).

29. According to the Bible, a person's response to Christianity has eternal consequences. For a Christian, apart from arguments based on religious freedom, it is therefore important *not* to remove religion from the public sphere (Matt 28:18-20). But on the other hand it is not possible to force anyone to believe (Mark 6:10-11; Luke 10:8-11).

3

The Decision

3.1 THE CHRISTIAN VIEW

FROM A BIBLICAL POINT of view the decision for or against Christianity can be thought of as a battle, with influences from God (through the Holy Spirit), the flesh, the outside world, and the devil.[1] God tries to connect to our spirit to become a Christian through the Holy Spirit. The devil tries to prevent this from happening, also by influencing our spirit.

But what does the decision to become a Christian mean? It is first of all more than a rational belief that Christian doctrine is true. The starting point is that God first calls us through the Holy Spirit by making a personal invitation to come to him.[2] If we answer this call by opening up our hearts,[3] the Holy Spirit may convince us that we have sinned.[4] It is then possible for us to make a genuine and repentant response to the gospel. But if we don't make such a response we will not become a Christian.

Second, even though most people try to live a worthy life, we can never earn the right to become a Christian by being good enough, since we all have sinned.[5] But it is still very easy to become a Christian, accessible to anyone regardless of age, life experience, or social, ethnic, or religious back-

---

1. This does not contradict the Christian doctrine that Jesus defeated the devil on Calvary cross. By doing so he gave us all the *option* of choosing him in order to have eternal life. But since God loves us he wants us to follow him by free will (see evidence 17). This leaves us with a choice of embracing Christianity or not.

2. John 6:44; Matt 11:28–30.

3. Exod 36:26–27. According to figure 4.8 the heart consists of the spirit and part of the soul.

4. John 16:8–10.

5. Rom 2:9–20; 3:23; Eph 2:8.

ground. The only requirement is that we *want* to become a Christian and are honest to God. This is the good news which the Bible describes as salvation by grace, because of Jesus' sacrifice on Calvary.

Third, the consequences of becoming a Christian are dramatic also in this life. The Bible refers to this as being "born again,"[6] which is the moment when our spirit is filled with the Holy Spirit. This means a completely changed direction of life. After this has happened, we can *choose* to follow the influences of the renewed spirit rather than the flesh and the part of the outside world not in line with God's will. It was previously not possible to follow God by being good ourselves, but after conversion we are given the power of the Holy Spirit to do so.[7] Baptism is then a way of making official that the old life has been replaced by a new one,[8] although some Christians regard it as part of the conversion. In the new Christian life, *sanctification* is the process of following the direction and guidance of the Holy Spirit. The influence of the fall is then gradually removed through changed priorities, and manifested in all aspects of our life as visible *fruits of the Spirit*.[9] It amounts to giving up self-control and being lead by God—like following a wind[10]—so that God takes part in all of our subsequent decisions after the biggest one to become a Christian.[11]

Fourth, the timing of the decision varies between individuals. Some persons know when they became a Christian, although this moment was often preceded by a period of seeking God.[12] Others may not be able to tell exactly when they decided for Christ; it was rather a process that extended over some time. Or perhaps they grew up in a Christian family and feel they have been a Christian as long as they remember. This means they cannot tell themselves when they became a Christian—only God knows. In any case, one of the gifts of the Holy Spirit is assurance of salvation.[13]

---

6. John 3:3; 1 Pet 1:23.
7. Rom 8:1–17.
8. Rom 6.
9. Matt 7:15–20; Gal 5:22–26.
10. John 3:8.
11. Col 1:9; Eph 5:17; Ps 32:8.
12. This is very much the idea of the Alpha course concept. People are given plenty of time to learn about Christianity and the message of the gospel. See Gumbel, *Telling Others*.
13. Rom 8:15–16. It is true that Christians may have seasons of doubts in life where God seems far away. But if we are totally honest to God about this our faith may actually mature and get stronger after such periods.

Fifth, as a Christian you have been adopted as a child of God[14] into a worldwide family of believers—the church, the head of which is Christ. The members of the church have different gifts and tasks,[15] and are united in love by the Holy Spirit. This is much like stones that form a spiritual house[16]—a unity that is supposed to be visible to others.

3.2 THE NATURALISTIC VIEW

If naturalism is true, we cease to exist after death and the decision for or against Christianity has no eternal consequences. Deciding against Christianity is then a realistic way of holding on to the truth. This insight often leads existentialism. According to this view the meaning of life cannot be imposed from outside—it is rather shaped by our own individual decisions. Often one tries to find meaning in life through work, family, hobbies, and various types of social engagement. Bertrand Russell honestly wrote about the consequences his atheism had on his view of life:

> That Man is the product of causes which had no prevision of the end they were achieving; that his origin, his growth, his hopes and fears, his loves and beliefs, are but the outcomes of accidental collocations of atoms; that no fire, no heroism, no intensity of thought and feeling, can preserve individual life beyond the grave; that all the labours of the ages, all the devotion, all the inspiration, all the noonday brightness of human genius, are destined to extinction in the vast death of the solar system, and that the whole temple of Man's achievement must inevitably be buried beneath the debris of a universe in ruins—all these things, if not quite beyond dispute, are yet so nearly certain, that no philosophy which rejects them can hope to stand. Only within the scaffolding of these truths, only on the firm foundation of unyielding despair, can the soul's habitation henceforth be safely built.[17]

Existentialists often take a step further and stress the absurdity of life. But it is hard for many to live with such a worldview, and the *life-without-God argument* is a persuasive effort in favor of Christianity based on the

---

14. John 1:12; Rom 8:14–17.
15. Rom 12.
16. 1 Pet 2:4–6.
17. Russell, *Why I Am Not a Christian*, 107.

meaningless of life without God.[18] For instance, Pascal gave a vivid description of the human condition:

> Imagine a number of men in chains, all under the sentence of death, some of whom are each day butchered in the sight of the others; those remaining see their own condition in that of their fellows, and looking at each other with grief and despair await their turn. This is an image of the human condition.[19]

Although himself a Christian, Pascal was writing this passage from a naturalistic point of view.

Whether one regards life as meaningful or not, if naturalism is true then Christians live on a myth. Belief in God is then a way to make life more endurable, but since there is no spiritual world and in particular no God, such a faith is a mental defense mechanism rather than a relation with Christ, and the decision for or against Christianity is a psychological rather than a spiritual struggle. It is sometimes thought to be caused by a mental weakness or a desire for social context. Richard Dawkins and others have also suggested that our religious disposition has a genetic component, or at least it is a byproduct of other inherited traits.[20]

3.3 CONSEQUENCES OF THE DECISION FOR THE DECISION-MAKER

Let us identify ourselves with the decision maker *before* the decision is taken. From what has been said so far, the meaning of the four possible ways to combine truth and decision in figure 1.4 can be summarized as follows:

Rightly deciding against Christianity: Christianity is not true. If you decide not to become a Christian you have realized correctly that life finishes after death. This will give you no hope for eternal life, but on the other hand you can control it yourself. You will try to create meaning in life through career, family, sports, music, and other types of social engagement. But you admit there is no eternal meaning of life.

Wrongly deciding for Christianity: Christianity is not true. But if you become a Christian anyway you will live by a myth. The decision is a way for you to create meaning, and by doing so you have not much to loose. Occasionally you will feel good to think about God, but since he does not exist and there is no Holy Spirit, your thoughts are only created by your own

---
18. Craig, *Reasonable Faith*, chapter 2.
19. Pascal, *Pensées*, note 434.
20. See for instance Dawkins, *God Delusion*, chapter 5 and the references therein.

mind. Your choice of Christianity is a kind of religious drug that is not based on a true relationship with God.

Wrongly deciding against Christianity: Christianity is true. But if you do not become a Christian, since there is eternal life after death, your soul and spirit will be separated from God forever after you die. On the other hand, you will be able to control your life here and now, and you don't have to worry too much about the opinion of others. Chances are small that anyone will try to force you to change your mind. You will try to create meaning in this life through career, family, sports, music, and other types of social engagement. But you admit there is a risk that things will not turn out well after you die.

Rightly deciding for Christianity: Christianity is true. If you decide to become a Christian, you will enter a personal relationship with Jesus, and you will be saved for eternity together with God. It is your hope that your deep feelings of emptiness and lack of meaning will disappear. You have heard that God has a plan for you already in this life, but at the cost of giving up self-control. Your decision might be questioned by relatives, friends, and others. In fact, it is possible that people will find you a bit crazy,[21] and in some countries you will even face the risk of persecution.[22]

---

21. 1 Cor 1:18–31; John 15:18–25.
22. 1 Pet 2:21–25; Phil 3:10–11. See also evidence 6 and 22.

4

The Aposteriori Wager

IN THIS CHAPTER WE will describe the Aposteriori Wager—a model for the decision to become a Christian. In the first two sections we give some general comments on belief, rationality, faith, and probabilities. Then we turn to a formal definition of the Aposteriori Wager, with Christian as well as naturalistic interpretations. Finally, we summarize and respond to the most comment objections against the Wager.

Part of the material in sections 4.2 and 4.3 is more mathematical. In order make the text more accessible we have put all the formulas in the appendices. If you still find these two sections too technical, you may concentrate on the discussion related to figures 4.5, 4.6, and 4.7.

4.1 BELIEF, RATIONALITY, AND FAITH

Belief is a mental state of ours, and we all believe in a number of things that influence the way we act. Although we have an intuitive idea of what belief is, it is still a delicate matter to define in exact terms.[1] A very basic requirement is that in order to believe in a certain statement there has to be some alternative. For instance,

> C1: Red cars are red

is merely a tautology. Since there is no alternative, our certainty of C1 is not a belief (other than a belief in the laws of logic). On the other hand, consider the sentence

---

1. Swinburne, *Epistemic Justification*, chapter 2.

> C2: Christopher Columbus set out for his voyage from Spain to America in 1492.

This is a statement in which we may believe, since there are at least two alternatives: that Columbus did not go to America at all, or that he did so but not in 1492. The American philosopher J. P. Moreland (1948–) writes:

> A belief's impact on behavior is a function of three of the belief's traits; its content, strength and centrality.[2]

The *content* refers to what we believe, the *strength* of the belief depends on how convinced we are that it is true, and the *centrality* of the belief quantifies how important it is for our worldview—that is, how much we value it. The importance of a belief is related to our purposes to achieve certain goals and this typically requires some action of ours. We may believe very strongly in C2 although it very seldom influences the way we act. It is therefore not a central belief. On the other hand,

> C3: The political program of the right-wing party is preferable to that of the left-wing party.

is also statement that we may believe in strongly since there is an alternative—that the left-wing party is preferable. Depending on how central C3 is for us, if we believe in C3 we may vote for and even join the right-wing party.

Although the content of the belief is very important, I would argue that it is the strength and centrality of the belief that make us act. The influence of the content is rather indirect. For instance, someone who enters politics at a young age may strongly believe that the right-wing party is superior and value political engagement not because he has great knowledge of the right wing's political program but rather because his parents or friends influenced him.

In the book of Acts, when Paul preaches in Athens he starts the sermon as follows:

> People of Athens! I see that in every way you are very religious. For as I walked around and looked carefully at your objects of worship, I even found an altar with this inscription: to an unknown god. So you are ignorant of the very thing you worship, and this is what I am going to proclaim to you.[3]

Obviously the Greeks had very vague ideas about the nature of this unknown god. But for at least some of them their belief was strong enough to make them act and build an altar of worship. In figure 4.1 we have illustrated

---

2. Moreland, *Love Your God*, 73. See also Sire, *Why Should Anyone Believe?*
3. Acts 17:22–23.

how action may depend on the strength and centrality of the belief. For statement C3, the further to the right along the strength of belief axis we are, the more we believe that the right-wing party is preferable; and the higher along the centrality axis we are, the more important we think the program of the right-wing part is. The further northeast we are along the action axis, the more inclined we are to *act in accordance with our belief*—that is, to vote for and join the right-wing party.

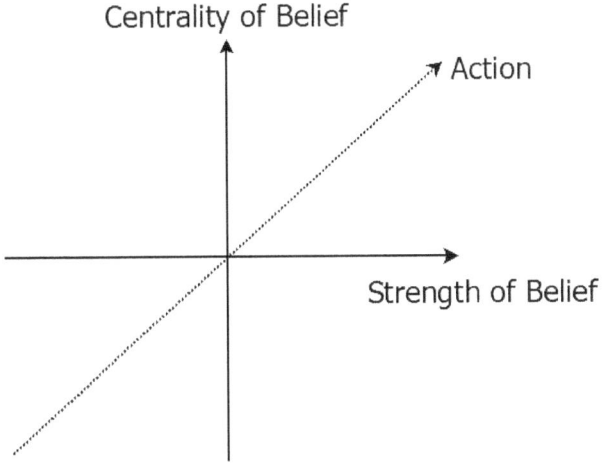

Figure 4.1: Illustration of how the strength and centrality of our beliefs jointly affect our tendency to act in accordance with them.

If we consider religious beliefs, then action is typically related to some kind of spirituality. The British philosopher Peter S. Williams (1974–) writes that

> Spirituality concerns how humans relate to reality—to themselves, to each other, to the world around them and (most importantly) to ultimate reality via their worldview beliefs, concomitant attitudes and subsequent behavior . . . A person's actions are "spiritual" insofar as they are an organic outworking of their beliefs about reality and their attitudes.[4]

For Christian belief, that is, belief in the statement C that Christianity is true, we will distinguish between the action of *becoming* a Christian, whether we can define a particular moment when this happened or not, and

---

4. Williams, "Apologetics in 3D," 8.

the subsequent action of *practicing Christian faith*. It is the former kind of action that we will focus on when we define and analyze the Aposteriori Wager.

In the sequel, it will be tacitly understood that "belief" means *rational belief*, and we will use the two terms synonymously. Rationality can be of several types, for instance, epistemic rationality—a desire to believe true things—and instrumental rationality—a desire to make rational decisions, that is, to achieve certain goals.[5] When speaking of rational belief, it is the former kind of rationality we have in mind. Such a rational belief involves our prior conceptions *and* all the evidence we know of. In particular, the *strength of our rational belief* in a proposition depends on how much we believe it is true, based on prior conceptions and evidence.

The American philosopher Lara Buchak[6] (1981–) views faith as something closely related to action. We will follow this approach and assume that faith in a proposition (for instance, that Christianity is true, C) leads to action (becoming a Christian). Faith is in this way different from strength of rational belief, since it also involves how much we value C.

4.2 PROBABILITIES

In the previous section we defined the strength of (rational) belief in a statement C as dependent on our prior conceptions and evidence, and in the introduction we mentioned that probabilities are used for quantifying strength of belief.[7] We mentioned that there is a mathematical tool called Bayes' Theorem that is very well suited for this purpose. It allows us to distinguish between apriori probabilities, which only involve our prior conceptions, and aposteriori probabilities, which also take evidence into account.[8]

It is the aposteriori probability of statement C (Christianity is true) that we will use to model the decision to become a Christian. Our aposteriori probability of Christianity depends on an inborn apriori tendency from birth to connect to God, as well as the evidence we experience in life. This is related to work by the British philosopher of religion Richard Swinburne (1934–) and Stephen Unwin. Whereas they consider the aposteriori probability for the existence of God,[9] we will focus on the narrower proposition that Christianity is true.

---

5. Kelly, "Epistemic Rationality as Instrumental Rationality" and Buchak, "Instrumental Rationality."
6. Buchak, "Can It Be Rational to Have Faith?"
7. Sections 1.3 and 1.4.
8. See appendix A for formal definitions.
9. Swinburne, *Existence of God*; Unwin, *Probability of God*.

In order to illustrate this consider two persons, Adam and Ben. The apriori probability 0.5 for Christianity and 0.5 for Non-Christianity is the same for both of them. Adam has a neutral interpretation of his life experience—that is, he regards the evidence as making it equally likely that Christianity is true or not true. His aposteriori probability of Christianity is therefore the same, 0.5, as his apriori probability. On the other hand, Ben interprets evidence in favor of Non-Christianity. He regards evidence as making it 19 times more likely that Non-Christianity is true compared to the probability that Christianity is true. This makes Ben's aposteriori probability 0.05 of Christianity ten times smaller than his apriori probability 0.5 of Christianity.[10]

In the sequel and unless otherwise stated, whenever we write "probability" it is aposteriori probability that we have in mind. Later on in the book we will argue that (aposteriori) probabilities are subjective. This essentially means that they vary a lot between persons that have access to similar information. Since degrees of belief are based on these probabilities, they are subjective as well.

Before proceeding with the Wager we will mention some other notions of probability that should not be confused with subjective (aposteriori) probabilities. The *physical probability* of an event C quantifies the degree by which we know the outcome of C when *all* possible background information is available. Historical events such as "Jesus resurrected from death" are of this sort since they either happened or not. The physical probability of a historical event is therefore zero if it did not happen or 1 if it happened, although we may not know which is true. By assigning a subjective probability of 0.8 to the claim that Jesus resurrected from death, we are more inclined to *believe* that this happened rather than the opposite, given the knowledge we have. However, this does not reflect any real uncertainty as to whether Jesus resurrected or not (so-called ontological chance). It only reflects our own lack of knowledge (so-called epistemic chance).

Mathematical statements are reminiscent of historical events. They are always based on certain assumptions—the system of axioms—and they are regarded as true if they follow logically from these axioms, and false if they do not. The physical probability of a mathematical statement is therefore zero or 1 given the system of axioms.[11] If a theorem has not yet been proved or disproved, it is called a *conjecture*. In 1742 the German mathematician Christian Goldbach (1690–1764) brought forward a famous conjecture. It

---

10. See appendix F for more details.

11. See however the discussion on the incompleteness of mathematics in evidence 16, chapter 11.

concerns an important class of numbers called prime numbers. A prime number is greater than 1 and it is only divisible by 1 and itself. These numbers have many intriguing properties, and the first of them are 2, 3, 5, 7, 11,... Goldbach's idea is very easy to formulate:

> Every even integer greater than 2 can be expressed as the sum of two prime numbers.

But this conjecture has not yet been proved in spite of many efforts. It is easy to check that the statement is true for the first few even integers (4=2+2, 6=3+3, 8=3+5, and so on) and it has in fact been verified[12] for integers up to at least 4×10^{18}. Most mathematicians therefore believe the statement is true, and they would assign it a subjective probability close to but slightly lower than 1.

A deterministic event is predetermined by its causes to either happen or not, and therefore its physical probability is zero or 1. Determinism is the belief that all processes in the natural world are fully determined by their causes with only one possible outcome, so that not only historical events but also all future events have a physical probability of zero or 1. Indeterminism is the opposite belief that some events are truly random in the ontological sense referred to above. There are proponents of determinism and indeterminism among Christians, and one's opinion crucially depends on how the free will of man is interpreted.[13]

Many physicists advocate indeterminism. For instance, if we regard the decay of nuclear isotopes as purely (ontologically) random, the physical probability is 0.5 that a specific carbon 14 atom decays within 5730 years. Quantum mechanics (for instance, Heisenberg's uncertainty principle) seems to indicate indeterminism. But it is also possible that in the future we may be able to explain things that look random today.[14]

A subjective probability (like 0.8 for the belief that Jesus resurrected) can be thought of as a prediction of a physical probability, given our finite amount of background information and our incomplete cognitive ability to process it. The terms *epistemic probabilities* and *inductive probabilities* are closely related to subjective probabilities, although a distinction is often

---

12. Oliviera e Silva, "Goldbach Conjecture Verification."

13. Bradley and Howell, *Mathematics through the Eyes of Faith*, chapter 5. See also the discussion on Molinism in evidence 17.

14. Indeed, it is well known that Albert Einstein interpreted the uncertainties of quantum mechanics in terms of incomplete knowledge (epistemic chance) rather than true randomness (ontological chance). And there is some recent research that seems to support Einstein's arguments; see Harrigan and Spekkens, "Einstein, Incompleteness."

made.[15] There is also the notion of *frequentist probability* (also referred to as *statistical probability*). It is applicable to events that are repeatable under identical circumstances a large number of times. For instance, if we roll a dice, the frequentist probability 1/6 of having four eyes means that if we roll the dice a large number of times the relative proportion of fours will approach 1/6. But the physical probability of each single roll is zero or 1, if we assume that the outcome is a deterministic function of the initial conditions (height, speed, momentum . . .). But if we have no idea of the initial conditions and believe that the dice is symmetric, we assign for each roll a subjective probability 1/6 to the event that four eyes come up.

From now on we will tacitly assume that all probabilities are subjective unless otherwise stated. The reason is that we are mainly concerned with the statement C that Christianity is true. We don't have the background information required in order to use physical probabilities. Frequentist probabilities are not very useful either when we focus on events that only happened once. In particular, they are not appropriate to use for assessing whether Christianity is true or not.

4.3 DEFINING THE APOSTERIORI WAGER

We will apply the concepts of (subjective aposteriori) probability, belief, rationality, faith, and action to the Aposteriori Wager. This will lead us to a model that is very similar to the one that was illustrated in figure 4.1.

In the previous section we argued that a person's strength of rational belief in a statement can be assessed through his aposteriori probability that the statement is true. We have formalized this reasoning in appendix A by introducing Strength of Rational Belief, which is an abbreviation of "the strength of rational belief in Christianity a person has." It is essentially the aposteriori (subjective) probability of Christianity being true, although presented on a different scale.[16] Christianity is favored on this scale when Strength of Rational Belief is positive, that is, when the probability of Christianity being true exceeds 0.5. Analogously, Christianity is disfavored when Strength of Rational Belief is negative, that is, when the probability of Christianity being true is less than 0.5.

---

15. See for instance Keynes, *Treatise on Probability*; Plantinga, *Warrant and Proper Function*, chapters 8–9; Collins, "Teleological Argument"; Swinburne, *Epistemic Justification*, chapters 3–4; Swinburne, *Existence of God*, chapter 1; and Swinburne, *Faith and Reason*, chapter 1.

16. In mathematical terms we use a log odds or a logit scale. That is, if P is the subjective aposteriori probability assigned to Christianity, Strength of Rational Belief equals $\log P/(1-P)$. See appendix A for details.

It is shown in appendix A that Bayes' Theorem is equivalent to saying that Strength of Rational Belief is the sum of Strength of Prior Belief and Strength of Evidence, as illustrated in figure 4.2. The first of these two terms, Strength of Prior Belief, is an abbreviation of "the strength of an individual's prior belief in Christianity," and it is positive when our prior conceptions favor Christianity and negative when they favor Non-Christianity. We can think of Strength of Prior Belief as a quantifier of our desire (implanted from birth) to connect to God. The other part, Strength of Evidence, is an abbreviation of "the strength of evidence in favor of Christianity that a person has." It is positive or negative depending on whether our assessment of evidence favors Christianity or not.

Strength of Rational Belief combines prior belief and evidence, and it quantifies the extent to which we believe Christianity is true by means of self-evident knowledge[17] implanted from birth, and beliefs inferred from other kinds of knowledge through perceptions, memories, deductions and reasoning, testimonies, and various kinds of authorities. It is subjective in that it differs between persons with similar life experience. With a naturalistic interpretation, there is no spiritual world and therefore no spiritual influences on rational belief. From a Christian point of view, rational belief is to some extent influenced by the spiritual world, although before conversion it has not yet reached the heart in a transforming way. We will argue in section 4.4 and chapter 14 that once a person has taken an active decision to become a Christian the spiritual influence will increase Strength of Rational Belief.

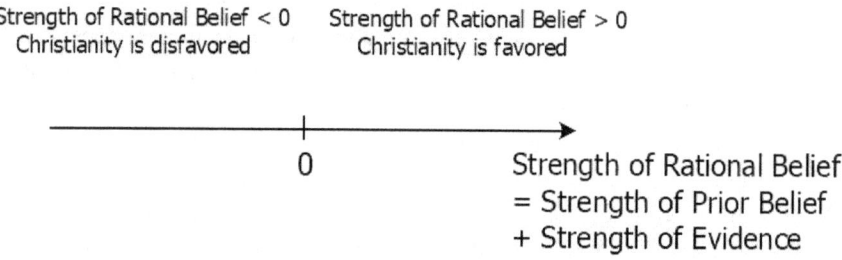

Figure 4.2: Illustration of Strength of Rational Belief. Christianity is favored when it is positive, whereas Christianity is disfavored when it is negative.

Since we don't always act according to our (rational) beliefs, these beliefs only constitute part of the decision to become a Christian. Richard Swinburne writes:

17. Clouser, *Knowing with the Heart*. See also chapter 5.

> Yet, people are often criticized for not "acting on" their beliefs. This seems to suggest that it is one thing to have a belief, another to act on it.[18]

He then gives several examples of why our actions are not always in accordance with our beliefs, although he argues that this belief-action discrepancy is not the common rule. According to the Danish philosopher and theologian Søren Kierkegaard (1813–55) we can never arrive at faith by empirical evidence alone. It always requires an act of will. He even argues that since faith requires full commitment we show a lack of faith when we look at evidence. Buchak proposes a somewhat different model where faith involves evidence acquired *so far*, but then we stop looking at *further* evidence in order to act and make a decision.[19] But this does not exclude the possibility of using further evidence in order to understand in retrospect the consequences of the decision we already made.[20]

We will follow Buchak's approach. As in figure 1.4, this involves an assignment of rewards to all four combinations of truth and decision, where each reward represents the strength of our will to act according to a specific combination of truth and decision. This definition is more general than interpreting reward as something that benefits ourselves, since our motives to act can be numerous, such as fear, longing for inner peace, feelings of unworthiness, or simply being too busy with other things in life.[21] In the sequel we will therefore refer to figure 1.3 as a *willingness table* and say that the four rewards of the table define a *willingness assignment*. This willingness assignment corresponds to a *willingness attitude* of ours.

It turns out that the willingness assignment can be summarized by one single number, which we refer to as Strength of Will. It is an abbreviation of "the extent to which a person's willingness assignment favors Christianity" or "the strength of a person's willingness assignment in terms of favoring Christianity." We show in appendix B that the willingness assignment favors Christianity when Strength of Will is positive, whereas it disfavors Christianity when Strength of Will is negative (see figure 4.3). We can also interpret Strength of Will as a quantifier of how central of our belief in Christianity is, as illustrated in figure 4.1, or as a quantifier of how

---

18. Swinburne, *Faith and Reason*, 28.

19. Kierkegaard's view is also referred to as fideism. See for instance Kierkegaard, *Concluding Unscientific Postscript*; Adams, "Kirkegaard's Arguments against Objective Reasoning"; and Buchak, "Can It Be Rational to Have Faith?"

20. Section 4.5.1 provides more details on whether a decision always requires full evidence or not.

21. Recall the discussion about this in chapter 1.

much our desire to achieve goals in life (instrumental rationality) are in line with those of the Bible.

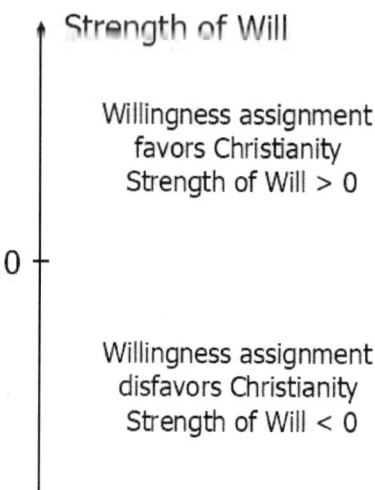

Figure 4.3: Illustration of Strength of Will. Christianity is disfavored when it is negative (below the origin) and favored when it is positive (above the origin).

Willingness tables will be discussed more extensively in chapter 7. Just to make you familiar with the concept, let us give two introductory examples. We first recall the willingness assignment in figure 1.4 of a person who wants to live according to the truth but still favors Christianity a bit. It is shown in appendix F that Strength of Will equals 1. On the other hand, a person who knows very little about Christianity may prefer to act solely based on what is true and use the neutral willingness assignment of figure 4.4, where each true alternative is assigned a reward of 1 and the false ones are given a reward of zero. In this case Strength of Will equals zero.

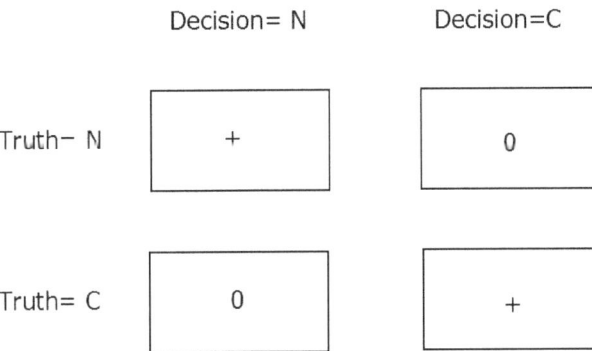

Figure 4.4: Illustration of a neutral willingness table for the decision between Christianity (C) and Non-Christianity (N). A true alternative gets a reward of 1 and a false alternative a reward of zero. Strength of Will in figure 4.3 equals zero.

We will use a version of the Wager where the choice between Christianity and Non-Christianity depends on which alternative gets the highest expected reward.[22] In appendix C we show that such a decision rule can be formulated in the following equivalent and perhaps more transparent way: A person becomes a Christian when Action, defined as the sum of Strength of Rational Belief and Strength of Will, gets positive (see figure 4.5). Action can be interpreted as "a person's total willingness to act and become a Christian." It has three main ingredients: Strength of Prior Belief, Strength of Evidence, and Strength of Will. Figure 4.5 provides a graphical summary of the Aposteriori Wager model, and it has great similarities to figure 4.1. It also has some connections to Stephen Unwin's faith math approach.[23]

To summarize, the Aposteriori Wager models the decision to become a Christian as an interplay between rational belief and a willingness to act.

---

22. This is the Expectation rule for the Wager, defined in section 1.4.

23. The faith math formula for Christianity C in Unwin, *Probability of God* is $B(C)=P(C|E)+F(C)$, where $P(C|E)$ is the aposteriori probability of C given evidence E, $F(C)$ is the faith factor for C, which depends on will, and $B(C)$ quantifies the total degree of belief in C based on prior belief, evidence, and will. Although Unwin did not connect his faith factor and total degree of belief with the Aposteriori Wager, it is in fact possible to do so, at least heuristically. This is achieved by transforming Action back to a probability scale between zero and 1. More specifically, given that $P(C|E)$ and Action are available from the Aposteriori Wager, we first define $B(C)=10^{Action}/(1+10^{Action})$ as the antilogit transformation of Action. The faith factor is then computed as $F(C)=B(C)-P(C|E)$. Whereas $P(C|E)$ and $B(C)$ are numbers between zero and 1, $F(C)$ can be positive or negative, depending on whether the willingness assignment favors Christianity or not.

This raises the question of whether belief formation is voluntary or not.[24] We argue that it is, since belief is based on evidence. Indeed, the choices we make affect how we evaluate the evidence we already have, and also to some extent what kind of new evidence we will encounter later on in life. In the next section we will find that this is particularly clear from a Christian point of view, since our decision to become a Christian will open up for new evidence in terms of revelations, which strongly affects our beliefs.

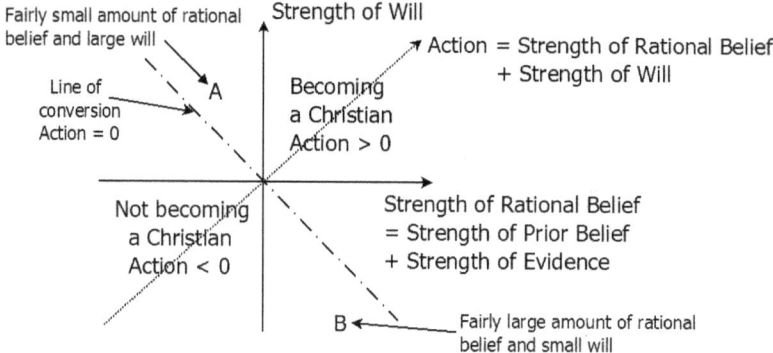

Figure 4.5: Illustration of which combinations of Strength of Rational Belief and Strength of Will lead to conversion. Strength of Rational Belief is positive to the right of the vertical axis and negative on the left side of it, whereas Strength of Will is positive above the horizontal axis and negative below it. According to the Aposteriori Wager a person becomes a Christian when Action—the sum of Strength of Rational Belief and Strength of Will—gets positive. This means that conversion happens when someone crosses the dash-dotted line. Points A and B represent two persons whose rational beliefs and willingness to act are very different. This illustrates that people may not always act according to their rational beliefs. On the other hand, if every person was located (say) along the dotted diagonal from the lower left to the upper right, then there would always be full concordance between Strength of Rational Belief and Strength of Will.

---

24. Whether belief formation is voluntary or not is a controversial topic among philosophers, with different points of view. According to doxastic voluntarism people have at least some voluntary control over their beliefs, whereas doxastic involuntarists claim the opposite. See for instance Moreland and Craig, *Philosophical Foundations*, chapter 3; and Chignell, "Ethics of Belief," section 3.3 for more details and further references.

4.4 INTERPRETING THE DECISION PROCESS

In chapter 3 we gave a Christian and naturalistic interpretation of the decision for and against Christianity. We will now put this into the context of the Aposteriori Wager.

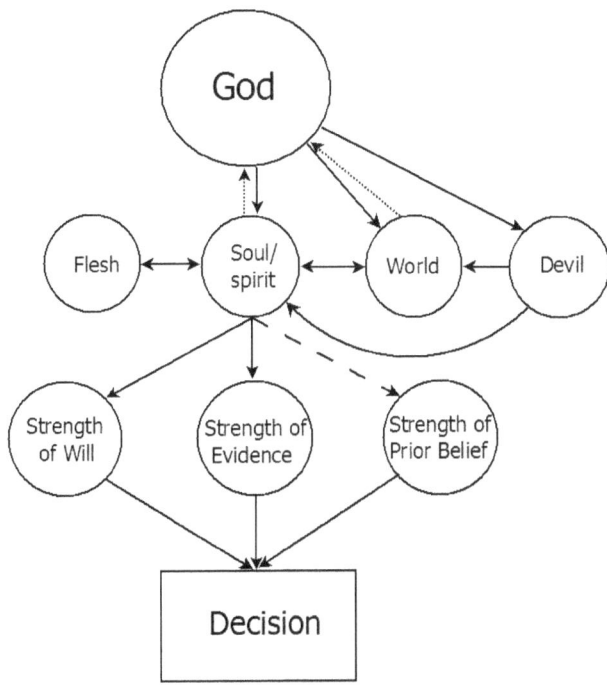

Figure 4.6: Christian interpretation of the Aposteriori Wager for the decision to become a Christian. All non-dotted arrows indicate causal relationships. The soul—the decision maker—gets influence from the flesh, the visible world, and the outside spiritual world (God and devil). The dashed arrow from the soul to prior belief corresponds to an apriori longing for God implanted *from birth* (see chapter 5). There is an arrow directed towards the devil, since his destructive actions are restricted by God's power,[25] and the arrow from God to the world illustrates God as the creator and upholder of the universe. The two dotted arrows represent the effect of prayers of the individual who makes the decision (directed from soul/spirit) and other individuals (directed from the world). They can be thought of as secondary causal events, ultimately controlled by the power of God.

Starting with the Christian interpretation, we recall that the decision can be viewed as a battle where God through the Holy Spirit tries to *increase*

---

25. Job 1:8–13; Eph 6:10–18; Rev 12:10–13.

our Strength of Evidence and Strength of Will, whereas the influence of the devil and the flesh is the opposite—to *lower* Strength of Evidence and Strength of Will. The impact of the outside world depends on which type of influence we are exposed to. The effect can either be to increase or decrease Strength of Evidence and Strength of Will. The causal relationships relevant for the decision to become a Christian are illustrated in figure 4.6. The corresponding naturalistic interpretation is given in figure 4.7. Regardless of whether we use the Christian or the naturalistic model, the decision is highly subjective and therefore it varies a lot—also between people with similar life experience. This is because we interpret evidence very differently and since our willingness attitudes are not the same.

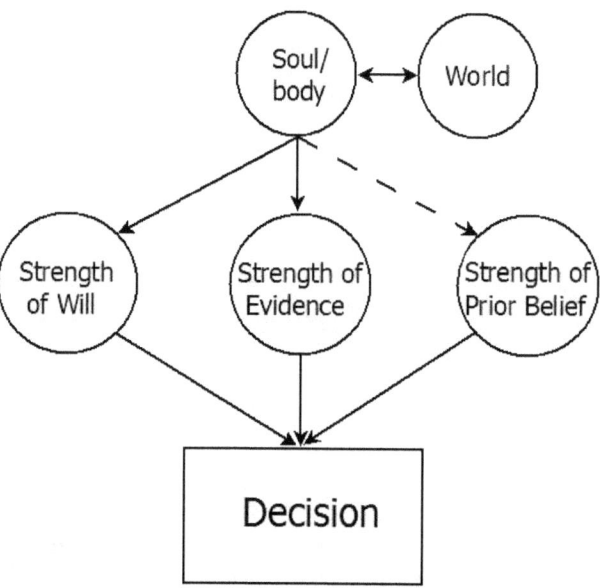

Figure 4.7: Naturalistic interpretation of the Aposteriori Wager for the decision to become a Christian. Arrows indicate causal relationships. The body and soul is essentially one unit determining the decision. The dashed arrow, directed from the soul/body to Strength of Prior Belief, represents a genetically and/or environmentally caused predisposition from birth to be religious.[26]

It is very important to emphasize that from a Christian point of view figure 4.5 describes what triggers a person to *become* a Christian. When God makes a call he complements and adds to our rational belief when we *feel his presence*. This starts a process that involves confession, a statement

26. See section 3.2.

of faith in Christ, and surrender to him, so that we *get filled* with the Holy Spirit. Then the line of conversion is crossed and Action changes from negative to positive.

The different meanings of Action and Strength of Rational Belief (before conversion) can be illustrated by an episode from the life of Jean Francois Gravelet, a French tightrope walker and acrobat, also known as Blondin.[27] He is well known for having crossed the gorge below the Niagara Falls, 1100 feet long and 160 feet above the water, on a tightrope. This he did a number of times, either blindfolded, in a sack, trundling a wheelbarrow, carrying his manager on his back, or sitting down midway while cooking and eating omelet on a single-legged chair. During one performance in 1860 he asked the Duke of New Castle, who was among the audience, if he believed Blondin could carry a person over the gorge in his wheelbarrow. The Duke answered yes. But nevertheless he declined when Blondin asked if he would like to volunteer, and so did everyone else in the audience except for one old woman—Blondin's own mother. Lots of people had a rational belief in Blondin's ability, but only his mother was willing to act and put her trust in him. That is, she was the only person in the audience whose Strength of Will was sufficiently large to act.

In the same way a rational belief alone in Jesus doesn't necessarily imply a willingness to receive him as Savior. There will always be a leap of faith based on trust in God:

> Now faith is confidence in what we hope for and assurance about what we do not see.[28]

We also gain insight into what Action means by looking at Engel's scale of spiritual decision. It is named after missiologist James Engel (1934–2016) and summarized in table 4.1.[29] The steps of Engel's scale could represent how Action changes from negative to positive during conversion.

---

27. Gumbel, *Questions of Life*.
28. Heb 11:1.
29. See Engel and Norton, *What's Gone Wrong*, and sections 2.1 and 3.1 of this book. The Internet Evangelism Day website gives more details on Engel's scale of spiritual decision, and its extension due to Frank Gray—the so-called Gray matrix. Gray proposed that Engel's scale (which corresponds to Action in our model) should be complemented with a second antagonism/enthusiasm scale, which is close to our Strength of Will. The Gray matrix is therefore similar to plotting Action on a vertical against Strength of Will on a horizontal scale. Internet Evangelism Day, "Gray's Is the Color."

Table 4.1: Engel's scale of spiritual decision

Although the exact details of a decision for Christ vary, this table suggests how belief by heart may change when a person becomes a Christian. It corresponds to crossing the line of conversion in figure 4.5, so that Action changes from negative to positive.

−8	Awareness of supreme being, no knowledge of gospel
−7	Initial awareness of gospel
−6	Awareness of fundamentals of gospel
−5	Grasp implications of gospel
−4	Positive attitude towards gospel
−3	Personal problem recognition
−2	Decision to act
−1	Repentance and faith in Christ
0	New birth
+1	Post-decision evaluation
+2	Incorporation into Body
+3	Conceptual and behavioral growth
+4	Communion with God
+5	Stewardship

When a person becomes a Christian he starts to *believe by heart*, not only rationally, even though his strength of rational belief in Christianity might have been small just before the decision.[30] Pascal summarized this work of the Holy Spirit this way:

> The heart has its reasons which the reason does not know.[31]

Anselm of Canterbury (1033–1109) expressed similar thoughts even more strongly:

---

30. However, Strength of Rational Belief and Strength of Will cannot be fully separated from each other. Indeed, it is likely that a person with a willingness assignment that strongly favors Christianity has at least some degree of rational belief in it, even just before the decision.

31. Pascal, *Pensées* (ebook), 62. Belief by heart can also be regarded as an instance of self-evident knowledge; see Clouser, *Knowing with the Heart*, chapter 4. With this terminology, belief by heart is that kind of self-evident knowledge that is to a large extent the work of the Holy Spirit. This does not contradict that God has put eternity in the heart of man from birth (prior belief 1 of chapter 5), as a longing for and conception of God as existing and real. This is slightly different from the belief by heart one obtains after conversion—an understanding of the fullness of the whole gospel. See also section 4.3.

I do not seek to understand in order to believe, but I believe in order to understand. For I believe even this: that I shall not understand unless I believe.[32]

For both of these quotations figure 4.8 gives a possible way of interpreting belief by heart. The heart includes a person's spirit, but also the deepest thoughts, beliefs, purposes, and motives of the soul. The spirit gets connected to and filled with the Holy Spirit after conversion, and only the Word of God can discern the dividing line between the spirit and the soul.[33] This is the line that separates our emotions from a deep relationship with and belief in God.

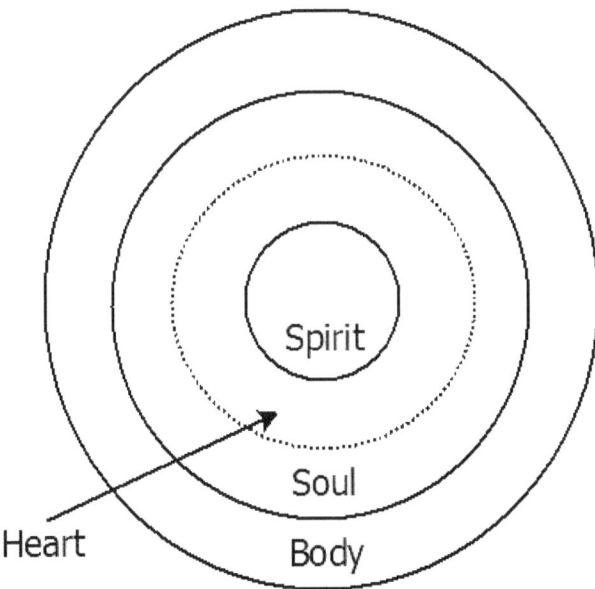

Figure 4.8: A possible interpretation of the human heart.[34] It presupposes a trichotomy view of man, according to which each one of us has a body, soul, and spirit. The heart is represented by the dashed circle. It consists of the spirit and parts of the soul.

Many Bible passages illustrate that God welcomes a person—such as A of figure 4.5—whose rational belief is small but still takes a leap in faith, as

---

32. Saint Anselm, "Proslogium," 7.
33. Heb 4:12.
34. Bevere, *Extraordinary*, chapter 16.

an act of will, in order to get to know him. Indeed, in the Gospel of Matthew we read about the rewards of seeking God:

> Ask and it will be given to you; seek and you will find; knock and the door will be opened to you. For everyone who asks receives; the one who seeks finds; and to the one who knocks, the door will be opened.[35]

And from another chapter of the same gospel we learn that rational belief as small as a mustard seed may be sufficient.[36] Swinburne divides interpretations of Christian faith into three main categories: the pragmatic, Lutheran, and Thomist views.[37] Pragmatic faith is close to Pascal's view, according to which one may *start* practicing Christianity with only a small amount of rational belief:

> You would like to attain faith, and do not know the way; you would like to cure yourself of unbelief, and ask the remedy for it. Learn of those who have been bound like you, and who now stake all their possessions. These are people who know the way which you would follow, and who are cured of an ill of which you would be cured. Follow the way by which they began; by acting as if they believed, taking the holy water, having masses said, etc. Even this will naturally make you believe . . .[38]

If this practice is sincere, Pascal contended that it will gradually turn into a belief by heart. The Lutheran view of faith is closest to Engel's interpretation of Action in table 4.1, involving both knowledge and trust in God by heart. As for the pragmatic view, one could start off by a small amount of rational belief, but the moment of conversion is emphasized more. The Thomist view is named after Thomas Aquinas (1225–75). It offers a more intellectual understanding of Christian faith, although it still includes more than rational belief. Richard Swinburne summarizes:

> So, although Thomist faith by itself is a very intellectual thing, a faith of the head and not the heart, a faith which may be held without any fruit in Christian living, the meritorious faith which the Thomist commends, the saving faith which puts the person of faith on the way to salvation, involves the whole person.[39]

---

35. Matt 7:7–8.
36. Matt 17:20.
37. Swinburne, *Faith and Reason*, chapter 4.
38. Pascal, *Pensées* (ebook), 54–55.
39. Swinburne, *Faith and Reason*, 141.

According to Aquinas such meritorious faith requires that it should "come into being in the right way" and "be formed by love." On the other hand, someone with a large amount of rational belief may still not want to become a Christian—such as person B of figure 4.5. An extreme example of this attitude is the devil or the demons, who know that God exists:

> You believe that there is one God. Good! Even the demons believe that and shudder.[40]

In spite of this knowledge they are totally unwilling to submit to God. But there are also several reasons why we as humans may have a willingness attitude that strongly disfavors Christianity.[41]

4.5 OBJECTIONS AGAINST THE WAGER

The Wager has been controversial and much debated for centuries. In this section we will discuss three of the most common objections.[42]

4.5.1 The Non-Evidence Objection

The Wager has been criticized for providing *pragmatic arguments*. Such arguments intend to motivate Christian belief even when the evidence is inconclusive. This is in contrast to *epistemic reasons*, which aim to convince that statements are true solely based on evidence. It is argued that it is impossible or at least not rational to have faith in something without believing it to be true from evidence in the natural. One of the most well-known proponents of *evidentialism* was the British mathematician and philosopher William Kingdon Clifford (1845–79), who famously commented:

> It is wrong always, everywhere, and for any one, and to believe anything upon insufficient evidence.[43]

The validity of this objection depends a lot on whether a naturalistic or Christian worldview is favored. From a naturalistic point of view, the only way to find out whether a statement is true or not is to test it empirically and

---

40. Jas 2:19; see also Job 1–2.
41. Willingness attitudes of this kind are treated in section 7.3.
42. For more details on these and other objections, such as questioning whether wagering is compatible with the doctrine of predestination, see Morris, *Making Sense of It All*; Groothuis, *On Pascal*; Jordan, *Pascal's Wager*; Rota, *Taking Pascal's Wager*; and evidence 17 of this book.
43. Clifford, "Ethics of Beliefs," 186.

evaluate the evidence.[44] And this is to some extent a sound attitude, since most people would gather at least some information before making any of the big decisions in life. From a Christian point of view, testing evidence is also good start. Something that is true will stand testing and Christian faith is not blind.[45] This view was also expressed by Pascal:

> The prophecies, even the miracles and proofs of our religion, are not of such a kind that they can be said to be absolutely convincing, but they are at the same time such that it cannot be said to be unreasonable to believe in them. There is thus evidence and obscurity, to enlighten some and obfuscate others. But the evidence is such as to exceed, or at least equal, the evidence to the contrary, so that it cannot be reason that decides us against following it, and can therefore only be concupiscence and wickedness of heart.[46]

As a top-class scientist Pascal knew that evidence is important for our beliefs, and in the *Pensées* he presented various kinds of evidence in favor of Christianity. In subsequent chapters of this book we will also discuss different types of evidence. Although we argue that this makes Christianity a very rational option, evidence before the decision is still only part of the story—it will never give us a strict proof for or against Christianity.

Having said this, one may also raise several objections against evidentialism. Since it cannot be tested empirically, it is first of all self-refuting. And the American philosopher William James (1842–1910) brought forward another *will-to-believe argument* against evidentialism in 1896. He contended that it is not rational to require full evidence in order to believe:

> A rule of thinking which would absolutely prevent me from acknowledging certain kinds of truth if those kinds of truth were really there, would be an irrational rule.[47]

James thought his principle applied very well to religious decisions, since there is much at stake and we are forced to make them. In particular, it applies very well to becoming a Christian, since humans cannot understand their broken relationship with God by rational arguments and evidence alone. Pascal analyzes the human condition in his anthropological

---

44. This is related to the discussion on methodological naturalism in evidence 10.
45. The view that faith is independent of and even hostile to reason is called fideism.
46. Pascal, *Pensées*, note 835.
47. James, *Will to Believe*, 31–32.

argument and contends that man is both noble—as created in God's image—and wretched—because he is fallen. This is vividly expressed as:

> What kind of freak is man! What a novelty he is, how absurd he is, how chaotic and what a mess of contradictions, and yet what a prodigy! He is judge of all things, yet a feeble worm. He is repository of truth, and yet sinks in such doubt and error. He is the glory and the scum of the universe.[48]

Pascal argues that it is a sign of human greatness when we recognize our limitations. This self-consciousness should motivate us to take a step in faith in order to acquire more conclusive evidence. And God has deliberately chosen a way for us to reach him that is accessible to anyone regardless of age, intelligence, or ethnic and social background:

> At that time Jesus said, "I praise you, Father, Lord of heaven and earth, because you have hidden these things from the wise and learned, and revealed them to little children. Yes, Father, for this is what you were pleased to do."[49]

Somewhat related to evidentialism is the thought that Christians have the *burden of proof*, since they hold on to a faith that adds something to naturalism. Although proof should not be interpreted in a strict logical sense, the view is anyhow that Christians have the responsibility to verify that their position is more likely than naturalism. When choosing between two worldviews, it is contended that one should use a parsimony argument and go for the simpler explanation.[50] Bertrand Russell once used a teapot argument along this line:

> Many orthodox people speak as though it were the business of skeptics to disprove received dogmas rather than of dogmatists to prove them. This is, of course, a mistake. If I were to suggest that between the Earth and Mars there is a china teapot revolving about the sun in an elliptical orbit, nobody would be able to disprove my assertion provided I were careful to add that the teapot is too small to be revealed even by our most powerful telescopes. But if I were to go on to say that, since my assertion cannot be disproved, it is intolerable presumption on the part of human reason to doubt it, I should rightly be thought to be talking nonsense. If, however, the existence of such a teapot were affirmed in ancient books, taught as the

---

48. Pascal, *Pensées*, note 131; and Groothuis, *Christian Apologetics*, chapter 18.
49. Matt 11:25–26.
50. See also evidence 15.

sacred truth every Sunday, and instilled into the minds of
children at school, hesitation to believe in its existence would
become a mark of eccentricity and entitle the doubter to the
attentions of the psychiatrist in an enlightened age or of the
Inquisitor in an earlier time.[51]

The Christian response is that there is enough evidence in order to take the first steps in order to *become* a Christian.[52] Indeed, the Wager argument concerns the decision to take such a step more than *holding on* to Christian faith. We have already mentioned[53] that God will reward those who seek him by revealing his presence through the Holy Spirit, thereby supplying more evidence and increasing the amount of rational belief in Christianity after the decision has been made. But Christianity does not mean holding on to something one does not believe to be true. The Bible is indeed very honest—it says that if Jesus has not resurrected then Christianity is not true and Christian faith has little or no value.[54] But there is still a leap of faith and an act of will involved in becoming a Christian. This leap is based on evidence that is less conclusive before the decision than after.

4.5.2 The Cupidity Objection

The Cupidity Objection emphasizes that the Wager gives *prudential reasons* for Christian faith. It promises various types of benefits for Christianity, in particular an eternal life together with God without any suffering or pain. The British philosopher of religion Dewi Z. Phillips (1934-2006) argued that if someone's belief includes promises of eternal salvation, he will be indifferent to this life—an attitude that is not morally right:

> Construing belief in the immortality of the soul as the final state which gives men good reasons for acting in certain ways now falsifies the character of moral regard. It certainly allows no room for anything that might be meant by the spirituality of the soul. It seems to me that if people lead a certain kind of life simply because of the final set of consequences to which it leads, they are indifferent to that way of life.[55]

51. Russell, "Is There a God?," 547–48. See also Selander, "Gud och bevisbördan" for more on the burden of proof between atheists and Christians.

52. This is discussed in chapters 9–13, in particular in evidence 19.

53. Section 4.4.

54. See willingness attitude 5.

55. Phillips, *Death and Immortality*, 30. See also Swinburne, *Faith and Reason*, chapter 5.

But Christianity is meant to have the opposite effect. A life in service and honor to God is intended to be meaningful here and now, and influence the way we treat others. It is not just a route to afterlife.

A related objection—*ethical evidentialism*—regards it as unethical not to follow evidence alone, and in particular considers it not right to acquire faith in something because of promised benefits. According to the *Avarice charge* the Wager also violates a moral duty of prohibiting injury to oneself (for instance caused by impaired cognitive health) or others by believing in something without enough evidence. These objections would certainly have some credibility if Christian faith was totally blind. But since (we argue) strong evidence for Christianity is available, it is neither unethical nor immoral to hold on to it. And the Avarice charge becomes self-refuting, since there is no conclusive evidence against Christianity, and therefore *any* decision (also the decision not to take a stand) becomes immoral according to this principle. Instead it seems much more reasonable that the healthiest option is to believe in the truth, whether it is Christianity, naturalism, or some other philosophy of life.

Even when the motive of becoming a Christian is one's personal good, this doesn't make it egoistic. Self-interest need not be selfish in the sense of hurting others. On the contrary, Christianity is meant to have visible effects in this life. The second most important command of the whole Bible,

> Love your neighbor as you love yourself,[56]

emphasizes that it *is* possible to care for others *and* ourselves. Indeed, if I don't like myself I will have *more* difficulties loving others. And Christianity is not a zero-sum game where the benefits of some are compensated by the loss of others, neither in this life nor in afterlife. Becoming a Christian is rather an *individual decision*, and the Bible states that God wants everyone to be saved:

> The Lord is not slow in keeping his promise, as some understand slowness. Instead he is patient with you, not wanting anyone to perish, but everyone to come to repentance.[57]

4.5.3 The Many Gods Objection

We will discuss various willingness attitudes in chapter 7. One version of Pascal's Wager gives Christianity an infinitely positive large reward and

---

56. Lev 19:34; Matt 19:19; 22:39; Mark 12:31; Luke 10:27.

57. 2 Pet 3:9.

naturalism an infinitely negative reward if Christianity is true.[58] The many gods objection asserts that the same rewards could be used for any other theistic religion that promises eternal good, such as Judaism or Islam. The French philosopher and writer Denis Diderot (1713–84) once commented:

> Pascal has said that if your religion is false, you have risked nothing by believing it true; if it is true, you have risked all by believing it is false. An Imam could have said as much.[59]

One may extend Diderot's objection by saying that infinitely many gods other than the Christian one could exist. If each one of these gods or religions promises an infinitely high reward, it may be argued that none of them should be dismissed apriori.

A first response to the many gods objection is to change the Wager argument into an *Ecumenical Wager* in order to distinguish between naturalism and theism. This type of Wager could be employed as a first step for a person to start believing in a spiritual reality outside the visible world. This includes arguments of *natural theology*, such as the existence of the universe, design, morality, reason, and consciousness. But this is just a start, since the consequence of not making a final decision between several theistic religions is the same as deciding against them all. For instance, Christianity and Islam make several conflicting statements—in particular whether Jesus was only a prophet or the Son of God and the unique way to salvation. Both religions cannot be true and one has to make a choice—either between them or against both of them.[60]

In the beginning of chapter 2 we emphasized that the Wager can also be used to choose between Christianity and one or several other religions. The only requirement is that one of the religions is true.[61] Suppose, for in-

---

58. See the table of figure 7.1.

59. Diderot, "Additions to the Philosophical Thoughts," para. lix. See also Jordan, *Pascal's Wager*; and Bartha "Many Gods, Many Wagers."

60. See evidence 1.

61. See appendix D for how to use the Wager when choosing between Christianity and several alternatives. There is a technical problem though when the Expectation rule is used for distinguishing between two religions that both (say) give an infinitely positive reward if true and an infinitely negative reward if the other religion is true. As soon as both of them is assigned a positive probability, no matter how small, the expected reward is not well defined for either of the two religions and therefore a choice cannot be made. But if the *Jamesian Wager* (based on the Next Best Thing principle) is used instead of the Canonical Wager (based on the Expectation rule) it is possible to retain infinite utilities for both religions; see Jordan, *Pascal's Wager*, section 3.4. This is also related to Schlesinger's principle, according to which one could choose between several alternatives with infinitely large expected utility by choosing the one with highest probability of having an infinite utility. Schlesinger's principle can be deduced from

stance, that David chooses between Christianity and Islam, and gives both religions a reward of 10 if true and -10 if false. Then the willingness table is neutral, and David will choose the religion he believes most likely to be true. He will therefore base his decision on prior belief (implanted from birth) and evidence. From a theistic perspective, one could argue that prior belief is similar for both religions, since it is hard for a child to know which god he naturally relates to, because of lack of information.[62] Then evidence alone will determine whether David chooses Christianity or Islam. Pascal compared evidence of the two religions and argued that, unlike Jesus, Mohammad was not foretold by prophecies, he did not prophecy himself, and he did not perform miracles. Pascal contended that the Qur'an is less historically and logically credible than the Bible, largely dependent on one person's claimed divine revelation.[63] We could add that Christianity is the most universal religion that has penetrated almost all cultural and ethnic groups. It has very much been spread during periods of oppression and persecution, whereas Islam to a larger extent spread through the sword.[64] This pattern seems to have prevailed to this day. In fact, a recent study among German young men revealed that Christians are less involved in violent behavior than Muslims.[65] It also seems that Christianity gives a more realistic view of human nature, with man fallen but yet created in the image of God. There are also several testimonies of the changed lives of people who became Christians. Many others regarded these witnesses as strong evidence for their own choice.[66] Since the Qur'an claims that Jesus never died, perhaps the ultimate piece of evidence when deciding between Christianity and Islam (or any other religion) is whether or not Jesus resurrected from

---

relative utility theory, of which Bartha, "Many Gods, Many Wagers" gives an account. In chapter 7 we argue though that infinite utilities are less realistic since rewards correspond to an act of will. With finite utilities the Canonical Wager is also well defined.

62. If a person assigns the true religion a reward of 10 and the false one a reward of -10, it follows from appendix B that the willingness assignment is neutral, since Strength of Will =0. We know from appendix A that Strength of Prior Belief =0 if no religion is favored apriori. It then follows from formula C.7 of appendix C that Action=Strength of Prior Belief+Strength of Evidence+Strength of Will=Strength of Evidence. This person will therefore choose religion based on evidence alone. However, we will argue in section 5.2 that from a Christian perspective a small child belongs to Christ, and under this assumption Strength of Prior Belief is positive.

63. Groothuis, *Christian Apologetics*, chapter 9, and evidence 22 of this book.

64. Ibid., chapter 24. See also evidence 6 and evidence 18.

65. The study was based on interviews with more than 16,500 Christian or Muslim adolescents. Among the Christians, a higher degree of religiosity was correlated with a lower rate of violent behavior, whereas for Muslims the correlation was in the opposite direction. Baier, "Influence of Religiosity."

66. Evidence 23.

death. And a majority of theologians regard the resurrection as historically credible.[67]

But it is not necessary to have a neutral reward assignment between Christianity and Islam. Even though both religions promise eternal good, one may still use a reward argument in favor of Christianity, either since the message of salvation is a free gift by grace, not by works, or because of awareness of sinfulness and longing for inner peace through belief in Christ. Our main point is that the Aposteriori Wager can be used to distinguish between two religions based on willingness assignments, prior beliefs, and evidence.

The infinitely-many-gods objection can be answered in a similar way. If finite rewards are assigned to all competing religions and all of them are given at least some positive apriori probability, evidence will be important for choosing between them, whereas the rewards may or may not be the same.

---

67. Evidence 22.

5

Prior Belief

IN THE PREVIOUS CHAPTER we introduced the Aposteriori Wager and raised various objections against Pascal's Wager. In the next three chapters we will analyze the three major components of the decision to become a Christian: prior belief, evidence, and willingness assignment. This will be illustrated with a number of examples that are written from a Christian perspective.

In this chapter we look more closely at prior belief. Section 5.1 starts with a general discussion on how to choose priors. This part is a bit technical. If you are more interested in the Christian interpretation of prior belief you may proceed to section 5.2.

5.1 CHOOSING PRIOR

We have previously formulated the decision as one between Christianity (C) and Non-Christianity (N). It is possible to split Non-Christianity into a number of different alternatives. For instance, we may formulate the decision as one between:

$\quad$ C: Christianity
$\quad$ N_1: Naturalism
$\quad$ N_2: Judaism
$\quad$ N_3: Islam
$\quad$ N_4: Buddhism
$\quad$ N_5: Hinduism

In this case Non-Christianity (N={N_1, ... N_5}) includes five alternatives. This list could of course be extended to include many other known or yet unknown philosophies of life.[1]

We have previously discussed how to extend the Aposteriori Wager to choose between Christianity and other monotheistic religions, on one hand, and other polytheistic religions or philosophies of life, on the other—the Ecumenical Wager.[2] It can be phrased as choosing between Theism (T) and Non-Theism (NT). Using the six alternatives above, this corresponds to selecting one of these categories:

T = {C, N_2, N_3}: There is one God,
NT = {N_1, N_4, N_5}: There is not one God.

Regardless of whether we choose between Christianity and Non-Christianity, or between Theism and Non-Theism, we need to know how likely the six alternatives (C, N_1, ... N_5) are based on background knowledge (K), which is part of the prior, and evidence (E).

The choice of prior involves several ambiguities that have been discussed a lot within the statistics and philosophy literature. The first ambiguity concerns whether the prior can be changed after having seen the evidence.[3] This can be illustrated with the *bridge player's fallacy*. The player finds the cards of his bridge hand in a certain order, and there are two competing and apriori equally likely hypotheses: N, that the deck of cards was mixed randomly with any possible hand of cards being equally likely, and C, that someone cheated and put them in a specific predetermined order that the player does not know of. If the bridge player, after having seen the cards, asserts that his hand is identical to the rigged hand he will choose C because the evidence (his bridge hand) overwhelmingly supports C in favor of N. This is usually not regarded as a valid kind of inductive argument in planned experiments, since the player uses his evidence in order to change the prior so that the conclusion gets biased—a fallacy.

Suppose however that the player receives a piece of paper that was written *before* the hand was distributed but nevertheless given to him afterwards. The text on this paper says that the hand he obtained was rigged. It is

1. See evidence 1 for a discussion about the differences between various religions.
2. Section 4.5.3 and appendix D.
3. See for instance Mellor, "God and Probability"; Swinburne, *Existence of God*, chapter 6; and Swinburne, *Epistemic Justification*, appendix. In the latter reference a distinction is made between *predictivist* and *timeless* theories, depending on whether the prior is allowed to change when new evidence is encountered; evidence that gives information about whether previous evidence was obtained before a hypothesis was formulated or not.

then a valid inductive inference to choose C. The piece of paper can either be regarded as new evidence or as new background information for the old evidence. In the latter case it is completely valid to change the prior and let evidence be restricted to recognizing the hand of cards.

The ambiguity of the bridge player example concerns how to distinguish evidence from background knowledge. In his book *The Existence of God*, Richard Swinburne writes:

> However, . . . any division between evidence and background knowledge will be a somewhat arbitrary one. Normally it is convenient to call the latest piece of observational evidence E and the rest K; but sometimes it is convenient to let E be all observational evidence and letting K be mere "tautological evidence."[4]

In the former case, when E only incorporates the latest piece of observational evidence the prior can sometimes be changed, even after having seen the evidence—as for the bridge player. I will follow the latter approach though. When applied to the decision to become a Christian, it means that E will include all evidence acquired during life, whereas background knowledge (K) only involves *self-evident knowledge* and desires that I regard as implanted from birth. The prior is therefore fixed over time and does not change. One may object to this interpretation of prior since a small child does not know of Christianity, nor of any other religion. However, my interpretation of prior is our *inborn tendency* of accepting a certain statement the first time it is heard, before taking evidence into account.

The second ambiguity concerns which apriori probabilities the six alternatives (C, $N_1 \ldots N_5$) should have. One option is to choose prior from some objective criterion. If the six alternatives (C, $N_1, \ldots N_5$) were all of the same kind, they would be assigned the same apriori probability 1/6 by any of these objective criteria.[5] This is much like guessing which face of a dice will come up before we roll it, and it is usually referred to as an *uninformative prior* or the *principle of indifference*.

---

4. Swinburne, *Existence of God*, 67. We have modified the symbols of the original text to conform with our notation.

5. The most common objective criterion for distinguishing between alternatives of the same kind is an *uninformative prior*. When the number of alternatives is finite this criterion assigns the same apriori probability to each one of them. When the number of alternatives is infinite there are many possibilities. Jeffrey's prior is often used for a continuous scale of alternatives such as real numbers, since it is invariant with respect to choice of scale (transformations). See for instance Berger, *Statistical Decision Theory* or Rubin et al., *Bayesian Data Analysis*. The prior could also be selected from the maximum entropy principle; see Jaynes, *Probability Theory*.

But philosophies of life are not of the same kind, and it is also important how we group them. For instance, if we merge Buddhism and Hinduism into a new category of Eastern religions we get five alternatives

C: Christianity
N_1: Naturalism
N_2: Judaism
N_3: Islam
N_4: Eastern Religions

rather than six, and subsequently one has to choose between Buddhism and Hinduism if N_4 is selected at first. The principle of indifference assigns Christianity an apriori probability of 1/5, which differs from the 1/6 we had before. The reason for this contradiction[6] is that the principle of indifference was used for two different sets of alternatives.

In order to avoid dependence on how we label alternatives we have to assign priors by some other rule. A common principle in science is to give higher apriori probabilities to simpler alternatives whereas more complicated ones are regarded as less likely. This is referred to as Occam's razor or the principle of parsimony. Richard Swinburne writes:

> The practice of scientists historians etc. shows that they judge a *very* simple theory to be very much more probable than less simple theories. If you can explain many clues by the hypothesis that one agent caused them, that is far more probable than a theory with the same explanatory power to explain the clues that postulates that two agents caused the clues.[7]

Simplicity includes the number of initial conditions and laws of nature needed to formulate the theory and also how understandable it is.[8] A related but yet different concept is scope. The higher the scope of a theory is the more information it provides, the more predictions it makes about the world, and the easier it is to falsify. For instance, if a theory postulates that all heavenly bodies move either in elliptic orbits (around some other object, which is in one of the ellipse's focal points) or in parabolic orbits, it has a larger scope than a theory that only allows bodies to move in elliptic orbits. A theory with smaller scope is usually given larger apriori probability, al-

---

6. This contradiction is related to Bertrand's paradox.

7. Swinburne, *Existence of God*, 70. See also Swinburne, *Epistemic Justification*, chapter 4. In *Bayesian model selection*, simpler models and models with smaller scope are usually assigned higher apriori probabilities.

8. Evidence 10 provides more details about the nature of scientific theories.

though Swinburne argues that the simplicity criterion is more important for assigning apriori probabilities.

Since theism postulates one single agent—an eternal, omnipotent, omniscient, and perfectly free God, who needs no causation—it is often regarded as a simple alternative and therefore one assigns it a high apriori probability. In order to finalize the choice of prior we must divide the (high) apriori probability of theism into apriori probabilities of Christianity, Judaism, and Islam, and analogously divide the apriori less likely alternative of Non-Theism into its subalternatives.

Are there yet other rules for making a prior choice between religions? I will argue that the there are indeed other criteria for choosing the prior. Since this is an individual decision, it is crucial that the prior is selected from the perspective of the decision maker and therefore reflects the nature of man according to some religion or philosophy of life. When the prior for different religions only involves background knowledge implanted from birth, it corresponds to the *inborn tendency* of a small child to relate to a personal god. Although this way of choosing apriori probabilities slightly differs from Swinburne's simplicity criterion, I would argue that it also leads to a high apriori probability for theism, but for the reason that children seem to have a very natural conception of one single god.[9] When choosing between theistic religions, one could argue from a theistic perspective that it is reasonable to assign the same prior to Christianity and Islam, since a small child does not know which god she naturally holds on to.[10] An atheist could make the same argument based on an assumed genetic disposition of being religious in general. But in the next section I will discuss choice of prior from a Christian perspective. I will argue that the apriori probability of Christianity quantifies our inborn desire to connect to God. It should be high in order to reflect how children's belief in God is described in the Bible.

5.2 CHRISTIAN INTERPRETATION OF PRIOR

We will now be more specific about what to include in the prior for the decision to become a Christian. That is, we will look at what influences our tendency to favor Christianity (C) or Non-Christianity (N) before evidence is taken into account. In the previous section we argued that the prior includes

---

9. See for instance the work of Coles, whose interviews with boys and girls of various backgrounds indicate that many children express advanced thoughts and questions relating to God. Coles, *Spiritual Life of Children*.

10. This argument was used in section 4.5.3 as a response to the many gods objection.

our inborn desire to connect to God, which includes an inborn desire to be loved and to live a life with meaning, purpose, and goals. From a Christian perspective, these desires are consequences of the longing of our spirit to be reconnected to the Holy Spirit of God. Indeed, Jesus valued the strong faith of a child who very easily believes and has a natural way of accepting God without questioning:

> People were also bringing babies to Jesus for him to place his hands on them. When the disciples saw this, they rebuked them. But Jesus called the children to him and said, "Let the little children come to me, and do not hinder them, for the kingdom of God belongs to such as these. Truly I tell you, anyone who will not receive the kingdom of God like a little child will never enter it."[11]

The meaning of these verses is that a child belongs to Christ purely based of prior conceptions. He needs no overwhelming evidence, nor does he require a strong act of will in order to believe. The following verses from Paul's Letter to the Romans also indicate that God doesn't make a child morally accountable for sin, since it is too small to understand that a law has been broken:

> But sin, seizing the opportunity afforded by the commandment, produced in me every kind of coveting. For apart from the law, sin was dead. Once I was alive apart from the law; but when the commandment came, sin sprang to life and I died. I found that the very commandment that was intended to bring life actually brought death.[12]

---

11. Luke 18:15–17.

12. Rom 7:8–10. Although theologians have different opinions on this, several other Bible passages indicate that a child that dies before the age of moral accountability goes to heaven (Isa 7:16; 2 Sam 12:23; John 9:41). In our context this means that a positive Strength of Prior Belief leads to Christ. A morally accountable individual, on the other hand, has the ability to understand the implications of the decision for and against Christianity. He will therefore include evidence and willingness assignment in the decision process (figure 4.5 and formula C.8 of appendix C). One may object, saying that the cognitive and social development of humans is gradual, and for this reason it is difficult to know when someone becomes morally accountable. Yes, this *is* indeed difficult for *us* to know. We simply have to trust God as a completely righteous and fair judge and be grateful that we are not to decide about the eternal destiny of others, since we have far too little information for this.

If so, the decision of a child is solely based on an apriori probability of Christianity larger than 50 percent.[13] And if God has implanted a longing for him that is equally strong for all children, this prior will not be subjective.

Prior belief can be of different forms. *Foundationalism* is a school of thought within philosophy that asserts that all belief systems have some foundational components. They are called "basic" or "properly basic" beliefs, and they don't need other beliefs in order to be justified. Within this framework we could interpret prior beliefs as those basic beliefs that are of relevance for the decision to become a Christian, such that we either have them or at least have a capability to acquire them from birth.[14] We will suggest a model by which our prior belief in Christianity has four such basic belief components (prior belief 1–4). This is illustrated in figure 5.1 and explained in more detail below.

---

13. If the decision only involves prior belief, there is no evidence involved, so that Strength of Evidence=0. Assuming that the reward table of a child is neutral (cf. figure 4.4), it follows that Strength of Will=0. According to figure 4.5 this implies that Action=Strength of Prior Belief. From equation C.8 of appendix C we conclude that an apriori probability of Christianity larger than 0.5 is equivalent to a positive value of Strength of Prior Belief, which is equivalent to a positive value of Action, which leads to Christ.

14. By definition, a (proper) basic belief does not need support from any other belief in order to be valid. Although foundationalists differ in their views on what a basic belief is, they often include self-evident knowledge (such as beliefs in logic and reasoning), ordinary life perceptions, and beliefs in certain moral and theological values. In section 5.1 we used a convention of including in the prior only those things that are implanted from birth. Therefore, only those basic beliefs that are implanted form birth are part of the prior belief in Christianity; all other basic beliefs (such as perceptions) are part of the evidence. Among the remaining basic beliefs, we have only included those we consider important for the decision to become a Christian. For more details on foundationalism, see Moreland and Craig, *Philosophical Foundations*, chapter 5.

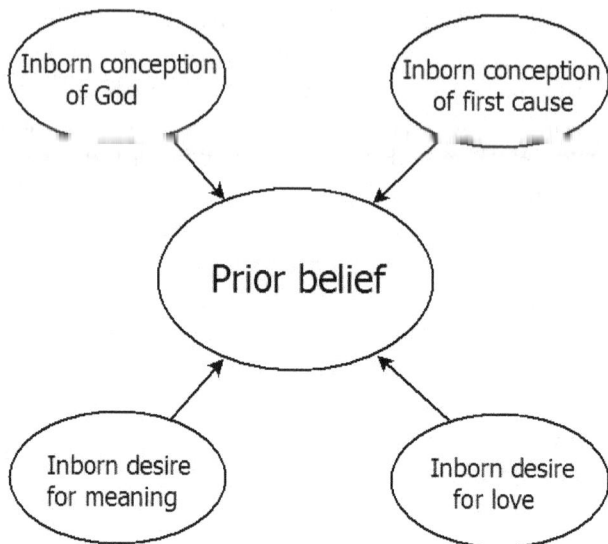

Figure 5.1: A model with four components of prior belief. It is based on a Christian perspective, since all four components reflect our inborn desire from birth to have a relationship with God.

Prior Belief 1: Inborn conception of and longing for God. Many people—even those that regard themselves as non-religious—tend to pray to God when they are facing extreme pressure. Indeed, it seems that from early childhood we all have an inbuilt conception of God as our true Father—someone who knows everything we do. The Bible tells that God has put eternity into the heart of man:

> He has made everything beautiful in its time. He has also set eternity in the human heart; yet no one can fathom what God has done from beginning to end.[15]

This is manifested as a longing for a God that knows of our thoughts and completely embeds us with his love at each moment.[16] But since our personal relation with him is broken after the fall of man, we have a lack of inner peace.

In the eleventh century Anselm, the archbishop of Canterbury, reasoned that if God exists in the mind of all humans as the greatest possible

---

15. Eccl 3:11.
16. Ps 139:1–18.

being then he must exist in reality as well, otherwise he would not be the greatest possible being. This is usually referred to as the *ontological argument* for the existence of God.[17] Indeed, if God only exists in our mind our conception of and longing for him is just a psychological construct, the purpose of which is to create a false belief of happiness and safety in life.

Prior Belief 2: Inborn conception of a first cause. Causality is a more intellectual kind of prior belief. Our conception of causality is to some extent dependent on experience, but yet we seem to have an inbuilt idea that everything with a beginning has a cause. The *cosmological argument* for the existence of God[18] is based on the premise that a first cause or sufficient reason exists. It raises the question, "Who created God?" However, if we accept as a logical premise the fact that everything with a beginning has a cause and regress backwards in time we get a whole chain of causes. Two possibilities then is to either have a first eternal cause without beginning or an infinite sequence of causes. The cosmological argument is based on the premise that the first explanation—an ever-existing God—gives a more stable worldview. Indeed, it is easier to explain why the present has arrived given a finite number of events in the past. Later on we will find that a first cause is also more in line with modern cosmology.[19]

Another related *argument from simplicity* is that an infinitely capable first cause—God—has more explanatory power and provides a simpler rather than a more complicated explanation of the universe.[20] The Bible refers to God in Trinity as a *transcendent* first cause, which is eternal, present from the beginning, and outside our notion of space and time. It also describes Christ as the Word and that everything was created *through* him:

> In the beginning was the Word, and the Word was with God, and the Word was God. He was with God in the beginning. Through him all things were made; without him nothing was made that has been made. In him was life, and that life was the

17. Ontology focuses on the nature of being, existence, or reality of various entities. It is part of a major branch of philosophy called metaphysics. Kurt Gödel, Alvin Plantinga, and others have presented modern versions of the ontological argument based on modal logic. See for instance Plantinga, *Nature of Necessity*. An automated and computerized version of Gödel's proof has recently been implemented by Benzmüller and Woltzenlogel Paleo, "Formalization, Mechanization and Automation."

18. For more details on the cosmological argument, see Craig, *Reasonable Faith* and the references therein.

19. See for instance Craig and Sinclair, "*Kalam* Cosmological Argument" and evidence 12 and 13 of this book.

20. Swinburne, *Existence of God*.

light of all mankind. The light shines in the darkness, and the darkness has not overcome it.[21]

Some other powerful verses about Christ can be found in the first chapter of Paul's Letter to the Colossians.

> For in him all things were created: things in heaven and on earth, visible and invisible, whether thrones or powers or rulers or authorities; all things have been created through him and for him. He is before all things, and in him all things hold together. And he is the head of the body, the church; he is the beginning and the firstborn from among the dead, so that in everything he might have the supremacy. For God was pleased to have all his fullness dwell in him.[22]

This passage tells us that creation is not only through Christ; it is also *in* him, *to* him, and *upholded by* him.

Prior Belief 3: Inborn desire for meaning and purpose. Our purpose and perceived meaning of life is like the engine of a car—it drives and motivates much of what we do. From a Christian point of view our inborn *desire* for meaning and purpose reflects a longing for a life in line with God's will. And as such it is part of our prior belief.

According to the Bible life's true meaning and purpose is obtained by entering a relationship with God, since he created us for the purpose of glorifying his name.[23] He had a plan designed for each one of us already before we were born:

> For you created my inmost being; you knit me together in my mother's womb. I praise you because I am fearfully and wonderfully made; your works are wonderful, I know that full well. My frame was not hidden from you when I was made in the secret place, when I was woven together in the depths of the earth. Your eyes saw my unformed body; all the days ordained for me were written in your book before one of them came to be.[24]

But unfortunately we often miss this. We are so occupied with duties and prefer to follow our own sometimes rather selfish motives. Then later, when we look back at life, we tend to acquire a more realistic view of it. Things

21. John 1:1–4; see also Gen 1.
22. Col 1:16–19.
23. 1 Cor 10:31.
24. Ps 139:13–16.

that once seemed important suddenly strike us as trivial and sometimes we even regret them. Other small acts of unselfishness that once appeared to be unimportant now make our heart warm. Hardly no one regrets at the end of his life that he worked too little, rather he regrets that he didn't spend more time doing what really matters, like helping others and showing love to people. Jesus once said that the whole Law boils down to two commandments:

> Love God with all your heart, and love your neighbor as yourself.[25]

Following this way of living gives life true meaning—an investment in heavenly treasures that never fades away.[26]

Prior Belief 4: Inborn desire for unconditional love. We are often judged by what we do. This is to some extent natural since we are responsible for our deeds and they tell others quite a lot about who we are.[27] But we all seem to have an inborn *desire to be loved unconditionally*, and this is part of our prior belief. Ideally our parents and family should fulfill this role, but any human love is imperfect and sadly enough many families are broken.

Whereas meaning and purpose are related to our outward missions in life, our need for love is even more foundational. This is beautifully illustrated in Paul's Letter to the Ephesian Church:

> . . . so that Christ may dwell in your hearts through faith. And I pray that you, being rooted and established in love, may have power, together with all the Lord's holy people, to grasp how wide and long and high and deep is the love of Christ, and to know this love that surpasses knowledge—that you may be filled to the measure of all the fullness of God.[28]

God's love for us is usually referred to as *agape* love. It is perfect, unconditional, and manifests itself in that Jesus died for us on Calvary while we were still sinners.[29] It is not until we get deeply rooted in the love of Christ that we are able to live an unselfish life for others with true meaning and purpose. But unconditional love doesn't mean that God approves everything we do. On the contrary, God is not only loving but he is also holy and therefore he cannot tolerate sin. He is willing to forgive us everything,

25. Luke 10:27; Matt 22:36–40.
26. Matt 6:19–20.
27. Jas 2:14–26.
28. Eph 3:17–19.
29. Eph 2:1–6.

but he wants us to follow him. If we stumble and fall again he still wants to forgive us when we sincerely regret what we did.

God's unconditional love is beautifully illustrated in the Parable of the Lost Son who squandered his father's wealth in wild living and ended up in poverty and starvation. He then sincerely regretted himself and returned to his father in humbleness:

> When he came to his senses, he said, "How many of my father's hired servants have food to spare, and here I am starving to death! I will set out and go back to my father and say to him: Father, I have sinned against heaven and against you. I am no longer worthy to be called your son; make me like one of your hired servants." So he got up and went to his father. But while he was still a long way off, his father saw him and was filled with compassion for him; he ran to his son, threw his arms around him and kissed him. The son said to him, "Father, I have sinned against heaven and against you. I am no longer worthy to be called your son." But the father said to his servants, "Quick! Bring the best robe and put it on him. Put a ring on his finger and sandals on his feet. Bring the fattened calf and kill it. Let's have a feast and celebrate. For this son of mine was dead and is alive again; he was lost and is found." So they began to celebrate.[30]

The father reacted out of mercy, happiness, and true love. But he also acknowledged that his son was figuratively dead before coming back to life. Just as the son longed for his father's love, the love of God ultimately comes from the Father of the Trinity—whose primary characteristic is love. Indeed, Jesus' mission was to open up for us the way to the Father, so that we may get to know him through Christ.[31]

---

30. Luke 15:11–32.
31. John 1:18; 14:6–7.

6

Adding Evidence

IN THE PREVIOUS CHAPTER we looked at prior belief, the first part of the decision for Christianity. In this chapter we focus on the second part—evidence.

Lots of people would not consider Christianity an option unless they first acquired some positive evidence in favor of it in order to strengthen their rational belief.[1] The apostle Thomas belonged to this category. The Gospel of John retells the episode when Thomas was finally confronted with overwhelming evidence:

> Now Thomas (also known as Didymus), one of the Twelve, was not with the disciples when Jesus came. So the other disciples told him, "We have seen the Lord!" But he said to them, "Unless I see the nail marks in his hands and put my finger where the nails were, and put my hand into his side, I will not believe." A week later his disciples were in the house again, and Thomas was with them. Though the doors were locked, Jesus came and stood among them and said, "Peace be with you!" Then he said to Thomas, "Put your finger here; see my hands. Reach out your hand and put it into my side. Stop doubting and believe." Thomas said to him, "My Lord and my God!" Then Jesus told him, "Because you have seen me, you have believed; blessed are those who have not seen and yet have believed."[2]

This strong evidence of the risen Christ was enough for Thomas to acknowledge Jesus as his Lord and Savior. Jesus answers Thomas by appreciating those whose faith is so strong that they believe like a child, without requiring

---

1. This is treated more extensively in willingness attitude 5 of the next chapter. It is also related to the discussion on evidentialism in section 4.5.1.
2. John 20:24–29.

overwhelming evidence.³ However, since God loves us he sometimes provides us with evidence when our rational belief and willingness to become Christians are not strong enough.⁴ If we are Christians already he may provide us with new evidence in order to strengthen our faith. On the other hand, if we are exposed to evidence for Christianity this also increases our responsibility to respond. Jesus criticized the inhabitants of several Galilean cities who had not come to faith in spite of his ministry there,⁵ and the Bible even contends we are foolish when we say in our heart that there is no God in spite of all the evidence.⁶

Our judgment of evidence is highly subjective. From a Christian perspective the Holy Spirit and the devil both try to influence the way in which we evaluate evidence, as shown in figure 4.6. Jesus illustrates this in the Parable of the Rich Man and Lazarus. The rich man wanted his brothers to get saved, asking Abraham to send them very strong evidence—an encounter with a person that had risen from death. The brothers had previously not listened to Moses and the prophets, and Abraham answered the rich man that they would not be convinced to change their way of living even if someone came back from death.⁷ Why? Their subjective interpretation of evidence was simply very much against God. At another instance,⁸ the Pharisees and Sadducees came to Jesus in order to test him by asking for a sign from heaven. Jesus knew in his heart they would not come to faith if he showed them another miracle. He replied that they had enough of signs already, and that his future resurrection—referred to as the sign of Jonah—would be the ultimate one.

3. Luke 10:21.

4. John 14:11.

5. Matt 11:20–24. See also Luke 12:48 and John 15:22–25. For mathematical models of when it is rational to look for more evidence before making a decision, see Good, "Principle of Total Evidence"; Buchak, "Can It Be Rational to Have Faith?"; and Buchak, "Instrumental Rationality."

6. Ps 14:1–3.

7. Luke 16:31.

8. Matt 16:1–4.

ADDING EVIDENCE 73

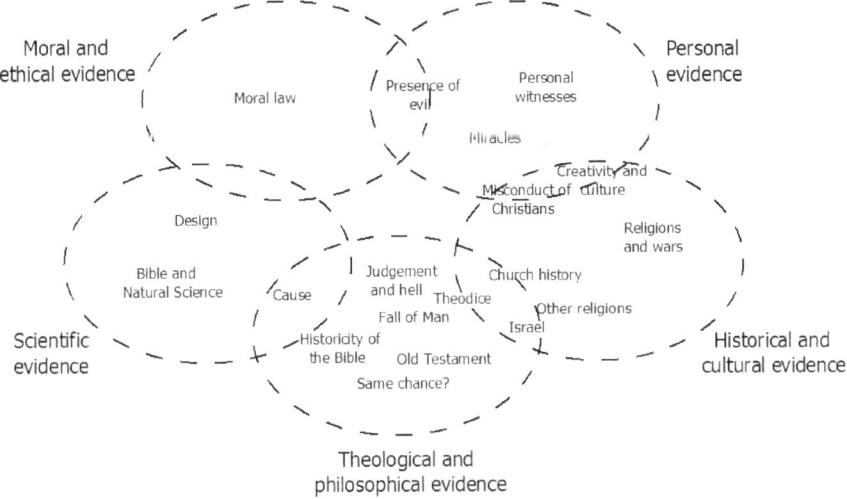

Figure 6.1: Illustration of how the evidence of figure 4.6 is divided into various units. With some overlap these are grouped into five categories: historical/cultural, consciousness/moral, scientific, theological/philosophical, and personal evidence.

74   PART I: MODELING THE DECISION TO BECOME A CHRISTIAN

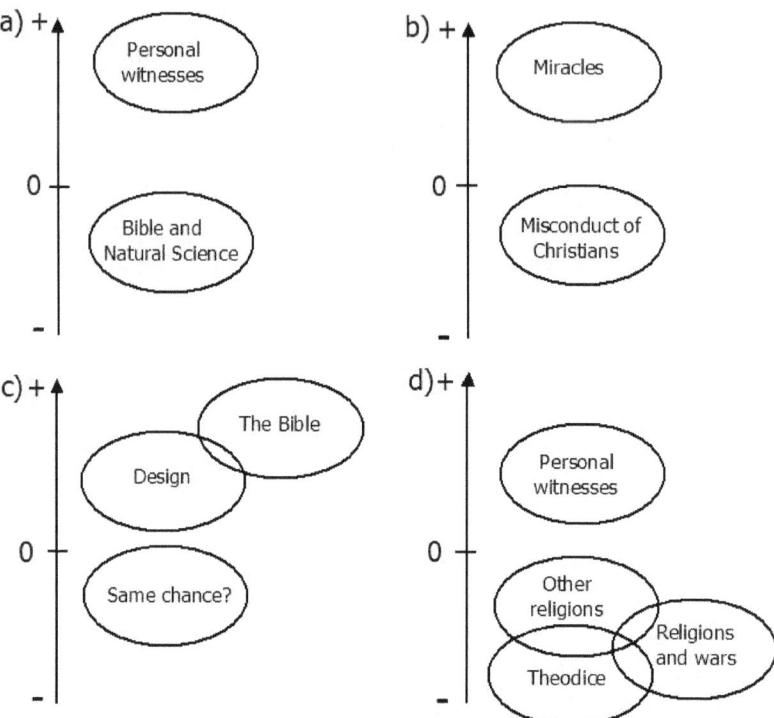

Figure 6.2: Illustration of how different types of evidence are pieced together for four persons. In a) a former atheist witnesses a personal testimony of a close friend and this overrules his previous negative evidence for the Bible from science. In b) a person with bad experiences of Christians from his childhood suddenly experiences an extraordinary event that he interprets as miraculous. In c) an agnostic biologist thinks the teaching of salvation is unfair since he believes people have different chances of hearing the gospel. The he learns more about the human cell. The signatures of a designer become such strong evidence for Christianity that he starts reading the Bible. In d) a man's wife becomes a Christian. This personal testimony is not strong enough though to balance his previous view that religion has caused wars, hatred, and prejudice. The vertical position of each unit of evidence in figures a)–d) quantifies its strength of support of Christianity, with positive values assigned to those units that favor Christianity and negative values to those that don't. In the simplest case the overall Strength of Evidence is obtained by adding the strength of evidence of all the subunits.[9]

We will penetrate the various types of evidence in more detail in chapters 9–13. They are divided into five groups: historical/cultural, consciousness/

---

9. This corresponds to the naive Bayes assumption in formula E.2 of appendix E.

moral, scientific, theological/philosophical, and personal evidence, as illustrated in figure 6.1. There are no distinct boundaries between them and some pieces of evidence belong to several categories. The first-cause evidence, for instance, is both philosophical and scientific, and the history of the Jewish people is not only historical but also theological evidence.

Cumulative-case apologetics is a method whereby many types of evidence or arguments for Christianity are pieced together, with a claim that Christianity explains data a lot better than any other hypothesis.[10] This is no doubt an effective apologetic method. But nevertheless we argue that our subjective interpretation of evidence makes it highly individual what kind of evidence is important for the decision to become a Christian. For Pascal it seems that personal evidence carried the highest weight—the bonesetters, his sister, and his visionary dream. Theological evidence was no doubt important as well, including both his reading of the Bible and his acquaintance with Jansenism.[11] For others it may be scientific evidence. For instance, a biologist may learn about the remarkable organization of the human cell and contend that a designer must exist, which then motivates him to start reading the Bible. Figure 6.2 illustrates the reaction to Christianity of four different persons by plotting the strength of the relevant units of evidence along a vertical scale. A positive value means that Christianity is favored and a negative value the opposite. For each person it is just a few units of evidence that are crucial for their conversion, although other types of evidence may later influence and strengthen the faith they already have.

---

10. See for instance Feinberg, "Cumulative Case Apologetics" and Swinburne, *Existence of God*, chapter 1.

11. Section 1.1.

7

Willingness Assignment

IN THE PREVIOUS TWO chapters we focused on prior belief and evidence, the first two parts of the decision to become a Christian. In order to make the decision we have to take a final step and act, based on the rewards and costs that we assign to a Christian and non-Christian life. This is the third part of the decision and the topic of this chapter. It complies very well with Jesus' teaching: Before we make a decision we are challenged to first calculate the reward and cost of being his follower:

> And whoever does not carry their cross and follow me cannot be my disciple. Suppose one of you wants to build a tower. Won't you first sit down and estimate the cost to see if you have enough money to complete it? For if you lay the foundation and are not able to finish it, everyone who sees it will ridicule you, saying. This person began to build and wasn't able to finish.[1]

In these verses Jesus contrasts the short-term costs for his followers—being questioned, ridiculed, or even persecuted—from the long-term rewards of inner peace and eternal life. The Bible never promises that the Christian life is easy—only that it is the most meaningful one.

Since the reward assignment represents an act of will,[2] we will follow the convention of chapter 4 and speak of a willingness assignment (which reflects our willingness attitude) that is displayed in a willingness table. This assignment depends on the ultimate goals and desires we have in life, such as striving for happiness, self-control, inner peace, meaning, love of power or richness, a desire for social acceptance or context, or a hunger to know

---

1. Luke 14:27–30; see also Matt 13:20–21.
2. Recall the discussion about this in chapters 1 and 4.

the truth. It turns out that our attitude to Christianity can be grouped into three main categories depending on the types of goals we have. In the next three sections we present each one of them in more detail.

7.1 A SMALL AMOUNT OF RATIONAL BELIEF SUFFICIENT

In this section we consider willingness attitudes with such a large reward of choosing Christianity that no matter how small our rational belief is we still act and become a Christian. At first this sounds questionable—is it reasonable that Christianity gets a reward at least as large as Non-Christianity, regardless of which alternative is true? Such an attitude seems to indicate that one is primarily not interested in the truth. But willingness assignments of this kind can be warranted since more information will be available after the decision to become a Christian has been made. And this information is not attainable unless we first take a step in faith and approach God.[3]

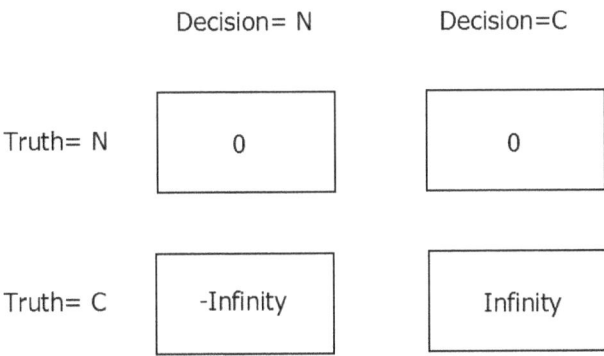

Figure 7.1: The figure illustrates Pascal's willingness table for the decision between Christianity (C) and Non-Christianity (N). If Christianity is chosen its reward is infinitely large if it is true, whereas one loses nothing (zero reward) if it is false. If Non-Christianity is chosen one wins nothing (zero reward) if it is true, whereas one loses everything (reward negative infinity) if it is false. Strength of Will (defined in figure 4.3) is infinitely positive.

---

3. Chapter 8 motivates this kind of reasoning, in particular the sixth criterion of section 8.1.

Willingness Attitude 1: Nothing to lose. Of the four willingness attitudes in this section, this one relies most on pragmatic thinking. It was advocated by Pascal[4] and the rewards are shown in figure 7.1.

The argument is as follows: A decision for Christ has an infinite reward in terms of eternal life if Christianity is true, whereas one loses nothing if Christianity is not true. On the other hand, a decision against Christianity is an infinite loss if Christianity is true, whereas one gains nothing if it is not. It therefore suffices with a very small amount of rational belief for a person with such reward assignment to become a Christian.[5]

From a Christian perspective, it is likely that the Holy Spirit has influenced a person to have such a reward table, although one may argue that the infinite reward of Christianity in Pascal's table is more realistic for a person *after* his conversion than before. Indeed, before the decision the prospect of giving up self-control of life may feel scary. But the longer one has been a Christian the more rewarding it seems when we realize that God the creator has a plan for each one of us and knows better than anyone else—including ourselves—what is best for us.[6] Similarly, the reward of wrongly deciding against Christianity will tend to decrease dramatically after a person comes to Christ, since then the prospect of getting eternally separated from God is even more frightening than before the decision.

There is a slight variation of Pascal's argument. Its willingness assignment is perhaps a bit more realistic and it is illustrated in figure 7.2. A person with this attitude still believes he is better off as a Christian whether Christianity is true or not. Even though the reward numbers are more moderate than in Pascal's example, the strength of will in favor of Christianity is still infinitely large.

A person with a willingness assignment of figure 7.2 thinks the quality of life before death will increase anyway if one becomes a Christian. For instance, Foreli Kremarik, the mother of Akiane,[7] writes about the discus-

---

4. To be more precise, there are different interpretations of what kind of reward table Pascal advocated; see Hájek, "Pacal's Wager." It is in any case clear that in the third and most well-known version of his Wager argument (the so-called *argument from dominating expectation*), Pascal proposed an infinite reward when Truth as well as Decision equal C, which gives an infinitely positive Strength of Will. More details on the reward assignments of the other two versions of Pascal's Wager can be found in Hacking, "Logic of Pacal's Wager" and Hájek, "Blaise and Bayes."

5. It suffices that the aposteriori probability of Christianity is larger than zero or, equivalently, that Strength of Rational Belief is larger than negative infinity.

6. Acts 20:24; Phil 3:7–16.

7. The story of Akiane is described in Kremarik, *Akiane*, part 1. Neither of her parents were Christian when she was born. But already as a small child Akiane told

sions she and her husband had when they found out about their daughter's extraordinary and apparently God-given talents: "After several discussions we ended up with the conclusion that it was better believing in God and be wrong than not believing in God and be right. We concluded we had nothing to lose in believing in God." As a result they decided to become Christians. It seems that the Holy Spirit influenced their choice of reward table. Then, after conversion and a growing relationship with Christ, the nothing-to-lose argument lost some of its impact since the belief was now by heart.[8] Foreli Kremarik writes: "Because of our newly found belief in God we were drawn even closer to God. For the first time in our life we experienced an indescribable joy, harmony, and peace."

Philosopher Kevin More has recently defended the nothing-to-lose argument in terms of human wisdom—a "know-how for protecting one's threatened interests." He argues that wisdom should prompt us to start living as if God existed in order to find out more.[9] More concludes that this also makes sense of one of the psalms:

The fool has said in his heart "there is no God."[10]

According to this Bible passage it is even foolish of us to bet on atheism without first trying to find out whether God exists.

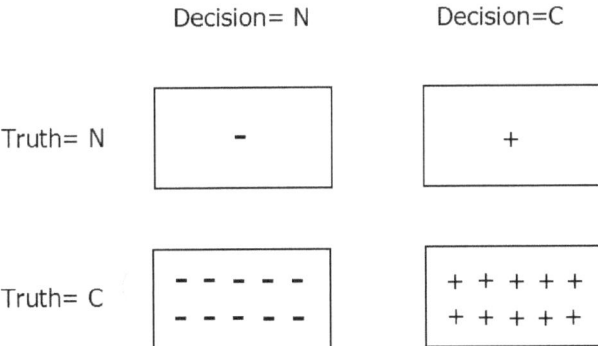

Figure 7.2: A possible willingness assignment for a person with a nothing-to-lose attitude towards Christianity (C) and Non-Christianity (N). Christianity

---

them about her encounters with God, who taught her how to draw. Soon thereafter she started to make remarkable drawings at the age of 4, paintings at 6 years of age, and poetry at 7. These extraordinary paintings portrayed natural sceneries, angels, and Jesus. In conversations with the parents it was also obvious that she had very deep insights about the nature of God.

8. Recall the discussion on self-evident knowledge from section 4.4.
9. Moore, *Untrumpable*, chapter 1.
10. Ibid., preface; and Ps 14:1.

gets a higher reward (10 and 1 respectively) than Non-Christianity (-10 and -1 respectively) regardless of which alternative is true. Strength of Will (defined in figure 4.3) is therefore infinitely positive.

Willingness Attitude 2: Desire for inner peace. We have previously mentioned an inborn conception of God as one part of our prior belief.[11] Since our relationship with God is broken after the fall, there is an empty space of our soul/spirit that manifests itself as a lack of inner peace. Our desire for inner peace might be so strong that it triggers us to put higher reward on Christianity (as in figures 7.1 and 7.2) even if our rational belief in Christianity is low.[12] Jesus probably had this in mind when he said:

> Come to me, all you who are weary and burdened, and I will give you rest. Take my yoke upon you and learn from me, for I am gentle and humble in heart, and you will find rest for your souls. For my yoke is easy and my burden is light.[13]

Another example of this willingness attitude is from the book of Acts. On the first day of Pentecost[14] the disciples gathered in Jerusalem, ten days after Jesus was taken up to heaven. Suddenly they got filled with the Holy Spirit and began to speak in other tongues as the Spirit enabled them. Since this was the Festival of Weeks many Jews were visiting Jerusalem. And they got utterly surprised by what happened. The apostle Peter stood up and gave a bold sermon where he explained what he and his friends had experienced, quoting passages from the Old Testament that foretold the resurrection of Jesus and a future outpouring of the Holy Spirit. The reaction of the audience was instantaneous:

> When the people heard this, they were cut to the heart and said to Peter and the other apostles, "Brothers, what shall we do?" Peter replied, "Repent and be baptized, every one of you, in the name of Jesus Christ for the forgiveness of your sins. And you will receive the gift of the Holy Spirit. The promise is for you and your children and for all who are far off—for all whom the Lord our God will call."[15]

---

11. This is prior belief 1 of chapter 5.

12. In evidence 1 we argue that a desire for inner peace may also drive people towards other religions.

13. Matt 11:28–30.

14. Acts 2:1–41.

15. Acts 2:37–39.

After this sermon about 3,000 persons became Christians. One may argue that the manifestations of the Spirit and Peter's preaching increased the evidence in favor of Christianity for people in the audience. To some extent this is true. However, the fact that they were *cut to their heart* and asked the question "What shall we do?" reveals that the Holy Spirit created a longing for Christ within them. It is likely that they had not yet fully understood the meaning of the conversion and rather had their willingness attitude changed. The message they heard created a strong desire for inner peace in their lives, even though their intellect had not yet fully grasped what was going on. The strength of their rational belief was therefore still not very high.

Willingness Attitude 3: Desire for meaning. Although an inborn desire for meaning in life is part of our prior belief,[16] this desire may suddenly increase for adults as well. Perhaps we look back on life and start to question its meaning, or we experience something that we hope will open up a new door for us. As in figures 7.1 and 7.2, this may trigger us to give a higher reward to Christianity than to Non-Christianity, even though we may not yet understand rationally what is going on.

When Jesus called Simon Peter, Andrew, James, and John as disciples they had been out fishing all night and Jesus had just finished a sermon:

> When he had finished speaking, he said to Simon, "Put out into deep water, and let down the nets for a catch." Simon answered, "Master, we've worked hard all night and haven't caught anything. But because you say so, I will let down the nets." When they had done so, they caught such a large number of fish that their nets began to break. So they signaled their partners in the other boat to come and help them, and they came and filled both boats so full that they began to sink. When Simon Peter saw this, he fell at Jesus' knees and said, "Go away from me, Lord; I am a sinful man!" For he and all his companions were astonished at the catch of fish they had taken, and so were James and John, the sons of Zebedee, Simon's partners. Then Jesus said to Simon, "Don't be afraid; from now on you will fish for people." So they pulled their boats up on shore, left everything and followed him.[17]

---

16. See prior belief 3.
17. Luke 5:1–11; see also Matt 4:18–22 and Mark 1:14–20.

Peter had already known Jesus for some time,[18] and probably recognized him as a man called by God since he approved Jesus' suggestion to let down the nets. For Peter, his previous acquaintance with Jesus and the miraculous big catch of fish increased his evidence for this powerful rabbi being a man sent by God, perhaps even the Messiah. But it was still a big step to leave everything and become a follower of Jesus. It seems that Peter suddenly realized his own shortcomings and the holiness of God. Although he had not yet fully understood what was going in his mind, when Jesus challenged him he pursued his instinct and decided that it would be more meaningful to follow God's plan for his life and become a disciple of Christ.

Willingness Attitude 4: Desire to be loved unconditionally. Another part of prior belief is our inborn desire to be loved unconditionally.[19] Even as adults we may long for someone to love us so strongly that we put higher reward on Christianity than naturalism—as in figures 7.1 and 7.2. This may happen during a life crisis—for instance, when we feel lonely or betrayed—even though our rational belief in Christianity is still rather small.

We mentioned earlier the attitude of the father in the Parable of the Lost Son as an example of unconditional love.[20] If we focus instead on the lost son, we recall that initially he felt no need to stay with his father but preferred to live in a foreign country.[21] Later he ended up in a very difficult situation, facing the risk of starvation and a life in extreme poverty. When he re-evaluated his previous life *he came to his senses* and recalled the love of his father. This not only increased the strength of his evidence, but he also changed his *desire* to receive the unconditional love of his father and return to him. That is, he changed his willingness attitude.

7.2 SOME RATIONAL BELIEF REQUIRED

In this section we consider willingness attitudes that treat Christianity and Non-Christianity equally or favor one alternative weakly. This will make evidence and rational belief in Christianity more important for the decision.

---

18. John 1:35–51.
19. See prior belief 4.
20. Ibid.
21. That is, he wanted to control his own life, see willingness attitude 6.

Willingness Attitude 5: Getting to know the truth at first. Recall that a person with a neutral willingness attitude—as in figure 4.4—bases his decision solely on prior belief and evidence. A small child, for instance, has very little evidence. He still belongs to Christ based on a prior belief that favors Christianity.[22] A grown-up, on the other hand, may have a neutral willingness assignment because he thinks this is a rational attitude, or simply because he knows very little about Christianity. In order to become a Christian he may either require more evidence for Christianity or re-evaluate his old evidence.

During Paul's second missionary journey he was sent to prison in Philippi together with his travel companion, Silas, as described in the book of Acts. While they were still in jail the following happened:

> About midnight Paul and Silas were praying and singing hymns to God, and the other prisoners were listening to them. Suddenly there was such a violent earthquake that the foundations of the prison were shaken. At once all the prison doors flew open, and everyone's chains came loose. The jailer woke up, and when he saw the prison doors open, he drew his sword and was about to kill himself because he thought the prisoners had escaped. But Paul shouted, "Don't harm yourself! We are all here!" The jailer called for lights, rushed in and fell trembling before Paul and Silas. He then brought them out and asked, "Sirs, what must I do to be saved?" They replied, "Believe in the Lord Jesus, and you will be saved—you and your household." Then they spoke the word of the Lord to him and to all the others in his house. At that hour of the night the jailer took them and washed their wounds; then immediately he and all his household were baptized. The jailer brought them into his house and set a meal before them; he was filled with joy because he had come to believe in God—he and his whole household.[23]

We may assume that the jailer knew quite little about Christianity. Indeed, Paul and his followers had not been in Philippi for long and they were probably the first missionaries to arrive there. The jailer therefore had a fairly neutral willingness attitude. But the unexpected release of the prisoners was so overwhelming that his evidence for Christianity increased to the extent that he became a Christian. Another possibility is that the Holy Spirit

---

22. Recall the discussion from the beginning of section 5.2 on the belief of a child.
23. Acts 16:22–34.

influenced the jailer so that he started to long for inner peace. If this was the case his willingness assignment suddenly favored Christianity.[24]

As another example, assume that Adam and Ben[25] both have the willingness table of figure 1.4. They have some knowledge of Christianity and Non-Christianity, and give Christianity a larger reward if it is true. It could be promised eternal life and inner peace that make them favor Christianity. But their desire to follow the truth still makes the reward of wrongly deciding for Christ smaller than the reward of rightly deciding against Christ, if Christianity is not true. Although Christianity is favored a bit, some amount of rational belief in Christianity is still required for them to become Christians. Whereas Adam's amount of rational belief is large enough for conversion, Ben's is not. Although Ben's rewards favor Christianity, he may say: "In principle I think Christianity is fine and I would certainly embrace it if I believed that it is true. However, my belief just isn't strong enough and I want to live according to the truth." In a way this is an honest attitude, and from a Christian point of view Ben has already started to open up his spirit to God. He just needs some more evidence for Christianity (or to re-evaluate the evidence he already has) in order to be convinced. On the other hand, we will never be sure about Christianity until we take a step in faith and receive Jesus into our lives. It can therefore be a risky strategy to postpone the decision until we are totally convinced.

There are many others who argue similarly as Ben.[26] Thomas, one of the 12 disciples, had a positive attitude to Jesus' teaching and he was also prepared to die for his teacher.[27] But Thomas still required more evidence after Jesus' resurrection in order to be convinced that Jesus was not only human but also God—he needed to see that his rabbi had risen from death. The American journalist Lee Strobel (1952–) was once an atheist. But after his wife became a Christian and he saw her changed way of living he wanted to find out whether Jesus had resurrected from death or not before he would receive Christ into his own life. After several years of study he found the evidence for Jesus' resurrection so overwhelming that he became a Christian.[28]

A similar view is reflected in Paul's First Letter to the Corinthian Church, where he firmly states that if Jesus has not resurrected then Christianity is not true and Christian faith has no value:

---

24. See willingness attitude 2.
25. This example is taken from section 4.2 and appendix F.
26. See also the beginning of chapter 6.
27. John 11:16.
28. Strobel, *Case for Christ*.

> If there is no resurrection of the dead, then not even Christ has been raised. And if Christ has not been raised, our preaching is useless and so is your faith. More than that, we are then found to be false witnesses about God, for we have testified about God that he raised Christ from the dead. But he did not raise him if in fact the dead are not raised. For if the dead are not raised, then Christ has not been raised either. And if Christ has not been raised, your faith is futile; you are still in your sins. Then those also who have fallen asleep in Christ are lost. If only for this life we have hope in Christ, we are of all people most to be pitied.[29]

However, this is part of a letter written to the Christian church of Corinth. As such it is not only relevant for the decision to become a Christian but also important for Christians to *hold on* to the faith they already have.

7.3 STRONG RATIONAL BELIEF NOT ENOUGH

In this section we present willingness assignments that disfavor Christianity to the extent that no evidence is enough for becoming a Christian. Unless the rewards are changed a person with such an attitude will not convert.

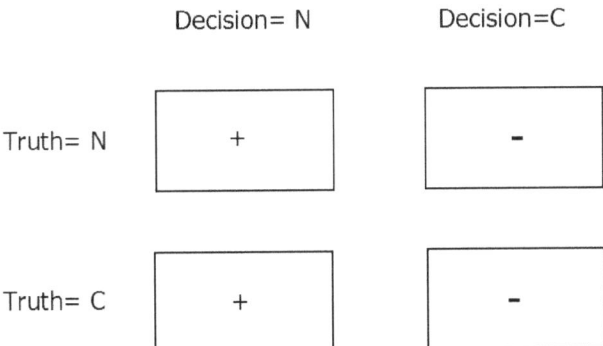

Figure 7.3: A possible willingness table when the reward of becoming a Christian (C) is smaller than the reward of Non-Christianity (N), regardless of truth. Strength of Will, which was defined in figure 4.3, is in this case infinitely negative.

---

29. 1 Cor 15:13–19.

Willingness Attitude 6: Self-control. An obstacle for us to becoming a Christian is a reluctance to give up what we have. We may worry about the opinions of relatives, friends, and colleagues. Because of fear or pride we may want to keep self-control. From a Christian point of view this is an influence of the flesh, and figure 7.3 gives a possible willingness assignment for a person with such an attitude. In order for him to become a Christian he must first revalue his desires and goals in life.[30]

When Jesus had preached in Jerusalem shortly before he died on Calvary, many of the religious leaders believed in him. But because of the Pharisees they would not confess their faith out of fear they would be put out of the synagogue—they loved praise of men more than praise of God.[31] This is not to say that a person who keeps his faith in private doesn't believe by heart. But a natural consequence of a true conversion is a desire to tell others.[32]

The high priest, Caiaphas, had a major role in the decision to hand over Jesus to Roman court and have him killed. He was then confronted with new evidence when Jesus resurrected. But the personal prestige was probably too high for him to humble himself and acknowledge that Jesus was indeed God. In an attempt to hide the resurrection event, he took part in a plan to bribe the guards. They were instructed to report that Jesus' followers had stolen his body from the tomb.[33]

Willingness Attitude 7: Too busy with life. As Pascal writes, we often divert ourselves from thinking about the big decisions in life:

> Being unable to cure death, wretchedness and ignorance, men have decided, in order to be happy, not to think about such things . . . From childhood on men are made responsible for the care of their honour, their property, their friends, and even on the property of honour of their friends; they are burdened with duties, language-training and exercises, and given to understand that they can never be happy unless their health, their honour, their fortune and those of their friends are in good shape, and that it needs only one thing to go wrong to make them unhappy. So they are given responsibilities and duties which harass them from the first moment of each day. You will say that is an odd way to make them happy: what better means could one devise

---

30. This is further discussed in chapter 14.
31. John 12:42–43.
32. Matt 28:18–20; Rom 10:9–10.
33. John 11:45–53; Matt 28:11–15.

to make them unhappy? What could one do? You would only have to take away all their cares, and then they would see themselves and think about what they are, where they come from, and where they are going. That is why men cannot be too much occupied and distracted, and that is why, when they have been given so many things to do, if they have some time off they are advised to spend it on diversion and sport, and always to keep themselves occupied.[34]

Many of the responsibilities that Pascal mentions are good. But they tend to distract us, even more so today than for Pascal's seventeenth-century contemporaries. Jesus illustrates the same attitude in the Parable of the Great Banquet, to which many guest were invited:

> A certain man was preparing a great banquet and invited many guests. At the time of the banquet he sent his servant to tell those who had been invited, "Come, for everything is now ready." But they all alike began to make excuses. The first said, "I have just bought a field, and I must go and see it. Please excuse me." Another said, "I have just bought five yoke of oxen, and I'm on my way to try them out. Please excuse me." Still another said, "I just got married, so I can't come." The servant came back and reported this to his master. Then the owner of the house became angry and ordered his servant, "Go out quickly into the streets and alleys of the town and bring in the poor, the crippled, the blind and the lame." "Sir," the servant said, "what you ordered has been done, but there is still room." Then the master told his servant, "Go out to the roads and country lanes and compel them to come in, so that my house will be full. I tell you, not one of those who were invited will get a taste of my banquet."[35]

A similar attitude is described in the Parable of the Sower.[36] One of the responses to the sown seed is found among people who initially hear the Word of God joyfully. But then the seed is suppressed by worries of life, the deceitfulness of wealth, and desires for other things that occupy their thoughts.

Whereas the person with self-control at least calculates the rewards for and against Christianity, the busy person does not—at least not consciously. He is more indifferent and doesn't take the time to think about the meaning and purpose of life or simply keeps postponing or suppressing such thoughts. Perhaps he feels there is plenty of time to make the decision

34. Pascal, *Pensées*, notes 133 and 139.
35. Luke 14:15–23.
36. Mark 4:1–20.

later. Such a person tends to cheat himself and doesn't seriously consider the option of becoming a Christian. This is also an example of the influence of the flesh.

Since our priorities in life are reflected in how we spend our time, being too busy with life is also an act of will. It is rooted in a more or less subconscious assignment of a larger reward to not becoming a Christian than to the opposite, even if Christianity is true. The busy person's actual willingness assignment is typically as in figure 7.3, with an infinitely negative strength of will of becoming a Christian. He will therefore not take this step unless he first changes his priorities.

Willingness Attitude 8: Not good enough. Maybe some of us feel oppressed by things we did that were wrong. Or we don't feel good enough to give our lives to Christ. Even though *in principle* we would like to have a reward table that favors Christianity, our *actual* reward table is rather as in figure 7.3. From a Christian point of view, this lack of self-consciousness is a destructive influence on the spirit that effects the decision for Christianity. Indeed, the devil not only tempts us to do things against the will of God, but once we have he also accuses us for doing so.[37] However, the core message of the gospel is that no one is good enough by himself:

> This righteousness is given through faith in Jesus Christ to all who believe. There is no difference between Jew and Gentile, for all have sinned and fall short of the glory of God, and all are justified freely by his grace through the redemption that came by Christ Jesus. God presented Christ as a sacrifice of atonement, through the shedding of his blood—to be received by faith.[38]

This is precisely why Jesus had to come down from heaven, live among us, and pay for our sins.

Willingness Attitude 9: Too simple, foolish, offenseive, or odd. We often think that everything valuable has a price and that nothing in life can be earned for free. A free gift seems unfair to those that do not receive it. For this reason it may be hard for us to accept that restored peace with God and eternal life *are* free gifts. But this is exactly what makes Christianity unique—by the

---

37. See for instance Job 1–2 and Zech 3:1–3.
38. Rom 3:22–25.

grace of God salvation *is* free. But it was not free for Christ, who had to pay the price for us.[39]

The gospel may also challenge our view of God as almighty and powerful. It is almost inconceivable that through incarnation God the creator became one of us. Jesus was born as a helpless baby; he had to escape from Herod (c. 73–4 B.C.)—the client king of Judea—and flee with his family, Joseph and Mary, to Egypt. Then they went back to Galilee, where his parents brought him up. He was obedient to them, grew, and became strong.[40] He was finally willing to humble himself and die for us on a cross in Jerusalem. A religion with such a weak God may be thought of as foolish,[41] even more so since Christians are expected to act in the same way by serving others, loving, and praying for their critics and enemies—not paying back injustice.[42] Jesus taught the disciples about their duty to serve others by washing their feet. Even the apostle Peter had a difficult time understanding this, since it challenged his usual way of thinking.[43]

When Paul went out for missionary journeys and preached the gospel, most Jews anticipated a Messiah that would restore Israel as a nation and liberate them from Roman oppression, not a suffering Messiah that claimed to be God, died on a cross, and a few days later resurrected from death. For many of them the gospel either seemed to be foolish or an offensive heresy.[44] A large number of Gentiles could not accept a God that showed such weakness in contrast to the powerful properties that the gods of Greek mythology possessed. Although parts of pagan literature opened up for an afterlife, a bodily resurrection and its victory over death was not a possibility. The gospel message was therefore even more odd for many Gentiles than for the Jews.[45]

The thought of the gospel as too simple, foolish, offensive, or odd either represents evidence against the Bible or a willingness assignment as in figure 7.3, with Christianity having a smaller reward whether true or not. One may rationally believe that Christianity is true after having experienced a strong testimony of a friend or a seemingly miraculous event, and yet still have difficulty *accepting* Christ into one's heart since the core of the gospel

39. Rom 3:21–31.
40. Matt 1–2; Luke 2.
41. 1 Cor 1:18–25.
42. Matt 5:38–48; Matt 20:25–28; Rom 12:14; 1 Pet 3:9.
43. John 13:1–17.
44. However, according to Boyarin there were a number of different messianic expectations among the Jews in the first century A.D. Some Jews anticipated that Messiah would be the divine Son of Man referred to in Dan 7:13–14. Boyarin, *Jewish Gospels*.
45. 1 Cor 1:23; Acts 17:32–33. See also Wright, "Jesus' Resurrection."

seems too different from our usual way of thinking. From a Christian point of view, this person's spirit has not yet opened up for the influence of the Holy Spirit of God.[46]

Willingness Attitude 10: Doesn't need God. We mentioned that many become Christians because of a desire for inner peace.[47] But other people don't feel they need God, and in particular feel no need for forgiveness and restored peace. This self-righteous attitude also leads to a willingness assignment as in figure 7.3. It is typically not the flesh but rather the spirit that narrows down the possibility for God to reach out, although a changed life situation may trigger this person to reconsider his attitude.

Jesus once talked to a group of Pharisees at the temple courts of Jerusalem, telling them that they had to be set free from their sins. The Pharisees didn't think they needed to change anything in their lives. They rather said their ancestry from Abraham and religious zeal was enough. But Jesus told them that their sin consisted in not believing in him as a man sent from God.[48]

Willingness Attitude 11: Doesn't want God. Some individuals may even be hostile against God,[49] as illustrated in figure 7.4. Such a person doesn't want to acquaint with God. The reward of becoming a Christian is therefore low, although the amount of rational belief in God might be high. Indeed, it is difficult to be hostile towards someone you don't believe in. As in the previous example, it is not the flesh but rather the spirit that has influenced this attitude the most. To some extent this person has opened up for destructive influence from the spiritual world.[50] The Bible refers to this as getting a hardened heart,[51] which is a way of hurting the Holy Spirit. Although the situation for such a person might be worse than for people with other kinds of willingness attitudes, nothing is impossible for God. Any person who changes his mind in order to get to know God is most welcome to do so.

---

46. 1 Cor 2:13–16.
47. See willingness attitude 2.
48. John 8:31–59.
49. John 15:23–25.
50. Strength of Rational Belief is in this case not only affected by the soul—it also includes destructive spiritual components. See also the discussion on Strength of Rational Belief and self-evident knowledge in sections 4.3 and 4.4.
51. Heb 3:13.

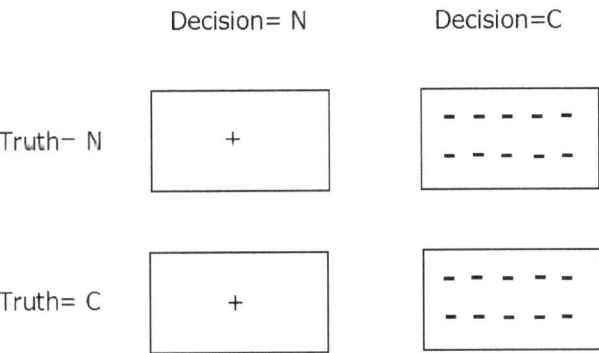

Figure 7.4: A possible willingness table for a person who is hostile towards God in his choice between Christianity (C) and Non-Christianity (N). The reward -10 of Christianity is lower than the reward 1 for Non-Christianity, regardless of truth. Strength of Will (defined in figure 4.3) is infinitely negative.

8

Justifying Christian Belief

IN CHAPTERS 4–7 WE defined and analyzed the main ingredients of the Aposteriori Wager, whereby the decision to become a Christian combines prior belief (our deepest needs, desires, and inborn conceptions of God), evidence (perceptions, memories, testimonies, and various types of authorities), and—depending on our goals in life—a willingness to act. We stressed that the way we interpret evidence and act are both very subjective since it varies a lot between individuals with similar life experience.

A question arises whether we are justified in holding beliefs and acting on subjective grounds. The fact that decisions are subjective doesn't necessarily mean there are no objective criteria for checking how justified they are. We addressed this when responding to various objections against the Wager.[1] In this chapter we will deepen the discussion by using concepts from epistemology, the part of philosophy that deals with the theory of knowledge.[2] Our conclusion is that most of the commonly used justification criteria are subjective, since we interpret them in a way that often depends on our worldview. Based on this, we argue that Christian belief is warranted[3] unless one can show that Christianity is false. The discussion in section 8.1 is a bit technical and it is not required for the rest of the book. If it suffices

---

1. See section 4.5.

2. For a more extensive treatment, see for instance Plantinga, *Warrant and Proper Function* and *Warranted Christian Belief*; Moreland and Craig, *Philosophical Foundations*, chapters 5 and 7; Swinburne, *Faith and Reason*, chapter 2 and references therein.

3. We will assume that warranted belief is equivalent to justified belief, although it is more common to use Plantinga's definition that a belief is warranted if the belief has also been turned into knowledge. Plantinga, *Warrant and Proper Function*, chapters 1–2.

for you to know the main points of the argument I suggest you go directly to the parable of section 8.2.

8.1 JUSTIFICATION CRITERIA

A (rational) belief is generated from prior conceptions and evidence when these are processed in our mind. This belief-generating process has similarities to how a scientific theory is formed, and in both cases we need some *inductive criteria*.[4] A willingness attitude, on the other hand, depends on the goals we have in life and the actions that will achieve these goals. Richard Swinburne has provided justification criteria for rational beliefs and actions. Motivated by these, we list six different criteria that make a belief and willingness assignment more justified:[5]

1. A specific belief should be internally coherent with other beliefs of ours. For instance, do we regard the Bible as reliable given our knowledge of natural science, history, religious beliefs, and ethics?

2. The inductive criteria we use to form a belief—based on prior beliefs and evidence—should be objective. Simplicity, ability to explain what has happened, and ability to predict what will happen are often regarded as such criteria. For instance, if we consider the (apparent?) design in nature as evidence, do these criteria lead us to believe that blind evolution or a creative mind explains it the best?

3. Our belief should be generated from a reliable source—that is, a source that is likely to give true information. For instance, how reliable is the information obtained from a specific book or Internet site? How much can we trust the testimony of a person based what we know of him, his general behavior, or what others have said about him? Is a belief controlled by some paradigm of thought that makes it less reliable even though it might be held by a majority of people?

4. We have a duty to acquire enough evidence or to check the reliability of the sources so that the probability that the belief is true is acceptably large given the environment we live in.

5. The belief should be formed by someone with a functioning cognitive ability. For instance, are we using all the information we have in a proper way? Or is the belief formed in a more ad hoc way, either

---

4. See evidence 10.

5. In Swinburne's terminology there are different types of rationality. Our classification is reminiscent but somewhat different. Swinburne, *Faith and Reason*, chapter 2.

consciously, due to impaired memory, or because our brain has been damaged in some other way? Do we have some prejudice that makes our conclusions biased?

6. Is the willingness attitude consistent with our goals in life and are these goals reasonable? For instance, are we postponing the decision to become a Christian because of anxiety of what others would think—in conflict with our deepest goals in life? Do we want to live a life controlled by ourselves or do we accept being led by someone else? What do we value the most—the short- or the long-term goals?

It is usually not possible for a belief and willingness attitude to fully satisfy all these criteria, and epistemic theories emphasize their importance differently. *Internalist* theories focus on the agent's own belief formation, regarding variants of 1 (subjective version) or 2 (objective version) as most fundamental. *Externalist* theories differ from internalist ones. They relate more to the outside world and emphasize variants of 3. Theories can also be categorized based on time, where a *synchronic* theory deals with belief formation at a given moment (criteria 1–3), whereas *diachronic* theories additionally stress the importance of forming a belief over a longer period of time (criterion 4). Epistemic theories can further be distinguished based on how beliefs are related. In *coherentism* there is no hierarchy between beliefs and the only requirement for them to be justified is internal coherence (criterion 1). *Foundationalism* does not treat the beliefs symmetrically but divide them into basic beliefs (those that are foundational and need no support from other beliefs[6]) and non-basic beliefs (those that need support from other beliefs). Notice that coherence theories are always internalist, whereas foundational theories can either be internalist (close to criterion 2) or externalist (criterion 3).

Most of the propositions we use in daily life, such as "I will live longer if I exercise regularly and eat nutritious food," only involve phenomena of the natural world. Our beliefs in them and willingness to act upon them can be justified by (variants of) criteria 1–6 in more or less the same way whether we have a naturalistic or Christian perspective.[7] For propositions of this sort we may regard 1–6 as more or less objectively valid criteria.

The proposition "Christianity is true" is different, since it involves claims about the supernatural world. Criteria 1–6 are still important for checking how justified Christian belief is and how well grounded a decision

---

6. Basic beliefs should not be confused with prior beliefs. See section 5.2 for more on the difference between basic and prior beliefs.

7. For simplicity we assume, as in chapter 2, that the two alternatives are naturalism and Christianity.

for Christianity is. But we claim that criteria 1–6 will all be interpreted differently—at least to some extent—depending on whether one has a naturalistic or a Christian perspective. In particular, the objections to Christian belief that presuppose a naturalistic interpretation are subjective.

In order to motivate that the interpretation of criteria 1–6 depends on our worldview, we will use some concepts from the American philosophers Jeff Jordan (1959-) and Alvin Plantinga (1932-).[8] If we hold a belief for which evidence is not (yet) fully conclusive, it often relies on *truth-independent pragmatic arguments* or *truth-dependent pragmatic arguments*. They differ as to whether we get benefits from holding the belief independently of truth or not. An objection towards Christian belief can either be a *de facto objection* that aims to show that Christian claims are false, or a *de jure objection* that contends a Christian has no right to hold his belief even if it is true. Below we will give examples of objections to Christian belief. They are all based on claims for which at least one of criteria 1–6 is not fulfilled. We argue that none of them is a valid de jure objection, since they either aim to show that Christianity is false (a valid de facto objection) or they implicitly presuppose that Christianity is false. Given that these examples are representative, they indicate that Christian belief is warranted unless one can show that it is false.[9]

Let us start with criterion 1. It looks very uncontroversial at first, since a naturalist and Christian would agree that it is not a good thing to have contradictory beliefs, whatever we believe. If a claimed contradiction turns out to be true, this is a valid de facto objection since true beliefs cannot contradict each other. For instance, *if* undisputable evidence was found that Jesus did not resurrect from death, then a Christian's belief in this evidence would contradict his belief in texts from the Bible claiming that the resurrection took place. This would surely undermine this person's Christian belief. But a claimed contradiction sometimes relies on more or less hidden assumptions. Perhaps the most well-known example is the logical problem of evil, where belief in an omnipotent and loving God is thought to contradict all evil and suffering in the world. But, as we will see,[10] this argument is based on assumptions regarding God's omnipotence and love that are not necessarily valid if Christianity is true. The logical problem of evil is therefore neither a valid de facto nor a valid de jure objection.

---

8. Moreland and Craig, *Philosophical Foundations*, chapter 7.

9. For a more in depth discussion, we refer to Plantinga, *Warranted Christian Belief*. Plantinga distinguishes between three types of de jure objections: those that claim Christian belief is unjustified, irrational, or unwarranted. He argues that none of these objections are valid.

10. See evidence 17.

For criterion 2 a naturalist could undermine Christian belief in a designer by saying that science has verified common descent of species—driven by blind evolution. If this claim is based on evidence it is a valid de facto objection. But if the criticism relies on *methodological naturalism*[11]—that only natural explanations are allowed in science—its is a prior assumption that rules out a designer from the start and makes blind evolution the only possible option. It is therefore not a de facto objection and not a valid de jure objection either, since if Christianity is true we can allow for personal explanations and thereby make the designer alternative much more likely.

A naturalist could use criterion 3 and claim that the *historical critical method* has shown that the Bible is not a reliable source. This method grew out of the Enlightenment of the eighteenth century in order to investigate the reliability of written texts. To a large extent it was developed by Johann Semler (1725–91) and other German theologians who applied it to the Bible.[12] The method is very similar to methodological naturalism and parts of it are uncontroversial, such as trying to find the original sources of the biblical material—in particular, the process of transforming oral tradition into written text, the historical context of each of the 66 biblical books, and its coherence with other contemporary texts regarding context and style of writing. We can agree on the importance of this whether we have a naturalistic or Christian perspective, since it amounts to checking if there are any de facto objections towards Christianity. But the fundamental assumptions of the historical critical method are partly naturalistic: that there is a uniform and universal reality that is accessible to human reason and investigation, that events in the present and past are interconnected and comparable to analogy, and that objective criteria are used for checking them. The "interconnection by analogy" effectively means that the universe is regarded as a closed system so that fulfilled prophecies, miracles, and other direct interventions by God are invalidated. It is therefore not a de facto objection to criticize the Bible because it includes supernatural events. It is not a valid de jure objection either, since God may actively intervene in his creation if Christianity is true—thereby causing the supernatural events.

For criterion 4, we recall that the decision to become a Christian always involves a leap of faith that leads to action based on some evidence and a willingness to act, even if this evidence is never fully conclusive just before the decision.[13] From a naturalistic perspective, Christian faith (at least the

---

11. See evidence 10.

12. Vanhoozer, *Is There a Meaning in This Text?*; Thiselton, *Hermeneutics* and references therein.

13. See chapter 4, in particular sections 4.4 and 4.5.1.

pragmatic or Lutheran versions of it[14]) violates criterion 4, since it relies on pragmatic arguments with inconclusive evidence at the time of the decision. It is therefore claimed that a Christian is not justified in holding his belief. This criticism is not de facto, since it only questions the motives of having a Christian belief. But many would say that becoming a Christian is a truth-dependent pragmatic argument. We would never get full assurance before the decision is made since the most conclusive evidence comes afterwards—a revelation of God through the work of the Holy Spirit.[15] Therefore the last part of criterion 4—"given the environment we live in"—is crucial. If Christianity is true, we can argue that criterion 4 is satisfied whenever we have collected enough evidence before the decision in order to make Christianity a viable option. Given that we live in the natural world, this is the best we can do, and then by the grace of God he will reward our action in terms of increased evidence. To criticize these pragmatic reasons for becoming a Christian is therefore not a valid de jure objection. Some would claim even more—that belief in Christianity relies on a truth-independent pragmatic argument. Indeed, if Christianity is false and someone decides to become a Christian he will not get post-decisional evidence in favor of Christianity if naturalism is true, and no one will force him to hold on to his faith.

Criterion 6 seems to require that our goals should always accord with what we believe is true. A naturalist may say that Pascal's nothing-to-lose argument violates criterion 6: Since the reward for Christianity is always at least as large as for Non-Christianity *regardless* of what is true,[16] one is not justified in having Christian belief. This is clearly not a de facto objection, but is it a valid de jure objection? Again, one may argue that from a Christian point of view the truth will not be fully revealed to us unless we first make a decision for Christ. This is not because we can *decide* to believe that Christianity is true or not.[17] If it is true, it is rather *God* that reveals himself and increases our strength of belief after the decision has been made. Then it becomes less relevant that we put higher reward on Christianity before the decision even if it were false. Therefore, this is not a valid de jure objection to Christian belief since it loses force if Christianity is true. But one may argue that the objection is not necessarily valid either if Christianity is false. Then we will either find out (by lack of revelation from God) that we live based on a myth and no one will force us to hold on to the decision we

14. The concepts were defined in section 4.4.
15. Evidence 19 and 24 gives more details on various types of revelations from God.
16. Section 7.1 describes willingness attitudes of this kind, including the nothing to loose argument.
17. Swinburne, *Faith and Reason*, 24–26.

made, or we will continue to sincerely believe in the myth for the rest of our life. But if the alternative to Christianity is naturalism there is no afterlife and then we will never find out that we were wrong.

For criterion 5, finally, we refer to a 1998 survey among top scientists of the National Academy of Sciences of the USA. Only 7 percent of the respondents reported that they believed in God; 72 percent claimed to be atheist; and the remaining 21 percent were agnostic and did not know whether God exists.[18] Polls like these are sometimes used to question the credibility of Christian faith, since many persons with a high cognitive ability do not believe in God. This is not a de facto objection, since it does not present evidence against the main dogma of Christianity. In order to check whether it is a valid jure objection, the interpretation of *cognitive ability* is crucial. For many propositions about the natural, like "There are more than 200 billion stars in the Milky Way galaxy," we regard a person's belief in it as more justified if we know he has studied astronomy, which requires some cognitive skills. But if Christianity is true we rather think of a Christian's belief as justified by the way he lives, since people look for visible fruits in his life. This is partly a different kind of knowledge that the Bible refers to as *wisdom*. It is attainable for anyone who has first been justified in Christ by grace by the work of the Holy Spirit, through a relationship with God. This kind of knowledge is frequently described in the wisdom literature of the Old Testament.[19] When Jesus prayed to his Father he said:

> Now this is eternal life: that they know you, the only true God, and Jesus Christ, whom you have sent.[20]

From a biblical perspective, our cognitive ability before the decision to become a Christian is not as important as for other decisions. Why? Because the gospel is equally accessible to anyone! Pascal reminds us about the split human condition. After the fall of man we cannot fully trust our own minds when deciding for Christ. A work of the Holy Spirit is always required,[21] and some would argue that a top scientist is more likely to be too busy with life in order to take his time and think about the big questions, or perhaps he is pressed by his peers to have certain opinions. The cognitive ability argument is therefore not a valid de jure objection. This is not to say that we shouldn't use our cognitive skills when making the decision for or against Christianity. For instance, if we first study many different religions and philosophies

---

18. Lennox, *God's Undertaker*, chapter 1.
19. In particular, this includes Prov 1–4, 8–9 and many of the psalms.
20. John 17:3.
21. See chapters 2 and 3.

of life as objectively as we can and then decide that Christianity is the best option, our decision is more informed. This is not a bad thing, although it is possible that the Holy Spirit prompted us to undertake the study.

8.2 A PARABLE

Christian belief is very often challenged by the claim that a decision has to rely on enough evidence. Although it is always a good thing to look for evidence, we have already responded to this objection against Christianity.[22] Here we will give another response by extending the following parable of Jesus:

> The kingdom of heaven is like treasure hidden in a field. When a man found it, he hid it again, and then in his joy went and sold all he had and bought that field.[23]

In the extended parable the man is a shepherd and the owner of a second field, next to the first one. He hasn't found the treasure yet and he doesn't even know for sure whether it exists. But *if* it does it can only be in the other field, which is separated from the man's own field by a high fence. It is only possible to enter the other field from the man's field through a gate that is built into the fence. If the treasure exists it must have been put in the other field by someone else who first carried it through the man's field, then through the gate, and finally buried it in the other field. If the treasure exists it is easy to find once the other field is entered, but some traces of its transport through the man's own field can be found as well. These traces are fairly strong but not fully conclusive, since they have been mixed with traces from other people that have visited the man's field.

What is the best strategy for the man to use in order to find out whether the treasure exists or not, given that time is limited (the gate will close at an unknown time point)? He values the treasure—if it exists—so much that he is prepared to sell everything he has in order to get it. But in view of what is at stake he first makes a careful investigation of his own field to check if there are traces of the treasure transport. After having investigated some but not all parts of his field, he finds some evidence that is not fully conclusive. If he is skilled at distinguishing different kinds of traces, he is tempted to spend some more time on that, almost forgetting that there is a simpler way out—the gate. But knowing that time is limited and that his own efforts will never give him full evidence, he finally decides to sell everything he has and enter the other field through the gate.

---

22. See section 4.5.1 and criterion 4 of section 8.1.
23. Matt 13:44.

In this parable the man's field is the natural world and the traces of the treasure in the man's field represent all evidence we can find in the natural world. The treasure in the other field is the kingdom of heaven and the gate is Jesus:

> Therefore Jesus said again, "Very truly I tell you, I am the gate for the sheep. All who have come before me are thieves and robbers, but the sheep have not listened to them. I am the gate; whoever enters through me will be saved. They will come in and go out, and find pasture. The thief comes only to steal and kill and destroy; I have come that they may have life, and have it to the full."[24]

Entrance through the gate is free and it requires no special skills. The money represents everything in life the man is prepared to sacrifice in order to get the treasure, and therefore his willingness attitude favors Christianity a lot. The time point when the gate closes is either the moment when the man dies or when Jesus returns a second time, whichever comes first.

24. John 10:7–10.

PART II

Penetrating the Evidence

9

Historical and Cultural Evidence

IN CHAPTER 6 WE introduced five categories of evidence of relevance for Christianity. In the following five chapters we will analyze each one of them in more detail. Our first category of evidence is obtained from history, other religions, and culture. This includes Christian impact on culture, the history of the Jewish people, and the history of the church. We will address these issues one by one, keeping in mind that the interpretation of all this evidence—in particular, whether Christian impact has been good or bad—varies a lot between people.

Evidence 1: Why Christianity and not some other religion? Christian belief is based on a number of truth claims, in particular that the Bible is the Word of God and that Jesus is the only way to salvation. Followers of Jesus believe that Christianity alone is true, and that no other religion or philosophy of life is. But isn't such an attitude presumptuous? For many people this is a stumbling block and a negative evidence for Christianity, much related to the many gods objection against Pascal's Wager.[1]

Various solutions have been proposed in order to modify the Christian uniqueness claims. The first one is *universalism* or *perennialism*. A version of it holds that all religions are different ways of getting to know a spiritual reality. After all, there are common features of all religions. This includes a diagnosis of what is wrong in human life, a notion of an ideal human existence, and a path to reach this existence through salvation. At a first glance this sounds sympathetic. But a closer look reveals that religions make very different claims. For pantheistic religions (Hinduism, Buddhism, Taoism)

---

1. See section 4.5.3.

the spiritual reality is impersonal and embedded in nature. The ultimate existence in Hinduism is an impersonal god (Brahman) and in Buddhism an impersonal state of being (nirvana). Theistic religions (Christianity, Judaism, Islam) all have a personal and omnipotent creator God but there are still important differences. It is true, for instance, that the Qur'an regards Moses, David, Jesus, and other biblical persons as prophets, and Jesus is even thought of as a sinless miracle worker. But the Qur'an claims that important parts of the Bible have been distorted from Allah's original revelation—that Jesus neither died on the cross nor was divine, and in particular that Allah is not triune.[2]

But what about Christianity and Judaism? It is true that they share the same roots, since the Old Testament is part of the Christian Bible. Christians hold that the God of the Old Testament is the same as God of the New Testament, as revealed in Jesus Christ. The first followers of Jesus were all Jews. They did not think belief in Jesus as the promised Messiah threatened their Jewish identity. But later on Christianity and Judaism gradually drifted apart. Although Orthodox Judaism regards the Old Testament as sacred scripture, they complement it with the oral law of Mishnah and its scholarly interpretations in Talmud. And most importantly it is not believed that Jesus is the Messiah.

The most fundamental difference is the way religions teach salvation—*soteriology*. It is only within Christianity that salvation is a gift by grace through belief in Jesus Christ. Other religions require works in some form or the other, such as obedience to the five pillars in Islam. The core of the New Testament is that belief in Jesus as Redeemer and Savior is the *only* way of getting to know God and having eternal life with him.[3] Since Christianity is the only religion for which Jesus is Redeemer and Savior, universalism and classical Christianity cannot both be true. But on the other hand, there are many liberal interpretations of Christianity where the Bible is not the inerrant and unequivocal Word of God and Jesus is not the only way to salvation. Some of them attempt to combine Christianity with other religions, such as the religious pluralism proposed by the British theologian and philosopher of religion John Hick (1922–2012).[4]

Second, one may adhere to postmodern thinking and argue that there is no objective truth. Any person's belief is true for him in a subjective way. This line of thought is often combined with syncretism of religions, so that each individual is encouraged to build his own mixture of belief systems.

---

2. Groothuis, *Christian Apologetics*, chapters 23 and 24.
3. John 14:6.
4. Hick, *Interpretation of Religion*.

But since the Bible does not allow for this, the classical interpretation of Christianity cannot be mixed with other religions. In the first commandment of the Mosaic Law it is told that man should have no other gods except God himself.[5] There is also a logical objection to the statement "There is no absolute truth." It defines a philosophy of life that, according to its own principles, cannot be true. This form of thinking is therefore self-contradicting and self-refuting.

Third, one may argue that some other philosophy of life than Christianity is true. This view is completely logical and related to religious *particularism*—the view that only one religion is correct. In fact, this book is all about describing the decision between Christianity and other philosophies of life, such as naturalism. But if Christianity is true then no other religion can be true.

It is interesting to note that the Bible in fact explains the existence of other religions. According to Christianity the fall of man involved a broken relationship with God.[6] Yet man is created in his image and therefore we have an inbuilt desire to restore the broken connection with God. It is much like an inborn empty space of our spirit that is longing for him.[7] This longing for God should ideally lead us to Christian belief. On the other hand, other religions are human attempts to restore the broken relation with the spiritual world by efforts of our own. At best this creates non-spiritual strongholds in our soul,[8] but there is also a risk that we connect to the spiritual world in a destructive way.[9] According to Christianity it is simply not possible for man to reach God by himself. It is only faith in Jesus that can restore the relation, so that the empty space of our spirit is filled with the Holy Spirit of God.[10]

Evidence 2: Are religions mostly about fights and wars? Many people think that religions have mostly contributed to society in a negative way. In particular, they believe that lots of wars and fights in history were caused by them.[11] This becomes positive evidence for naturalism and negative evidence for Christianity—and for other religions as well.

5. Exod 20:3.
6. See section 2.1.
7. This corresponds to prior belief 1 and willingness attitude 2.
8. Jer 10:1–16.
9. 1 Cor 9:14–22.
10. Rom 8:1–17.
11. For instance, a worldwide Ipsos poll was commissioned in November 2010, where more than 18,000 citizens from 23 nations were asked about their views on

As a response we recall that from a Christian perspective religious activity reflects man's desire to have the broken relation with God restored.[12] Humans are religious by nature and most people believe in something. It seems that any attempt to remove religion is doomed to fail. Indeed, in societies with a state controlled atheistic dictatorship political leaders have sometimes been celebrated in a religious way. Perhaps the most extreme example is the Juche Idea of North Korea, with its own divine scriptures and priests. The first two rulers—Kim Il-Sung and Kim Jong-Il (1941-2011)—were treated as divine characters in terms of a personal cult.[13]

If religion is oppressed it still pops up in disguised forms in fantasy films, adventure books, and other parts of culture. The secularization of Western Europe has created a religious vacuum, a process that took off during the Enlightenment of the late eighteenth century and then accelerated after World War II. Since the 1960s the vacuum has very much been filled by the New Age movement and the new spirituality. Today transcendental meditation, yoga (inspired from Hinduism), mindfulness (inspired from Buddhism), and similar practices are widespread. This mixture of Western and Eastern religious thoughts is similar to when Indian pantheism and Neoplatonism influenced Europe in the third century. Religion has not been removed, not even in the most secular states. The New Age emphasis on "all is one" has rather affected our worldview in terms of how we view individuality, the outside world, and—not the least—morality, good, and evil.[14]

Second, even though religion has caused many conflicts and wars in history, there are very often more fundamental causes behind these. Either religion has been used by people in power for political purposes or it has been a marker of ethnic and cultural identity in various conflicts. However, the deepest and most fundamental cause is the fall of man, by which we tend to be selfish rather than acting out of love. In the long run this causes all kinds of disagreement between humans.[15] It is primarily not religions but humans that we should blame for the conflicts.

---

religion. About half of the respondents thought "religion provides the common values and ethical foundations that diverse societies need to thrive in the twenty-first century," whereas the other half agreed that "deeply held religious beliefs promote intolerance, exacerbate ethnic divisions, and impede social progress in developing and developed nations alike." Ipsos Global @dvisory, "Is Religion a Force for Good in the World?"

12. Evidence 1.

13. Martin and Bach, *Back to the Jerusalem of the East*.

14. Groothuis, *Unmasking the New Age*; Pearcey, *Total Truth*, appendix 2; and Ewert, *Vem tänder stjärnorna?*

15. See for instance Gal 5:19–21 for the acts of the flesh.

But people may respond that some religious doctrines in fact *command* people to start conflicts that lead to oppression of others, like the jihad of Islam. Well, this is not surprising from a Christian point of view as far as *other* religions are concerned, since they reflect man's attempts to reach God[16] and thereby are limited by human weaknesses from the fall. This does not contradict that other religions may include portions of true wisdom. We are all created in the image of God and to some extent we know what is right and wrong.[17] But humans are still responsible for religious doctrines that oppose the will of God, including oppression of others.

Third, atheism is a relatively new phenomenon. It grew out from the Enlightenment in the nineteenth and twentieth centuries.[18] But in spite of this short history there is still no lack of data on how secular states have functioned. Many of the worst crimes of the twentieth century were committed by atheistic communist regimes. In fact, the number of people killed by atheist or secular regimes during the twentieth century alone has been estimated at over 100 million—more than 100 times the number of total deaths caused by Christians, from the Crusades until this day.[19] This includes Joseph Stalin's (1878-1953) Gulags in the Soviet Union, Mao Zedong's (1893-1976) Cultural Revolution in China, the Khmer Rouge's Killing Fields in Cambodia, and the labor camps of North Korea. Although the Nazi regime was not atheistic, Adolf Hitler (1889-1945) was much inspired by Nietzsche's Übermensch philosophy and not an articulated friend of Christianity.[20]

Evidence 3: Has there been mainly misconduct or a good impact by Christians? Fights between people with non-Christian beliefs is one thing. But since Christians claim to practice the *only true* religion, how should we explain any oppression from or division among them? People may know of Christians whom they regard as hypocrites; they might have read about believers who were not able to live up to their faith, and for many this easily becomes a stumbling block. Such a reaction is to some extent understandable and it is in fact even biblical. Christianity is primarily not a religion but a transforming relation with Christ. It is intended to produce visible results.[21]

16. Evidence 1.
17. Evidence 8.
18. Section 2.2.
19. See for instance D'Souza, *What's So Great about Christianity*; Habermas, "Plight of the New Atheism" and references therein.
20. Lennox, *Gunning for God*, chapter 3.
21. Eph 4:17–32.

On the individual level, when someone becomes a Christian a process of sanctification is meant to start that is guided by the Holy Spirit and ultimately will bear fruit and make this person more Christlike.[22] Sadly though, as Christians we do not always make use of or realize the life-transforming power that is accessible to us through the Holy Spirit. This easily leads to a life without salt and light[23] that makes no difference to people. And the Bible is very honest. It actually acknowledges this and warns that it may ultimately lead to false teaching and ungodly behavior.[24] But Christians also have personal weaknesses to fight, like jars of clay with a treasure—God—living within them.[25]

On the collective level, Christians are meant to love each other by the work of the Holy Spirit. This is a way for the church to reveal God to rest of the world:

> I pray also for those who will believe in me through their message, that all of them may be one. Father, just as you are in me and I am in you. May they also be in us so that the world may believe that you have sent me. I have given them the glory that you gave me, that they may be one as we are one, I in them and you in me, so that they may be brought to complete unity. Then the world will know that you sent me and have loved them even as you have loved me.[26]

Any division among or fight between Christians is an example of destructive spiritual influence from the world.[27] It is often used by the devil in order to oppose the spread of Christianity.

Having said this, it should be added that many bad things have been done *in the name of* Christianity by monopolistic state churches and other regimes. Apart from oppression of religious minorities, two of the most cited examples are the Crusades to Israel during the Middle Ages and the burning of witches, which culminated in Europe during the fifteenth, sixteenth, and seventeenth centuries. But the fact that something bad has been done in the name of Christianity doesn't necessarily mean it was conducted by Christians who gave their hearts and lives to Jesus. The Bible rather teaches that it is impossible to consistently rebel against the will of God and at the

---

22. Section 3.1.
23. Matt 5:12–14.
24. 1 Tim 1:18–20; 2 Pet 2.
25. 2 Cor 4:7.
26. John 17:21–23; see also Ps 133 and John 13:35.
27. This is illustrated in figure 4.6.

same time nurture a relationship with him. In his Sermon on the Mount Jesus said:

> Watch out for false prophets. They come to you in sheep's clothing, but inwardly they are ferocious wolves. By their fruit you will recognize them. Do people pick grapes from thornbushes, or figs from thistles? Likewise, every good tree bears good fruit, but a bad tree bears bad fruit. A good tree cannot bear bad fruit, and a bad tree cannot bear good fruit.[28]

This problem is often reinforced when media gives a biased view. It is true that misbehavior and disagreement has higher news value than peacefulness in any organization, political party, or religion. But this is particularly so for Christianity. Indeed, if Christianity is true it is a scent of life for those who believe and often a source bad conscience for those who don't. This is vividly expressed by Paul in his Second Letter to the Corinthian Church:

> But thanks be to God, who always leads us as captives in Christ's triumphal procession and uses us to spread the aroma of the knowledge of him everywhere. For we are to God the pleasing aroma of Christ among those who are being saved and those who are perishing. To the one we are an aroma that brings death; to the other, an aroma that brings life. And who is equal to such a task? Unlike so many, we do not peddle the word of God for profit. On the contrary, in Christ we speak before God with sincerity, as those sent from God.[29]

One way of suppressing such a bad conscience is to report news in a biased way and to favor one's own worldview. For instance, the American sociologist Rodney Stark (1934–) argues that our Western view of the Crusades—as brutal European colonialism with Christian motives—has been very biased.[30] The first Crusade in 1096–99 was not unprovoked but a response to Muslim aggression towards Christian pilgrims and defilement of churches and holy places in Jerusalem, when the Seljuk Turks became the new rulers of Asia Minor. The emperor of Byzantium wrote a letter to Pope Urban II (c. 1042–1099) in which he asked for help, and this initiated the first Crusade. The primary reason was to liberate the Holy Land, not to convert Muslims by force. During the battles cruelties were sadly conducted on both sides. And the knight orders were not pure military trusts. On the contrary, quite a large bit of their work involved charity and medical care.

28. Matt 7:15–18; see also 1 John 3:8–9.
29. 2 Cor 2:14–17.
30. Stark, *Triumph of Christianity*, chapter 13 and references therein.

Several influential writers including Francois-Marie Arouet Voltaire (1694-1778), Edward Gibbons (1737-94), John William Draper (1811-82), and Andrew Dickson White (1832-1918) spread a negative view of the Middle Ages in the eighteenth and nineteenth centuries. It was described as a time of superstition—dominated by a Catholic Church that opposed science. In contrast, classical antiquity and the Renaissance-Enlightenment were referred to as periods of great progress.[31] But this is a very biased picture. The scholastic theologians argued that Christianity was rational and founded the first European universities. They were very influential from the twelfth century, with Thomas Aquinas the most well-known representative. But since they were more inspired by Aristotelian natural philosophy than Aristotelian logic they tended to hold the view that God was logically restricted in his creation to follow the forms that Aristotle (384-22 B.C.) had discovered. By the end of the thirteenth century a group of voluntarist theologians reacted against scholastic theology. They emphasized even more that nature should be studied by experiments, since our mental capabilities are too limited to deduce the intentions of an omniscient God.[32] Although this emphasis on empirical induction was also more true to Aristotle himself than is normally recognized,[33] it is anyhow clear that Christians of the Middle Ages contributed a lot to the advancement of science.

Many reported conflicts between science and the church have also been biased. For instance, when Galileo Galilei (1564-1642)—a committed Christian—advocated a heliocentric worldview in the early seventeenth century he was opposed only by parts of the church. This was a conflict between Christians with different interpretations of the Bible, where Galileo advocated experiments as a way of learning more about God's creation. He did not want to be constrained by Ptolemaic astronomy and Aristotelian physics, which influenced not only the church but also secular scientists at the time.[34]

Even though cruelties have been done in the name of Christianity, the trademark of the church during its 2,000 years has rather been to follow the golden rule of the Bible:

---

31. Stark, *Triumph of Christianity*, chapter 14; Pearcy and Thaxton, *Soul of Science*; Gordon, "Rise of Naturalism"; Stenumgaard, *Vetenskapens illusioner*; and Landgren, "Tro och vetenskap."

32. Pearcey and Thaxton, *Soul of Science*.

33. Landgren, "Aristotelian Concept of History."

34. See also evidence 10 of chapter 11.

> So in everything, do to others what you would have them do to you, for this sums up the Law and the Prophets.[35]

This includes taking care of the poor and needy, as beautifully illustrated in the parable of the Good Samaritan in the New Testament[36] and repeatedly commanded in the Old Testament.[37] Although no one can fully accomplish these goals they are still not utopian. It is well known among sociologists that during the first three centuries A.D. many slaves and people of the lower classes became Christians, and the church grew by deeds of love and mercy. When Christianity became the state church of Rome in the fourth century, lots of hospitals were built, slavery decreased dramatically, infanticide was forbidden, and the brutal gladiatorial games were prohibited.[38] Monks, nuns, and missionaries followed the traditions of the first Christians to do charity work and to start schools, giving people hope for their future. Today there are many worldwide Christian aid organizations, such as Caritas Internationalis, Samaritan's Purse, and Christian Aid Mission—to mention just a few. And some studies clearly suggest that Christians are more engaged in charity work compared to atheists or agnostics.[39] But people seldom read about all this care for the poor and needy done by Christians all over the world. It is well known for instance that Christian rehabilitation and health clinics are often very effective. When people in miserable conditions suddenly get a new hope in life they are usually liberated from all kinds of addictions.[40]

Christianity also had a big impact on human rights, democracy, and prosperity, rooted in the biblical idea that all humans are created in the image of God, with dignity, worth, and equal value. Christians of the Middle Ages and Renaissance proposed natural and international law as a reflection of God's creation.[41] The teaching of the reformers Martin Luther (1483–1546) and John Calvin (1509–64) inspired daily work as a fulfillment of God's calling. This was reinforced by the Pietists and Methodists of the seventeenth and eighteenth centuries and laid an important foundation for future economic welfare.[42] The Bible was translated into many languages and mass education was encouraged. The Protestant free churches empha-

---

35. Matt 7:12.
36. Luke 10:25–37.
37. Evidence 18.
38. Copan, *Is God a Moral Monster?*, chapter 20 and references therein.
39. Barna Group, "Atheists and Agnostics Take Aim."
40. Pearcey gives more details on religious activity as a positive source for mental well-being. Pearcey, *Total Truth*, chapter 1. See also evidence 23.
41. Evidence 9.
42. Weber, *Protestant Ethic*.

sized human rights, such as John Wesley's (1703–91) fight for slavery trade abolition. This movement was later carried on and very successfully led by William Wilberforce (1759–1833).

But what caused the development of modern western democracies? It was indeed paralleled by secularization, but this does not imply that the latter caused the former. On the contrary, the American sociologist Robert Woodberry argues that Protestantism in particular facilitated rise of modern democracy. He also found a very strong statistical association between missionary work and development of representative democracies all over the world.[43] In countries where Protestant missionaries were allowed to minister and evangelize with an emphasis on salvation by grace, their work catalyzed religious liberty, mass education, mass printing of newspapers, founding of voluntary organizations, new colonial reforms, and legal protections for non-whites. These changes inspired stable democracies to develop, whether many people became Christians or not through their work. Most of these missionaries were not financed by state-controlled churches. On the contrary, some of them belonged to churches that were oppressed by the state.

Sometimes it seems that people outside of Europe are better at recognizing the remarkable influence that Christianity has had on Western society. The following is a quote from a talk by a Chinese scholar that represented the Chinese Academy of Social Sciences. It was given to a group of American tourists.

> "One of the things that we were asked to look into was what accounted for the success, in fact, the pre-eminence of the West all over the world," he said. "We studied everything we could from the historical, economic, and cultural perspectives. At first, we thought it was because you had more powerful guns than we had. Then we thought it was because you had the best political system. Next we focused on your economic system. But in the past twenty years, we have realized that the heart of your culture is your religion: Christianity. That is why the West has been so powerful. The Christian moral foundation of social and cultural life was what made possible the emergence of capitalism and then the successful transition to democratic politics. We don't have any doubts about this."[44]

---

43. Woodberry, "Missionary Roots" and Leijon, "Lutheranism or Secularism."
44. Aikman, *Jesus in Beijing*, chapter 1.

Evidence 4: Culture and creativity in arts and science. Although Europe is quite secularized today, the 2,000 years of Christian impact have influenced society much more than most of us think. This includes not only human rights, democracy, charity, and economy, but also culture.[45] This is to some extent expected, since Christianity has been the dominant worldview. But much of the work of Christian artists, composers, and writers show signs of great creativity, with influence far outside the Christian community. The complexity and beauty of Johann Sebastian Bach's (1685–1750) music seems to reflect the greatness of God; John Bunyan's (1628–68) book *Pilgrim's Progress* illustrates our journey through life; the books of Fyodor Dostoyevsky (1821–81) portray man's struggle with sin; and the works of J. R. R. Tolkien and C. S. Lewis depict the fight between good and evil. These persons have managed to convey either beauty or very deep insights of what it means to be human. For many people this is strong evidence for—and even a route to—Christianity. Several of the most prominent scientists have also been Christians. Their strong faith was not only important in their daily life, it also inspired their creative thinking.[46]

It is described in the book of Exodus how God filled Bezalel and Oholiab with his Spirit. This gave them skill, ability, and knowledge in all kinds of crafts to make artistic designs in order to build the Tent of Meeting and the Ark of the Covenant.[47] God also encouraged and equipped Moses, Joshua, and Gideon with creative leadership skills under very difficult circumstances.[48] The style of writing of many biblical books reflects creativity as well. There is beauty, encouragement, and comfort in the Psalms, poetry in the Song of Solomon, wisdom in Proverbs and Ecclesiastes, historical and scholarly writing in Luke and the book of Acts, theological insights and systematic teaching in Paul's letters, and metaphysical qualities in the gospel and letters that John the apostle wrote.

There is also much non-Christian culture with great impact, for instance, from Greek antiquity. Christians are of course not more creative than others per se. The core of the gospel is rather that anyone is welcome to receive the message of salvation. But from a Christian perspective, the only way for a person to reach his full potential is to receive Jesus into his heart and discover God's plan for his life. When someone takes this step his spirit is filled with God's Holy Spirit. And if God is allowed to penetrate

45. Hill, *What Has Christianity Ever Done*.
46. Evidence 10 and 15.
47. Exod 31:1–11.
48. Exod 2; Josh 1:1–9; Judg 6:11—8:21.

more and more aspects of life, creativity will increase in a way that reflects God's creativity.[49] The work of a Christian artist may therefore reveal what it means to be human, since we are all created in the image of God. Although this image was distorted, it was yet not destroyed after the fall of man [50]

It is much more challenging to motivate creativity from a naturalistic point of view. Indeed, with such a worldview it is difficult to explain why we should trust our senses in the first place.[51]

Evidence 5: Israel and the Jewish people. The Jews have been scattered around the world for thousands of years. This was caused by a series of events; in particular, the Assyrian captivity of the Northern Kingdom of Israel in 722 B.C., the Babylonian captivity of the Southern Kingdom of Judah in 586 B.C., the siege of Jerusalem in A.D. 70, and the Roman crushing of Simon bar Kokhba's revolt in A.D. 134. In spite of this the Jews survived and kept their religious traditions. They have also been extremely successful in finance, business, science, arts, and music. Today they comprise only 0.2 percent of the worldwide population, but yet more than 20 percent of Nobel Prize winners have a Jewish origin. Many worldwide corporations such as Facebook, Dell, Oracle, WhatsApp, Google, and Ben & Jerrys were founded by Jews. This success is particularly remarkable in view of the strong opposition and persecution they have faced for centuries.

From the Middle Ages the Jews in Europe[52] were often not allowed as guild members, but were compelled to live in ghettos within the cities. And sadly, this was often instituted by the surrounding Christian authorities. Jews have often been accused of various things like killing of children and plotting to control the world. The rise of religious freedom and other human rights in Europe during the nineteenth century made it possible for Jews to enter trade, science, and politics. Because of their success within all these spheres, antagonism towards them increased. The Dreyfus affair by the end of the nineteenth century convinced Teodor Herzl (1860–1904) that the Jews could not hope for fair treatment in Europe. This encouraged him to start a *Zionist movement.* The increased wave of anti-Semitism from the late nineteenth century culminated in the Holocaust of World War II 50 years later. When the shocking news of the concentration camps reached the world, people in most countries got a guilty conscience over what hap-

---

49. Bevere, *Extraordinary.*
50. Section 2.1.
51. Evidence 7.
52. See evidence 22 for more on Jewish history.

pened. This led the newly founded United Nations to act so that modern Israel was established in 1948. The nation of Israel has fought for its survival for almost 70 years since then. And it just takes a few generations for people to forget. The positive attitude towards modern Israel and the Jews after World War II has gradually drifted back to a normal state of skepticism and anti-Semitism. The political and military activities of no other nation is scrutinized in the same way as for modern Israel—the only democracy of the Near East where all inhabitants have human rights, regardless of ethnicity and religion.

The remarkable history of the Jews has struck people for centuries, and many explanations for their prosperity have been proposed. For instance, persecution and discrimination may increase problem-solving skills and the willingness to take risks. Their religious traditions have kept the Jews together, with an emphasis on memorizing scriptures so that their literacy and degree of education has been high. Their vision to return to the homeland Israel has also given them hope. Another possibility is the high intelligence among Ashkenazis, who comprise about 75 percent of the worldwide Jewish population today. They immigrated to Central and Eastern Europe in early medieval times, and since they were forced to have occupations that required literacy, mathematical, and economic skills it has been proposed that natural selection increased their intelligence.[53] There may be some truth in all of these natural explanations, but they appear inadequate to fully unravel the Jewish success story.

It seems that we have to look for supernatural answers as well, either directly or indirectly through natural explanations. Over 300 years ago King Louis XIV (1638-1715) of France asked Pascal to give him proof of the supernatural. Pascal answered:

Why, the Jews, your Majesty, the Jews.

Pascal believed that Jewish history confirms the credibility of the Bible, and in the *Pensées* he presented many details about the Jews. Many others regard not only the ancient but also the modern history of Israel as very strong evidence for Christianity. In order to understand more about Jewish history we have to look more closely into the Bible's record of Israel and the chronology of figure 9.1.[54]

---

53. Cochran et al., "Natural History of Ashkenazi Intelligence."

54. For more details on the Bible's record of Israel and Jewish history, see for instance Walvoord, *Israel in Prophecy*; Reichmann, *Judarna*; and Scharfstein, *Understanding Jewish History*.

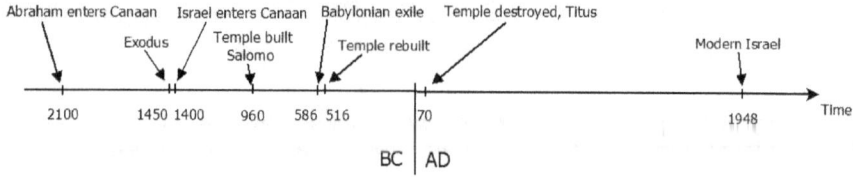

Figure 9.1: Approximate timing of some major events in the history of Israel based on a literal chronological interpretation of the Bible from Abraham and onwards.

God called Abraham out of Ur of the Chaldeans around 2100 B.C. He made a covenant with Abraham[55] that was later confirmed and specified on several occasions.[56] This covenant can be summarized as follows:

1. Abraham would have a son and become the father of a nation (Israel). His name would be made great.
2. The people of Israel were promised the land of Canaan after 400 years of slavery in Egypt.
3. Abraham and his descendants would be greatly blessed.
4. God would bless those that blessed Abraham and his descendants.
5. God would curse those that cursed Abraham and his descendants.
6. All nations on Earth would be blessed through Abraham and his descendants.

Item 1 was a covenant between God on one hand and Abraham and his descendants on the other. As a sign of this the Israelites were to circumcise each male baby eight days after birth. God's first part of this promise came true when Abraham and Sarah, in spite of their high age, had a son—Isaac.[57]

Item 2 was initiated around 1450 B.C. when Moses led the Israelites out of Egypt, and it was finalized 40 years later when his successor Joshua brought them into the Promised Land.

Item 3 was specified shortly after the exodus from Egypt as a covenant on Mount Sinai when God gave the Law to Israel.[58] He promised to bless them greatly as a nation when they had entered into the Promised Land, under one *condition*—that they obeyed God. When Israelites started to worship the

---

55. Gen 12:1–3.
56. Gen 13:14–17; 15:1–20; 17:1–18.
57. Gen 21:1–6. God also promised to bless Abraham's other son, Ishmael, with a promise of having many descendants. This was confirmed by circumcision as well, although God made the special covenant through Isaac and Israel (Gen 17:20–27).
58. Exod 20–30.

gods of the surrounding nations they were first warned through prophets and later punished, although God forgave and helped them once they repented. This circle of punishment and repentance was repeated, although the overall spiritual climate gradually declined until God allowed Jerusalem to be conquered by Babylonian troops around 600 B.C. The temple—which had been built under Solomon's reign around 960 B.C. as the religious center of worship—was destroyed. When the Jews were sent to captivity in Babylon they once again repented. A fraction of them returned in 539 B.C. and started to rebuild the temple in order to restore the Jewish nation. For the next several hundred years Israel was constantly surrounded by great powers. Although the Jews had periods of political freedom, in 63 B.C. they were occupied by the Romans. But a large number of Jews remained in Israel until the son of the Roman emperor—Titus (A.D. 39-81)—destroyed the temple in A.D. 70 and conquered Jerusalem. A final destruction of Jerusalem took place when bar Kokhba's revolt was defeated about 65 years later. Most of the Jews of Israel were scattered around the world again and it was not until 1948 that the modern nation of Israel was proclaimed in the land once promised to Abraham.

This history of Israel reveals a pattern. From the time of Abraham until this day we find that God never forgot his chosen people, although he sometimes punished them but very often he greatly blessed them. This blessing of Israel as a nation was often regarded as evidence of God already in the Old Testament. For instance, when Joshua sent out two Israeli spies to Jericho to prepare for an attack, they were protected by the prostitute Rahab. It was obvious to her by the way the Israelites had been rescued out of Egypt and protected in the Sinai desert that the God of Israel was the God of all nations.[59] Isaiah prophesied that the Jewish descendants would be known and honored by all people as a nation truly blessed by God.[60] Around 520 B.C. the prophet Zechariah encouraged the Jews that returned from the Babylonian exile to finish the rebuilding of the temple. The forthcoming blessings of Israel would be a sign for many people from powerful nations, and they would come and celebrate festivals together with the Jews.[61]

The reader is urged to find modern examples of items 4 and 5, where good treatment of Jews has blessed nations whereas a more hostile attitude has had the opposite effect. Whether or not there are natural explanations for this, on a deeper level there may still be spiritual reasons behind it, since God usually operates within the laws of our world.[62] In the Old Testament

---

59. Josh 2:9-13 and evidence 18.
60. Isa 61:8-9.
61. Zech 8:18-23.
62. Another possible cause of a nation's prosperity is Christianity itself; see evidence 3.

we find the same pattern. Nations with a hostile attitude towards Israel were punished and those with a friendly attitude were not. For instance, when Saul was the king of Israel around 1050 B.C. the Amalekites were punished for not waylaying the Israelites when they came out of Egypt, whereas God wanted to protect the Kenites for showing kindness towards Israel when they came out of Egypt.[63]

The prophecy of item 6 was reinforced and detailed when God spoke through Moses of a coming prophet,[64] when he later spoke to King David of an eternal kingdom,[65] and through many of the Old Testament prophets and psalm writers of a coming Messiah that would suffer[66] and become King and Ruler[67] of a kingdom that would last forever.[68] It was finally fulfilled when Jesus, the Savior of all mankind, was born as a Jew.

Christians have interpreted the Old Testament promises to the Jewish people very differently. Some theologians hold the view that the Christian church replaced Israel as God's chosen people. This is referred to as replacement theology or supersessionism. It arose when Christianity and Judaism gradually drifted apart the first few centuries A.D. Some early traces of this view can be found already in the writings of Justin Martyr (A.D. 100–65) and Melito of Sardis (died c. A.D. 180). This negative view of Jews has persisted in the church since then, for instance, in the sermons of John Chrysostom (c. 349–407) in the fourth century and in some of the later writings of Martin Luther in the sixteenth century. Sadly, this sometimes inspired oppression against Jews.

But can replacement theology be warranted? It is true, on one hand, that the Law is now replaced by faith in Christ through grace,[69] and by him the Law gets implanted in our hearts.[70] The Bible even refers to the church as Israel.[71] However, this doesn't mean that a messianic Jew who accepts Christ as his Lord and Savior has to abandon his cultural identity and stop celebrating Jewish festivals. Nor has God forgotten Israel as a nation. It rather seems clear from the Bible that he still has a plan for them, will continue to bless them in various ways, and at the end of time many Jews will come to

63. 1 Sam 15:1–6. See also evidence 18.
64. Deut 18:18–19.
65. 1 Chr 17:14.
66. Isa 53.
67. Ps 110, Jes 9:7.
68. Ps 89:35–38.
69. Gal 2:15–21.
70. Hebr 10:15–17.
71. Rom 9:6–8.

Christ.⁷² And modern history seems to confirm this. Although the number messianic Jews is still relatively small, in recent years it has increased.⁷³

A friendlier attitude towards the Jews grew out from John Calvin's Reformed tradition in the sixteenth century. His teaching emphasized that the Old and New Testaments should be harmonized, and from the seventeenth century this had a big impact in the Netherlands and among the Puritans in England. In the nineteenth century John Nelson Darby (1800–82) and many other leaders of Protestant churches continued this *Christian Zionism* tradition. They recognized God's promises to his chosen people, their right to return to Israel, and the apocalyptic prophecies about the Jews before and after the second coming of Christ. These Christians realized that several passages of the Old Testament strongly indicate a return of the Jewish people from *many* nations,⁷⁴ and their teaching inspired the Jewish Zionist movement at the end of the century. This theology also accords very well with the foundation of the modern state of Israel. Indeed, a large number of Jews have migrated there from many countries, whereas they mainly returned from *one* country after the Babylonian exile.

To summarize, God did not choose Israel because they were morally more qualified than other nations.⁷⁵ It rather seems that God's major purpose with Israel was to reveal himself to a world that had forgotten about him. First of all, his blessing and protection of Israel would remind the people of other nations of his existence and sovereignty, not only in the Old Testament but also today. Second, the failure of the Jews to follow the Law motivated a Redeemer as a necessity for mankind.⁷⁶ Third, this Redeemer—Jesus Christ—needed a Jewish environment to be born into. Fourth, the modern history of Israel agrees well with the biblical promises to the Jews.

Evidence 6: Church history. After Jesus had died, resurrected, and ascended to heaven the first church included a handful of followers that regularly gathered and prayed in private, frightened to share their faith in public.

---

72. Rom 11:25–32; Jer 32:38–41; Zech 12; Rev 12.

73. According to some estimates there are about 350,000 messianic Jews worldwide, a majority of which lives in the US, and a smaller fraction (10,000–20,000) in Israel. Although the counts vary, it seems that the number of messianic Jews is growing. Posner, "Kosher Jesus."

74. See for instance Isa 11:10–12; Jer 32:37; Ezek 38:8; and Jer 31:35–36. These passages strongly indicate that Israel will remain as a nation.

75. Deut 7:7–8.

76. Evidence 18.

Shortly thereafter a tremendous growth initiated on the day of Pentecost[77] and very soon Christendom started to spread around the Roman Empire. Christianity is today the largest world religion, with more than two billion followers—almost a third of the human worldwide population.[78]

The history and growth of the church is for many people strong evidence for Christianity. One may object, saying that all world religions have grown from a tiny start and one of them has to be the largest. Although this is a logical response, it is not only the fact that church *has* grown but even more *the manner in which it has grown* that is strong evidence for Christianity.

Religious beliefs are first of all deeply rooted in humans. Often they mark ethnic and cultural identity, and religious conflicts have caused much division between nations and cultures. But Christianity is meant have the opposite influence and unite people with different backgrounds.[79] Indeed, if we look at the history of the church it turns out that Christianity has penetrated ethnic and cultural barriers like no other religion. It first spread among Jews from Jerusalem to Judea and Samaria,[80] and then to Damascus,[81] Cyprus, Phoenicia in present Lebanon, and Antioch in present Syria.[82] Antioch was one of the places where many Gentiles (non-Jews) first became Christians. Paul and Barnabas were sent out from the church of this city as missionaries to present-day Turkey,[83] and later Paul extended his missionary journeys to Greece.[84] He was later sent to Rome, where a church had already been established.[85] There he continued his ministry while he was still under house arrest.

In the following centuries Christianity spread throughout the Roman Empire in present-day Europe, North Africa, and the Middle East. The Muslim expansion that started in the seventh century greatly diminished Christian influence in the Middle East and North Africa. But Europe gradually became and largely remained a Christian continent until the nineteenth

---

77. Acts 2:1–47.

78. For more detailed statistics, see Johnson and Ross, *Atlas of Global Christianity*. It is a very challenging to estimate the number of Christians. Not only because the number varies over time and across continents, but more importantly—whether someone is a Christian or not is ultimately something between that person and God (see section 3.1).

79. This is discussed in evidence 3.

80. Acts 8.

81. Acts 9:10–25.

82. Acts 11:19–30.

83. Acts 13–14.

84. Acts 15:36—20:38.

85. Acts 28:11–31.

and twentieth centuries. The Christian influence of Europe then gradually diminished as it was replaced by secularized thinking. However, through missionary work Christianity continued to spread in the sixteenth century from Europe to South and North America, and also to other continents. The largest revivals in the history of the church came in the twentieth and twenty-first centuries, though. They have generated an enormous growth of Christianity, especially in southern Africa, but also in Asia and South America. There are still quite few Christians in the Muslim world, but in the last few decades the church has been growing faster than ever in many of these countries.

To summarize, the history of the church reveals that most of the larger ethnic groups have been penetrated by the gospel. It is simply wrong to say that Christianity is rooted in a specific culture, except its Jewish Old Testament origin. The first believers were either Jews or they came from countries of the Middle East or Europe—regions where comparatively few are Christians today. A typical Christian of the twenty-first century rather lives in Nigeria, China, South Korea, or Brazil. This development accords well with the Great Commission, in which Jesus commanded his followers to make disciples of *all nations*.[86] Just before his ascension to heaven he told his followers that the church would spread, starting in Jerusalem and then proceeding to Judea, Samaria, and to the end of the world.[87] God is not the God of one people but of all nations.

Second, there are many misconceptions about *how* Christianity grew. It is often believed that Christianity to a large extent spread through Western colonization. On the contrary, some of the most intensive periods of church growth—the first three centuries A.D. and the last 200 years—were characterized by revivals, the work of missionary organizations, and the personal evangelization of local churches.[88] Although nations have been conquered in the name of Christianity and missionaries followed the European colonists, no one can be forced to become a true follower of Jesus since this is a matter of giving your heart to him. Indeed, when Jesus sent out his disciples to minister, he instructed them to leave those villages where the message was not received and go to others.[89] A church whose members are forced to adopt Christian faith is less likely to survive for a longer period of time. And it is much more vulnerable to syncretism, whereby Christianity is melted

---

86. Matt 28:18–20; Luke 24:47.

87. Acts 1:8.

88. See for instance Hill, *History of Christianity*, Sahlberg, *Missionens historia* and Stark, *Triumph of Christianity* for more details.

89. Mark 6:6–13.

with other religions. Western cultural imperialism should therefore not be confused with spread of Christianity. On the contrary, missionary work is much more likely to bear fruit if the gospel of Jesus Christ is presented within the given cultural and ethnic framework. It is only those parts of culture that relate worship of other gods that have to be abandoned.

In fact, Christianity has often grown under periods of oppression and persecution from the outside world. Jesus was very well aware of this, and therefore he gave a last promise to the disciples before the ascension to heaven that they would be filled with the Holy Spirit as a source of power, especially during times of opposition. Ten days later—on the day of Pentecost—the Holy Spirit manifested himself, people started to speak in foreign tongues, and Peter boldly held a sermon after which many came to faith.[90] The Christians in Jerusalem were well liked by the people,[91] but gradually the opposition from the religious leaders increased until Stephen, the first-Christian martyr, was killed.[92] This started a period of persecution that scattered the followers around Jerusalem so that Christianity spread.[93]

This pattern of oppression and church growth has continued ever since. The church father Tertullian (c. 160–c. 225) stated that "the blood of the martyrs is seed of the church." One of the worst persecutions of Christians, which took place in the beginning of the fourth century, was lead by the Roman emperors Diocletian (244–312) and Galerius (260–311). But Christianity was not eradicated. On the contrary, ten years later Christianity was officially allowed by the new emperor, Constantine (272–337). And within a century Christendom became the state religion of the Roman Empire.

A modern example is the development in China during the twentieth century. The Christians in China numbered a few millions after World War II. Then Christianity was regarded as a Western religion after the communist revolution of 1949. All foreign missionaries were expelled from the country and the state control of the church quickly increased. This culminated during the cultural revolution of the 1960s, and after that it has continued to various extents. The majority of Christians refused to enter the state-controlled church, many of them were sentenced to long-term imprisonment, and underground house churches were founded. These churches experienced tremendous growth and today the number of Christians in

---

90. Acts 2:1–40.
91. Acts 2:47.
92. Acts 7:54–60.
93. Acts 8.

China is at least 100 million![94] Another even more recent example is the current rapid church growth in Iran and many other Muslim countries, in spite of strong opposition and persecution.[95]

Although outside pressure may create unity among the oppressed ones, it is still very hard to explain the expansion of Christianity by natural means. Many people in countries with rapid church growth turn to Christ when they encounter Jesus in a dream, witness a healing, or notice the changed life of a friend that gave his life to Jesus. A much more reasonable explanation for the growth is that persecution of Christianity is a way of fighting God, who cannot be defeated. The Pharisee Gamaliel realized this. In the book of Acts we read about his wise advice to the elders of Israel, when they discussed how to respond to the spread of the early church in Jerusalem. They had just witnessed a miraculous release of some of the apostles from jail, and Gamaliel urged the other religious leaders not to persecute the first Christians.[96]

Third, it seems that churches that teach a classical Christian doctrine often grow more quickly—regardless of denomination.[97] This indicates that their interpretation of Christianity is more appealing to people (and to God). This is true in particular for charismatic churches, and many of them experienced remarkable growth in the last 100 years within many denominations. Their signature is the presence of the gifts of the Holy Spirit, including, for instance, speaking in tongues and the gifts of prophecy, knowledge, and wisdom, as well as a positive attitude toward signs and wonders—not as a goal in itself, but as a way of getting to know Jesus more deeply, and as a help for the church members to make Christ known to others. This is very much in line with Joel's prophecy in the Old Testament:

> And afterward, I will pour out my Spirit on all people. Your sons and daughters will prophesy, your old men will dream dreams, your young men will see visions. Even on my servants, both men and women, I will pour out my Spirit in those days.[98]

These verses were quoted by Peter on the first day of Pentecost. And many of the churches the first three centuries were charismatic, for instance, in Corinth in the book of Acts. In modern times the charismatic influence came back after revivals in Europe and North America in the eighteenth and nineteenth centuries. Then it increased even more when the worldwide

94. Aikman, *Jesus in Beijing*.
95. Garrison, *Wind in the House of Islam* and Doyle, *Killing Christians*.
96. Acts 5:33–39.
97. Kelley, *Why Conservative Churches Are Growing*.
98. See Joel 2:28–29 for the Old Testament prophecy and Rom 12:4–8; 1 Cor 12:4–10; 1 Cor 14; Eph 4:11–13 for teaching about the gifts of the Holy Spirit.

Pentecostal revival appeared in the beginning of the twentieth century.[99] Fifty years later a charismatic revival entered many Protestant, Catholic, and other groups around the world. Today many of these churches are growing very fast.[100] One of the most remarkable examples is the Yoido Full Gospel Church of South Korea. It started with a handful of believers in the late 1950s and today it has more than half a million members—including several planted satellite churches.

---

99. Most well known is the revival that started at Azusa Street, Los Angeles, in 1906. But other revivals appeared about same time in Wales, Mumbai India, Pyongyang North Korea, and in Valpraiso Chile.

100. The annual growth of charismatic churches has been (point) estimated to 2.4 percent, which is higher than for other churches. Johnson et al., "View from the New Atlas of Global Christianity." For historical details about the charismatic revival, see Bennett, *Nine O'Clock in the Morning*; Plessis, *Man Called Mr. Pentecost*; and Aronsson, *Guds eld över Sverige*, chapter 1.

10

Evidence from Reason, Consciousness, and Morality

THERE ARE A NUMBER of things that distinguish humans from animals, such as our self-awareness, ability to reason, and a capacity to distinguish right from wrong. In this chapter we will look at the origin of these skills. Depending on our response we either get evidence in favor of or against Christianity.

Evidence 7: Reason and consciousness. From a Christian perspective, human creativity and ability to reason are both gifts from God and part of the soul.[1] With a naturalistic worldview, our senses have rather evolved—more or less blindly—from lower forms of life. The question is which of these two explanations is most credible. It turns out that the naturalistic, evolutionary theory faces several challenges. It is first of all difficult then to know why we should trust our mental capabilities. This objection against naturalism is usually referred to as the *argument from reason* in favor of a Creator. And it was noted already by Charles Darwin in a private mail correspondence:

> But then with me the horrid doubt always arises whether the convictions of man's mind, which has developed from the minds of lower animals, are of any value of at all trustworthy. Would anyone trust in the convictions of a monkey's mind, if there are any convictions in such a mind.[2]

---

1. Section 2.1 and evidence 4.
2. Darwin, "Letter to William Graham," lines 19–23.

This quote—Darwin's doubt—was later developed by the British politician Sir Arthur Belfour (1848–1930), the geneticist J. B. S. Haldane (1892–1964) and others. It also inspired C. S. Lewis to write:

> Supposing there was no Intelligence behind the universe, no creative mind. In that case, nobody designed my brain for the purpose of thinking. It is merely that when the atoms inside my skull happen, for physical or chemical reasons, to arrange themselves in a certain way, this gives me, as a by-product, the sensation I call thought. But, if so, how can I trust my own thinking to be true? It's like upsetting a milk jug and hoping that the way it splashes itself will give you a map of London. But if I can't trust my own thinking, of course I can't trust the arguments leading to Atheism, and therefore have no reason to be an Atheist, or anything else. Unless I believe in God, I cannot believe in thought: so I can never use thought to disbelieve in God.[3]

And there are many others who more or less agree with this statement. Philosopher Thomas Nagel (1939–), for instance, is not a theist but he has nevertheless offered an argument against blind evolution similar to that of Lewis.[4]

Consciousness is a property even more basic than our ability to reason. An *argument from consciousness* for the existence of God has been developed by Richard Swinburne, among others.[5] The first part of the argument concludes that consciousness is a mental entity that is correlated with physical observables. For instance, when I lift a cup of coffee (a physical thing) I must first think about doing so (a mental thing). A pain caused by physical injuries is another example. It will affect our mind, and certain *psychosomatic disorders* such as lower back pain and high blood pressure have a stress-related mental component. *Neuroplasticity* is another physical phenomenon that is correlated with mental properties. It is that part of neuroscience that studies the ability of the brain and nervous system to change structurally and functionally as a result of inputs from the environment, even when we meditate and practice religions.

The second part of the argument from consciousness concludes that the correlation between physical and mental entities must have a personal explanation rather than a natural one. This very much points to dualism,

---

3. Lewis, *Case for Christianity*, 32. Lewis's original argument from reason can be found in the essay "Is Theology Poetry?" It was published in Lewis, *Weight of Glory*, chapter 5.

4. Nagel, *Mind and Cosmos*.

5. Swinburne, *Existence of God*, chapter 9. See also Moreland, "Argument from Consciousness," and sections 2.1–2 of this book.

by which we have a soul (the personal agent) that exists independently of our body, although the two communicate.[6] J. P. Moreland has reviewed a number of alternative naturalistic theories. According to one of these, consciousness does not exist independently of the body but has *emerged* from it.[7] He concludes that none of these theories have a plausible way of explaining consciousness or other mental properties. They are rather explained by theism, whereby God infuses a soul into us. In fact, many atheists admit that consciousness from their perspective remains a mystery.

There is actually plenty of evidence for dualism from near-death experiences, which often occur after clinical death when pulse, heartbeat, and measured brain activity (in terms of EEG) have ceased. This is first of all different from biological death, which is thought to be irreversible. And Christians claim that Jesus is the first person that resurrected after biological death with his body transformed into a new form.[8] When persons with near-death experiences come back to life in their old body after a clinical death, they often tell about things they could possibly not know from the natural. This includes resuscitation attempts in the hospital and reports of having met friends that recently died—although the person with the near-death experience didn't know of this before their clinical death. Often they mention the dead and loved ones with joy, not sorrow.

The strength of these testimonies increases by the fact that many of their details were confirmed independently by other persons. In fact, many experts acknowledge the difficulty of interpreting them by natural physiological or psychological mechanisms, such as hallucinations.[9] But from a naturalistic and monistic perspective these are the only possible explanations, since no soul and consciousness are believed to exist independently of the body. This is a strong argument in favor of a spiritual reality outside of the natural. But it is possible to push the argument further, more specifically towards Christianity. Indeed, people with near-death experiences—including children who have not heard of near-death experiences and not read about heaven—often report very concurrent details of paradise and of Jesus.[10]

---

6. See sections 2.1–2 for more on monism/dualism and the nature of man according to Christianity and naturalism.

7. See Moreland, "Argument from Consciousness", Groothuis, *Christian Apologetics*, Chapter 17, and references therein.

8. See for instance Wright, *Jesus' Resurrection* and references therein.

9. Habermas, "Paradigm Shift."

10. For instance, the story of Colton Burpo's near-death experiences before he was four years old are told in Burpo, *Heaven Is for Real*.

Evidence 8: Morality. Why are there moral values that tell us about right and wrong? For many people their existence is strong evidence for God. For instance, our conscience tells us that lying, stealing, killing, and adultery are wrong. It also seems that these values have been more or less the same for thousands of years. For instance, Greek philosophers and verses from the Bible have inspired people to list good and bad virtues, and in A.D. 590 Pope Gregory I (c. 540–604) coined the seven deadly sins (wrath, greed, sloth, pride, lust, envy, and gluttony) as the origin of many others.[11] The church fathers listed the seven virtues (prudence, justice, temperance, courage, faith, hope, and love) as examples of good behavior.[12]

The so-called *moral argument* for a Creator can be phrased as follows:

1. If God does not exist, there is no objective morality.

2. Objective moral values do exist.

3. Hence God exists.

It has two premises (1 and 2) and one conclusion (3). The British philosopher William Sorley (1855–1935) was one of the first to develop a longer argument for morality.[13] He reasoned as follows: Although we perceive that objective values exist in general, this does not mean we have full knowledge of all specific moral values, as some of these can be learned. But we still have an overall awareness that certain things *ought* to be done. Richard Swinburne points out[14] that the moral argument is weaker than one based on our *mental awareness of morality*. This latter argument can formally be expressed as follows:

1'. If God does not exist, we are not aware of moral right and wrong.

2'. We are aware of what is right and wrong.

3. Hence God exists.

Indeed, it requires even more to explain existence *and* awareness of morality by whatever other hypothesis than God. Many find it quite astonishing that people all over the world from their childhood have similar conceptions of right and wrong, regardless of cultural and ethnic differences. This strong instinct of ours has been named the *moral law*. The existence of

---

11. Prov 6:16–19, and desires of the flesh in Gal 5:16–21.

12. This includes the fruits of the Spirit in Gal 5:22–26.

13. Craig, *Reasonable Faith*, chapter 3.

14. Swinburne, *Existence of God*, chapter 9; and Swinburne, *Faith and Reason*, chapter 5.

the moral law can be developed further to an argument for Christianity if we add sin to the moral awareness premises:

0. If Christianity is not true, man is not fallen.
I. If man is not fallen, we are not aware of a moral law of right and wrong that we repeatedly break.
II. We are aware of a moral law of right and wrong that we repeatedly break.
III. Hence Christianity is true.

According to premise 0, the fall of man is specific to Christianity. It is true that Judaism and Islam also acknowledge that humans sin, but it is only in Christianity that the fall of man marks a turning point in history after which man's nature changed into an inclination of sinfulness. Premise I claims that it is only the fall of man that explains our awareness of a law of right and wrong *and* our failure to follow it. Some naturalistic theories of morality will be discussed below, but let us first look at the biblical explanation of the moral law. The fall of man can be found in Genesis, when Adam and Eve ate from the tree of knowledge. Then their relation with God was not only distorted, but something else happened as well. They were also given the *knowledge of good and evil*.[15] This knowledge is the moral law, which God summarized in the Ten Commandments[16] given to the people of Israel. Premise II is based on the empirical observation that everyone (or at least most of us) has a conscience related to a moral law of right and wrong. This is vividly expressed by Paul in his Letter to the Roman Church:

> Indeed, when Gentiles, who do not have the law, do by nature things required by the law, they are a law for themselves, even though they do not have the law. They show that the requirements of the law are written on their hearts, their consciences also bearing witness, and their thoughts sometimes accusing them and at other times even defending them.[17]

In these verses Paul hints that we frequently oppose what our conscience tells us to do. But often we want others to get a good impression of us, and therefore we try to hide our failures and shortcomings. The moral law is in this sense very different from the natural laws of science. Whereas the natural laws are set aside very rarely under exceptional circumstances, the moral

---

15. Gen 3:5,22; see also Rom 2:14–15 and Deut 30:11–14.
16. Exod 20:3.
17. Rom 2:14–15.

laws are violated quite frequently.[18] A good example of this is the failure of the Jews to follow the Law of the Old Testament. Since the same would have happened to any other group of people if the Law had been given to them, this explains why it was necessary for a Redeemer to enter our world.[19]

Jesus explained that the entire moral law can be summarized in one single golden rule—to treat others as you want to be treated yourself.[20] In his Roman Epistle, Paul gives an even stronger picture of our failure to follow the standards of the Law:

> So I find this law at work: Although I want to do good, evil is right there with me. For in my inner being I delight in God's law; but I see another law at work in me, waging war against the law of my mind and making me a prisoner of the law of sin at work within me. What a wretched man I am! Who will rescue me from this body that is subject to death? Thanks be to God, who delivers me through Jesus Christ our Lord! So then, I myself in my mind am a slave to God's law, but in my sinful nature a slave to the law of sin.[21]

Although the Law is holy by itself, it is also our curse, since it makes us even more aware of our sins. And there is only one possible way out—to be filled with the Holy Spirit through faith in Christ:

> For what the law was powerless to do because it was weakened by the flesh, God did by sending his own Son in the likeness of sinful flesh to be a sin offering. And so he condemned sin in the flesh, in order that the righteous requirement of the law might be fully met in us, who do not live according to the flesh but according to the Spirit. Those who live according to the flesh have their minds set on what the flesh desires; but those who live in accordance with the Spirit have their minds set on what the Spirit desires. The mind governed by the flesh is death, but the mind governed by the Spirit is life and peace.[22]

Then we are given the ability to *choose* to follow the renewed spirit rather than the desires of the flesh. The universal validity of a moral law across human cultures has for many been so striking that it led them to Christ. It had

---

18. In evidence 11 and 24 we interpret miracles as instances when the natural laws are set aside.
19. Rom 5:20–21.
20. Matt 7:12.
21. Rom 7:21–25.
22. Rom 8:3–6.

a big impact, for instance, on C. S. Lewis[23] and the well-known molecular biologist Francis Collins[24] (1950–) in their decisions to become Christians.

Adherents of the alternative sociobiological view argue that moral awareness can be deduced from biology, so that premises 1' and I are false. But there are several difficulties associated with such a theory by which conscience has a biological origin. The Scottish philosopher David Hume (1711–76) pointed out the difficulty of drawing ethical conclusions about what *ought* to be from observations and statements of what *is*.[25] From a naturalistic point of view this is indeed a challenge. But there is no problem to take such a step from is to ought if God—the Lawgiver—exists.

Social Darwinism was developed, in spite of Hume's warning, by the English philosopher and biologist Herbert Spencer (1820–1903). It was based on the very optimistic view that evolution and the survival of the fittest guarantees progress in all parts of life, and therefore it would give us reliable grounds not only for biology, but also for ethics and morality. Morality was defined as the goal of evolutionary theory in terms of a perfect man. This view was partially shared by Darwin, and since it inspired racism, eugenics, and ultimately the Holocaust of World War II, it was very much discredited after the 1940s.

Modern evolutionary theorists try to avoid what Hume classified as a category mistake, that is, not regarding morality as an entity of its own but somewhat more cryptically as a tool that makes reproduction and survival more efficient. Ultimately it is therefore a kind of illusion. Evolutionary biologists Michael Ruse (1940–) and E. O. Wilson (1929–) categorized morality along these lines as a "corporate illusion" that has been "fobbed off on us by our genes to get us to cooperate."[26]

But if reproduction and survival are the main goals of society it is difficult to motivate altruistic and unselfish actions like saving the life of a sick person. Various mechanisms have been proposed in order to account for such behavior, like selfish genes, evolutionary game theory, group selection, kinship selection, and pleiotropy (when a single gene affects several traits). People have different views on how much these mechanisms can achieve, but is seems difficult for all of them to explain why the life of an old person should be saved even if this involves personal risks, or why promises should be kept to a dying person if there is no afterlife. These deeds seem to have no obvious evolutionary advantages, not even collectively for groups

23. Lewis, *Mere Christianity*.
24. Collins, *Language of God*.
25. Lennox, *Gunning for God*, chapter 4.
26. Ruse and Wilson, "Evolution of Ethics."

of people. And still we characterize them as good.²⁷ In any case, even if an evolutionary explanation of altruistic behavior *were* to be found, a tendency to do what is morally good doesn't imply a *belief* that this action is good—in line with Hume's critique. The latter would require evolution of a type of consciousness that also includes ethical values.²⁸

With an evolutionary perspective—whatever version of it one has—moral awareness becomes highly subjective and transformable over time. This was very vividly pointed out by Fyodor Dostoyevsky in *The Brothers Karamazov*. He argued that morality requires God, since

> Without God and the future life . . . everything is permitted . . .²⁹

Indeed, most people realize that it is difficult for us to act consistently if we believe that morality is subjective. Even if we believe *in theory* that our awareness of morality has evolved, it is difficult *in practice* to hold on to this view. We all get upset over various kinds of injustice, not least when we are the victims. But on which grounds do we react in such a way? It is indeed difficult to justify these reactions if awareness of morality is either subjective or if it exists objectively in some way that we don't know of. It is only awareness of an objective morality rooted in personhood that makes it legitimate to be upset.

Evidence 9: Social law and human rights. Our view of morality has crucial consequences for society and how to organize it. If we believe that humans are aware of an objective morality, it is possible to deduce a *natural law* that gives socially and personally binding rules of behavior. Such ideas were present already among the ancient Greek philosophers, and the Dominican priest Thomas Aquinas developed them further within a Christian context. According to Aquinas the natural law is a reflection of God's creation. This motivated the Dutch philosopher and theologian Hugo Grotius (1583–1645) to formulate his ideas of international law.³⁰ A century earlier the Dutch humanist and Catholic priest Desiderius Erasmus (1466–1536)

---

27. See for instance section 2.2; Dawkins, *God Delusion*; Smith, *Evolution and the Theory of Games*; Taylor, "Group Theory in Homogeneous Populations"; Jansen, "On Kin and Group Selection"; Selander, "Richard Dawkins moralsyn" and references therein.

28. Swinburne, *Existence of God*, chapter 9.

29. Dostoyevsky, *Brothers Karamazov*, 589.

30. Nordström, "De mänskliga rättigheternas grund."

had urged rulers to subject themselves to Christian ethical values instead of seeking power for its own sake.[31]

This doesn't mean that a state with a Christian majority should be a theocracy (like Sharia law in Islam), since religious freedom is one of the cornerstones of a godly society. In fact, a consequence of the golden rule is to treat others as you wish to be treated yourself. The Israeli theocracy of the Old Testament was unique and part of God's plan to save mankind.[32] We cannot apply this theocracy to modern states right away, and many believe that the history of Christianity has too much been dominated by monopoly churches after Constantine's conversion in the fourth century.[33] The Christian interpretation of natural law rather means that the value system of a society should rely on unchanging virtues such as justice, forgiveness, grace, and respect for life, family, the disabled, the poor, and the unborn. This agrees well with Jesus' teaching—that the kingdom of God is not forced upon us from above but rather grows from within. It starts in the heart of those who have been filled with the Holy Spirit through belief in Christ:

> He also said, "This is what the kingdom of God is like. A man scatters seed on the ground. Night and day, whether he sleeps or gets up, the seed sprouts and grows, though he does not know how. All by itself the soil produces grain, first the stalk, then the head, then the full kernel in the head. As soon as the grain is ripe, he puts the sickle to it, because the harvest has come."[34]

The Dutch politician and theologian Abraham Kuyper (1837–1920) developed ideas along these lines. All parts of Christian life are an honor to God within a society that consists of independent sovereign spheres. The state and church should be separated, different faith communities should have the right to start their own schools and universities, and families should be granted freedom to choose education for their children. Pope Leo XIII (1810–1903) had similar political ideas within a Catholic framework. He modernized Catholic social ethics in the encyclical *Rerum Novarum*, and argued that many political and social decisions could be taken at a local level with an emphasis on social justice. These ideas of Kuyper and Leo XIII have been very influential until this day for politics in Europe and the United States.

---

31. His most well-known publication on this subject is Erasmus, *Education of a Christian Prince*.
32. Evidence 18.
33. Stark, *Triumph of Christianity*.
34. Mark 4:26–32; see also Luke 13:18–21; 17:20–21; and Rom 14:17.

On the other hand, if morality is subjective the legal system is only a social construct. The Italian historian and writer Niccolò Machiavelli (1469–1527) advocated that rulers sometimes need to resort to unethical principles in order to stabilize the nation and stay in power.[35] The British philosopher and lawyer Jeremy Bentham (1748–1832) introduced *legal positivism*, by which utilitarian principles should be used to ensure the greatest happiness for the greatest number of people. But this requires a definition of happiness, and it easily leads to a society where the majority's vote defines morality. The value system of the society is then correct by definition, although it is easily manipulated and controlled by people in power. If so, how can we know for sure that the acts of the Nazis during World War II were wrong?

One message of the Bible is that any society that abandons the principles of God will develop in a destructive manner.[36] After World War II the Universal Declaration of Human Rights was formulated in an attempt to prevent new cruelties of the sort mankind had just experienced. Its Article 18 states:

> Everyone has the right to freedom of thought, conscience and religion; this right includes freedom to change his religion or belief, and freedom, either in community with others and in public or private, to manifest his religion or belief in teaching, practice, worship, and observance.

This agrees well with a Christian value system—with an emphasis on freedom of thought, conscience, and religion—since these are the most fundamental of rights. If they fail, other kinds of political rights such as freedom of speech, liberty of the press and media, freedom of assembly, and freedom to start political parties will sooner or later be jeopardized. It is therefore an important task of schools and journalism to promote a pluralistic society with freedom of conscience and other basic human rights.[37] A report by the United Nations Global Compact and the Religious Freedom & Business Foundation contains a number a case studies in different countries.[38] They reveal the importance of religious freedom and tolerance for economic welfare and prosperity. There are many historical examples where freedoms of thought, conscience, and religion have been restricted, not least in the com-

---

35. Machiavelli, *Prince* and Landgren, "*Makt eller rätt.*"

36. See for instance evidence 18.

37. Melhus argues that a Christian perspective on journalism education, research, and communication presupposes a commitment to democracy and pluralism. Melhus, "Discipline of Journalism."

38. Grim et al., "BUSINESS."

munist states of the twentieth century. Some of these fundamental rights are threatened today in European secularized states (often in the name of tolerance) and even more in some religious states in the Middle East.

In order to meet the increased challenge to follow Article 18, Os Guinness (1941–) took the initiative to formulate the Global Charter of Conscience together with people of many faiths, politicians, academics, and others. It was published at the European Union Parliament in Brussels, with a purpose of bringing religious tolerance back to the center of public debate and to help future generations to engage freely in the public life.[39]

---

39. Bielefeldt et al., "Global Character of Conscience."

11

Scientific Evidence

THE SCIENTIFIC REVOLUTION OF the sixteenth and seventeenth centuries and the Enlightenment of the eighteenth century elevated belief in human reason. Christianity or theism was still the dominant worldview among scientists in Europe, but gradually Western culture became more secularized and naturalistic. The process elevated in the nineteenth century, and by the mid-twentieth century it was not uncommon in academia to believe that science had disproved many fundamental Christianity claims. Although others argued that Christianity and science could be harmonized, this view was still quite marginalized, at least in the public sphere. From the late 1960s metaphysical ideas in general and Christianity in particular had an upswing though at philosophy departments—a trend that has continued until this day.[1] But in most other fields of study Christian academics tend to separate their scholarly work from their beliefs. The naturalistic approach has an overwhelming dominance in experimental disciplines—a fact that is most evident for those branches of science that investigate the history of the universe, the origin of life, and its diversity on Earth. The question is whether such a bias is warranted. In this chapter we will look at scientific evidence and its interpretation, and we will investigate whether it favors a Christian or a naturalistic worldview. We will discuss whether natural science has disproved the Bible, with a particular focus on miracles, the age of the universe, Darwinian macroevolution, design, and the origin of mathematics.

Evidence 10: The Bible and natural science. In order to answer the question whether (natural) science has disproved the Bible, we first need to address

[1]. Pearcey, *Total Truth*, 58–59 and references therein.

two other questions—how to interpret the Bible and what science is. It turns out that this is not at all easy. The answer to the first question depends on our theology and the second question relates to the *demarcation problem* of philosophy of science: How do we distinguish science from other kinds of knowledge? Depending on how these two questions are answered, we get at least three perspectives on how science relates to Christianity.

The first point of view is that Christianity and science are *complementary* and should not interfere, since science deals with facts and rational thinking whereas Christianity (and other religions) concerns moral values and the meaning of life. This view was advocated by the American paleontologist and evolutionary biologist Stephen Gould (1941–2002) in his Non-Overlapping MAgisteria (NOMA) principle. Somewhat related is fideism, according to which faith is independent of or even hostile to *reason*.[2] It is indeed true that Christianity and science to some extent focus on different questions—why and how this world came about and functions. Most scientific research can therefore be conducted regardless of which faith one holds on to. But there are other reasons why science and Christianity (or religion in general) cannot be fully separated. First of all, the Bible makes several claims that can be checked empirically, whereas the NOMA principle reduces Christian belief to subjective experience. Second, a scientific theory is not only based on empirical observations; it also relies on *unproved assumptions* that must be accepted by faith.

The second point of view is shared, for instance, by the New Atheists. The advocates of this view often believe that science has no real boundaries. In particular they acknowledge that Christianity makes testable claims. And based on this they conclude that science has disproved the Bible, and hence that science and Christianity are in *conflict*. For instance, former Oxford Chemistry Professor Peter Atkins (1940–) writes:

> Humanity should accept that science has eliminated the justification for believing in cosmic purpose, and that any survival of purpose is inspired only by sentiment.[3]

According to the third *coherence* point of view, science and Christianity are friends that interfere a lot. Its proponents agree with adherents of the conflict scenario that many (but not all) Christian claims can be tested. But they interpret evidence very differently from those that view science as a defeater of Christianity. This third group includes many Christian scientists

---

2. Gould, *Rock of Ages*.
3. Atkins, "Will Science Ever Fail?"

who emphasize that the Bible also provides great *motivation for conducting science*. There are several reasons why they make this claim:[4]

1. The Bible tells that the universe is created by a rational and trustworthy God in a unified and coherent way.[5] We can therefore expect to find laws of nature and logic that reflect the order of God's creation. This is related to the *transcendental argument* for God.

2. God created the universe from nothing—*ex nihilo*—all by himself.[6] He has full control over creation, and it is therefore reasonable to assume that apparent irregularities in nature only reflect our current lack of knowledge.

3. God made his creation good[7] but not a god. We can therefore study it with pleasure and without fear.

4. Humans are created in the image of God[8] with the ability to reason. This makes it possible to attain knowledge of the world by observing it and "thinking God's thoughts after him." This is the *argument from reason* in favor of theism.[9]

5. God is sovereign and free to create the universe as he wishes. Although he is bound by his own nature, his intellectual capability is so much larger ours.[10] Therefore, as humans with finite abilities, we cannot deduce how the universe is ordered by logical reasoning alone. We have to collect empirical observations from nature and based on these repeatedly formulate, reject, and validate new models.[11]

6. God has given humans dominion over creation and a mandate to cultivate and take care of it, but not to exploit it in a negative way.[12]

7. An important aspect of being a follower of Christ is truthfulness, which includes taking all empirical evidence into account and not hiding anything that would threaten one's own worldview.

---

4. Pearcey and Thaxton, *Soul of Science*.
5. Gen 1.
6. John 1:3; Col 1:16–17; Heb 11:3.
7. Gen 1:31.
8. Gen 1:27.
9. However, Christianity also involves revelations from God (section 2.1), and therefore it leads to questions that we cannot fully answer by reason alone.
10. Isa 55:9.
11. See the comment on voluntarist theology in evidence 3.
12. Gen 1:28.

It is not surprising in view of this that historically belief in a rational God was important for the development of science. We have already mentioned that during the Middle Ages scholastic theologians founded the first European universities and voluntarist theologians stressed the importance of experiments.[13] Many of the universe's natural laws were then discovered in the seventeenth, eighteenth, and nineteenth centuries by Christian scientists like Galileo Galilei, Isaac Newton (1642–1727), Michael Faraday (1791–1867), and James Clerk Maxwell (1831–79). Their Christian conviction was not an obstacle for them. On the contrary, their faith in God motivated their research.[14] The British biochemist, historian, and sinologist Joseph Needham (1900–95) wanted to find out why China in spite of its early innovations had fallen behind Europe in terms of advancement of science and technology. He concluded that scientists in Europe had been motivated by a widespread belief in God—a designer who made all scientific laws understandable—and so they very much expected to find such laws.[15]

The question to ask then is which of these three perspectives of science versus Christianity is correct. We have already argued that the first complementary point of view is not reasonable. It therefore remains to find out whether science and Christianity are friends or in conflict, and this hinges on whether there is evidence that contradicts Christianity or not. Francis Bacon (1561–1626), Galileo, and others reasoned that God apart from the Bible had written a second book of nature—his creation. If we believe that God is truthful and trustworthy these two books should not contradict each other. If they did this would definitely be evidence against classical Christianity, according to which the Bible is the Word of God that he inspired humans to write different parts of according to his will, and for a special purpose.[16] The details of the Bible should therefore be reliable.

But one should be cautious about reporting conflicts between the Bible and science. A stated conflict between a biblical *interpretation* and a scientific *theory* is not necessarily a conflict between the Bible and empirical data. Both the interpretation and the theory have to be scrutinized before a real conflict can be established. Figure 11.1 classifies tentative conflicts between the Bible and science into four types (A–D). This classification is due to the Swedish philosopher Mats Selander (1967-), and it is only an A conflict that is regarded as serious.[17] A type-A conflict would occur for instance if

13. Evidence 3.
14. Stenumgaard, *Vetenskap och tro*.
15. Needham, *Grand Titration*.
16. 2 Tim 3:16.
17. Selander, "Vetenskap och tro" and *Utan Jesus ingen mobil*, 119.

indisputable empirical evidence of Jesus' body was found. This would prove that Jesus never resurrected from death.

In order to apply figure 11.1 we first need to make some comments on Bible interpretations and scientific theories. Starting with Bible interpretations, believing that the Bible is the Word of God doesn't imply that we know the exact meaning of all its details. The Holy Spirit may lead us and open up the meaning of certain Bible passages, and hermeneutics is a scholarly discipline that gives us principles of Bible interpretation.[18] Around 400 Augustine of Hippo (354–430) cautioned against making too definite interpretations of certain Bible passages.[19] It may easily lead to "God of the gaps" arguments, where things not yet explained by science are attributed to direct interventions of the Creator. Eyewitness accounts, records of the creation in Genesis, and the apocalyptic details of the book of Revelation have to be interpreted in different ways. Sometimes our understanding of a Bible passage increases by knowing the historical setting and details of whom the message was addressed to. It is also reasonable to assume that God included details in the Bible to make it understandable at the time it was written. For instance, we know today that the first verses of one of the psalms should not be interpreted literally as favoring a geocentric view, with Earth as a fixed object of the universe:

> The heavens declare the glory of God; the skies proclaim the work of his hands. Day after day they pour forth speech; night after night they reveal knowledge. They have no speech, they use no words; no sound is heard from them. Yet their voice goes out into all the earth, their words to the ends of the world. In the heavens God has pitched a tent for the sun. It is like a bridegroom coming out of his chamber, like a champion rejoicing to run his course. It rises at one end of the heavens and makes its circuit to the other; nothing is deprived of its warmth.[20]

From a Christian point of view, we can think of this psalm as praise to God for having created a universe by which we can view and marvel the sun's orbit in the sky from our point of view—as observers on Earth—although this was not obvious to people of ancient times.

---

18. See for instance Vanhoozer, *Is There a Meaning in This Text?* and Thiselton, *Hermeneutics*.

19. Augustine, *Literal Meaning of Genesis* and Young, "Contemporary Relevance." See also evidence 22 of this book.

20. Ps 19:1–7.

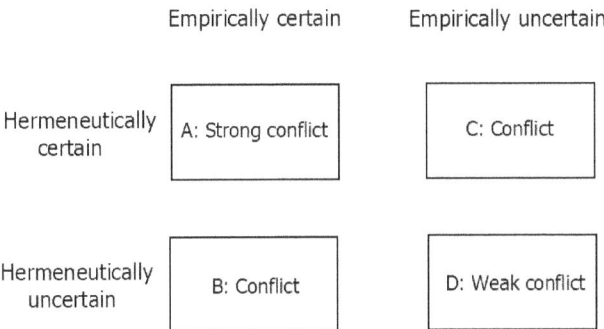

Figure 11.1: Categorization of a stated conflict between an interpretation of the Bible and a scientific theory. It is only A that represents a strong conflict whereby the Bible contradicts science. In B we may allow science to form our understanding of the Bible and in C our faith could influence our understanding of the world. In D the stated conflict is only weak.

In order to define what science is we use Hempel's model of *scientific explanations*.[21] As shown in figure 11.2a, it asserts that a scientific theory or model consists of deterministic laws of nature. These laws help us to deduce which phenomena will happen given certain initial conditions. They are often formulated with logical principles or mathematical equations. It was the French philosopher, mathematician, and writer René Descartes (1596–1650) who gave the first modern formulation of such laws: the conservation principles of motion. This later inspired Isaac Newton to derive his famous laws of gravity and motion. A law of nature can also be statistical, when things do not happen with certainty but different outcomes are possible with various probabilities. This is appropriate when (seemingly?) non-deterministic phenomena are modeled, such as in quantum physics, or when the decay of nuclear isotopes is studied. A statistical model can also give a simplified description of a more complicated deterministic reality.[22] A good scientific model should in any case explain observed data well and make good predictions for the future.

The *principle of induction* is the standard method to infer new models from observations, but there are several versions of it. *Logical positivism* was a philosophical school developed in Berlin and Vienna in the 1920s and 1930s. Its adherents downplayed the role of faith commitments in science.

21. Hempel, *Philosophy of Natural Science*; Swinburne, *Epistemic Justification*, chapter 4; and Swinburne, *Existence of God*, chapter 2.

22. Recall from section 4.2 that this randomness corresponds to our lack of knowledge (epistemic chance), whereas true randomness—if it exists—is referred to as ontological chance.

They believed that reliable knowledge could only be induced from empirical observations and deductive logic. But there is also an older version of the inductive method—the *hypothetico-deductive method*, an early form of which goes back to Aristotle.[23] It acknowledges that there are always assumptions involved in experimental science: A scientific investigation starts with a guess or hypothesis of possible laws of nature, which are tested with data from a number of experiments. If the hypothesized model fails to explain data it has been falsified, but if it explains data well its status is gradually elevated to a scientific theory. In this way the model has been induced from observations. However, the philosopher of science Karl Popper (1902–94) pointed out that it is impossible to verify that a model is true—no matter how many tests it survives. We can only disregard those models that have been falsified.

Although modern science relies on the principle of induction, philosophers have realized that it contains several layers of uncertainty.[24] The logical positivists were too optimistic and Popper's more realistic view of science has been acknowledged. For several reasons it is in fact even difficult to define one single universally valid scientific method.[25] Experimental science is first of all formed within a social and philosophical context.[26] For instance, the initial guess of the hypothetico-deductive method is to some extent ad hoc and sometimes influenced by the reigning worldview. Second, even if a model explains data well it may still not be the best one. There may be other (perhaps yet unknown) models that explain data at least as well, and then some criterion such as simplicity must be used in order to distinguish them. A well-known example is Johannes Kepler's (1571–1630) theory of elliptical orbits of planets around the sun, which supported astronomical data well. However, it was soon replaced by Newton's theory of gravity, which was not only simpler but it also explained more data by means of the law of gravity and the universal laws of motion. Third, the fact that a model has explained data well in the past does not guarantee that it will continue to do so in the future, as when Newtonian physics failed to interpret the Michelson-Morley experiment in 1887. In order to explain this light experiment Albert Einstein (1879–1955) proposed his theory of

---

23. Grant, *Scientific Method in Brief*, 36–37.

24. Chalmers, *What Is This Thing Called Science?* and Searle, "Contemporary Philosophy." It is common today to acknowledge and quantify apriori uncertainty of scientific reasoning by means of probabilities. See Howson and Urbach, *Scientific Reasoning* and section 1.4 of this book.

25. Feyerabend, *Against Method*.

26. This is not only the case for experimental sciences, but also for statistics and some other mathematical sciences. Geertsema, "Christian View."

special relativity in 1905, where the relative speeds of different objects were added in new ways. In the next decade he extended these new ideas to a general theory of relativity, whereby gravity was described as a geometric property of space and time.

The context dependency of science has been highlighted in the works of Thomas Kuhn (1922–96). He suggested in 1962 that science develops through a series of revolutions. A normal period is characterized by a well-established paradigm, until a series of anomalies are discovered that eventually lead to a crisis. This crisis is finally resolved by a new groundbreaking theory that explains the anomalies and produces a *shift of paradigm*.[27] This new theory often represents such a new way of thinking that it takes quite some time before it is accepted by the scientific community. The theory of relativity, for instance, was not firmly established until the 1920s, after a sufficient amount of astronomical data had confirmed it. Ernest Rutherford's (1871–1937) atom theory was less controversial, and it was therefore accepted more quickly. His experiment in 1911 with alpha particles passing through a gold foil led him to suggest a model in which most of the atom's mass was concentrated in a very small charged nucleus, around which electrons were orbiting. A similar swift transition occurred in the 1940s when DNA (deoxyribonucleic acid) was found to be the carrier of genetic information in the chromosomes, rather than proteins.

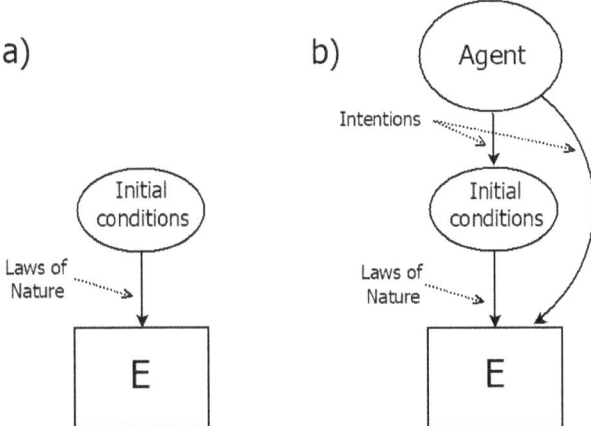

Figure 11.2: Hempel's model of scientific explanations. This is depicted in a), with evidence (E) caused by initial conditions and laws of nature. A personal explanation has been added in b) in terms of a powerful agent who intentionally acts, either by causing the initial conditions or by direct interventions—for instance, exceptions from the laws of nature.

27. Kuhn, *Structure of Scientific Revolutions*.

It is far more difficult for a new theory to be accepted if it threatens not only a scientific but also a philosophical paradigm. This happened to Galileo when his astronomical observations in the early seventeenth century led him to challenge Aristotelianism and confirm a heliocentric rather than a geocentric model.[28] Another example is *methodological naturalism*. It is a principle that requires all explanations of a scientific model to be natural, as in figure 11.2a. This is a philosophical assertion that cannot be validated by empirical evidence—it has to be accepted by faith. Methodological naturalism excludes any model with *personal explanations* in terms of an agent—as in figure 11.2b—and it also leaves the origin of the initial conditions and laws of nature unexplained. It is currently so well established within the scientific community that it seems difficult to challenge. The same is true for an ever more outspoken version, which I refer to as *strong methodological naturalism*.[29] It only allows for a subclass of the natural explanations in figure 11.2a for which initial conditions are not *inspired* by a design argument. Initial conditions with a design flavor are ruled out even if one defers the interpretation of them to a separate philosophical or theological discussion. A very honest and amazing admission of the strong assumptions behind methodological naturalism was given by evolutionary biologist and Harvard Professor Richard Lewontin (1929–):

> It is not that the methods and institutions of science somehow compel us to accept a material explanation of the phenomenal world, but, on the contrary, that we are forced by our a priori adherence to material causes to create an apparatus of investigation and a set of concepts that produce material explanations, no matter how counter-intuitive, no matter how mystifying to the uninitiated. Moreover, that materialism is absolute, for we cannot allow a Divine Foot in the door.[30]

(Strong) methodological naturalism is possible to use for most branches of science when delimited questions are being asked, like "How hot will a cup of coffee be in ten minutes?" In this case it suffices to know the initial conditions (the current temperatures of the cup and the surrounding air) and the law of nature (Newton's law of cooling) in order to get the answer.

---

28. Lennox, *God's Undertaker*. See also evidence 3.

29. A slightly different definition of weak and strong methodological naturalism (MN) is given by Plantinga. He defines weak MN as a principle according to which scientific theories should not include beliefs in the supernatural, nor denials of such beliefs. Strong MN goes further, since it includes in a theory denials of the supernatural. Plantinga, *Where the Conflict Really Lies*.

30. Lewontin, "Billions and Billions of Demons," para. 24.

And this answer can easily be confirmed by repeated experiments. But methodological naturalism is more problematic when we deal with single occurrences that cannot be repeated. In particular, it is very questionable to favor naturalism in this way when science starts to reach its natural boundaries and ask bigger questions like "How did the universe come about?" or "How did life on Earth appear?" When personal explanations are not allowed, the *how* questions will tend to push away the *why* questions like a cuckoo in the nest—and even more so when initial conditions, inspired by personal explanations, are not permitted because of a fear of using "God of the gaps" arguments.

This reluctance to fill out gaps is to some extent understandable. But methodological naturalism itself leads to "naturalism of the gaps" arguments just as easily, where unknown phenomena seemingly without function are explained by chance and blind evolution.[31] "God of the gaps" and "naturalism of the gaps" arguments are both arguments from ignorance.[32] Such an argument cannot be used to prove a proposition, although it may still be employed for deriving the most likely explanation. Karl Popper argued that hypotheses should not be dismissed as unscientific if they are to some extent inspired by metaphysical ideas.[33] They should only be abandoned if they have been falsified or are constructed in such a way that they cannot be falsified. If several possible falsifiable explanations remain, one could still propose the most likely one based on subjective apriori beliefs *and* (incomplete) evidence—as long as this is clearly stated.[34] It is not unscientific to pose an explanation that is partly based on belief or intuition as long as one *separates* such conjectures from observed data. A worse approach is to *pretend* that reasoning is purely evidence based when it involves more or less hidden assumptions, like methodological naturalism.

After this digression into hermeneutics and philosophy of science, let us go back to figure 11.1. Below we will discuss three of the most intensively debated tentative conflicts: existence of miracles, origin/age of universe, and Darwinian macroevolution. If methodological naturalism is abandoned we will argue that none of these conflicts is of type A,[35] and this suggests there is no deep conflict between Christianity and science. The British mathematician and philosopher of science John Lennox (1946–) argues that the real

31. See evidence 15 for more on "God of the gaps" and "naturalism of the gaps" arguments.

32. Hahn and Oaksford, "Rationality of Informal Argumentation."

33. Popper, *Conjectures and Refutations*.

34. This can be done, for instance, within a subjective Bayesian framework by assigning apriori probabilities to the competing explanations.

35. See evidence 11, 12, and 14.

conflict is rather between Christianity and naturalism.[36] Philosopher Alvin Plantinga claims even more in *Where the Conflict Really Lies*:

> My overall claim in this book: there is superficial conflict but deep concord between science and theistic religion, but superficial concord and deep conflict between science and naturalism.[37]

Plantinga uses a variant of the argument from reason in order to motivate this claim:[38] A naturalistic interpretation of science inevitably leads to blind evolution. But our own cognitive faculties are not reliable if they are formed by blind evolution. This includes all of our beliefs, in particular our belief in naturalism and blind evolution, which cannot be trusted—a contradiction.

Evidence 11: Miracles. The Bible reports a number of miraculous events: the division of the Red Sea during the exodus from Egypt, Jesus' virgin birth, the healing ministry of Jesus and the apostles, and most importantly the resurrection of Jesus. Other ancient sources also mention Jesus as a miracle worker and the history of the church is full of events that have been interpreted as miracles.[39]

These and other claimed miracles strongly suggest that things without known natural explanations happen. But critics tend to interpret them as deceptions or misinterpretations or argue that they have a known or yet unknown natural explanation. But even if such an explanation was found, it does not invalidate God as the first cause and ultimate reason for what happened.

David Hume presented a well-known and very influential argument for the rationality of not believing in miracles:

> A miracle is a violation of the laws of nature; and as a firm and unalterable experience has established these laws, the proof against a miracle, from the very nature of the fact, is as entire as any argument from experience can possibly be imagined. Why is it more than probable, that all men must die; that lead cannot, of itself, remain suspended in the air; that fire consumes wood,

---

36. Lennox, *God's Undertaker*.
37. Plantinga, *Where the Conflict Really Lies*, ix.
38. Evidence 7.
39. See for instance Keener, *Miracles* and Craig, *Reasonable Faith*, chapter 6 for comprehensive accounts of miracles. In this book we have a brief discussion of miracles in section 8.1 in connection with the historical critical method, and a longer one in evidence 24.

and is extinguished by water; unless it be, that these events are found agreeable to the laws of nature, and there is required a violation of these laws, or in other words, a miracle to prevent them? Nothing is esteemed a miracle, if it ever happen in the common course of nature. It is no miracle that a man, seemingly in good health, should die on a sudden: because such a kind of death, though more unusual than any other, has yet been frequently observed to happen. But it is a miracle, that a dead man should come to life; because that has never been observed in any age or country. There must, therefore, be a uniform experience against every miraculous event, otherwise the event would not merit that appellation.[40]

Hume makes a rightful distinction between a sudden event that has been seen before, like the death of a person, and one that has never been seen before, like resurrection from death before Jesus. The latter Hume defines as a miracle and he presents two main arguments for rejecting it. According to the first argument a miracle violates the uniformity of laws of nature. This is a matter of imposing a naturalistic worldview, which requires that the theory of scientific explanations in figure 11.2a holds for everything that ever happened in the universe without any intelligent agent interfering. The second argument is based on the uniformity of experience. But in this case Hume is not acknowledging the limitations of the principle of induction.[41] The fact that no one has seen a particular miracle before doesn't imply that there hasn't been one, since nobody has complete knowledge of everything that ever happened in the universe. In fact, as John Lennox points out, Hume's writing is somewhat contradictory, since elsewhere he acknowledges the limitations of our ability to induce the uniformity of nature from perceptions.[42]

Hume characterizes a miracle as a *violation* of the laws of nature. But if our worldview allows for an intervening personal agent (figure 11.2b) it is more appropriate to define a miracle as an *exception* of these laws. This is illustrated by C. S. Lewis in terms of the virgin birth of Jesus:

> If God annihilates or creates or deflects a unit of matter, he has created a new situation at that point. Immediately all nature domiciles this new situation, makes it at home in her realm, adapts all other events to it. It finds itself conforming to all laws. If God creates a miraculous spermatozoon in the body of a virgin, it

40. Hume, *Enquiry*, 58.
41. See evidence 10.
42. Lennox, *God's Undertaker*, chapter 12; and Keener, *Miracles*, chapters 4–6.

does not proceed to break any laws. Pregnancy follows, according to all normal laws, and nine months later a child is born.[43]

From this it follows that a miracle does not contradict natural science. It only contradicts naturalism, by which the universe (or a collection of universes) is a closed system where everything is governed by matter, energy, and laws of nature—not allowing for any outward influence or intervention by God. But within a Christian worldview miracles are completely logical, since an omnipotent God can intervene in his creation whenever he wishes. Although God continuously upholds and influences the world, most Christians would think that he mostly operates within his own created laws and that miracles are very exceptional events. Indeed, if they happened all the time it would be much more difficult to do science.

Our attitude towards miracles depends crucially on whether we accept personal explanations in addition to natural ones. But even if our worldview allows for supernatural events, we can never determine with certainty which events are miraculous and which are not. There is always a "God of the gaps" element involved, and ultimately it is a matter of faith if we accept an unusual event as a miracle or not. Following Lewis's definition of a miracle as an exception of the laws of nature, it is inherently difficult to design an experiment in order to test if miracles occur, since our knowledge of the laws of nature changes with time. Moreover, a personal agent can interfere with our planned experiment as he pleases.[44] But many claimed miracles are so strong that it seems highly unlikely that they are caused by a yet unknown natural law.

To summarize, the miracles of the Bible are hermeneutically certain, whereas the empirical evidence of there being no miracles is highly uncertain and rather based on philosophical assumptions. According to figure 11.1 the claimed conflict between miracles and science is therefore of type C.

---

43. Lewis, *Miracles*, 63.

44. It is questionable to criticize miracle claims on the ground that very few designed experiments have proved their existence. Claimed miracles are either observations from nature or reports of humans, neither of which are part of a planned experiment. This is a kind of *observational study* where observations exist already before the study; see Rosenbaum, *Design of Observational Studies*. Requiring a designed experiment relies on the assumption that it is possible for humans to control God, which the Bible warns us against believe; see Matt 4:7.

One may argue that a well-documented extraordinary event is evidence for the *existence* of a miracle whether it is part of a designed experiment or we just happened to observe it. See also evidence 24 for the *interpretation* of miracles, given that we believe they have happened.

Evidence 12: Cosmology, age of universe and Earth. Another claimed conflict is the age of the universe and Earth. Most scientists today believe that the universe and Earth are several billion years old—much different from what a literal interpretation of the Bible suggests. In the seventeenth century Archbishop of Ireland James Ussher (1581–1656) constructed a time line for all biblical events, going all the way back to creation of man and the universe. According to his chronology man is about 6,000 years old, with Adam and Eve created in 4004 B.C. And most Christians accepted this time line until geologists James Hutton (1726–1797) and Charles Lyell (1797–1875) proposed that Earth is a lot older.

Some scholars that interpret the ages of the Bible literally have suggested that time lines are not always complete. They argue that there has been telescoping of genealogies, where names for various reasons are left out intentionally. It is then hard to estimate the age of Adam of Eve precisely, but a range of 10,000–50,000 years has been suggested.[45] A literal young-Earth interpretation of Genesis therefore leads to an age of Earth that could vary between 6,000 and maybe up to 50,000 years. Old-Earth creationists may have similar estimates for the age of mankind, but they allow for a much older Earth and universe. Crucial for this discussion is how one interprets the Hebrew word *yom*, which is used for the six creation days of Genesis 1. It has been suggested that they represent longer periods of time.[46]

So what does empirical data say regarding the age of Earth and the universe? It is important to emphasize that any cosmological theory is necessarily based on a number of assumptions. The history of the universe and Earth cannot be observed directly, nor can it be confirmed by repeated experiments. We can only observe its indirect consequences and extrapolate back in time, using some type of clock. But such a clock must satisfy three conditions in order to be accurate: first, it needs a well-defined starting point; second, it must have a reliable ticking mechanism; and third, nothing should have interfered with the clock (or if it has, that must be corrected for).[47]

45. An argument for a 6,000-year-old Earth, and genealogies without gaps, is given in Pierce and Ham, "Are There Gaps?" A higher age is suggested in Kitchen, "On the Reliability of the Old Testament" and Milliam, "Genesis Genealogies."

46. Old-Earth creationists suggest that *yom* may refer to longer periods of time in some other Bible verses, e.g., Job 20:28; Ps 20:1; and Prov 11:4. For these and other old-age arguments, see Lennox, *Seven Days* and Grudem, *Systematic Theology*, chapter 15 (in particular pages 293–97). A young-Earth response is that creation in Gen 1 is compared to a regular week of six working days in Exod 31:15–17. For this and other young-age arguments, see Pierce and Ham, "Are There Gaps."

47. For a summary of different methods of dating, see Williams and Hartnett, *Dismantling the Big Bang*, chapter 5; and Renard, "Dateringsmetoder."

The age of Earth is currently estimated to 4.5 billion years using radiometric dating of old material such as meteorites (the isotope clock). Other methods to estimate old events rely on cyclic changes of Earth's orbit, intensity changes of its magnetic field (magnetic clock), cooling of Earth (heat clock), increasing sodium levels in the sea (salt clock), counting of sedimentary rock layers (sediment clock), or ice layers in the Antarctic. For the age of humanity and other species one uses mutational changes of DNA (molecular clock). But some assumptions of the dating methods have been questioned in spite of all these clocks. It is well known for instance that sedimentary layers can be produced quickly when a liquid carries an abundance of particles. Creationists claim that the flood of Noah[48] severely affected the sedimentary clock, with very visible and interpretable effects. As the name suggests, isotope clocks use radioactive decay of some isotope. The most well-known example, carbon-14, is mostly used for events that are recent compared to an old dating of Earth, whereas other isotopes are used for older events. Although the ticking mechanisms of isotope clocks are well characterized, the original amount of the radioactive isotope is often not known and interference cannot be ruled out.[49] Therefore, it seems that an old Earth is not empirically indisputable.

The currently dominating cosmological model is the Big Bang theory, also referred to as the Standard Model of cosmology or the Friedmann-Lemaître model. It posits that the universe started with a sudden explosion—a singularity—and after that expanded until this day. The Big Bang theory was proposed in 1927 by the Belgian priest and physicist George Lemaître (1894–1966) and it is supported by various kinds of empirical evidence. Edwin Hubble (1889–1953) observed the redshift of light from galaxies in 1929, consistent with an expanding universe. The next important discovery came 35 years later in 1964 when cosmic background radiation (low-energy photons) was detected. This thermal radiation is believed to have been "left over" from an early stage of the universe, emitted from particles of the non-empty space between stars and galaxies. The cosmic background radiation is important for cosmology since it is believed to reflect the state of the universe when it first became transparent. Before this happened the expanding universe consisted of charged particles that grew colder, so that protons and electrons eventually combined to form neutral atoms that no longer could absorb the thermal radiation. This is believed to have happened between

---

48. Gen 6:13—8:19.

49. For different points of view regarding the dating of old events on Earth, see Molen, *Vårt ursprung?*; Williams and Hartnett, *Dismantling the Big Bang*; Alexander, *Creation or Evolution*; and McIntosh, *Genesis for Today*.

300,000 and 400,000 years after the explosion.[50] When astronomers look in their telescopes the background radiation gives a snapshot of the first transparent universe. The striking feature is that this radiation has almost the same intensity in all directions, corresponding to an absolute temperature of about 3 Kelvins. There are some very small oscillations, and these are thought to give a blueprint on the sky of the slight density variations from the first transparent universe—variations that were necessary as a seed for future structure (stars and galaxies) to form through gravitation. Other evidence in support of the theory includes the relative abundance of different types of atomic nuclei of the universe and a roughly homogeneous spatial distribution of galaxies and quasars.

The detection of cosmic background radiation convinced most scientists of the Big Bang theory, rather than the competing Steady State model with an infinitely old universe. Much more is known today—50 years later—and cosmology has been integrated with particle physics in a new research field called astroparticle physics. For instance, the Higgs particle (or Higgs boson) was tentatively discovered in 2012. Its existence would confirm the standard model of particle physics, which gives a unified account of three forces: electromagnetic, weak, and strong nuclear interactions, of which the former two are closely connected. And it is likely that this discovery will impact future cosmology.

There are still many gaps and open problems related to the Big Bang theory. For instance, if the universe was a randomly distributed cloud of elementary particles just after the explosion, its rapid expansion could not have had time to equilibrate temperature during its first 300,000–400,000 years to an extent compatible with the observed very small background oscillations. In order to explain this, the American physicist Alan Guth (1947–) hypothesized in 1980 that a very fast inflationary epoch of space itself (rather than of matter) took place during the first fraction of a second after the Big Bang. The velocities of certain clusters of particles, stars, and galaxies have also surprised researchers. Since gravitation from the visible matter of the universe is too small to explain these high velocities, a hypothetical dark matter quantity has been introduced. It has further been discovered that the expansion of the universe seems to be accelerating. In order to account for this a notion of dark energy was proposed. Another difficulty relates to highly redshifted objects called quasars. The American astronomer Halton Arp (1927–2013) studied quasars and questioned the reigning paradigm to estimate distances solely from redshifts. Whereas Big Bang cosmology predicts these quasars as very

---

50. Jones et al., *Introduction to Galaxies and Cosmology*.

distant objects, Arp's experiments suggest rather that they are ejected from host galaxies much closer to us.[51]

Parts of the Big Bang theory rely on the Copernican principle. This assumption, named after Nicolaus Copernicus (1473–1543), posits that no place (including Earth) has a specially favored position in universe. It can sometimes be tested empirically, as when Galileo used planetary motion to reject a geocentric worldview in favor of a heliocentric one. But it is an instance of strong methodological naturalism[52] to enforce the Copernican principle, so that any cosmological theory with a center of the universe is ruled out from start. And this principle might be too restrictive, as some recent data indicates that our position in universe is favored. Indeed, it seems that galaxies are positioned along concentric spherical "onion shells," rather than homogeneously distributed as previously believed.[53]

The Big Bang theory suggests a 13.8 billion-years-old universe. This estimate is based on measurements of the cosmic background radiation, the expansion rate of the universe, and extrapolation back in time until the starting point—the explosion—is reached. Russell Humphreys (1942–) introduced in 1994 a new cosmology with a much younger universe. He abandoned the Copernican principle and assumed that the Milky Way galaxy is close to the center of an expanding universe. This gives a time dilation, so that the clocks at our galaxy run much more slowly than those at other parts of the universe. Earth and the universe are therefore young from our local time frame on Earth, whereas the rest of the universe is old as viewed from its own time frame. The Australian physicist John Hartnett (1952–) combined Humphrey's idea with a recently proposed generalization of Einstein's general theory of relativity. This theory is due to the Israeli physicist Moshe Carmeli (1933–2007). It adds a fifth dimension (velocity of space) to space and time and the resulting Carmeli-Hartnett cosmology is consistent with a literal young-Earth interpretation of Genesis 1. In particular, it focuses on the acceleration of the universe that took place during one single day when God stretched out the heavens:

> And God said, "Let there be lights in the vault of the sky to separate the day from the night, and let them serve as signs to mark sacred times, and days and years, and let them be lights in the vault of the sky to give light on the earth." And it was so. God made two great lights—the greater light to govern the day

---

51. Arp, *Seeing Red*.

52. See evidence 10. The Copernican principle is closely related to the cosmological principle that Albert Einstein introduced in his General Theory of Relativity. Gonzales and Richard, *Privileged Planet*, 248.

53. Hartnett, *Starlight, Time and the New Physics*.

and the lesser light to govern the night. He also made the stars. God set them in the vault of the sky to give light on the earth, to govern the day and the night, and to separate light from darkness. And God saw that it was good. And there was evening, and there was morning the fourth day.[54]

According to the Carmeli-Hartnett cosmology, the redshifts we see from galaxies is light emitted during the fourth day of the creation week. It seems to explain astronomical data (redshifts from galaxies, galaxy rotations, non-homogeneous distribution of galaxies) well, without any need to introduce the somewhat ambiguous concepts of inflation, dark matter, and dark energy.[55] But there are some mathematical inconsistencies with Carmeli's cosmology that haven't been resolved yet.[56] Another young-Earth cosmology, due to American astronomer Jason Lisle, is the anisotropic lightspeed convention, according to which the incoming speed of light is infinite.[57]

To summarize, what kind of conflict is there between the Bible and science regarding the age of Earth? From the perspective of a young-Earth creationist, the biblical claim of a young age is hermeneutically certain. But scientific evidence for an old Earth does not seem to be undisputable and therefore the conflict in figure 11.1 is of type C rather than type A. The old-Earth creationist, on the other hand, argues that the biblical claim of a young Earth is hermeneutically uncertain, and this makes the conflict even weaker (type D).

Evidence 13: Causality. The Standard Model and young-Earth cosmologies lead to a sudden start of the universe (figure 11.3). But if the universe has a start, does it have a first cause as well? Such a first cause would be consistent with the biblical view that God created everything out of nothing through his own Word, as powerfully described in the first verses of the Gospel of John:

> In the beginning was the Word, and the Word was with God, and the Word was God. He was with God in the beginning. Through him all things were made; without him nothing was made that has been made.[58]

---

54. Gen 1:14–19.

55. Humphreys, *Startlight and Time*; Carmeli, *Cosmological Relativity*; Hartnett, *Starlight, Time and the New Physics*; and Gärdeborn, *Intelligent skapelsetro*.

56. Hartnett, "Does My Use of Carmeli's Cosmology."

57. Hartnett, "Aberration of Startlight."

58. John 1:1–3; see also Gen 1:1–5.

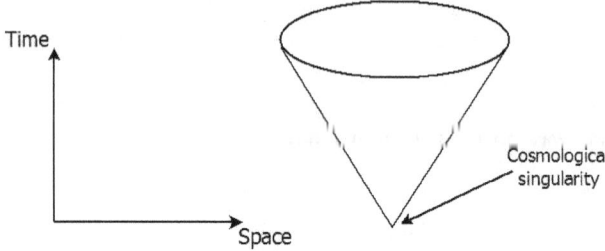

Figure 11.3: Illustration of time and space for a cosmological model with a first start.[59]

The relation between a first start and a first cause is addressed by the *kalām* cosmological argument. It motivates a first cause as follows:

1. Whatever begins to exist has a cause.
2. The universe began to exist.
3. Therefore the universe has a cause.

We have previously looked at causality from a philosophical point of view,[60] but here we will analyze the *kalām* argument in terms of cosmology. Its first two statements are premises and the third one is a conclusion. Premise 1 simply asserts that things cannot come into existence without a cause. Whereas the inflationary model of the Big Bang theory[61] tries to explain the early phase of the universe, it doesn't address the start itself. There are however *quantum cosmology models* that additionally try to explain the origin of the universe as a kind of quantum fluctuation of a primeval state of the universe, where the universe is thought to have had zero volume. An example of this kind of model is Vilenkin's quantum fluctuation model. One type of quantum fluctuation is the spontaneous "coming into being" of virtual particles in the quantum vacuum—and the uncertainty principle of quantum mechanics allows that to happen. These fluctuations are thought to be the original seed of the large-scale structures (planets, stars, galaxies) that we find in the universe today. At first this seems to violate premise 1 of the *kalām* argument. But a zero-volume vacuum fluctuation is not the same thing as "no cause"![62] We also noticed earlier that some of the proposed

---

59. See figure 3.2 of Craig, *Reasonable Faith* for a similar picture.
60. Prior belief 1 of section 5.2.
61. Evidence 12.
62. Craig and Sinclair, "*Kalam* Cosmological Argument" and Jones et al., *Introduction to Galaxies and Cosmology*.

young-Earth cosmologies don't seem to require any inflationary theory or quantum vacuum fluctuations.

Stephen Hawking (1942–) and Leonard Mlodinow (1954–) argue in *The Grand Design* that the universe came into being out of nothing.[63] Regarding premise 1 they believe it is at least possible for physical theories and laws of nature to come into existence as long as the balance between positive and negative energy of the universe is maintained. They also advocate a collection of theories called M-theory. This theory has not yet been empirically confirmed and it suggests that the universe is made up of high-dimensional, tiny, and vibrating superstrings. Some physicists hope it will become a "theory of everything" that unifies general relativity (large scale structure of space-time through gravity) and quantum field theory (small scale structure of matter). If M-theory—or some other theory of everything—was the first cause it would replace the personal agent of figure 11.2b and thereby allow laws of nature to act so that the universe (and in fact several universes) could be formed. But this can be questioned on several grounds: John Lennox points out that a scientific theory has no intentions and in particular not the capacity to *create* laws of nature; it only allows them to act. Nor have the laws of nature the capacity to create initial conditions (for instance quantum vacuum fluctuations) for them to act on.[64] Moreover, the mathematical equations of the M-theory represent information in terms of abstract ideas—information that is left unexplained. This all indicates that M-theory cannot explain why the universe came into existence.[65]

Hawking and Mlodinow also question premise 2 of the *kalām* argument. According to their model time can effectively be modeled as a dimension of space in the early universe and therefore we cannot say that the universe would have had its origin at a specific moment in time. But the *kalām* argument does not require that the universe started at a specific point in time—only that it started. There is a well-known result in cosmology due to Arvind Borde, Alexander Vilenkin, and Alan Guth that suggests that any universe that on average expands must have a start.[66]

---

63. Hawking and Mlodinow, *Grand Design*.

64. Lennox, *God and Stephen Hawking*; Högås, "grand design."

65. Plotnitsky addresses various theories for how quantum mechanics is thought to affect our understanding of causality and the relation between observations and underlying objects. For instance, the so-called EPR experiment and Bell's Theorem suggest that if quantum mechanics makes correct predictions there has to be strong instantaneous correlations of measurements of spins of electrons at very large distances—corresponding to an action faster than the speed of light. Plotnitsky, *Epistemology and Probability*.

66. Högås, "grand design."

Physicists have tried to come up with other cosmological theories that refute premise 2. Many of them are more in line with Aristotle's view of an eternal universe, and the most well known of these is the Steady State model. But none of these theories have yet been confirmed by evidence to the same extent as the Big Bang or some of the young-Earth cosmologies.[67] It is reasonable in view of this to say that premise 2 is well supported by cosmology, and together with premise 1 it implies conclusion 3, a first cause.

Evidence 14: Darwinian evolution. Is variation of life in plants, animals, and humans best explained by common descent or not? Are humans created unique? A literal reading of the Bible suggests that all humans descend from one first couple—Adam and Eve. The Darwinian theory of evolution, one the other hand, asserts that all living species evolved gradually from one or a few ancestral life forms and formed a tree—or web—of life. This is potentially a conflict between science and Christianity. In order to look into this claimed conflict we must first describe evolutionary theory in more detail and address how Christians interpret what the Bible has to say about the origin of life and species.

Starting with evolution, all scholars agree that it exists in one form or another. The main questions are how much of the diversity of life it explains and which mechanisms bring about this diversity. A modern version of evolutionary theory called neo-Darwinism asserts that evolution is driven by small molecular genetic changes when parents transmit their DNA to offspring. These changes accumulate gradually and they are governed by three mechanisms. The first, mutations, are changes in the DNA molecules of germ cells, such as misprints of single letters of DNA code (called nucleotides), insertion or deletion of stretches of DNA, or shuffling of DNA from one chromosome to the other. The second mechanism is randomness as to which parts of DNA parents will pass on to their offspring. The third one is competition in terms having many offspring, where natural selection favors individuals that are more fit for their environment.

Christians are basically divided into two camps regarding their views on evolution. Some of them advocate a *design hypothesis*, where some different life forms (*kinds* of animals or plants) were first *created* and then changed over time through *microevolution*. This includes evolution

---

67. Apart from the Steady State model, there are many other suggested cosmologies without a first point in time. This includes the Oscillating models, Vacuum Fluctuation models, the Chaotic Inflationary model, Quantum Gravity models, and String models. See Craig, *Reasonable Faith* and Craig and Sinclair, "*Kalam* Cosmological Argument" for more details.

within species, with classical textbook examples such as changes in coloring of pepper moths and size of Galápagos finch beaks. It also includes formation of new species in the wild within kinds through migration and subsequent separation, such as dogs and wolves; various horse-like creatures spread over Africa and Asia; and within the cat family Asian tigers, African jaguars, and American pumas.[68] This kind of evolution does not build any new organs with new functionality. It only modifies and changes structures that already exist. For instance, it regulates gene activity without changing the genes themselves. One creationist version of the design perspective asserts that microevolution started *after* the fall of man, when competition, death, and decay came into the world. In particular, human origin is unique. This means that all humans form one kind and that we all descend from a first couple.[69]

Other Christians follow the dominating evolutionary view in academia and believe that all life forms have descended from single cells. This requires not only microevolution, but also *macroevolution* into new kinds of species with new types of organs. Whereas secular scientists regard macroevolution as blind, Christians who advocate macroevolution think it is controlled or at least planned by God—so-called *theistic evolution*. They argue that God would know beforehand the effect of all mutations that ever happened, and how species reproduce and transmit their genes from one generation to the next. British paleontologist Simon Conway Morris (1951–) uses the metaphysical idea of biological convergence in order to describe theistic evolution as goal-directed.[70]

Let us compare theistic evolution with a creationist design hypothesis in terms of biblical interpretation. We first need to stress that it *is* possible for Christians to have different views on evolution and yet accept Jesus as Lord and Savior. But the hermeneutic consequences of Darwinian macroevolution are still quite substantial, since one of the mechanisms of evolution—natural selection—incorporates death and competition. The question is how well this accords with creation being good before the fall of man. It also makes the problem of evil more difficult to resolve, since God is then responsible for death. And the hope for eternity becomes less appealing. If carnivorousness, suffering, and death were built into life from start—also in the garden of Eden in the second chapter of

---

68. Jeanson and Lisle, "On the Origin of Eukaryotic."

69. More details on the design perspective can be found in Lennox, *God's Undertaker*; Nevin et al., *Should Christians Embrace Evolution?*; and Meyer, *Darwin's Doubt*.

70. Conway Morris, *Life's Solution*. Two other books with a theistic evolutionary perspective are Collins, *Language of God* and Alexander, *Creation or Evolution?*

Genesis—it seems difficult to interpret the new heavens and Earth in the book of Revelation as a restored Eden:

> Then the angel showed me the river of the water of life, as clear as crystal, flowing from the throne of God and of the Lamb down the middle of the great street of the city. On each side of the river stood the tree of life, bearing twelve crops of fruit, yielding its fruit every month. And the leaves of the tree are for the healing of the nations. No longer will there be any curse. The throne of God and of the Lamb will be in the city, and his servants will serve him.[71]

The question of human origin is even more important for Bible interpretation. Most evolutionary biologists believe that chimpanzees are our closest relatives and that the two lines split between four and seven million years ago. Then a hominid species—Homo erectus—evolved in Africa and spread to Europe and Asia about two million years ago. Various archaic species are thought to have evolved from Homo erectus in the last 500,000–800,000 years, including Neanderthals in Europe and Denisovans in Asia. It is believed that modern humans then evolved from Homo erectus in Africa more than 100,000 years ago, and there they went through a severe reduction in population size to 10,000 individuals or less. A large part of this group emigrated from Africa about 50,000 years ago to the Middle East, Europe, East Asia, and America—gradually replacing existing archaic species. After leaving Africa, all non-African populations have experienced much more recent and severe reductions in size (down to a few thousand individuals) before they started to grow. Then about 10,000 years ago the Neolithic Revolution changed the lifestyle from hunting and gathering to farming.[72]

If this common ancestry scenario of human history is true, Christians have to interpret the creation of man in Genesis 2 metaphorically since there was never a single human couple:

> Then the Lord God formed a man from the dust of the ground and breathed into his nostrils the breath of life, and the man became a living being . . . Then the Lord God made a woman from the rib he had taken out of the man, and he brought her to the man.[73]

---

71. Rev 22:1–3.

72. Mellars, "Going East" and Li and Durbin, "Inference of Human Population History."

73. Gen 2:7, 21.

It these verses are not taken literally and macroevolution is true, how should we interpret the fall of man—a doctrine that is central to Christianity and its teaching of original sin and atonement in Christ? Was it a historical event when Adam and Eve ate from the tree of knowledge, which lead to spiritual death, and when God after that cursed the ground because of Adam's sin?

> To Adam he said, "Because you listened to your wife and ate fruit from the tree about which I commanded you, 'You must not eat from it', cursed is the ground because of you; through painful toil you will eat food from it all the days of your life."[74]

The crucial question is whether it is possible to acknowledge the fall of man and yet advocate theistic evolution. The quantum physicist and philosopher Antoine Suarez summarizes various attempts to do so.[75] According to the retelling theory there was first a long process of growing moral awareness among early hominids and then another long process of growing human disobedience, metaphorically described as the fall of man in Genesis 3. A consequence of the retelling theory is that Adam and Eve were not historical persons but rather representatives of a larger group of people. This idea was present already in the writings of church father Origen (184–254). But this is very difficult to reconcile with Paul's teaching in the Roman Epistle, where he parallels Adam and Jesus and clearly thinks of Adam (and Eve) as historical persons:

> For if, by the trespass of the one man, death reigned through that one man, how much more will those who receive God's abundant provision of grace and of the gift of righteousness reign in life through the one man, Jesus Christ! Consequently, just as one trespass resulted in condemnation for all people, so also one righteous act resulted in justification and life for all people. For just as through the disobedience of the one man the many were made sinners, so also through the obedience of the one man the many will be made righteous.[76]

The genealogies of Genesis 5 and 11 and in Luke 3 also support the idea of Adam as a real person. A number of other theistic evolutionary interpretations of the fall of man have been suggested[77] whereby Adam and

---

74. Gen 3:17.

75. Suarez, "Can We Give Up the Origin of Humanity?"

76. Rom 5:17–19.

77. These theories include personal hominids, theological species, Homo divinus, and relational damage. For more details see Suarez, "Can We Give Up the Origin of Humanity?"

Eve are literal but God selected them among thousands of contemporaries. These theories differ in terms of when and how God chose the first couple. But since macroevolution is a gradual process they all have difficulties to explain God creating the first human couple as very unique and different from the animals, as Paul's teaching in the New Testament clearly suggests:

> Not all flesh is the same: People have one kind of flesh, animals have another, birds another and fish another.... So it is written: "The first man Adam became a living being"; the last Adam, a life-giving spirit.[78]

To summarize, it seems difficult to harmonize theistic evolution with the Bible. Why should God be responsible for death and competition and how can the theory explain the uniqueness of humans and the fall of man? These difficulties suggest that a unique origin of humanity in figure 11.1 is close to hermeneutically certain.

What about the empirical certainty of macroevolution? It is first of all only part of a larger evolutionary scenario. After the universe came into being, elementary particles and atoms were formed (particle evolution), then heavier chemical elements (chemical evolution), and after that planets and stars (planetary and stellar evolution). All this had to happen before life on our planet originated (organic evolution) so that macroevolution could start (biological evolution). From a naturalistic point of view each one of these evolutionary steps must have occurred spontaneously.

Particle, planetary, and stellar evolution first requires a high amount of fine tuning of various constants of nature.[79] The origin of life then involves a number of strong assumptions. It is required that a prebiotic soup of amino acids and other macromolecules were created from an early atmosphere on Earth that had to be almost free of oxygen. Then these molecules must have evolved by chance or necessity (so-called self-organization) through a series of chemical reactions to self-replicating and metabolizing cells. Since this requires proteins (replicator and metabolizer), DNA (information storing), and RNA[80] (messenger and translator of information), we have a classical chicken-or-egg problem of what came first. In the last few decades researchers have hoped to solve this challenge, assuming that life started with RNA, which stores information *and* metabolizes. It is believed that at a certain time in the history of Earth some RNA started to synthesize proteins whereas other RNA was transferred to DNA. But this theory has a number

---

78. 1 Cor 15:39, 45.
79. Evidence 15.
80. An abbreviation of ribonucleic acid.

of problems, for instance that RNAs are unstable and poor substitutes for proteins. But most importantly, there is no known spontaneous natural process by which the complicated information carrying RNA strings can be built. For instance, the building blocks of RNA (ribose) and many other chemical compounds have left- and right-handed mirror images that function in the same way. Both of them appear in chemical reactions but it is only the right-handed ribose version that is part of RNA.[81]

Given that life originated in some way or another, the first major obstacle for macroevolution itself is the fossil record of the rocks. Since macroevolution predicts slow changes, we would expect gradually changing fossils as well. But the rocks tell a very different story. The term *phylum* refers to the highest division in biological classification within the animal kingdom. Today there are about 35 animal phyla, each having its own unique architecture, blueprint, and structural body plan. Examples of phyla include chordates (all vertebrates, including humans), arthropods (insects, crustaceans, and trilobites), mollusks (squids and shellfish), and cnidarians (corals and jellyfish). Quite remarkably all phyla appear in the fossil record abruptly—not gradually, as the theory of macroevolution would predict. And a majority of phyla appear in Cambrian almost at the same time—about 550 million years ago (using an old-Earth geological time scale). This remarkable fact is referred to as the Cambrian explosion. But also within phyla we find very few transitional forms, i.e., fossil of species between those alive today. This problem was known to Darwin already. He thought that missing fossils would be found in the future, but even to this day there are at most very few of them. And it is not even clear whether these candidate missing fossils represent transitional forms or not.[82]

---

81. See for instance Schaefer, *Science and Christianity*; Meyer, *Signature of the Cell*; Meyer, *Darwin's Doubt*; Johnson, *Probability's Nature*, chapters 4–6; and Johnson, *Programming of Life* for a more comprehensive treatment of the various theories for the origin of life.

82. For an account of the Cambrian explosion, see for instance Meyer, *Darwin's Doubt* and Johnson, *Probability's Nature*, chapter 7. Regarding transitional forms, fossil have been found from Tiktaalik roseae, a species with some features in common with many four-legged animals (tetrapods) that live today; see Daeschler et al., "Devonian." It is believed to be a transition between fish and early tetrapods that lived about 375 million years ago (by old-Earth chronology), although paleontologists locate it differently in the alleged tree of life. Protistan organisms (or protists) are unicellular or multicellular without tissues. They are neither animals, plants, nor fungi. Farmer and Habura claim that protistan biology explains the Cambrian explosion. They argue that the animals that suddenly appear during Cambrium have protistan ancestors, and that several protistan transitional forms have been found. However, the claimed protistan ancestry of Cambrium animals is a bit speculative, and some of the alleged transitions among protists—if true—may also represent microevolution. Farmer and Habura,

The next obstacle for macroevolution is to explain the required molecular changes. The gene concept was unknown to Darwin when he published *On the Origin of Species* in 1859 and proposed natural selection as the most important driving force of evolution. The Austrian monk Gregor Mendel (1822–84) introduced genes in 1866, but this new concept was largely forgotten or at least not widely accepted until the beginning of the twentieth century. Then it took another 30–40 years before Darwin's theory was combined with mutational changes of genes and Mendel's laws of genetic inheritance. This *modern synthesis* (or neo-Darwinism) was widely believed to give macroevolution a solid theoretical basis. The chief architectures of neo-Darwinism were the prominent statisticians and geneticists Ronald Fisher (1890–1962), Sewall Wright (1889–1988), and J. B. S. Haldane. Their ideas where quickly embraced by Julian Huxley (1887–1975) and other evolutionary biologists.[83] Whereas Mendel discovered how genes are inherited *in individuals* from parents to children, Fisher, Wright, and Haldane created a mathematical discipline—population genetics—for how genes are transmitted *in a whole population* from one generation to the next. The way natural selection operates in this theory is that parents with certain genetic variants have a selective advantage and tend to have more offspring. After some generations, such a variant may have spread to the whole population and become fixed. Other genetic variants take over a population just by chance, without having such a selective advantage (so-called genetic drift). If we think of a population as a species, the idea of neo-Darwinism is that many variants become fixed after a sufficiently long time, and eventually the population evolves into a new species (so-called speciation). Or if two parts of the population get isolated, they evolve independently through a series of fixation events, so that eventually the original species splits into two.

Population genetics is in fact an excellent theory of microevolution. It gives the tools to describe how populations adapt to environmental changes and how some new species within the same kind (like wolves and dogs) develop from a common ancestor. But the theory has severe problems to explain macroevolution. When population genetics was first developed very little was known about how genes function on the molecular level, and cells were once believed to be simple "homogeneous globules of plasm."[84] Then a molecular genetics revolution started in 1953 when James Watson (1928–) and Francis Crick (1916–2004) discovered the double helix structure of DNA. Today we know that the DNA molecule and the

---

"Using Protistan Examples."

83. Huxley, *Evolution*.

84. Haeckel, *Evolution of Man*.

way it is expressed and coded into proteins in different cells is exceedingly complicated even for simple organisms. The human DNA molecules of all chromosomes have a total length of more than three billion nucleotides. They harbor more than 20,000 genes, many of which code for several proteins! Since macroevolution involves formation of new kinds of species, it requires totally novel organs with new functionality to emerge at some parts of the alleged tree (or web) of life. Many of these organs seem to be irreducibly complex[85] and require all their parts in order to function. A well-known example is a group of arthropods called tribolites, which suddenly appear in Cambrium with no record of ancestry. Their eyes use very advanced optics that function differently than for any other known animals. Other examples include evolution of wings and feathers in birds from dinosaurs, evolution of echolocation among whales from terrestial mammals, and evolution of photosynthesis among cyanobacteria. Darwinian theory has great difficulties explaining how such new organs or mechanisms develop, or how gender differences and sexual reproduction arise, since many beneficial mutations have to occur at once in order to initiate genetic changes at first, and then changes of the structural body plan (morphology). This requires some mechanism for creating new information. But mutations usually come one at a time at random positions of the DNA molecule, and most of them are neutral or damaging—just as misprints of a text. And the few beneficial mutations that we know of often represent a *loss* of information, such as antibiotic resistance of bacteria or sickle-cell anemia for protecting humans against malaria.[86]

Another problem for the macroevolution theory is to explain the distribution of genes between species. Many species have a number of orphan genes. As the name indicates, these genes seem to be species specific in the sense that they code for proteins that have no obvious similarity with proteins synthesized in other similar species. But genes are very complicated DNA strings with a number of structural components like start and stop sequences, exons, and introns. For humans they are on average a few thousand nucleotides long, although they vary a lot in length. It is a challenge to explain how orphan genes originated by purely natural processes.[87]

Macroevolution also requires new proteins to form. Each protein is a sequence of amino acids that corresponds to the coding part of some gene.

---

85. See Behe, *Darwin's Black Box* and evidence 15 for a definition of irreducible complexity.

86. Kimura, *Neutral Theory of Molecular Evolution* and Gauger et al., *Science and Human Origins*.

87. For recent attempts to explain orphan genes, see for instance Ruiz-Orera et al., "Origins of *de Novo* Genes" and references therein.

This amino acid sequence determines how the protein folds into a three-dimensional structure, and only a very small fraction of sequences result in functioning proteins. American biologists Doug Axe (1962-) and Ann Gauger (1953-) have shown that it is virtually impossible for macroevolution to produce new proteins, even from an amino acid sequence that is very similar to the target protein.[88]

These severe problems of gradual macroevolution led scientists to suggest other neo-Darwinian theories for the diversity of life. The most well known is *punctuated equilibrium*. It was proposed by paleontologists Niles Eldredge (1943-) and Stephen Gould already in 1972 in order to explain the missing intermediate fossils. The theory asserts that genetic and morphological changes appear abruptly, not gradually. There *have* been intermediate forms—we just cannot see their fossils since speciation did not happen gradually but very quickly. It is in fact difficult both to confirm and to refute this theory empirically, as Popper's falsification criterion would require, because of lack of data.[89] But there is another even more serious objection. In order to understand this objection we have to explain punctuated equilibrium in more detail. Its theory draws on population genetics, assuming that new genetic variants first appear in large populations through mutations, and then the original population must have split into several smaller and geographically subdivided subunits, in which fixation of new variants happened much more quickly. Eventually these subpopulations evolved to different, competing species and it is only the winning species that we see fossils of. But this process is governed by the same stepwise mechanisms of genetic change as gradual macroevolution, and therefore punctuated equilibrium faces the same problem: Even if speciation happened fast, how can new mutations create organs and structures with new functionality?[90]

American geneticist John Sanford (1950-) addresses another weakness of neo-Darwinism. He argues that it is not only difficult for natural selection and mutations to create new functionality. The DNA of humans—or of any other species—is actually *degrading* as weakly damaging mutations accumulate.[91] The number of such damaging mutations is of the order 10–100 per individual and generation for humans. It is simply not possible for natural selection to remove all these mutations. Not only is this an excellent

---

88. Gauger et al., *Science and Human Origins*. Experiments to generate RNA and protein sequences spontaneously from simple cells are reported in Hazen et al., "Functional Information." However, it has been argued that these experiments are too simple to mimic processes in natural populations; see Kozulic and Leisola, "Have Scientists."

89. See evidence 10.

90. Meyer, *Darwin's Doubt*.

91. Sanford, *Genetic Entropy*.

argument against macroevolution, it also indicates that the human species is young, since otherwise the accumulated mutations would have degraded our DNA too much.

If man is young, then we are not related to any apes in a tree of life. Indeed, the fossil record seems to indicate quite an abrupt discontinuity between ape-like and human-like forms.[92] There are also several important morphological differences between humans and apes in terms of brain function, dexterity, speech, and other traits with strong cognitive components. As we have seen, it is a big challenge for macroevolution to explain how such human skills arose through genetic changes from a common ancestor. But evolutionary biologists still argue that humans and chimps have a common ancestry, and they use two genetic arguments. The first one is the claimed DNA similarity between the two species. When the human and chimpanzee genomes were sequenced in 2003 and 2005, this DNA similarity was estimated to be around 99 percent. This number looks impressive at first, but it does not include all possible DNA differences between humans and chimpanzees. More recent estimates suggest that the DNA similarity between the two species is around 95 percent and that many human genes are absent among chimps.[93] DNA similarity is in any case not a proof of common ancestry, and it is not necessarily a very good measure of species similarity. As an analogy we may think of two very different buildings that are constructed with same types of bricks, used in different proportions. In a similar way the genes that humans and chimps share may be expressed very differently. It is often the non-coding parts of DNA that determine which proteins are active in different cells, and very small differences between such human and chimp DNA may still have a big impact on cell activity and body function. The gorilla and bonobo genomes were sequenced more recently and their DNA similarity with humans is about the same as for chimps. At some parts of the genome the gorilla's DNA is actually more similar to ours, so that different genomic regions suggest different trees of life. From a macroevolutionary point of view this is surprising—not what the theory would predict.[94]

The second argument for common ancestry of humans and chimps is based on the DNA variation *among* humans. It is slightly less than 0.1 percent and believed to be too large to warrant a unique founding couple—Adam and Eve. We mentioned above that population geneticists believe

---

92. Luskin, "Missing Transitions."

93. Gauger et al., "Genetic Evidence for Human Uniqueness" and references therein.

94. DeWitt, "What About the DNA Similarity?"; Gauger et al., *Science and Human Origins*; and Tomkins and Bergman, "Genomic Monkey Business."

humans originated from Africa, and they argue that for several hundred thousand years our ancestral population was never smaller than a few thousand individuals. The reason is that mutations would otherwise not be able to generate the diversity among humans we have today. But this argument has recently been criticized. If God created Adam and Eve with genetic diversity, this may indeed explain most of the genetic variation we see among humans today.[95]

In view of all these severe limitations of neo-Darwinism, evolutionary biologists have recently proposed a number of alternative theories in order to rescue the idea that humans share common ancestry with other species. The first of them—evo-devo—asserts that new species are formed abruptly, not gradually.[96] This is not achieved by increasing the speed at which small, gradual genetic changes occur (as for punctuated equilibrium), but rather through single mutations with very large effects. The most well known of these mutations occurs in *Hox* genes, which regulate the expression of many other protein-coding genes during animal embryological development. But these and other evo-devo mutations face severe problems, since the consequences of them seem to be harmful or lethal for all studied species.

A second alternative to neo-Darwinism does not focus on changes in the DNA molecules, but rather on epigenetic changes in the cell.[97] These changes are sometimes heritable and although they leave the DNA molecules intact they alter the way in which DNA is expressed into proteins. But such theories encounter a similar problem as neo-Darwinism. It is known for instance that some epigenetic information is important for animal embryological development. Since it is very difficult to alter such information without harmful consequences, one may ask how this information could be generated by random processes in the first place and then ultimately be transferred to changes in DNA.

A third theory that aims to replace or complement neo-Darwinism theory is due to the American biochemist Stuart Kauffman (1939–). It includes self-organization of cells during animal embryological development.[98] This development of body plans consists of two phases, where first cells differentiate into various types, and then they organize to form tissues. The first cell-differentiation phase requires genetic information whereas the second cell-organization phase requires epigenetic information. Kauffman

---

95. Sanford and Carter, "In Light of Genetics"; Jeanson and Lisle, "On the Origin of Eukaryotic"; and Hössjer et al., "Alternative Population Genetics Model."
96. See Meyer, *Darwin's Doubt*, chapter 16 and references therein.
97. Shapiro, *Evolution* and Noble, "Physiology Is Rocking the Foundations."
98. Kauffman, *Origins of Order* and Meyer, *Darwin's Doubt*, chapter 15.

proposes that the self-organization of both phases explain how new animal forms originated in the past. But this theory also faces a problem to explain how new information is generated.

To summarize, our conclusion is that unique origin of humans from a first couple is close to hermeneutically certain, whereas the empirical evidence of macroevolution is very uncertain. It seems that all proposed natural Darwinian explanations either do not account for how information emerged, or it is smuggled in from outside in some way or another.[99] We therefore argue that the claimed conflict between Darwinian macroevolution and the Bible in figure 11.1 is of type C. However, to question Darwinian macroevolution is more than challenging a scientific theory. It is also a matter of questioning a secular worldview and in particular the philosophical principle of (strong) methodological naturalism. We have illustrated this for the uncommon descent hypothesis of man and apes in figure 11.4.

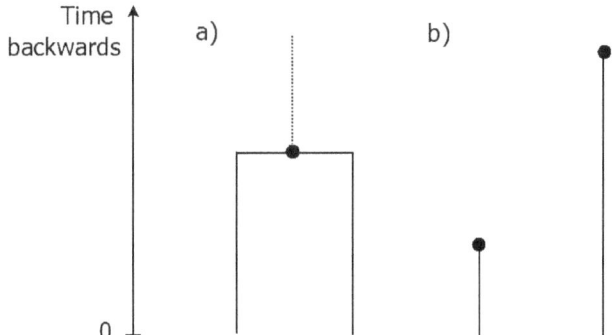

Figure 11.4: Models of human (left) and chimpanzee (right) ancestry according to common descent (a) and uncommon descent/unique origin (b) hypotheses. They are both models of scientific explanations (figure 11.2a) with different initial conditions. In a) the initial conditions are DNA of the most recent common ancestors of humans and chimps, and in b) it is DNA of the distinct founding couples of humans and chimps, both with created diversity. The laws of nature are the same for both scenarios—DNA change along the branches through natural selection, mutations, and genetic drift. The initial conditions in b) are inspired by a design argument. Rejecting b) from start is an instance of strong methodological naturalism.

---

99. See for instance Ewert et al., "Active Information in Metabiology" and references therein.

Evidence 15: Design. We all agree that the universe is well ordered, governed by natural laws, and that these laws are described by mathematical equations. Our planet even contains intelligent life and it is full of beauty. The question is: Did this order and beauty evolve by itself or was it planned by an intelligent designer? We have already treated Darwinian macroevolution,[100] but here we will broaden the discussion and focus also on the designed product itself.

Already the ancient Greek philosophers were impressed by the order in nature. Aristotle, for instance, thought it was caused by a first Unmoved Mover. A large number of people have emphasized design since then. One of the most famous arguments is due to the English philosopher and apologist William Paley (1743–1805). He motivated design through a watchmaker analogy:

> In crossing a heath, suppose I pitched my foot against a stone, and were asked how the stone came to be there; I might possibly answer, that, for anything I knew to the contrary, it had lain there forever: nor would it perhaps be very easy to show the absurdity of this answer. But suppose I had found a watch upon the ground, and it should be inquired how the watch happened to be in that place; I should hardly think of the answer I had before given, that for anything I knew, the watch might have always been there. . . . There must have existed, at some time, and at some place or other, an artificer or artificers, who formed [the watch] for the purpose which we find it actually to answer; who comprehended its construction, and designed its use. . . . Every indication of contrivance, every manifestation of design, which existed in the watch, exists in the works of nature; with the difference, on the side of nature, of being greater or more, and that in a degree which exceeds all computation.[101]

Just as a pedestrian recognizes the craft of a watchmaker, who created the watch for a purpose, we recognize an intelligent designer in nature. A Christian would say that this designer is God, who either provides us with laws of nature front-loaded with initial conditions or acts through direct interventions. The Bible tells that the evidence of a designer in nature is so strong

---

100. Evidence 14.
101. Paley, *Natural Theology*, chapters 1 and 3.

that we have no excuses for rejecting God.[102] Several of the psalms proclaim that the order and beauty of the universe bear strong witness of him.[103]

Figure 11.5: William Paley, an English apologist from the late eighteenth and early nineteenth century.[104] He is most famous for his watchmaker analogy of design in nature.

The *teleological argument* for the existence of God[105] uses design in order to motivate a Creator. It can be formulated as follows:

1. Nature has an order that fills a special purpose.
2. This order is either designed, exists out of necessity, or has occurred by chance.
3. The order we see around us does not exist out of necessity nor has it occurred by chance.
4. Therefore a designer must exist.

102. Rom 1:18–23.
103. See for instance Ps 8 and 19.
104. Image is in the public domain and taken from https://en.wikipedia.org/wiki/William_Paley#/media/File:William_Paley_by_George_Romney.jpg.
105. Craig, *Reasonable Faith* and Lennox, *God's Undertaker* provide more theological, historic, and scientific details about the teleological argument.

The first three sentences are the premises whereas the last one is a conclusion. The teleological argument has received a lot of attention in recent years. The main reason is that modern science has strengthened premise 1. First of all, a large number of cosmologists and physicists of various religious professions agree that the universe is extremely *fine-tuned* for life to exist on our planet.[106] For instance, in order to avoid collapsing after its beginning or expanding too rapidly into a chaos of elementary particles, initial conditions (expansion rate, density fluctuations, . . .), laws of nature (regulation of forces, charges, motion, . . .) and constants of physics (masses and charges of elementary particles, strength of forces, . . .) must all be calibrated very accurately. The existence of stars requires a similar detailed balance between attracting and expanding forces. There is also a considerable amount of local fine-tuning of our galaxy and solar system in order for Earth to be *habitable* and facilitate life. The solar system seems to have a very favorable position within one of the spiral arms of the Milky Way, quite far away from its center. Within our solar system, the distance between Earth and the sun, the almost circular orbit of Earth, and the angle between Earth's axis and orbit give optimal conditions for life in terms of average heat as well as seasonal and daily temperature variations. At the micro level, the existence of atomic nuclei requires a delicate balance between repelling electromagnetic and attracting strong nuclear forces. But our universe is not only habitable; it is also *discoverable*, since it is possible to observe other planets, stars, and galaxies from Earth. Astrophysicist Guillermo Gonzales (1963-) and philosopher Jay Richards (1967-) argue that the chances of a discoverable universe are very small, given that we live in a habitable universe.[107]

Modern biology provides even more evidence for premise 1 of the design argument. A cell can be pictured as a breathtaking, extremely complicated city with factories (ribosomes) for synthesis of proteins, power stations (mitochondria) that release chemical energy, roads (microtubules) for transportation, and surrounding walls (lipoprotein cell membrane) that regulate what comes in and out. The long DNA molecule in the cell nucleus contains all information needed for protein synthesis. It is ingeniously folded, written in a four-letter alphabet of nucleotides, and it translates into

---

106. Collins provides a probability argument for that fine-tuning makes the existence of God very likely. Collins "Teleological Argument." Halvorsen objects to this. His main argument is that fine-tuning cannot be used to deduce the existence of God, since he can possibly create any kind of initial conditions for the universe; also those that don't bring about life. Halvorsen, "Probability Problem." Although this is to some extent true, if we use Scripture to deduce what kind of universe God wants to create it seems clear that it is one where life exists.

107. Gonzales and Richards, *The Privileged Planet*.

amino acids—the building blocks of proteins—through the genetic code.[108] The non-coding part of DNA does not translate into amino acids, and it comprises more than 98 percent of the human genome. It was previously labeled as "junk DNA"—remnants of blind evolution without function. But through the ENCODE consortium it has recently been found that a dominate fraction of non-coding DNA is biologically active and seems to have important functions for various cellular activities, including regulation of which genes that are expressed in different cells.[109]

From our everyday experience and the above-mentioned evidence of modern science, most of us would agree that premise 1 is correct. Premise 2 is also quite uncontroversial. The crucial part of the teleological argument is whether premise 3 holds, or if the design is only apparent and a product of chance or necessity. The leading atheist Antony Flew (1923–2010) started to believe in design late in life. He thought the perceived order in nature (premise 1) was so strong that design was the only conceivable explanation. This led him to abandon his naturalistic worldview shortly before he died. The development of modern science—in particular biology—convinced him. He simply pursued the suggestion of Socrates to "follow the evidence where it leads" and deduced that a designer—God—must exist.[110]

But others disagree with Flew and try to refute premise 3 of the design argument. Many attempts have been made to do so. The most common objection to premise 3 is to view it as a *"God of the gaps" argument*.[111] If a claimed design by God finds a natural explanation, the reference to God is thought to be invalidated. This reasoning is to some extent understandable and history is full of "God of the gaps" arguments. But if we broaden our perspective then the occurrence of a natural explanation does not invalidate the design argument per se. Even though a very design-like phenomenon has a natural explanation we can still apply the cosmological argument and think of a regressing chain of explanations that eventually leads us to a first cause—God, the ultimate planner of everything in universe (see figure 11.2b).[112]

---

108. See for instance Sanford, *Genetic Entropy*, Johnson, *Probability's Nature*, chapter 6, and Johnson, *Programming of Life*, for more on the functional information of the cell.

109. The non-coding parts of the genome include various types of non-coding RNAs, regulatory elements, coding in introns for alternative ways of splicing out exons in genes, repetitive DNA, pseudogenes, and jumping genes. See for instance Wells, "Myth of Junk DNA" and ENCODE Project, "Encyclopedia of DNA Elements."

110. Flew, *There Is a God*.

111. Evidence 10.

112. The alternative would be to accept either an infinite chain of causes or a first

A second objection to premise 3 is the *argument of poor design*. It is claimed that the order around us is not perfect. For instance, it has been argued that some organs of the human body either have no function or at least they do not function in the optimal way. And as mentioned above, it was also believed that non-coding DNA is "junk" with no purpose. But these are all "naturalism of the gaps" arguments, and many of them turned out to be false when the functionality of many organs and of non-coding DNA was found. It is reasonable to assume that future discoveries will reveal even more function. But even if the argument of poor design was correct it is still not an argument against a designer. At best it is an argument against a designer that creates a perfect world. But even an omnipotent and good Creator may choose to give the created persons free will. In the Bible we read that creation was originally good, but after the fall it was subject to decay.[113]

A third critique of premise 3 is *reductionism*, by which a complex system can be reduced to its fundamental parts and ultimately explained by mathematical equations. The Hungarian chemist Michael Polanyi (1891–1976) criticized reductionism and argued for a holistic view where systems are organized hierarchically into different levels, in such a way that a higher level cannot be reduced to lower ones. The DNA molecule, for instance, cannot be reduced to chemistry and physics, since it carries information to synthesize proteins.[114] At the next level chemistry and physics cannot be reduced to mathematics, and mathematics itself is incomplete.[115] The German engineering Professor Werner Gitt (1937–) argues that design reflects information, which is not a property of matter or energy but rather a coded message from an intelligent sender that uses some language that is organized hierarchically into different levels.[116]

The fourth objection to premise 3 is more constructive. It attempts to find a *chance or necessity mechanism* that explains how a complex system arose. Such a blind designer includes self-organization to justify the origin of life or Darwinian macroevolution to explain the diversity of life. Richard Dawkins famously argues for biological evolution in his book *The Blind Watchmaker*:

> Paley's argument is made with passionate sincerity and is informed by the best biological scholarship of his day, but it is

---

cause whose creation we cannot explain; see prior belief 1 of section 5.2.

113. Gen 1:31; Rom 8:19–22.
114. Polyani, "Life's Irreducible Structure."
115. Evidence 16.
116. Gitt, *In the Beginning Was Information*.

> wrong, gloriously and utterly wrong.... A true watchmaker has foresight: he designs his cogs and springs, and plans their interconnections, with a future purpose in this mind's eye. Natural selection, the blind, unconscious, automatic process which Darwin discovered, and which we now know is the explanation for the existence and apparently purposeful form of all life, has no purpose in mind. It has no mind and no mind's eye. It has no vision, no foresight, no sight at all. If it can be said to play the role of a watchmaker in nature, it is the blind watchmaker.[117]

But we have seen already that macroevolution has several gaps.[118] Perhaps the largest obstacle for Dawkins' argument is that most mutations are neutral or damaging, and this makes it very difficult for blind evolution to produce an irreducibly complex system. This concept was introduced by biologist Michael Behe (1952–), and its definition is a refinement of Paley's watchmaker analogy:

> A single system composed of several well-matched, interacting parts that contribute to the basic function, wherein the removal of any one of the parts causes the system to effectively cease functioning.[119]

Behe argued that a number of biological systems are irreducibly complex, for instance the bacterial flagellum, the blood-clotting cascade, and the mammalian immune system. It would require a number of more or less simultaneous beneficial mutations to generate structures of this complexity, and evolution has not been observed to produce any system like this. For instance, the American evolutionary biologist Richard Lenski (1956–) has studied E. coli for over 25 years. About 10^{13} bacteria have been produced but no novel complex biological structures were found.[120] Nor have the natural experiments of HIV and malaria evolution generated new structures that we know of, in spite of 10^{20} viruses or cells a year. A number of attempts have been made with computer simulations to produce digital irreducibly complex systems, but none of them satisfy all criteria of Behe's definition.[121]

---

117. Dawkins, *Blind Watchmaker*, 5.
118. Evidence 14.
119. Behe, *Darwin's Black Box*, 39.
120. In a recent publication from Lenski's research group 264 genomes from various E. coli populations were sequenced. They found a number of fixed beneficial mutations that seem to represent microevolution in a planned experiment; see Tenaillon et al., "Tempo and Mode of Genome Evolution."
121. Ewert "Digital Irreducible Complexity"; Johnson, *Programming of Life*, chapter 10; and evidence 14 of this book.

Any attempt to explain the occurrence of complex systems by a chance or necessity mechanism seems to require that information is created out of nothing. The second law of thermodynamics suggests that this is not possible, at least for the isolated systems of non-living matter that this law applies to. The law postulates that disorder—or entropy—with extremely high probability increases to a limit of chaos, whereas a blind designer is claimed to operate in the opposite way.[122]

A fifth critique of premise 3 is the *argument from parsimony*. The idea is that a simpler explanation should be advocated over a more complicated one when both have similar explanatory power. And a universe without a designer is thought to be simpler. Although the argument from parsimony is a well-established scientific principle, it can be questioned whether it can be used to advocate a blind designer—not only because the proposed chance and necessity mechanisms seem to lack the claimed explanatory power, but also since theism is sometimes regarded as a simpler explanation than blind design.[123]

The sixth objection against premise 3 is usually applied to cosmology, but it can also be applied to macroevolution and some other chance/necessity mechanisms. It is called the *weak anthropic principle* for the fine-tuning of intelligent life. Given that we live in a habitable universe, this principle asserts that we are prone to *selection bias* since we *must* observe the universe we live in. Since a habitable universe requires fine-tuning, the conclusion of the argument is that fine-tuning should not surprise us. Applying this principle to our everyday life means that we should not be surprised by (or thankful for?) anything that we experience.

Astronomer and physicist Luke Barnes (1983-) has recently written a detailed overview on fine-tuning, and he refutes previous attempts to

---

122. There are three main views on how information is generated. 1) A purely materialistic and mathematical definition in terms of Shannon entropy. Blind evolution in biological systems is then explained by means of self-organization or mutations and natural selection. Although the second law of thermodynamics is often not applied to living systems, this approach is still challenged by the concept of irreducible complexity. 2) Information is defined for non-material structure through a bottom-up approach. With this approach blind evolution is explained by allowing the entropy to increase locally when energy is fed into a unit. 3) According the top-down approach, blind evolution is not possible (or most unlikely). Information is viewed as something that constrains the local thermodynamics. It is argued that the influx of energy into a local system requires a machine to make use of it for increased information, and occurrence of new machines requires additional information (intelligence). For more discussion and further references, see the review paper by McIntosh, "Information and Entropy," where the third approach is advocated. The difficulty of algorithms to generate new information is also highlighted in Marks et al., *Introduction to Evolutionary Informatics*.

123. See section 5.1.

explain it by means of laws of physics within one single universe.[124] Given what we know of physics today, it seems that the weak anthropic principle requires the existence of other universes. Several multiverse theories have been proposed, including the above-mentioned M-theory.[125] Swedish-American cosmologist Max Tegmark (1967–) has created a taxonomy for some of the other multiverse theories.[126] His Level I multiverse is based on a concept called eternal inflation. This is an extension of the Big Bang theory where the claimed initial inflation phase[127] of the universe does not come to an end, so that the expansion always continues at some place. The result is one infinitely large universe. It can also be thought of as a multiverse in which "our universe" is the part (the so-called Hubble volume) that can be seen through a telescope from Earth. The initial conditions (recall figure 11.2a) for the densities and motion of the matter that we see in our Hubble volume today are determined by the pattern of quantum vacuum fluctuations before it started to expand. Similarly, each other Hubble volume is determined by its original pattern of quantum vacuum fluctuations. Since there is only a finite (though very large) number of such fluctuation patterns there will be many other Hubble volumes identical to ours, and therefore it is claimed that our universe is not fine-tuned. For other multiverse theories the argument against fine-tuning is quite similar.

But many regard multiverse theories as speculative. For instance, physicist Paul Davies (1946–) writes:

> For a start, how is the existence of the other universes to be tested? To be sure, all cosmologists accept that there are some regions of the universe that lie beyond the reach of our telescopes, but somewhere on the slippery slope between that and the idea that there are an infinite number of universes, credibility reaches a limit. As one slips down that slope, more and more must be accepted on faith, and less and less is open to scientific verification.[128]

This leads to the question whether multiverse theories can be falsified or not. Although the answer to some extent depends on which multiverse one wishes to test, it has been suggested that large irregularities of the cosmic background radiation in terms of cold and hot spots would provide evidence for collisions between our universe and some others. It remains to be seen

124. Barnes, "Fine-Tuning of the Universe."
125. Evidence 13.
126. Tegmark "Multiverse Hierarchy."
127. Evidence 12 and 13 give more details on the inflationary theory of Big Bang.
128. Davies, "Brief History of the Multiverse," para. 10.

if such evidence for a multiverse will be found. Even if this were to happen, and in any case if a multiverse exists, this doesn't invalidate God as designer since it remains to answer who created the multiverse.[129] For similar reasons Richard Swinburne argues that the multiverse theory is more complicated than theism and therefore apriori less likely.[130] In contrast, the multiverse argument relies heavily on methodological naturalism. It favors naturalistic models of the universe where personal explanations are excluded (figure 11.2a) over models that (indirectly) offer a personal explanation in terms of fine-tuning (figure 11.2b).

To summarize the teleological argument, most people would agree that premises 1 and 2 are correct. We have reasoned that the attempts to refute premise 3 have not been successful. This strongly points to conclusion 4, that a designer exists.

Evidence 16: Effectiveness, beauty, and limitations of mathematics. In the previous examples of this chapter we looked at inductive sciences, and in particular their relevance for Christianity. This includes biology, chemistry, physics, and other disciplines whose objective is to develop models and theories in order to explain experimental data as well as possible, and to make good predictions.

Mathematics, on the other hand, is a deductive science with theories that do not include experimental data. It is more like a building whose foundation includes unproved statements called axioms (such as Euclid's axioms of geometry, Peano's axioms for the integers, and Zermelo-Fraenkel's axioms for sets), definitions, and undefined terms (such as points or lines of geometry). The house is gradually built higher when new bricks are added. Each such brick is either a new statement (a theorem) that is proved or deduced or a new definition that is introduced. The building materials are the laws of logic, and each new brick relies on what is in already in the house. Mathematics has, in spite of its deductive nature, been very successful and effective to provide models for experimental sciences, especially physics and chemistry, and more recently biology and social sciences as well. This success story took off during the scientific revolution of the sixteenth and seventeenth centuries when prominent Christian scientists such as Kepler, Galileo, and Newton formulated laws of nature and physics in mathematical terms, when Pascal and Fermat used probabilities for studying gambling problems, and when John Graunt (1620–74) introduced statistics for

---

129. This is similar to the argument against M-theory as a first cause in evidence 13.

130. Swinburne, *Existence of God*, chapter 8; and Swinburne, "Bayes, God and the Multiverse."

studying English mortality tables. By the eighteenth century mathematics had replaced theology as a foundation of many other sciences, and in the nineteenth century the prominent German mathematician Carl Friedrich Gauss (1777–1855) referred to it as the queen of science.

Mathematical theories often rely on axioms that we think of as self-evident, since they seem to reflect a reality. An example is the axiom of transitivity in the theory of integers: If x=y and y=z, then x=z as well. Very few would question this. And when new bricks of the building are added to these axioms they are often motivated by practical problems. A prime example is Newton's discovery of doing math with infinitely small quantities (infinitesimal calculus),[131] which enabled him to deduce elliptic planetary orbits from his laws of gravity and motion. But other mathematical theories have been built solely out of scientific curiosity, without thinking of practical applications. For instance, complex numbers include not only real numbers but also square roots of negative numbers. They were used by Italian mathematicians in the sixteenth century in order to solve certain equations. By the early nineteenth century this had developed into a rich theory. The remarkable thing is that although the theory of complex numbers was developed very much out of curiosity it later found numerous applications in many parts of experimental science. It is for instance an indispensable tool for describing electromagnetic waves and quantum phenomena of physics. And there are many other examples like this. Non-Euclidean geometry in curved spaces was developed in the nineteenth century by changing one of the axioms of Euclidean geometry, for instance, allowing "parallel lines" to intersect. More than 50 years later it found applications in Einstein's general theory of relativity.[132]

The Hungarian physicist, mathematician, and Nobel Prize winner Eugene Wigner (1902–95) found the effectiveness of mathematics so striking that he wrote:

> The miracle of the appropriateness of the language of mathematics for the formulation of the laws of physics is a wonderful gift which we neither deserve or understand. We should be grateful for it and hope that it will remain valid in future research and that it will extend, for the better or for worse, to our pleasure, even though perhaps also to our bafflement, to wide branches of learning.[133]

---

131. This discovery of infinitesimal calculus was made independently by Gottfried Leibnitz (1646–1716).

132. This is usually referred to as the *future-valued argument* for the worth of mathematics. Howell, "Matter of Mathematics," 84.

133. Wigner, "Unreasonable Effectiveness of Mathematics," 14.

178 PART II: PENETRATING THE EVIDENCE

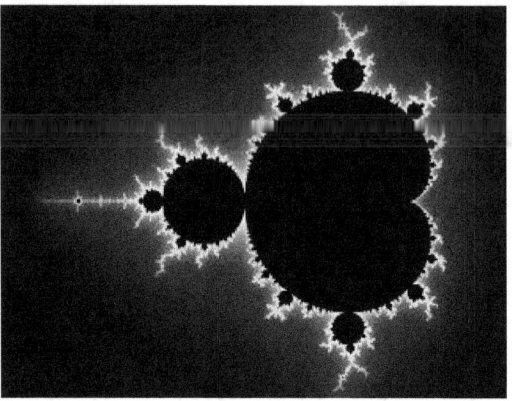

Figure 11.6: A Mandelbrot set, whose boundary repeats itself when magnified[134] (so-called self-similarity). The mathematical definition is the set of complex numbers c for which the infinite sequence $z_0 = (0,0), z_1 = z_0^2 + c, z_2 = z_1^2 + c, \ldots$ is bounded.

But mathematics is not only effective, it has aesthetic qualities as well.[135] For instance, fractals objects are self-similar, meaning they repeat themselves when you look at them through a magnifying glass. They are often regarded as beautiful (as is the Mandelbrot set of figure 11.6) and yet described in precise mathematical terms. A rectangle that frequently appears in art and whose shape is often thought of as elegant has one side that is approximately 1.618 times as large as the other. This number is referred to as the golden ratio (see figure 11.7). A mathematician is like a painting artist. Even though he proves a theorem, he may not be satisfied with the proof because it is too technical, too long, or too difficult to understand. The British mathematician G. H. Hardy (1847–1977) actually regarded beauty as an important quality of good mathematics,[136] since deep results are often simple and elegant, with surprising connections to other parts of mathematics.

---

134. Image is in the public domain and taken from https://en.wikipedia.org/wiki/Mandelbrot_set#/media/File:Mandel_zoom_00_mandelbrot_set.jpg. CC BY-SA 3.0.

135. This is usually referred to as the *aesthetic argument* for the worth of mathematics. Howell, "Matter of Mathematics," 84.

136. Hardy, *Mathematician's Apology*.

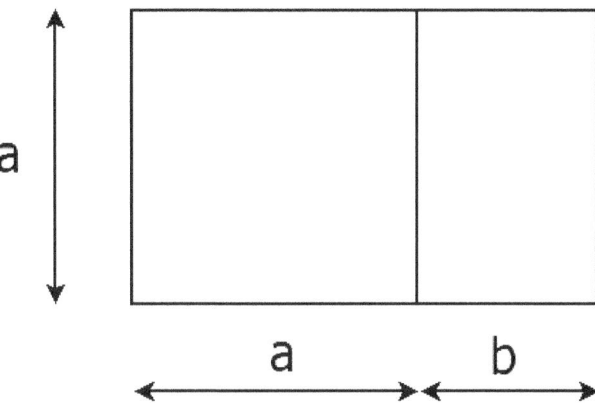

Figure 11.7: Illustration of the golden ratio 1.6180.... It is the ratio (a+b)/a between the side lengths of the combined rectangle, but also the ratio a/b between the side lengths of the small rectangle.

It seems natural in view of this to give the effectiveness and beauty of mathematics a Christian interpretation. This essentially boils down to merging Christianity with some theory of abstract objects.[137] *Christian Platonism* asserts that mathematical objects have real existence (ontological realism) as part of God's character. This view has been the dominant one among Christians, including the church father Augustine of Hippo,[138] scientists of the Renaissance like Galileo and Newton, and believers of today. *Christian mathematical empiricism* is more in line with an Aristotelian tradition. It was promoted by voluntarist theologians of the Middle Ages[139] and has recently regained some interest.[140] Although empiricists assert that some concepts like the law of non-contradiction and the Trinity are part of God's nature, they regard most mathematical objects as the result of human activity. They believe these objects have no independent existence, but view them as convenient ways of naming abstractions of real and existing things (ontological nominalism). According to both schools mathematical work is viewed as part of our God-given creativity and mandate to take care of creation. Through mathematics we may reveal some of the beauty of God, either directly as part of his character or indirectly since he created humans in his image with an ability to do mathematics.

137. Various interpretations of abstract objects can be found in Craig and Sinclair, "*Kalam* Cosmological Argument," figure 3.1.
138. Bradley, "Augustinian Perspective" and Howell, "The Matter of Mathematics," 79.
139. Evidence 3 and 10.
140. Bradley and Howell, *Mathematics Through the Eyes of Faith*, chapter 10.

What about naturalistic theories of mathematics? In the early seventeenth century Descartes proposed that mathematics is the language of a mechanistic world, and this view was adopted by Enlightenment thinkers as well. Some attempts have been made to explain the origin and effectiveness of mathematics within this framework. For instance, the American computer scientist and mathematician Richard Hamming (1915-98) argued that the effectiveness of mathematics is not surprising, since scientists tend to look for equations that fit their data well and select the kind of mathematics that suits it the most.[141] This is actually a good description of the way inductive science works,[142] but it seems inadequate to justify the beauty, elegance, and surprising applications of mathematics that we referred to above. It has also been proposed that the ability to do mathematics has evolved blindly over a period of time. But this can be questioned on several grounds. First, mathematical discoveries are typically at most a few thousand years old, which is a very short time frame for blind evolution to operate on. Second, different isolated cultures (for instance ancient Greece and premodern China) have often developed similar mathematics, and this seems to suggests that the ability to do mathematics is designed. Third, if the ability to do mathematics evolved blindly we may question whether it can be trusted in the first place. This is essentially the argument against the evolution of cognitive abilities in general.[143]

---

141. Hamming, "Unreasonable Effectiveness of Mathematics" and Bradley and Howell, *Mathematics Through the Eyes of Faith*, chapter 8.

142. Recall the discussion in evidence 10 on principles of inductive science.

143. Evidence 7 and 10.

Figure 11.8: Kurt Gödel, who is most famous for having proved that mathematics is incomplete.[144]

The success of mathematics in other sciences inspired many prominent mathematicians and philosophers of the early twentieth century, including Alfred North Whitehead, Bertrand Russell, and David Hilbert (1862–1943), to believe that all mathematical results could either be proved or disproved using only a small set of axioms. If this was true it would imply that mathematics is a complete science. Some people have held the reductionist view that other sciences can ultimately be reduced to mathematics, and this would imply that much of creation could ultimately be explained in terms of a few mathematical principles. Then things changed. It was shocking news when the Austrian mathematician and philosopher Kurt Gödel (1906–78) published his two incompleteness theorems (see figure 11.8). Gödel proved that any mathematical system that is without contradictions and is strong enough to contain arithmetic with natural numbers will contain statements that cannot be proved without adding new axioms. Moreover, we cannot

---

144. Image taken from https://en.wikipedia.org/wiki/File:Kurt_g%C3%B6del.jpg. Copyright has expired.

use a mathematical system to prove that it is free of contradictions. For a Christian these results are very comforting. While mathematics is a powerful, elegant, and beautiful gift from God to mankind, we will never be able to master or control it completely, just as creation continuously reveals new aspects of itself. We may admire and awe it but ultimately worship the Creator of it.

12

Theological Evidence

THE FOURTH CATEGORY OF evidence concerns theology and philosophy of religion. Why is there evil in the world? Is God of the Old Testament a loving God? Why does God hide himself? Aren't some Christian doctrines difficult to combine with a loving God, such as the fall of man and the existence of hell? Some of these topics are stumbling blocks for people to become Christians. Others find that Christianity has the best answers to these tough questions. The style of writing and historical credibility of the Bible is also important, and often considered as strong pieces of evidence in favor of Christianity. In this chapter we deal with six units of evidence that address these topics.

Evidence 17: The problem of evil and free will. Presence of evil and suffering is something we all face in some way or the other. Religions and philosophies of life have different answers to why we have to endure various kinds of hardships. According to pantheistic religions, such as Hinduism and Buddhism, suffering is not unfair. It is rather caused by our own misbehavior, either in this life or in earlier ones. From a naturalistic point of view it is even difficult to define suffering and evil in the first place, since objective moral values are not believed to exist. This made C. S. Lewis question and ultimately abandon his own naturalism:

> My argument against God was that the universe seemed so cruel and unjust. But how had I got this idea of just and unjust? . . . Of course I could have given up my idea of justice by saying it was nothing but a private idea of my own. But if I did that, then my argument against God collapsed too—for the argument

> depended on saying that the world was really unjust, not simply that it did not happen to please my private fancies. Thus in the very act of trying to prove that God did not exist—in other words, that the whole of reality was senseless—I found I was forced to assume that one part of reality—namely my idea of justice—was full of sense. Consequently, atheism turns out to be too simple.[1]

The question of evil is more subtle within Christianity, since at first it seems to contradict the existence of an almighty and benevolent God.[2] This can formally be summarized as the *logical problem of evil*:

1. If God exists, he is omnipotent and good.
2. An omnipotent being can create the world as he wishes to.
3. A good being wants to create a world without evil.
4. If God exists, there is no evil in the world.
5. There is evil in the world.
6. Hence there is no God.

In this argument 1, 2, 3, and 5 are the premises; 4 is a consequence of 1, 2, and 3; and 6 is a consequence of 4 and 5. Attempts to resolve the problem of evil are usually referred to as *theodicies*. Premises 1 and 5 are both indisputable from a biblical point of view, so a Christian has to show that at least one of premises 2 and 3 is false.[3] Premise 2 concerns the abilities of God. Even though God is omnipotent, he will only do things that are consequences of his own character. But this includes all the things he wishes or wants to do. Therefore it seems that premise 2 is correct, and we have to show that premise 3 is wrong.

Before dealing with premise 3 of the logical problem of evil, we will ask an even more basic question: Why did God create the world in the first place? According to the *no-reason argument*, an omnipotent and omniscient God has no needs or desires since these concepts are subjectively human, and therefore God has no reason to create the universe. The biblical view is that the members of Trinity indeed had perfect love and fellowship already

---

1. Lewis, *Mere Christianity*, 45–56. Habermas discusses atheistic objections to the problem of evil and theistic responses to them. Habermas, "Atheism and Evil."

2. For more details on the problem of evil, see for instance Craig, *No Easy Answers*, Grudem, *Systematic Theology*, and references therein.

3. Premises 2 and 3 of the logical problem of evil are closely related to the *argument from unbelief*—that God should gather believers only since he is omnipotent and wants humans to believe in him.

before the universe was created.[4] Therefore, God did not create us because he was lonely or *needed* companionship. We were rather created to glorify his name,[5] although he very much *wants* to spend time with us in a loving relationship. In order for this to happen he could not make us like robots—programmed to do good. He rather gave humans (and angels) the unique ability of making choices with long-term consequences. And this makes us morally accountable for what we do.

According to the Bible, God did not create evil, but sin and suffering came into the world as a consequence of the moral responsibility of angels and humans when they decided to rebel against God.[6] One may ask whether this fall of angels and men was a miscalculation on God's part. No—already before creation God knew what was going to happen. And he had a rescue plan—to send Jesus as Redeemer:

> With all wisdom and understanding, he made known to us the mystery of his will according to his good pleasure, which he purposed in Christ, to be put into effect when the times reach their fulfillment—to bring unity to all things in heaven and on earth under Christ.[7]

God knew the price that had to be paid for giving man moral responsibility and that he had to pay that price himself. Still he valued humans so much that he chose to carry out the creation he had planned.

But what does moral responsibility mean? Does it mean "free will"? According to the Bible no one can make choices outside God's providence and control of the world.[8] The term "free will" should therefore be cautiously interpreted, and Christians have somewhat different views on this matter. In Calvinist or Reformed theology free will only means the ability to make willing choices, i.e., choices that one approves of that have real effects. In Arminian theology free will also includes the ability to make choices not caused by anything outside ourselves. But since God is outside our notion of time he has the ability to respond to our choices in a way that assures his overall control of the world. In any case, humans are considered morally responsible for their acts. According to *Molinism* the two interpretations need not be contradictory, given that God transcends our notion of time and can foretell how we *would* react under circumstances that will never

---

4. John 17:5, 24.
5. Isa 43:7; Eph 1:11–12. See also prior belief 3.
6. See section 2.1.
7. Eph 1:9–10.
8. Heb 1:3.

happen. In the sequel we will therefore continue to speak of free will, having both interpretations in mind.⁹

After these comments we may return to premise 3 of the logical problem of evil. It is part of God's love to create angels and humans capable of loving him. This requires that we are given a free will to say either yes or no to him—with an ability to do either good or bad—without God overruling our choices. Therefore God took a risk of evil entering the world when he created angels and humans in this way. But because of God's divine foresight this is not a risk in our sense, since he knew before creation that evil *would* enter the world. This makes premise 3 invalid.

Even though presence of evil does not contradict an omnipotent and good God, as the logical problem evil would suggest, it may still be difficult to understand all the evil in the world and the various kinds of hardships that people face. Although this does not make God's existence logically impossible, the *evidential problem of evil* asserts that it makes his existence unlikely. The kinds of suffering that we face can be of several types, and some of them are more difficult to cope with than others. Most of us would accept that when we do what is wrong, such as gossiping, stealing, being jealous, or committing adultery, we will sooner or later suffer when other people react or when our conscience gives us a lack of inner peace.¹⁰ The good news is that inner peace can be restored by genuine repentance when we ask God and sometimes other people for forgiveness. It is more difficult to accept when we are victims of moral evil even though we have done nothing wrong, such as victimization and harassment, or persecution for political and religious beliefs. But from a Christian perspective we realize that these are also consequences of the fall of man. The Bible offers a very radical way of handling it, a way that protects us from bitterness and hatred:

> You have heard that it was said, "Eye for eye, and tooth for tooth." But I tell you, do not resist an evil person. If anyone slaps you on the right cheek, turn to them the other cheek also. And if anyone wants to sue you and take your shirt, hand over your coat as well. If anyone forces you to go one mile, go with them two miles. Give to the one who asks you, and do not turn away

---

9. Various interpretations of free will are discussed in Grudem, *Systematic Theology*, chapter 16. For an account of Molinism, see Craig, *Only Wise God* and Perszyk, *Molinism, the Contemporary Debate*. Very briefly, it asserts that God has middle knowledge before creation of what *would* happen if things turned out differently in the universe. Although this middle knowledge comes ahead of creation, it is dependent on God first having *knowledge of necessary truths*. It also differs from God's *foreknowledge* of what *will* happen in this world.

10. 1 Pet 4:15.

from the one who wants to borrow from you. You have heard that it was said, "Love your neighbor and hate your enemy." But I tell you, love your enemies and pray for those who persecute you, that you may be children of your Father in heaven.[11]

It is even more difficult to understand *natural evil*, such as sickness, injuries, deaths, and natural catastrophes, not the least when children, the disabled, or the poor are the victims. But such events are indirectly a consequence of us living in a fallen world. In Paul's Letter to the Roman Church we read:

> For the creation waits in eager expectation for the children of God to be revealed. For the creation was subjected to frustration, not by its own choice, but by the will of the one who subjected it, in hope that the creation itself will be liberated from its bondage to decay and brought into the freedom and glory of the children of God. We know that the whole creation has been groaning as in the pains of childbirth right up to the present time.[12]

Even though creation is subject to decay it still seems that the Bible doesn't provide any definite explanations for natural evil. But the book of Job in the Old Testament very honestly acknowledges that innocent people may suffer. Job was a most godly man who lost his children, much of his property, and his health. Three of his friends came to visit him, suggesting that his suffering was caused by his own sin, which they claimed Job had to confess. Job, on the other hand, insisted that he was innocent. Even though he complained a lot and felt abandoned by God, he never ceased to believe in him. At the end of the book God answered, telling Job that he was not in a position to judge since he had only a very limited knowledge of God's creation and intentions with the world. Although he never told why Job was made to suffer, he made it clear that Job's friends were all wrong.[13]

The conclusion is that God does not explain the origin of all suffering and evil in the world, and we lack sufficient background information to give answers. And presence of evil does not necessarily make God's existence unlikely, as the evidential problem of evil suggests. What we *do* know is that God's highest desire is for people to get to know him and have eternal life. Many people who have experienced suffering of various sorts have testified that such a period drew them closer to God and changed their perspectives in life, although they would usually not like to have their miseries

---

11. Matt 5:38–45.
12. Rom 8:19–22.
13. Job; Luke 13:1–5; John 9; Matt 5:11; Luke 6:22; 1 Pet 4:14.

repeated.¹⁴ As a Christian you have God's promises that justice will finally prevail and in heaven we are assured of complete joy and no suffering. This makes all hardships in this world—no matter how painful—only temporary and not final.¹⁵

Suffering and evil may not only draw us closer to God as a comforter. It could also motivate us to turn to God in the first place and become followers of Christ. We may agree with C.S. Lewis and argue that presence of evil presupposes an objective moral law with right and wrong, which is strong evidence for a law giver—God.¹⁶ The American philosopher of religion William Lane Craig (1949–) has summarized this argument as follows:¹⁷

1. If God does not exist, there are no objective moral values.
2. Evil exists.
3. Hence objective moral values exist.
4. Hence God exists.

Just as when you find yourself in a dark room and want to light it up, people who experienced real darkness and evil often search God by all their heart. They might have been victims of war, had a destructive growth, or involved themselves in various kinds of occult practices. These persons are often well aware of the existence of a spiritual world, but they have encountered it in a destructive way. What they believed would end in happiness gave them fear and anxiety. Some of them come to a point when they cry out to God to save and protect them. It may also be evil in the outside world that affects us. For instance, for most of us it is hard to explain the Holocaust of World War II without referring to evil. Such an insight may eventually lead us to God.

A father had a son who possessed an evil spirit since childhood. He was desperate for help and came to Jesus and the disciples:

> When they (Jesus and three of his disciples) came to the other disciples, they saw a large crowd around them and the teachers of the law arguing with them. As soon as all the people saw Jesus, they were overwhelmed with wonder and ran to greet him. "What are you arguing with them about?" he asked. A man in the crowd answered, "Teacher, I brought you my son, who is possessed by a spirit that has robbed him of speech. Whenever it seizes him, it throws him to the ground. He foams at the mouth,

---

14. Chapter 14.
15. Ps 73; Hab 1–2; Rev 21:1–7.
16. Evidence 8.
17. Craig, *No Easy Answers*, chapter 5.

> gnashes his teeth and becomes rigid. I asked your disciples to drive out the spirit, but they could not." . . . So they brought him. When the spirit saw Jesus, it immediately threw the boy into a convulsion. He fell to the ground and rolled around, foaming at the mouth. Jesus asked the boy's father, "How long has he been like this?" "From childhood," he answered. "It has often thrown him into fire or water to kill him. But if you can do anything, take pity on us and help us." "If you can?" said Jesus. "Everything is possible for one who believes." Immediately the boy's father exclaimed, "I do believe; help me overcome my unbelief!"[18]

Obviously, evil was a very evident reality for the father. He decided to put his faith in Jesus, who responded and healed the boy.

Even if there are reasons for evil that we don't know of, sometimes we still want to cry out to God, as one of the prophets of the Old Testament—Habakkuk—did. Habakkuk asked God why he tolerated so much injustice:

> How long, Lord, must I call for help, but you do not listen? Or cry out to you, "Violence!" but you do not save? Why do you make me look at injustice? Why do you tolerate wrongdoing? Destruction and violence are before me; there is strife, and conflict abounds. Therefore the law is paralyzed, and justice never prevails. The wicked hem in the righteous, so that justice is perverted.[19]

Since God wants to have an honest relationship with us he very much welcomes questions about the hardships that sometimes strike ourselves and others. When we face all sorts of trouble and feel that God is silent, the Bible promises that he is still present, even more so when we suffer.

> Therefore, since we have a great high priest who has ascended into heaven, Jesus the Son of God, let us hold firmly to the faith we profess. For we do not have a high priest who is unable to empathize with our weaknesses, but we have one who has been tempted in every way, just as we are—yet he did not sin. Let us then approach God's throne of grace with confidence, so that we may receive mercy and find grace to help us in our time of need.[20]

The Word of God tells that no one feels compassion with those that suffer as much as God, since he has experienced suffering himself through Jesus

---

18. Mark 9:14–26.
19. Hab 1:2–4.
20. Heb 4:14–16; see also Ps 139:5.

Christ. Jesus was innocently killed by those he loved and cared for, and therefore Jesus knows more than anyone what injustice and physical pain means.

Evidence 18: The Old Testament. There are passages in the Old Testament where God punishes individuals, cities, and even nations. Many people—even Christians—have difficulties to unify this with a loving God. For non-Christians it becomes negative evidence for Christianity, since they question whether the God of the Old Testament is the same as the God of the New Testament as revealed in Christ.

This critique is not at all new—it has a long history. Marcion of Sinope (c. 85–c. 160) argued that God of the Old Testament was incompatible with Jesus' teaching. He therefore proposed a canon that only included parts of the Gospel of Luke and ten of Paul's letters. His thoughts were regarded as heresy by the church, but similar ideas have prevailed among some theologians over the centuries until this day. The Old Testament has also been one of the main targets of the New Atheists. For instance, Richard Dawkins gives the following portrait of the Old Testament God in *The God Delusion*:

> The God of the Old Testament is arguably the most unpleasant character in all fiction: jealous and proud of it; a petty, unjust, unforgiving control-freak; a vindictive, bloodthirsty ethnic cleanser; a misogynistic, homophobic, racist, infanticidal, genocidal, filicidal, pestilential, megalomaniacal, sadomasochistic, capriciously malevolent bully.[21]

One may ask on which grounds Dawkins criticizes the God of the Old Testament. Earlier we found that from an atheistic perspective it is not easy to give a basis for moral values.[22] We still have to take his critique seriously and highlight some arguments in defense of the Old Testament. For a more detailed account we refer to the book *Is God a Moral Monster?* by the American theologian and philosopher Paul Copan (1962–).[23] But before we look into the Old Testament it must be emphasized that even if we regard the

---

21. Dawkins, *God Delusion*, 31.
22. Evidence 8 and 9.
23. Copan, *Is God a Moral Monster?* For other accounts of the Old Testament, see Geisler and Howe, *Big Book of Bible Difficulties*; Edsinger, *Krigen i gamla testamentet*; Lennox, *Gunning for God*, chapter 5; and Gustavsson, "Är Gud ett ondskefullt monster?"

whole Bible as divinely inspired we have to be humble about its interpretation[24] and acknowledge our limits to fully understand all parts of it.[25]

As a first response to the Old Testament critique we notice that Jesus,[26] the apostles Paul,[27] and Peter[28] all viewed it as divine Scripture and frequently referred to it in their teaching. So if we regard the New Testament as the inerrant Word of God we must give the Old Testament the same status.

Second, in order to fully understand the Old Testament portrait of God we have to keep the big picture in mind. The main message of the whole Bible is God's love and grace. This is very well described by David in one of the psalms:

> The Lord is compassionate and gracious, slow to anger, abounding in love. He will not always accuse, nor will he harbor his anger forever; he does not treat us as our sins deserve or repay us according to our iniquities. For as high as the heavens are above the earth, so great is his love for those who fear him; as far as the east is from the west, so far has he removed our transgressions from us. As a father has compassion on his children, so the Lord has compassion on those who fear him; for he knows how we are formed, he remembers that we are dust. The life of mortals is like grass, they flourish like a flower of the field; the wind blows over it and it is gone, and its place remembers it no more. But from everlasting to everlasting the Lord's love is with those who fear him, and his righteousness with their children's children—with those who keep his covenant and remember to obey his precepts.[29]

Indeed, the Bible tells us about a loving *and* holy God who created a world that was good. Humans where made in his image in order to take care of and explore it. Although God gave us free will he still makes it clear that he is the omnipotent creator who wants us to follow and worship him. This is not arrogance. It rather expresses divine humility, where God speaks the truth and doesn't deny his own abilities. Neither is it a sign of vanity when he wants us to worship him, but an invitation to express the joy for anyone

---

24. See the discussion on Bible interpretation in evidence 10 in connection with natural science.
25. 1 Cor 13:12.
26. Matt 5:17–19.
27. 2 Tim 3:16.
28. 2 Pet 3:15–16.
29. Ps 103:8–18.

who has chosen to be part of a family that he extended beyond the Trinity to include humans as well.

God became jealous when humans misused their ability to make willing choices[30] and started to worship the created and other gods. This is not a bad, self-centered jealousy, but rather a divine one, motivated by a deep love and concern for our best. It is much like a wife that loves her husband and finds him cheating on her. She will most certainly get jealous and react in some way or another. And God's divine jealousy after the fall was so strong that he started a mission of restoring the broken relationship with man by sending his own Son as Redeemer and Savior—a true act of humility.

Third, the Old Testament gives a very honest picture of the world after the fall of man, with lots of violence, hatred, warfare, patriarchy, slavery, oppression of the poor, sexual abuse, and other departures from God's original intention with his creation. As humans we simply cannot handle our God-given mandate to take care of the world, and the morality of *any* human society that abandons God develops in a destructive way. According to the Bible this happened to the first generations of humans after the fall. Then God sent the flood to rescue Noah and his family in order to give humanity a new start. But gradually most people forgot about their Creator again. They began to worship other gods, although it seems that some people in each generation honestly tried to follow God, like Enoch, Noah, and Job.

Fourth, when Abraham lived most people had forgotten about God.[31] Then God launched his long-term saving mission for humanity. He promised Abraham a great nation Israel of heirs and more than 600 years later he gave the Law to Moses and the people of Israel at Mount Sinai. The Law is primarily described in Pentateuch, the first five books of the Old Testament, in particular Exodus, Leviticus, and Deuteronomy. When we interpret it, it is very important to be aware of its contemporary Near East context. The Sinai legislation was actually a remarked moral improvement over the laws of the surrounding nations, such as the Sumerian laws, the Babylonian laws of Hammurabi,[32] and the Hettite laws of Asia Minor. The Mosaic Law emphasizes justice, honesty, not being sentenced without witnesses, and equal rights regardless of ethnicity:

> You are to have the same law for the foreigner and the native-born. I am the Lord your God.[33]

30. See evidence 17.

31. Josh 24:2.

32. The most well-known law prior to Moses' law is perhaps Hammurabi's code, named after a king of Babylon that lived during the seventeenth century B.C.

33. Lev 24:22.

The Old Testament repeatedly emphasizes good treatment of the poor, needy, and slaves:

> If anyone is poor among your fellow Israelites in any of the towns of the land the Lord your God is giving you, do not be hardhearted or tightfisted toward them. Rather, be openhanded and freely lend them whatever they need. Be careful not to harbor this wicked thought: "The seventh year, the year for canceling debts, is near," so that you do not show ill will toward the needy among your fellow Israelites and give them nothing. They may then appeal to the Lord against you, and you will be found guilty of sin. Give generously to them and do so without a grudging heart; then because of this the Lord your God will bless you in all your work and in everything you put your hand to. There will always be poor people in the land. Therefore I command you to be openhanded toward your fellow Israelites who are poor and needy in your land.[34]

The Law also forbids enforced slavery, and sometimes people sold themselves as slaves in order to gain financial security.[35] For marriage polygamy was not part of God's original creation:

> That is why a man leaves his father and mother and is united to his wife, and they become one flesh.[36]

When polygamy occurs in the Old Testament it often causes problems. Between the lines we realize that this was not according to God's will. Neither was divorce God's intention with marriage, but under certain circumstances such as adultery the Law allowed it to happen. Jesus later explained this to the Pharisees in the New Testament:

> Some Pharisees came to him to test him. They asked, "Is it lawful for a man to divorce his wife for any and every reason?" "Haven't you read," he replied, "that at the beginning the Creator made them male and female," and said, "For this reason a man will leave his father and mother and be united to his wife, and the two will become one flesh? So they are no longer two, but one flesh. Therefore what God has joined together, let no one separate." "Why then," they asked, "did Moses command that a man give his wife a certificate of divorce and send her away?" Jesus replied, "Moses permitted you to divorce your wives

---

34. Deut 15:7–15.
35. Exod 21:16; Lev 25:39.
36. Gen 2:24.

because your hearts were hard. But it was not this way from the beginning."[37]

The rules of war were also humanitarian in a contemporary perspective. Men were released from military duty if they were scared, had just been engaged, built a house, or planted a vineyard. The normal rule was to seek peace at first, with war as a last resort.[38]

It is very tempting for us, in spite of these moral improvements of the Mosaic Law over ancient Near Eastern legislations, to adhere to what C. S. Lewis referred to as cultural snobbery[39]—a critique of the Hebrew law from a modern Western perspective. The Sinai legislation consists of several hundred laws, with regulations about sacrifices, food, skin diseases, and other matters, and with harsh punishments (even death penalty) for idolatry and adultery. But the Law was given to Israel as a *theocracy* (a state where God rules) in order to *protect* them from religious influences of the neighboring cultures. God knew how easily the Israelites would forget about him, and therefore he imposed strict rules in order to make all aspects of the Israelite's life holy and set apart. Since the Mosaic Law was a covenant it was not enforced upon the people of Israel, and foreigners were also welcomed to start worshiping Yahweh.

Since God chose to act *in* an ancient Near East context—with all its shortcomings—he did not completely overrule all of its social structures. We cannot compare the Old Testament Law right away with the laws and human rights of modern democratic societies—which, by the way, to a large extent were shaped by Christianity, not the least through the work of Christian missionaries.[40] We must also keep in mind that changing the attitudes of a whole nation takes time. The Mosaic Law was not God's final word, but rather a step towards his ultimate goal of restoring moral ideals from creation where all humans are treated with dignity, without any violence or oppression, and where God's original purpose of marriage is restored. The moral contents and the overall spiritual intention of the Law can still be summarized in the Ten Commandments. It boils down to loving and respecting God and following the golden rule—to treat others as you wish to be treated yourself. And these principles are equally valid today.[41]

---

37. Matt 19:3–8.
38. Deut 20:5–8, 10.
39. Lewis, *Surprised by Joy*.
40. Woodberry, " Missionary Roots" and evidence 3 of this book.
41. Lev 19:18; Deut 6:5; and Matt 7:12. See also evidence 8 for a discussion on how the moral law reflects the Law given to Israel.

Fifth, the Old Testament shows that the Jews could not follow the principles of the Law. In fact, no one can do that by their own effort. Even though the moral commands and sacrifices of the Law were meant to help the Israelites to prosper, remember God, and protect them from the influence of other religions,[42] the book of Judges reveals that the Israelites repeatedly forgot about him and started worshiping other gods. Then they turned back to God during times of hardship after falling into the hands of plundering raiders. The same thing happened later in the history of Israel, and God often criticized the political leadership and the priesthood, not only for idolatry but also for being corrupt. He repeatedly urged them to take care of the poor and needy.[43]

The Old Testament therefore points to a Redeemer very much as a *necessity*, so that the Law gets implanted into our hearts. Then we can *choose* to follow God's will. Several of the Old Testament prophets had this message, for instance Jeremiah:

> "The days are coming," declares the Lord, "when I will make a new covenant with the people of Israel and with the people of Judah. It will not be like the covenant I made with their ancestors when I took them by the hand to lead them out of Egypt, because they broke my covenant, though I was a husband to them," declares the Lord. "This is the covenant I will make with the people of Israel after that time," declares the Lord. "I will put my law in their minds and write it on their hearts. I will be their God, and they will be my people."[44]

Sixth, one may still ask why God punished Israel for violating the Law and the surrounding nations for immorality and violence. To answer this we cannot put a human perspective on God's actions. Instead of "punishment" it is more accurate to say that each cause must have an effect. God is the creator of the universe with a role much different from ours. And life is not a right but a gift of God. Even though humans are not allowed to kill one another, the creator has the right to decide when our lives end. Although we are created in God's image and most valuable to him,[45] it is part of God's holiness, justice, and righteousness that acts against his will have implications. The main message of the Bible is forgiveness, and through Christ we are completely forgiven by grace. But when we as humans consistently turn our

---

42. Deut 6:10–19; 13:1–4.

43. See for instance Exod 22:21–27; the Sabbath Year and the Year of Jubilee in Lev 25; Deut 24:10–22; Ps 41:2–3; Prov 11:24–31; Amos; Isa 10:1–4; and Mal 3:5.

44. Jer 31:31–33. See also evidence 8.

45. Gen 9:6; Exod 20:13.

ways from God he may ultimately remove his protection, sometimes with severe effects. And the ultimate consequence of unforgiven sin is death.[46]

But since God loves us he gives repeated warnings to individuals,[47] cities, and even nations when we are drifting away along the wrong track. He is also very patient, usually giving plenty of time for repentance. In the Old Testament God usually warned and urged not only the Jews but also the surrounding nations by sending prophets to change their way of living, very clearly telling them about the consequences if they did not. Often people did not listen and then God patiently sent new prophets. The book of Jonah illustrates God's mercy when people actually did repent. In the middle of the eighth century B.C., God gave Jonah a mission to warn the Assyrians in the city of Nineveh, because their way of living had reached a point when God reacted. He gave the inhabitants of the city 40 more days before destruction.[48] The prophet first disobeyed God out of fear, but eventually he went to Nineveh and preached, so that the citizens humbled themselves and repented. When God saw this he had compassion and saved the city.

However, there comes a time when no warnings help, when the hearts of people have hardened and a society has been trapped in a state of immorality. Then God allows for bad things to happen and sometimes this is the only way for him to get his message through.[49] Even at this point God forgives and restores the relation with anyone who humbles himself. God always wants to forgive and he constantly hopes that we turn our ways to him.[50] With an eternal perspective in mind, people who repent during disastrous events are saved.

Around 1400 B.C., when Joshua led the Israelites into their Promised Land Rahab hosted a tavern in Jericho. She protected the two Israeli spies that prepared for an attack of the city. Since Rahab acknowledged God she saved herself and her family's life during the battle of Jericho:

> Before the spies lay down for the night, she went up on the roof and said to them, "I know that the Lord has given you this land and that a great fear of you has fallen on us, so that all who live in this country are melting in fear because of you. We have heard how the Lord dried up the water of the Red Sea for you when you came out of Egypt . . . When we heard of it, our

---

46. See also section 2.1 and prior belief 4.
47. This is discussed in chapter 14.
48. Jon 1–4.
49. Isa 26:9–11.
50. There are several examples in the Old Testament of God's forgiving grace, for instance Ezek 18; Mic 7:9; 7:18–20; and Manasseh's life story (response 2 of chapter 14).

hearts melted in fear and everyone's courage failed because of you, for the Lord your God is God in heaven above and on the earth below."[51]

We learn from Rahab that those who encounter or survive tragic events have the chance to repent, seek God, and start over again. When the Babylonians had conquered and destroyed Jerusalem in 586 B.C., a hopeful message was given to the Jews that had been sent to captivity:

> This is what the Lord says: "When seventy years are completed for Babylon, I will come to you and fulfill my good promise to bring you back to this place. For I know the plans I have for you," declares the Lord, "plans to prosper you and not to harm you, plans to give you hope and a future."[52]

Seventh, although we acknowledge that God has a right to decide about his own creation and a mandate to discipline us, some people would still agree with Richard Dawkins' claim that the Old Testament supports genocide and ethnic cleansing of innocent people. But is this true? Well, first of all, humans actually started most of the battles in the Bible and tragic events happen during all wars. When Israel was attacked by enemies, God often helped them in combat in order to save them as a nation. And very often he wanted to minimize violence, as when he commanded the Israelites not to fight the Edomites, Moabites, or Ammonites during their exodus from Egypt.[53] It is true that God told Moses to take vengeance on the Midianites. But this was partly a defense war, since some of the Midianites threatened the nation of Israel morally and spiritually. Inspired by the pagan prophet Balaam, Midianite women had earlier seduced Israeli men sexually so that they started to sacrifice to Baal and other gods.[54]

Around 1030 B.C. God spoke to the prophet Samuel to tell Saul, the first king of Israel, that he should bring the Amalekites to destruction. For hundreds of years this nomadic people had been a major threat to Israel's existence. After the crossing of the Red Sea around 1450 B.C. they were the first to attack the Israelites, while they were exhausted and unprepared for fight. Then other unprovoked assaults took place for generations to come.[55]

But the most difficult war was the attempt of the Israelites under Joshua around 1400 B.C. to drive the Canaanites out from the land once promised to

---

51. Josh 2:8–11.
52. Jer 29:10–11; see also Isa 62; Jer 32:36—33:26.
53. Deut 2.
54. Num 25, 31.
55. Exod 17:8–16; Judg 3:13; 6:3–7; 6:33; 1 Sam 15.

Abraham. This was not a defense war but one that God commanded as part of his long-term plan to prepare space for Israel—ultimately a step towards salvation of all nations. But even though the Canaanites west of Jordan had not provoked the Israelites in a fight, they were far from innocent, neither morally nor spiritually. Inspired by the lives of their deities, the Canaanites were involved in various types of temple sex (which for instance included adultery), bestiality, and even child sacrifice.[56] But God still showed great patience with the Canaanites. Abraham was promised that his descendants would inhabit Israel more than 600 years before the Israelites conquered the land.[57] God did not allow this to happen earlier, since the iniquity of the Canaanites was not yet full. In the meantime God gave them plenty of time to turn away from their way of living.

It is important to remember that these "Yahweh wars" commanded by God were unique. They should not be repeated later in history. Although the Midianites, Amalekites, and Canaanites were far from innocent, there is still much evidence that ethnic cleansing did not take place. God knew that the Israelites would not annihilate them completely, and all three peoples occur frequently later in history.[58] The punishment against the Midianites was only against a particular tribe, and only against those that either were combatants or had seduced the Israelites (something the Law punished with death, also for the Israelites). Paul Copan argues that Moses, Joshua, and Samuel might have used a Near Eastern rhetoric where "complete destruction of everyone" was not to be interpreted literally. It was rather a metaphor for complete victory. In spite of the moral problems of the Canaanites, the ultimate goal of the war of conquest was not to annihilate them. It was rather religious—to remove altars and all other influence of idolatry. And archaeological findings indicate that destroyed cities like Jericho and Ai were military forts, dominated by a male population of combatants. Most other Canaan buildings remained intact.[59]

However, let us assume a worst-case scenario that some children and other innocent people were killed in the Yahweh wars. This is of course very hard for us to grasp. If so, one may argue that if these children would have grown up in a culture that turned its ways against God it would be very difficult for them to get to know him as adults, unless God in some way revealed himself directly to them. In principle this would of course be

---

56. Lev 18:20–30.

57. Gen 15:16; Josh 3. We assume that the promise to Abraham was given between 2100 and 2000 B.C., whereas Israel was conquered around 1400 B.C. See also figure 9.1 for a chronology of these events.

58. Deut 7:22; Josh 23:7, 12–13, Judg 2:10–13; 1 Sam 30; 1 Chr 4:43; Esth 3:10.

59. Copan, *Is God a Moral Monster?*, chapters 15–17, and Deut 6:10–11.

possible.⁶⁰ But God *knew* that the Canaanites would teach the Jews to start worshiping their gods and lead Israel away from him.⁶¹ This doesn't mean that a child or anyone else is judged for things they *would* do in the future. On the contrary, many Bible passages strongly indicate that children who die before the age of moral accountability are saved.⁶²

Does this type of argument warrant holy wars and the killing of innocents today? Not at all! We repeat that the Yahweh wars were unique in the history of Israel, and part of God's plan to send Jesus as Savior of *all* mankind. While it is legitimate to use military forces for defense wars, the New Testament teaches that Satan is the real enemy—not people. Christians should not use violence, but rather spiritual weapons like prayer, and above all love their enemies.⁶³ A person who takes things in his own hands and kills children or other innocents is sinning, not causing his victim any good. It is God who saves a child for eternity, not the perpetrator. And each person has the right to make willing choices and say yes or no to God within the life span given to him *by God*. Therefore, Christians cannot use the Yahweh wars as an excuse for violence today. The Crusades of the Middle Ages are often used as bad examples of such intolerable violence. But they started as a defense war in order to avoid massacres.⁶⁴ When some of the Crusaders later on used the Old Testament as an inspiration for a holy war, their motives were wrong and did not follow Jesus' teaching. Nor can the Yahweh wars be compared with jihad of Islam. The Islamic wars have first of all not been limited in time. They have rather been part of Muslim history ever since the religion was founded by Mohammad in the seventh century.⁶⁵ Nor has it been limited geographically, but directed towards the whole non-Muslim world. Muhammad also followed the teaching of the Qur'an himself and took part in a large number of military battles.

Eighth, Jesus did not come to change the conception of God of the Old Testament, but to *fulfill* the Law and a large number of prophecies in order to complete God's mission of saving humanity:

> Do not think that I have come to abolish the Law or the Prophets; I have not come to abolish them but to fulfill them. For truly I tell you, until heaven and earth disappear, not the smallest letter, not the least stroke of a pen, will by any means disappear

---

60. See the discussion in evidence 19.
61. Deut 20:16–18.
62. See section 5.2.
63. Matt 5:38–48; Eph 2:14–18; John 18:36; 2 Cor 10:3–5; Eph 6:10–18.
64. Stark, *Triumph of Christianity* and evidence 3 of this book.
65. See also evidence 2 and section 4.5.3.

from the Law until everything is accomplished. Therefore anyone who sets aside one of the least of these commands and teaches others accordingly will be called least in the kingdom of heaven, but whoever practices and teaches these commands will be called great in the kingdom of heaven. For I tell you that unless your righteousness surpasses that of the Pharisees and the teachers of the law, you will certainly not enter the kingdom of heaven.[66]

But what exactly did Jesus mean by not abolishing any aspect of the Law? After all he rejected the acts of many religious teachers who tried to follow the Law in every detail. One answer is that the Jewish rabbis had *added* many rules (the so-called oral law, or the "tradition of the elders"[67]) to the Sinai legislation. But apart from this Jesus was speaking about a *deeper meaning* or *intention* of the Law. In order to see this it is helpful to first look at the different parts of the Law. The purpose of the *ceremonial* parts, which stipulated rules for sacrifices and temple service, was to remind the Jews about God and ultimately to advert for Christ. After Jesus' death and resurrection there is no need to follow them, although their overall purpose to obey and love God remains. As we have seen, many of the *social* laws reflect the ancient Near East—a society radically different from ours. We need not and should not follow all of them in detail (like the death penalty for adultery), but their overall purpose still remains—to remind us to follow God. The *moral* laws, such as the Ten Commandments and the golden rule, are absolute and reveal God's timeless character and will. When Jesus came he gave these moral laws a deeper meaning. He criticized any condition of our heart (such as anger, desire, and jealousy) that ultimately may lead to a literal violation of the Law. This is where the Pharisees (and we all) so often fail. But Jesus followed the moral laws—both literally and in the deeper sense—and this is also a goal for us. Not as a path towards salvation, but as a gratitude for being saved by grace, with Christ giving us a new heart that has the moral law written into it.

So the God of the New Testament is actually the same as the God of the Old Testament. When critics say the Jesus' teaching differs radically from that of the Old Testament, they think of his message of divine grace and forgiveness. But this is also present in the Old Testament, although not yet fully revealed. And our choices have consequences in the New Testament as much as they have in the Old Testament. For instance, Jesus was sometimes very harsh towards people who did not repent and turn their ways to him

---

66. Matt 5:17–20. See also evidence 22.

67. Mark 7:1–9; Matt 15:1–2. See also Hill and Walton, *Survey of the Old Testament*, 343; and Boyarin, *Jewish Gospels*, 104.

in spite of much evidence. There are also New Testament passages where God interferes directly as a judge in our world,[68] and then a *final* judgment will take place after the second coming of Christ. The main difference of the New Testament compared to the Old Testament is the possibility for man to receive, as a free gift, a personal relationship with God through belief in Christ. But we still have a choice to take this step or not, just as there was a choice to follow God or not in the Old Testament.[69] And the consequences of saying no are the same.[70]

To summarize; the Old Testament is necessary in order for us to get a deeper understanding of the New Testament—why Jesus had to come as Redeemer. The Old Testament also reveals that when a culture rejects the grace of God it gradually leads itself towards destruction.[71] And this is a warning for our modern society. From a Christian point of view, if God is abandoned our wisdom will not keep pace with increased knowledge from science, technology, literature, and arts. We will then lack the tools for handling technical advancement and material good in a fruitful way. Typical characteristics of such a society are materialism, individualism, a decreased amount of empathy and forgiveness, questioning the nuclear family as a basic unit, less respect for human life before birth, and worsened treatment of the weak, poor, and disabled. Naturalistic humanism, on the other hand, has a very different and optimistic view that mankind is fully capable of taking care of itself.[72]

Evidence 19: Hiddenness of God. What about people that never heard of the gospel during their lifetime? Isn't God unfair if those that grew up in a Christian community have a larger chance of becoming Christians? Is God more silent to some people than to others? The first of these two questions is often referred to as the *destiny-of-the-unevangelized argument* against God, and the last question deals with the *hiddenness of God*. They both seem to contradict our view of God as good and righteous, and for many this is negative evidence against Christianity.

---

68. Luk 10:10–15; Acts 5:1–11; 12:20–23.
69. For a discussion of God as Savior in the Old Testament, see chapter 14 of this book.
70. Rev 20:11–15.
71. Prov 29:18; see also Eccl 3:18–20 and Rom 1:18–25.
72. This is discussed in section 2.2.

The Canadian philosopher J. L. Schellenberg (1959–) has written a book on the hiddenness of God. Part of the argument can be summarized as follows:[73]

1. If God exists, his love is perfect.
2. If a God full of love exists, there is no one who has justified unbelief.
3. Justified unbelief exists.
4. Hence there is no God full of perfect love.
5. Hence there is no God.

The first three of these statements are premises, conclusion 4 follows from premises 2 and 3, and conclusion 5 from premise 1 and conclusion 4. The crucial parts of the argument are premise 2—whether God would allow justified unbelief among persons that never heard of him—and premise 3—whether justified unbelief does exist. These questions are not easy to answer, but God very much wants us to be honest with him. He allows us to ask difficult questions although we may not always get a full answer. There is always a risk of speculating, but we will anyhow try to give some response to Schellenberg's argument.

First, one may argue that God *does* show himself to all of us, at least to some extent. He speaks to us as a designer in nature;[74] through reason, morality, conscience;[75] and by his general providence for each one of us. *Natural theology* argues for the existence of God based on such *general revelations*. In the Roman Epistle Paul writes:

> Since what may be known about God is plain to them, because God has made it plain to them. For since the creation of the world God's invisible qualities—his eternal power and divine nature—have been clearly seen, being understood from what has been made, so that people are without excuse.[76]

According to the Bible these general revelations of God are so obvious that we have no excuse for not seeking him. But God's primary goal is not just to prove his existence but to have a personal relationship with us. The Bible is very clear on this; God *wants* to show his grace and for everyone to come to him:

---

73. Schellenberg, *Divine Hiddenness and Human Reason* and Carlsson, "Guds gömdhet."
74. Evidence 15.
75. Evidence 7 and 8.
76. Rom 1:20; see also Matt 16:1–4.

> But do not forget this one thing, dear friends: With the Lord a day is like a thousand years, and a thousand years are like a day. The Lord is not slow in keeping his promise, as some understand slowness. Instead he is patient with you, not wanting anyone to perish, but everyone to come to repentance.[77]

But God is a gentleman who never forces himself upon anyone. He wants *us* to start longing for him. The general revelation is therefore meant to be a starting point for us to approach God actively. If we do so the Bible promises that he will reveal himself more directly, since everyone who seeks God will find him:

> Ask and it will be given to you; seek and you will find; knock and the door will be opened to you. For everyone who asks receives; the one who seeks finds; and to the one who knocks, the door will be opened.[78]

But God still takes the first step. Our very *desire* to seek him in the first place is a result of him first making a call through the Holy Spirit.[79] Once we have started this journey of seeking God he will manifest himself through various *special revelations*, for instance when we read the Bible[80] or encounter a testimony of Jesus.[81] He may also show himself to us through some *direct revelation*.[82] We may therefore argue that general revelations make justified unbelief non-existent. And this would make premise 3 of Schellenberg's argument invalid.

Second, even though it is possible for everyone to start seeking God, one may still argue that the chances for people of hearing the gospel are very different. But we can trust that God's judgment will be completely fair, since he knows of all our circumstances, thoughts, and inner motives in life. According to the Bible we will be judged based on the information we have about the gospel.[83] Hearing the gospel carries with it a certain responsibility, and growing up in a Christian environment or culture in no way guaran-

---

77. 2 Pet 3:8–9; see also Ezek 33:11; Joel 2:12–14; Luke 15:1–7; 1 Tim 2:4.

78. Matt 7:7–12; Luke 11:9–10.

79. This was discussed in section 3.1. Using the concepts of the Aposteriori Wager in chapter 4, Action is gradually enlarged as Strength of Evidence, Strength of Will or both of them increase while we are seeking God. In particular, this may happen after a changed life situation (chapter 14).

80. Evidence 22.

81. Evidence 23.

82. Miracles are examples of such direct revelations, as discussed in evidence 24.

83. This relates to the discussion in the beginning of chapter 6. See also Rom 2:14–16 and Heb 4:4–6.

tees that one receives Jesus as Savior. This is rather an individual decision between each person and God, and it is not for us to determine who gets saved. When a person dies we can never know whether Jesus had revealed himself shortly before death, giving that person a chance to respond. Since this happened to one of the two criminals that was crucified together with Jesus,[84] it may very well happen today.

Third, one may wonder whether all missionary activity that focuses on evangelism is invalidated if hearing the gospel increases our responsibility to react, and if people could be saved for eternity anyway. All Christian activity should then rather focus on meeting humanitarian needs. But the classical Christian view is that preaching the gospel *and* helping the poor and needy are two inseparable sides of one coin. Neither of them should be downplayed, as described for instance in the Cape Town Commitment of the Lausanne Movement.[85] Although our responsibility depends on how much of the gospel we know, the Bible still makes it clear that salvation is only through Christ,[86] and nowhere does it teach about giving people a second chance of salvation after death.[87] Such a doctrine may give people a false hope.

Some theologians are *inclusivists*. Although they agree that Jesus is the only agent of salvation, they still think that salvation is possible for those that never heard of the gospel. In contrast, *particularists* argue that knowledge of the gospel is required.[88] The latter view has been dominating throughout the history of the church and there are several Bible passages that point in this direction. In the Roman Epistle, for instance, we read:

> If you declare with your mouth, "Jesus is Lord," and believe in your heart that God raised him from the dead, you will be saved. For it is with your heart that you believe and are justified, and it is with your mouth that you profess your faith and are saved. As Scripture says . . . "Everyone who calls on the name of the Lord will be saved." How, then, can they call on the one they have not believed in? And how can they believe in the one of whom they have not heard? And how can they hear without someone preaching to them? And how can anyone preach unless they are sent?[89]

---

84. Luke 23:39–43.
85. Lausanne Movement, "Cape Town Commitment."
86. John 14:6. See also section 3.1 of this book.
87. Luke 16:24–26; Heb 9:27; 2 Cor 5:10.
88. For an overview with further references, see Groothuis, *Christian Apologetics*, chapter 23.
89. Rom 10:9–14.

And many Christians have testified throughout the history of the church that God not only called them to preach the gospel but also blessed and helped them in doing that. This very much confirms the importance of evangelism.

Fourth, although God wants everyone to come to him, he may deliberately hide himself for *some period of time*, so that we start longing for a relationship and then come to him in faith. In the Hebrew Letter of the New Testament we read:

> And without faith it is impossible to please God, because anyone who comes to him must believe that he exists and that he rewards those who earnestly seek him.[90]

This hiddenness of God may therefore be thought of as short-term justified unbelief. But it is not necessarily justified unbelief in the long run.

Fifth, what can we say about premise 2 of Schellenberg's argument? Perhaps it is not so obvious after all? Should we take it for granted that people will give their lives to Jesus if he shows himself very clearly? Or is it so that some would still turn away from him? We found in chapters 6 and 7 that our interpretation of evidence and our willingness to become Christians are both very subjective. Since God has given us a free will,[91] if we deliberately say no to him even though we know of the consequences he will not force us to come to him. God knows of the future and he also knows how each one of us *would* react if we heard the gospel. He may very well show himself directly to those he knows will respond to him in a positive way. And many people who grew up in a non-Christian environment have testified that they encountered Jesus for the first time in a dream.[92] Perhaps God also influences *where* we are born? Recall the Christian view of human nature[93] where the soul/spirit is separated from the body and determines our willingness to seek him. Since God can move outside our notion of time, he knows not only of our future response to the gospel but also of our *potential* reaction if our soul/spirit were born into a body within another

---

90. Heb 11:6.

91. This discussion depends to some extent on what is meant by "free will." Different interpretations of free will are given in evidence 17, as a response to the *argument from unbelief*.

92. See Ottosen, "Need for a Comprehensive Revlation" for a related argument against the hiddenness of God. Ottosen contends that it is not necessary for God to show his existence in a two-step procedure—first in a moderate way and then more personally. Instead, it is possible to enter a personal relationship with God directly through Jesus Christ.

93. Section 2.1.

culture. One may speculate that God lets everyone who wants to receive Jesus grow up in a community where he will hear the gospel preached.[94]

But although we accept that people have a freedom to say yes or no to God it may still be hard to accept this emotionally—not least for our family and close friends. Recall however that God wants everyone to get saved. He is forgiving and willing to accept our surrender to him until the moment when we die.[95] We can never know for sure whether a person has received Christ or not before death, and those who do may not be the ones we thought of.[96] After all, we are the lump of clay and God is the potter.

Evidence 20: Fall of man. The fall of man is very central to Christianity. It is crucial for understanding the problem of evil,[97] for interpreting the Old Testament,[98] and for explaining why Jesus had to come and save us. But many people criticize the fall of man. There are several reasons: that Christianity has a pessimistic view of man, that God is hard and unfair when punishing *all humans* so strongly for the obedience of Adam and Eve, and that the consequences of the fall were so profound. Couldn't God have forgiven Adam and Eve right away? For reasons such as these the fall of man becomes negative evidence and sometimes even a stumbling block for people to become Christians. For instance, Richard Dawkins writes:

> But now the sado-masochism, God incarnated himself as a man, Jesus, in order that he should be tortured and executed in atonement for the hereditary sin of Adam. Ever since Paul espoused this repellent doctrine, Jesus has been worshipped as the redeemer of all our sins. Not just the past sin of Adam: future sins as well, whether future people decided to commit them or not! . . . I have described atonement, the central doctrine of Christianity, as vicious, sado-masochistic and repellent. We should also dismiss it as barking mad, but for its ubiquitous familiarity which has dulled our objectivity. If God wanted to forgive our sins, why not just forgive them, without having himself tortured and executed in payment . . . ?[99]

---

94. This discussion is related to Molinism and God's knowledge of things that *would* happen under different circumstances. For more details, see Craig, *No Easy Answers*, chapter 8.

95. Matt 20:1–16.

96. Matt 25:31–40.

97. Evidence 17.

98. Evidence 18.

99. Dawkins, *God Delusion*, 286–87.

Dawkins correctly notes that the atonement is central to Christianity. However it was not invented in Paul's letters. It was planned even before creation, and the gospels as well as a number of prophecies of the Old Testament speak of Jesus as the Redeemer of our sins.[100] But even if we acknowledge the importance of the fall of man and the atonement we have to be humble and admit that no one fully understands all of their aspects. God wants us to be honest with him and therefore he welcomes difficult questions. And it is indeed common—even among Christians—to have a *sentimental* view and devalue the existence of evil, so that any discussion about the fall and sin gets troublesome.[101] But in spite of our different emotions and preconceptions about the fall, the most important question is still whether it is true or not. And if it is true, how serious are the implications?

There is first of all much indirect evidence for the fall of man in terms of human nature. The most obvious consequence of the fall is our tendency to be selfish—not as a desire but as an enslaving force. We break the moral laws implanted into our hearts, and this has caused lots of violence in human history.[102] But there is plenty other evidence, like feeling *alienated* from home, work, and society: feeling *empty* deep inside in spite of fame, friends, and social activities; *lack of meaning and goals* in life; *striving for spiritual fulfillment*;[103] *materialism*, caused by a desire to fill our emptiness within by riches of the world; and finally *moralism and legalism*, when we express things (even those that are right) in a judging and unloving way. Pascal argued that although the doctrine of the fall is incomprehensible it still has the best explanatory power:

> Certainly nothing jolts us more rudely than this doctrine, and yet, but for this mystery, the most incomprehensible of all, we remain incomprehensible to ourselves. The knot of our condition was twisted and turned in that abyss, so that it is harder to conceive of man without this mystery than for man to conceive it of it himself.[104]

Whereas naturalism has a hard time explaining all these aspects of human nature, for Christianity they make perfect sense. They are all consequences of our broken relationship with God. But Christianity not only offers a

---

100. Gen 3:15; Isa 53; Matt 1:21 and a number of other Bible passages.
101. Keyes, "Sentimentality . . . and It Costs."
102. This is discussed in more detail in evidence 8.
103. See the discussion in evidence 1 about other religions.
104. Pascal, *Pensées*, note 131; and Groothuis, *Christian Apologetics*, chapter 18.

realistic diagnosis of the human condition, it also provides a solution to the problem.[105]

Second, apart from the consequence of the fall, the event *itself* represents human weakness of not resisting temptations that we know are wrong. This weakness is fueled when our intellect makes us increasingly arrogant, although it was given by God in order for us to administer and take care of the world. Sooner or later we tend to cross and invisible line and start to revolt against God, first in order to control our own lives and finally to get rid of him.

Third, we tend to misunderstand the implications of the fall. It does not mean that people can do no good before they turn to Christ. Humans are created in the image of God, and one of the consequences of the fall is our ability to distinguish good from evil.[106] Although we argued that a society develops in a destructive manner if it abandons God,[107] there is still much good done all over the world by followers of various religions. It is true that Christians get filled with the Holy Spirit and are given resources to *choose* to follow God—resources that are meant to have visible effects. This is sadly not always the case though and each one of us will continue to make mistakes.[108] But the meaning of the fall of man is primarily a broken relationship between mankind and God. From this context we see that the largest sin of man is denial of being a sinner and not following God through belief in Christ.[109] The major consequence of the fall is therefore to spend eternity separated from God if one does not *want* to have a relation with him and become a Christian.

Fourth, theologians have different views of whether all humans were punished because of Adam and Eve or whether humanity merely became sinful because of this event. In the latter case we are not punished directly because of Adam and Eve but rather indirectly because of our own inherited tendency to do wrong.[110] In any case one may object that it is unfair to be punished—directly or indirectly—because of the act of one man. But on the other hand it is equally undeserved to be redeemed through belief in Jesus Christ, whose death and resurrection is available for each one of us![111] In

---

105. For more details see Lennox, *Gunning for God*, chapter 6.
106. Evidence 8.
107. Evidence 18.
108. Recall the discussion on this from section 3.1 and evidence 3.
109. John 16:9.
110. Rom 5:13–14, 18–19 and Grudem, *Systematic Theology*, chapter 24.
111. Recall the discussion on this in evidence 19.

fact, the apostle Paul compares the acts of Adam and Jesus as analogous but yet opposite:

> For since death came through a man, the resurrection of the dead comes also through a man. For as in Adam all die, so in Christ all will be made alive.[112]

Fifth, even if we acknowledge that each one of us does wrong, one may still ask why God didn't forgive Adam and Eve and the rest of humanity right away. Was a Redeemer needed? Why did Jesus have to die for our sins? The answers to these questions have to do with two things: the seriousness of our condition after the fall and the holiness of God.[113] Even though Adam and Eve were tempted by the serpent, what they did was still not a simple and thoughtless mistake. It was a deliberate rebellion against God. And since God is holy he cannot tolerate sin—it is against his very nature. Even as humans we often want the perpetrator of a severe crime to be sentenced—not because we want him to suffer but since we require justice and fairness. But as humans we only have a mandate to forgive those who wrong us. Only God can forgive our general tendency to sin and violate his laws. And in order to satisfy God's call for justice these sins have to be paid for in some way.

The Bible describes in detail, when the Law was given to Israel at Mount Sinai,[114] how payment of sins should be carried out through various forms of sacrifice. In order for the Israelites to understand God's holiness the priests were given very strict rules for their ministry in the tabernacle (and later the temple).[115] The Old Testament system of sacrifice culminated once a year on the Day of Atonement when the high priest made a sacrifice for the whole people of Israel including himself. It was only allowed on this day for someone to enter behind the curtain of the tabernacle (and later of the temple) in front of the atonement cover on the ark, where God appeared in a cloud.[116]

The quality of the sacrifice determines how much of the sin is paid.[117] To illustrate this, think of black ink that is dropped by mistake on a piece of white paper. The effectiveness of the cleanser determines how much of the ink is removed. The sacrifices of the Old Testament were just temporary—

112. 1 Cor 15:21–22; see also Rom 5:12–21.

113. See the discussion about Christianity in section 2.1, and the passage on unconditional love (prior belief 4) in section 5.2.

114. Lev 1–17. See also evidence 5.

115. Lev 8–10.

116. Lev 16, 23:26–32.

117. Heb 11:4.

a shadow foretelling of the perfect sacrifice of Jesus Christ, valid for all mankind through all time.[118] The Bible describes the blood of Jesus that was shed on Calvary as this perfect cleanser. Since blood represents life[119] and the life of Jesus was perfect, all who trust in him are given atonement. This is absolutely central to Christianity, and for this reason believers all over the world regularly celebrate Communion to memorize the sacrifice of Christ.[120]

The gospel combines in a very remarkable way two aspects God's character: His *holiness* requires a sacrifice to be made, and in Christ he gives us such an undeserved perfect sacrifice out of *love*. And we have to look into the Bible in order to understand a bit of God's holiness. It says that no one has seen him *face to face* in this world, since none of us would survive such an experience.[121] But we can still perceive the *presence of God*. It is like exposing a seemingly white blanket to light. Once the light is on all dust is made visible. Even many godly characters in the Bible kneeled down, trembled, or confessed their sins when they experienced God's presence in an extraordinary way. For instance, when Isaiah was called as a prophet, he experienced God in a most unusual way:

> In the year that King Uzziah died, I saw the Lord, high and exalted, seated on a throne; and the train of his robe filled the temple. Above him were seraphim, each with six wings: With two wings they covered their faces, with two they covered their feet, and with two they were flying. And they were calling to one another: "Holy, holy, holy is the Lord Almighty; the whole earth is full of his glory." At the sound of their voices the doorposts and thresholds shook and the temple was filled with smoke. "Woe to me!" I cried. "I am ruined! For I am a man of unclean lips, and I live among a people of unclean lips, and my eyes have seen the King, the Lord Almighty." Then one of the seraphim flew to me with a live coal in his hand, which he had taken with tongs from the altar. With it he touched my mouth and said, "See, this has touched your lips; your guilt is taken away and your sin atoned for." Then I heard the voice of the Lord saying, "Whom shall I send? And who will go for us?" And I said, "Here am I. Send me!"[122]

---

118. Heb 8–10.
119. Lev 17.
120. Matt 26:20–29; Mark 14:17–25; Luke 22:14–30; 1 Cor 11:23–32.
121. Exod 33:20.
122. Isa 6:1–8.

Many other biblical characters had a strong vision of God, for instance: Moses at Mount Sinai;[123] Ezekiel when he was called as a prophet;[124] Daniel when he had a revelation on the banks of the Tigris River;[125] the apostles Peter, James, and John when they saw Jesus transfigured on a mountain and heard God's voice;[126] and the apostle John when he encountered Jesus during his Patmos exile.[127] The Israelites wanted to have Moses as their mediator with God at Mount Sinai. They feared speaking directly to the Lord, although Moses urged them not to be afraid but to respect God.[128] When King Solomon had the ark brought into the most holy place of the newly built temple of Jerusalem around 960 B.C., a cloud filled the temple with the presence and glory of the Lord, so that the priests could not perform their service. Shortly thereafter the temple was dedicated, and when Solomon finished praying the glory of the Lord once again filled the temple so that the priests could not enter into it.[129]

Even humans with a close relation to God can sometimes reflect his glory to such an extent that others cannot stand it. For instance, when Moses came down from Mount Sinai with the two tablets of the covenant law his face was so radiant after having spoken with the Lord that the Israelites were afraid to come near him.[130] It has also been reported on several occasions that while the British plumber and preacher Smith Wigglesworth (1859–1947) was praying to God others in the room felt the atmosphere so strongly that they had to leave.[131]

Having experienced a bit of God's holiness, we realize the seriousness of our disease. It then becomes clear that reaching God by our own efforts is absolutely impossible. In order to have a relation with God we are rather totally dependent on his grace, which is reachable *only* through repentance and belief in Christ:

> No one has ever seen God, but the one and only Son, who is himself God and is in closest relationship with the Father, has made him known.[132]

123. Exod 33:12–23; 34:29–35; Heb 12:21.
124. Ezek 1–2.
125. Dan 10:1–10.
126. Matt 17:1–8; Mark 9:2–8; Luke 9:28–36; 2 Pet 1:16–18.
127. Rev 1:9–20.
128. Exod 20:18–19.
129. 1 Kgs 8:1–11; 2 Chr 7:1–2.
130. Exod 34:28–35; 2 Cor 3:7–8.
131. Wilson, *Wigglesworth*.
132. John 1:18.

Therefore, Jesus *had to* die for us.[133]

Evidence 21: Final judgment and hell. The final judgment[134] is a central doctrine of Christianity. It asserts that our final destiny—heaven or hell—is determined by how we respond to Jesus Christ. Many people—even Christians—sometimes ask why a loving God should send people to hell, especially if this is a place of everlasting burning fire with no possibility to repent. Is such a punishment proportional to the severity of the committed crime? What about persons who tried to live a descent life but never heard of the gospel? Questions like these lead us to the *problem of hell*. These thoughts about hell are evidence against Christianity for many, whereas others are drawn closer to Christ by them.

The doctrine of hell is rarely preached today, at least not very explicitly in churches of our Western society. To some extent this reflects a desire to avoid frightening people, and perhaps a fear of speculating. One focuses instead on the love and grace of God through the atoning work of Jesus Christ. This is to some degree sound. But it is also likely that we as Christians are influenced by secular humanistic thinking, according to which we are not accountable to anyone greater than ourselves. And then the question of judgment becomes offensive and makes people skeptical. But the Bible frequently mentions judgment and hell and therefore we have to take these questions seriously—not least for those who ask about our Christian faith and want honest answers. And the teaching of heaven and hell as two possible outcomes has always been central in the history of the church, especially during revivals.

The problem of hell is related to three questions that we discussed before: first of all the problem of evil (How is it possible that an almighty and loving God allows evil in the world, since otherwise no one would end up in hell eternally?), but also the fall of man and the destiny of those who never hear the gospel preached.[135] For this reason we concentrate here on the existence and nature of hell.

First, a minority of theologians advocate *universalism*. This includes a few of the church fathers and some other scholars up to this day.[136] There are different versions of universalism, but typically one argues that the punishment in hell is not eternal, and those who did not receive Christ before

---

133. Gal 2:21.
134. Matt 25:31–46; Rev 20:11–15.
135. See evidence 17, 19, and 20.
136. Baker, *En brännande fråga* and "Vår Gud är en förtärande eld."

death have the opportunity to repent and come to heaven. Maybe they will first spend some time in hell—a kind of rehabilitation—but not eternally. Of course, from our rather limited perspective this may sound appealing, since none of us wants relatives, friends, or others to be eternally separated from God. But the main question is still whether universalism is true or not. And there are many passages in Scripture that describe the consequences of the final judgment as eternal. Nowhere is there a clear indication of people getting a second chance.[137] Therefore it seems very difficult to combine universalism with classical Christianity. If some people deliberately say no to God even when he clearly manifests himself to them,[138] hypothetically the same may happen if they were offered a second chance after death. And it is hard to imagine that God would force anyone to heaven. Moreover—if universalism is wrong—lots of people are given false hopes, perhaps with eternal consequences.

Second, the vast majority of Christians throughout the history of the church believed in a definite judgment after death without a second chance, although the interpretation of this judgment differs. The most common view is *traditionalism*, by which hell is an eternal place where people are sent as part of God's judgment. The *issuant view of hell* is also an eternal place without return, but people get there as a consequence of saying no to Christ—not as a punishment. In any case hell is thought of as real. But how is it like? Bible speaks of hell both in terms of burning fire and complete darkness,[139] suggesting that these pictures should not be interpreted literally. The purpose of these passages could also be to describe hell as a place where the love, joy, and light of God is absent. *Conditionalism*, on the other hand, regards hell as a metaphor for the soul's termination after death rather than a physical reality.[140] In spite of their differences, all these three interpretations of the judgment emphasize that we are not punished *from* heaven to a state of not spending eternity with God after death. We are rather saved through belief in Christ[141] *to* heaven. And God wants by all means each morally accountable individual to accept his only begotten Son.[142] But he does not overrule our free will, whether or not we say yes to him.

---

137. See for instance Swärd, *Efter detta*, Matt 25:1–12, and Luke 14:22–30.
138. John 11:46–53; Rev 9:20–21.
139. See for instance Mark 9:43–48; Rev 20:10–14; and Matt 8:14.
140. Baker, *En brännande fråga*.
141. John 3:16–18.
142. Luke 15:1–10.

Third, in the parables of the New Testament Jesus frequently speaks about the final judgment and hell concurrently with the kingdom of God and heaven.[143] Why is that? In order to understand this we have to look into the Bible, which refers to Jesus as the Truth.[144] In his ministry he was totally honest and wanted the disciples to fully understand the severe consequences of saying no to him. This would help them to know more deeply not only what they were saved to, but also what they were saved from, so that their decision was more informed. This doesn't mean that we should overemphasize the teaching of judgment and hell. But it is still important to lay out the doctrines of the Bible as accurately as possible.

Evidence 22: Reliability and contents of the Bible. What kind of story does the Bible tell, and is the content historically reliable? The Bible is diverse but yet coherent. It contains many confirmed historical eyewitness reports, but also spiritual revelations and astonishingly honest portraits of all its characters. The biblical message is easy for a child to understand but yet full of surprises even for the most educated theologian. These and other aspects of the Bible are for many people strong evidence in favor of Christianity, and here we will look at them one by one.[145]

The Bible is first of all not one single document. It is rather a collection of 66 different books—39 in the Old Testament and 27 in the New Testament. It was written during a long period of 1,500 years by more than 40 different authors, including kings, philosophers, theologians, statesmen, fishermen, historians, and medical doctors. At first this may seem a mosaic of text. And indeed, the biblical books were not only written during different time periods, but the authors also used different original languages and literary styles. Yet the Bible gives an extremely coherent picture of the world, and it offers deep insights into the condition of humanity and human nature. It has a red thread by which God is the creator of a world that humans were given the responsibility to take care of. But men rebelled, the relationship was broken, and God initiated his rescue plan in Christ as described in the New Testament and foretold by prophecies of the Old Testament.

Second, the Bible contains a lot of wisdom. It takes more than a lifetime to fully grasp—even for the best-trained scholar. There are all kinds

---

143. See for instance Matt 13:24–30, 47–52.

144. John 14:6. This is very much in contrast to the devil. According to the Bible he often manifests himself as an angel of light (2 Cor 11:14) and in this way he tries to give people various kinds of false hopes.

145. We already discussed how the Bible relates to natural science in evidence 10, whereas here we focus on the biblical story itself.

of symbols, parallels, and prophecies with multiple meanings that give the text a deeper meaning. Yet the Bible is accessible and readable for anyone, not meant to be read by theologians only. It has often been said that if you cannot explain something simply you probably haven't understood it yourself (a principle that applies to the book you are reading as well). Classical Christianity interprets the Bible as the Word of God. Since it is most reasonable to assume that God understands his own creation, we should therefore expect that the Bible is accessible and comprehensible. And indeed, Jesus himself was a master of illustrating deep theological and philosophical principles in terms of parables, and many of the life stories of the Old Testament are taught in Sunday schools all over the world. The Bible can indeed be read at several different layers of depth like no other book. This is much like when you use a cheese cutter to eat a piece of cheese.

Third, many archaeological findings support the reliability of the Old Testament. More than 50 years ago archaeologist Nelson Glueck (1900–71) made the following statement:

> As a matter of fact . . . it may be stated categorically that no archaeological discovery has ever confronted a biblical reference. Scores of archaeological findings have been made which confirm in clear outline or exact detail historical statements in the Bible.[146]

The archaeological material is even larger today. This includes the names of a large number of Israeli, Judaic, Assyrian, Babylonian, or Egypt kings or places referred to in the Bible that have been found in old scriptures. During excavations archaeologists have found the ruins of Nineveh,[147] the remnants of the walls of Jericho,[148] the town of Gibea where Saul resided,[149] and Hezekiah's tunnel in Jerusalem,[150] to mention just a few. In fact, there are Assyrian sources confirming King Ahab of Israel as early as 853 B.C.,[151] and other findings from Jerusalem that possibly originate from the time of King David around 1000 B.C.[152]

---

146. Glueck, *Rivers in the Desert*, 31. See also Geisler, *Systematic Theology*.
147. Nah 1:13–15.
148. Josh 6:1–30.
149. 1 Sam 10:25–27.
150. 2 Kgs 20:20.
151. See 1 Kgs 22.
152. It should be added however that a large number of archaeologists regard Bible passages on the patriarchs (Abraham, Isaac, and Jacob) and the exodus as myths; see for instance Furuhagen, *Bibeln och arkeologerna*. This view is challenged for instance by Kitchen, *On the Reliability of the Old Testament*. It is well known that absence of

Fourth, population genetics can be used to trace the ancestry of Jewish populations in a way that seems to agree very well with the Old Testament account. For instance, some recent studies indicate that a large majority of all Jews alive today originate from the Middle East, although quite naturally there is some degree of admixture with the European and North African host populations.[153] This Middle East ancestry fits well with the biblical record, according to which the current worldwide Jewish population (except for the "lost tribes"[154]) are descendants of those Jews that were scattered during the Babylonian exile around 600 B.C.[155] Then some degree of admixture with the surrounding populations took place after this Diaspora.

Since Jewish origin is often determined by the mother it is of interest to analyze the maternal ancestry of Jews. This has been done for Ashkenazi Jews and the results suggest there are only four founders for almost half of this population.[156] The DNA of these founders is found at much lower frequency in non-Jewish populations, suggesting that their ancestry is from the Middle East. Most likely these founders lived no earlier than the

---

archaeological evidence is not necessarily evidence of absence, and Kitchen gives a number of indirect arguments for the reliability of the Old Testament. Regarding the Israeli exodus from Egypt, a major argument has been that the destruction of Jericho and Ai in Josh 6 and 8 did not take place around 1400 B.C., as claimed in the Bible. Others argue for a literal chronology of these events. Crucial for this discussion is the timing of Egyptian dynasties, which are often used as markers of other occurrences. See for instance Möller, *Exodus Case*.

153. Principal component analysis and admixture analysis has been conducted on genomic data for a large number of non-Jewish and Jewish diaspora communities. See Atzmon et al., "Abraham's Children in the Genome Era,"; Behar et al., "Genome-Wide Structure of the Jewish People"; and Bray et al., "Signatures of Founder Effects." The conclusion is that a vast majority of Jews (for instance Ashkenazi, Sephardi, Caucasian, and North African) have a significant Middle East ancestry, with some degree of admixture from the surrounding host populations. In contrast, the Ethiopian and Indian Jews seem to have a higher degree of genetic influence from their host populations. This does not contradict ancestry form the Middle East, since the degree of admixture could have been much larger for these (small) groups. According to one tradition the Ethiopian Jews are believed to be descendants of King Solomon and the Queen of Sheeba (1 Kgs 10:10–13). This corresponds to an early common ancestry with other Jews from the tenth century B.C. An alternative explanation would be that many Ethiopian Jews are descendants of proselytes.

154. 2 Kgs 17:7–41.

155. Evidence 5.

156. The Ashkenazi Jewish population is believed be descendants of an early medieval Jewish community along the Rhine in Germany, who migrated from northern Italy. Then their descendants spread to other parts of Europe and more recently to other continents, in particular North America. Today it comprises a majority of the worldwide Jewish population.

patriarch Jacob slightly before 1900 B.C.,[157] but no later than the medieval era, when the Ashkenazi community settled in Germany.[158]

The Jewish priesthood (Cohanim), on the other hand, is paternally inherited. According to the Bible these Jewish priests are descendants of Moses' brother Aaron, who lived around 1450 B.C.[159] Paternally inherited DNA (Y-chromosomes) has been analyzed for more than 200 Cohanims from *diverse* Jewish communities. The results revealed that almost half of them (46 percent) had lineages merging to a common ancestral lineage at a time that doesn't contradict that of Aaron about 3,500 years ago. Half of this subgroup of priests had part of their Y-chromosome identical. This variant occurs at a much lower frequency among other Jews and it is almost absent among non-Jews. In addition it seems that many of the remaining Cohanims (outside of the 46 percent group) are descendants of a few other persons of Middle East ancestry who lived at a time that does not contradict the Old Testament record. A possible explanation is that non-descendants of Aaron were ordained as priests and that some of their heirs are among the Cohanims alive today.[160]

Fifth, ancient documents strongly support Jesus as a historical person who lived and walked on Earth. These sources include not only the Bible but also a number of external texts. For instance, the first-century Roman historian Tacitus (c. 56–117) mentions Christians in his work *Annales*, and so

---

157. See figure 9.1 for the assumed chronology.

158. For an analysis of the ancestry of Ashkenazi Jews from patterns of mitochondrial DNA inheritance, see Behar et al., "Matrilineal Ancestry of Ashkenazi Jewry." It should be emphasized that estimates of age of founders rely on assumptions on how often mutations occur—the molecular clock. We use the word "founder" for the most recent merger of all the maternal lineages within each of the four groups of Ashkenazi Jews.

159. Exod 28–29.

160. All participants in the study self-reported themselves as Cohanim, Levite, other Jewish tribe, Jew with unknown origin, or non-Jew. The estimated frequency of the most common ancestral lineage was 46 percent, with a 95 percent confidence interval ranging between 39 and 53 percent for all Cohanims that belong to this group. The Cohen Modal haplotype is present among almost half of this group of Cohanims. It consists of 12 highly variable genetic markers along the Y-chromosome. The estimated time of the most recent common ancestor for the 46 percent group of Cohanims is 3,190 years plus or minus a standard error of 1,090 years. See Hammer et al., "Extended Y Chromosome Haplotypes." The Bible suggests a merging time which is at most 3,500 years. This is well within one standard error from the 3,190 years, given that the assumed molecular clock rate is correct. Previous studies with smaller data sets not overlapping the one used by Hammer et al. give similar but less definite conclusions. See Skorecki et al., "Y Chromosomes of Jewish Priests" and Thomas et al., "Origins of Old Testament Priests."

does the Jewish historian Josephus (37–c. 100) in *Antiquities of the Jews*.[161] Most people would therefore agree that Jesus is not a myth. They would rather say that he lived 2,000 years ago, and answer yes to the top question of figure 12.1.

But current research indicates not only that Jesus existed, but that the New Testament in general and the four gospels in particular are reliable eyewitness reports. The books of the New Testament are by far the antique manuscripts with the largest number of preserved hand-written copies that date comparatively close to the time when the original documents were written.[162] In view of the well-established Jewish oral and mnemonic tradition and the very accurate scribal techniques of copying text, many scholars believe this time gap between the original and the copies is too small for the contents to have been distorted in a substantial way and for myths to have been created. This is particularly so for creeds, hymns, poetry, and story summaries of the first Christians—they predate the writing of the New Testament and seem to have been copied into the text.[163] In fact, many scholars believe that three of the gospels (Matthew, Mark, and Luke) were written down while some persons contemporary to Jesus were still alive so that errors could easily have been revealed as fraud—not the least by the opponents of the early church. The authenticity of the New Testament is further strengthened by linguistic analyses which seem to indicate that the frequencies of personal names in the four gospels concord well with those of Jews that lived in Palestine 300 B.C.–A.D. 200.[164] Another very interesting finding is a Roman stone inscription that was found at Delphi close to Corinth in the early twentieth century. It reports Gallio as a proconsul of

161. Burge et al., *New Testament in Antiquity*.

162. For instance, the Dead Sea Scrolls were found in 1947–56, with manuscripts dated from the period 250 B.C.–A.D. 70. They contain parts of most Old Testament books. These texts have a very high degree of concordance with the previously oldest known copies from medieval times. Some scholars believe that Mark 6:52–53 is included among the Dead Sea Scrolls, although opinions differ on the origin of this text fragment; see Green, "Dödahavsrullarna." The oldest known New Testament manuscript is John Rylands Papyri, with three verses from the Gospel of John (18:31–33). It is dated to A.D. 125, only 30 years after a commonly claimed time of authorship. The Chester Beatty Papyri from A.D. 200 contains large parts of the New Testament.

163. Habermas and Licona, *Case of the Resurrection of Jesus* and Habermas, "Resurrection of Jesus' Timeline." Dodd suggested that 1 Cor 15:3–8 is a passage that Paul received from Peter and James a few years after his conversion during a visit to Jerusalem around A.D. 35 (Gal 1:18–19). Today most scholars believe that this is true. The creed then represents very early Christian church belief, created at most a handful of years after Jesus' resurrection. Dodd, *Founder of Christianity*.

164. See Bauckham, *Jesus and the Eye Witnesses* and the Jewish name statistics collected in Ilan, "Lexicon of Jewish Names in Late Antiquity."

Achaia during A.D. 51–52. This agrees very well with the book of Acts, where Junius Gallio (5 B.C.–A.D. 65) is mentioned while Paul stayed in Corinth as part of his second missionary journey.[165] There are also non-biblical Christian literary sources from some of the early church fathers. For instance, the remaining fragments of the writings of Papias (c. A.D. 60-130)—bishop of Hierapolis in modern Turkey in the early second century—give valuable details about the first church.[166] All this evidence strongly indicates that the New Testament is a reliable historical document. Many people would therefore answer yes also to the second question of figure 12.1, and believe that Jesus' life and ministry is accurately described in the Bible.

Sixth, if the gospels are reliable eyewitness reports their records of Jesus strongly indicate that he was not only human. He seemed to possess a number of qualities that were well in line with his divine claims. C. S. Lewis once commented that since Jesus identified himself with God, he was either speaking the truth, lying, or mentally sick[167] (see figure 12.1). But the last two alternatives are very difficult to harmonize with what we read in the gospels, where Jesus is described as a very loving person who cared for everyone and was appreciated by the outcast. He was not afraid of speaking up against religious hypocrisy and injustice,[168] even though it cost him his life. Nor did he seek political power for himself.[169] His disciples followed him daily for three years. It would have been remarkable if they did not discover traces of a distorted personality of someone that either lied of falsely believed he was divine. Another possibility is that the followers spread Christianity after Jesus' death because they were either deluded or lying. But the first chapters of the book of Acts give a very different picture. The disciples didn't firmly believe in Jesus as God until they saw him resurrected. And even thereafter they met in private until the first day of Pentecost. The Holy Spirit then gave them power and courage to speak out more boldly.[170] This clearly indicates they had not been fooled. Many of the disciples even died for their faith. This would have been remarkable if they knew they were lying about Christ and his resurrection from death.

165. Acts 18:12–17.
166. Bauckham, *Jesus and the Eye Witnesses*.
167. This argument is known as Lewis's trilemma. It was first used for apologetic purposes in nineteenth century, but today it is most well known from Lewis, *Mere Christianity*.
168. John 4; Luke 19:1–10; and Luke 19:47–48. For more on the identity of Jesus, see Craig, *Reasonable Faith*, chapter 7; Gustavsson, *Kristen på goda grunder*, chapter 7; and Ewert, *Vem tänder stjärnorna?*, chapter 1.
169. John 19:35–37.
170. Acts 1–2.

Since the resurrection of Jesus is at the core of Christianity, it is particularly important to address its authenticity. Interestingly, most scholars on the subject believe that the resurrection did take place in some way or another. This also includes more liberal theologians who are otherwise critical concerning the authenticity of the New Testament. The argument in favor of the resurrection is based on the following *minimal facts*, which a majority of scholars agree on:[171]

1. Jesus died by crucifixion.
2. Jesus' disciples not only claimed but also believed that he rose and appeared to them.
3. The church persecutor Paul was suddenly changed.
4. The skeptic James, brother of Jesus, was suddenly changed.
5. The tomb was empty.

These five facts are based on biblical as well as non-biblical sources. If they are true, all naturalistic interpretations of the resurrection seem very unlikely. These natural explanations include that Jesus never died on the cross, that the Roman soldiers stole Jesus' body, that the disciples lied and stole Jesus' body, that the women who first claimed he had resurrected came to the wrong tomb, that the resurrection story gradually embellished into a legend, that supernatural tales of other religions have to be taken equally seriously as Jesus' resurrection, that the disciples were deluded, that the disciples had illusions or that they were hallucinating. For a more detailed account of all of these explanations we refer to the book by Gary Habermas (1950–) and Michael Licona (1961–).[172]

But it is not only the gospels that give credibility to Jesus as the Son of God. The Old Testament contains a number of messianic prophecies that Jesus later fulfilled. We know from historical data alone (the Dead Sea Scrolls) that the Old Testament is older than the New Testament. And if Jesus was only human he could possibly not fix many of the messianic prophecies himself. Indeed, if Jesus was not God he could not influence being born in Bethlehem[173] by a woman not yet married,[174] growing up in Galilee,[175] being

---

171. Habermas and Licona, *Case of the Resurrection of Jesus* and Habermas, "Resurrection of Jesus' Timeline." A probabilistic argument for the plausibility of Jesus' resurrection is presented in McGrew and McGrew, "Argument from Miracles."

172. Ibid.

173. Mic 5:2; Luke 2:1–21.

174. Isa 7:14; Luke 1:26–38.

175. Isa 9:1–7; Matt 1:23.

betrayed for 30 pieces of silver, money that was used for buying the potter's field,[176] being punished in spite of the fact that Pilate couldn't find him guilty of any crime,[177] having his clothes divided by lottery between the Roman soldiers before the crucifixion,[178] being pierced and mourned for during the crucifixion,[179] not having his bones crushed after his death,[180] being buried in a rich man's grave,[181] resurrecting from death on the third day,[182] and getting many disciples after the resurrection with followers from all over the world.[183] There is also another remarkable messianic prophecy in the book of Daniel that concerns the timing of Jesus' crucifixion.[184] Daniel mediated it during the Babylonian exile, some decades after Jerusalem had been destroyed in 586 B.C. Although theologians interpret Daniel's prophecy differently, it possibly predicts Jesus' death on Calvary to occur 69 or 70 sabbatical years after Jerusalem started to be rebuilt. A sabbatical year is a seven-year cycle and the number of sabbatical years until the crucifixion depends on whether week 70 is assigned to the end of times or not. If not, the period is 7x70=490 years. Assuming that the reconstruction of Jerusalem started under the leadership of Ezra the priest in 458 B.C. after a decree from the Persian king Artaxerxes I (c. 465-24 B.C.),[185] the prophecy predicts that Jesus was crucified in A.D. 33. According to many New Testament scholars this is also the most likely year of Jesus' death and resurrection![186]

Combining all these accounts of Jesus from the Old Testament and the gospels, the only plausible explanation is that he was the one he claimed to be—our Lord and Savior, the leftmost alternative of figure 12.1.

---

176. Jer 18:1-4; Zech 11:12-13; Matt 27:9.
177. Isa 53:1-12; Matt 27:15-26.
178. Ps 22:19; Matt 27:35.
179. Zech 12:10; Luke 23:48; John 19:34-35.
180. Exod 12:46; Num 9:12; Ps 34:20; John 19:31-33, 36.
181. Isa 53:9. According to Matt 27:57-60 the tomb of Jesus belonged to Joseph, a rich man from Arimathea.
182. Ps 16:10; Hos 6:1-2; Jon 2:1; Matt 12:38-41.
183. Isa 53:10; Dan 7:13-14.
184. Dan 9:24-27.
185. Ezra 7.
186. If years before Christ are written as negative numbers we find that Daniel's prophecy predicts Jesus' crucifixion in year A.D. $-458+70 \times 7+1=33$. The extra term $+1$ accounts for the fact that year zero is left out in the Gregorian calendar. See for instance Almkvist, *Framtiden förutsagd* and references therein.

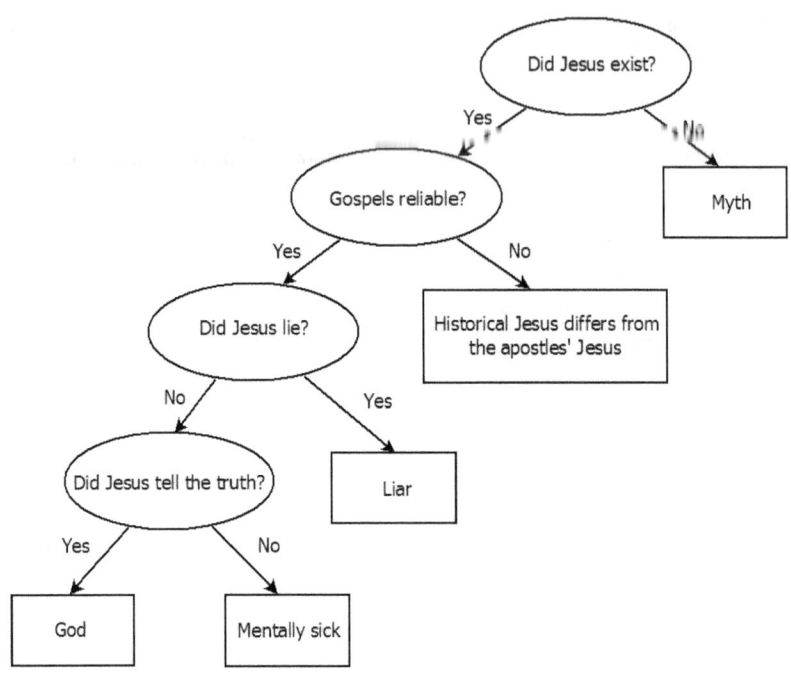

Figure 12.1: Who was Jesus? See the text for a discussion of the various possibilities.

Seventh, the Bible is remarkably honest. The shortcomings and weaknesses of several of its most important characters are described in detail. In the book of Genesis we read that Abraham told half a lie about Sarah being his sister, not his wife.[187] His son Isaac similarly lied about his wife, Rebekah,[188] and his grandson Jacob cheated Esau in order to receive his father's blessings.[189] Later on in the Old Testament we learn that Moses killed an Egyptian,[190] and that King David committed adultery and indirectly ordered the man he was cheating on to be killed.[191] In the New Testament we find that the apostles James and John seemed to be vengeful when they suggested that a Samaritan village should be destroyed[192] and proud when they asked for the best seats in the kingdom of heaven.[193] The apostle Peter denied Jesus three

---

187. Gen 20:1–17.
188. Gen 26:1–32.
189. Gen 27.
190. Exod 2:11–13.
191. 2 Sam 11.
192. Luke 9:51–56.
193. Matt 20:20–28.

times,[194] and in the book of Acts we read that Barnabas and the apostle Paul had a dispute and disagreed on whether or not Mark should follow them on a missionary journey.[195] The traditional opinion is that many of these persons are authors of large parts of the Bible. For instance, it is believed that Moses wrote about his own life story in Exodus, and Peter's denial of Jesus is vividly described in the Gospel of Mark, who probably was a disciple of Peter. It seems unlikely that their goal was to invent myths and start a new religious tradition based on their own ideas. A more credible explanation is that their writing was divinely inspired. Indeed, the main idea of the Bible is to tell about the broken relationship between God and mankind and the rescue plan for humanity. The shortcomings of otherwise very godly persons are very much in line with this, since *all* humans have sinned. The Bible also describes how these men humbled themselves, received God's forgiveness, and learned from their mistakes. In this way their life stories are good examples of the grace of God.

Eighth, many Christians believe that the Bible has something important to say about the world today, such as the establishment of modern Israel in 1948[196] and the second coming of Christ.[197] No one except God knows the exact time point of Jesus' return,[198] but the Bible speaks of signs[199] that will characterize the time before this event. Two such signs are the spread of the gospel to most parts of the world[200] and an increasingly individualistic and materialistic society.[201] The eschatological interpretation of some of these signs varies among Christians, in particular how to interpret the last part of the Bible—the book of Revelation.[202] According to the most literal (so-called futurist) interpretation, the book of Revelation describes

---

194. Mark 14:66–72; Matt 26:69–75; Luke 22:54–62.

195. Acts 15:36–41.

196. See evidence 5.

197. Acts 1:11.

198. Matt 24:32–36.

199. Dan 9, 12; Zech 14; Matt 24:1–22; Luke 21:7–24; 2 Thess 2:1–12; Rev 13.

200. Matt 24:14. The Joshua Project highlights ethnic groups with the smallest proportion of Christians. According to their statistics there is still some way to go in order to complete the Great Commission. More than 40 percent of the worldwide human population belongs to an unreached people group (less than 5 percent professing Christians and less than 2 percent evangelical Christians). Joshua Project, "Bringing Definition."

201. 2 Tim 3:1–9.

202. In Christian eschatology it is common to distinguish between four main views: futurist, preterist, historicist, and idealist. Among these the futurist approach is the most literal one. Since biblical prophecies may refer to multiple events the four approaches need not be contradictory. See Ibstedt, *Uppenbarelseboken* and references therein.

real events that will happen in the future before Jesus returns, with an evil-minded world ruler that will come to power, effectively control people, and enforce worship of him.[203] Although our globalized world with the Internet and a centralized economy has some advantages, many people regard it as a suitable environment for such a world ruler. Several Bible passages indicate that this period is characterized and/or preceded by a time of suffering of Christians and Jews and a rebuilding of the temple in Jerusalem.[204] The proclamation of the modern state of Israel and the political situation in the Middle East do not contradict this, nor does the fact that Christians are the most persecuted group of people today.[205]

Finally, most Christians witness that God speaks directly to them when they read from Scripture. The Bible refers to itself as the sword of the Spirit or as a double-edged sword:

> For the word of God is alive and active. Sharper than any double-edged sword, it penetrates even to dividing soul and spirit, joints and marrow; it judges the thoughts and attitudes of the heart.[206]

It is true that God may speak to us also when we read other books, but the Bible is still unique. For instance, the Holy Spirit may lead us to understand Bible passages that are very relevant for our life situation. This often happens when we face a decision, are longing for comfort, or need correction.

---

203. See in particular Rev 13.

204. See for instance Matt 24:1–22 and Rev 11:1–14.

205. For instance, the number of Christian martyrs during 2000–2010 has been estimated at 1 million, although this includes victims of war. There have been many periods of persecution of Christians during the history of the church (evidence 6), but these statistics show that our modern time is one of the worst; Johnson et al., "Christianity 2011." The evangelical Open Doors organization monitors persecution against Christians. They found that persecution is *increasing* today in many countries, with more than 100 million Christians worldwide facing some type of severe threat. Their statistics reveal that 2015 was the worst year in modern history for Christian persecution, with more than twice as many being killed for their faith compared to the year before. They also provide an annually updated list of countries with most opposition against Christians. This list ranks communist North Korea as the worst persecutor of Christians, followed by nine countries with a Muslim majority. Open Doors, "World Watch List." According the Pew Research Center, Christians faced governmental or social harassment in 108 nations, Muslims in 100 nations, and Jews in 81 nations in 2014. The last figure is very high since the Jews only comprise 0.2 percent of the worldwide population. It should also be noted that much of the persecution of Muslims takes place in Muslim countries. Henne et al., "Trends in Global Restrictions on Religion." For another recent and very comprehensive account of persecution against Christians, see Allen, *Global War on Christians*.

206. Heb 4:12.

Many people have even *become* Christians by reading the Bible. Augustine of Hippo lived in northern Africa and Italy around A.D. 400. After several years of struggle about Christianity, at the age of 32 he read two verses of Scripture from Paul's Letter to the Roman church:

> Let us behave decently, as in the daytime, not in carousing and drunkenness, not in sexual immorality and debauchery, not in dissension and jealousy. Rather, clothe yourselves with the Lord Jesus Christ, and do not think about how to gratify the desires of the flesh.[207]

This Bible passage spoke directly into his life and it had a great impact on his conversion. He then became one of the most influential theologians and church fathers of all time.[208]

Nicky Gumbel (1955–) is the main developer of the Alpha course concept. He wanted to persuade two of his friends that had recently become Christians to abandon their faith, because he thought they were wrong. In order to get more information he started to read through the New Testament—the four gospels, the book of Acts, and the first of Paul's letters. Although he grew up in a Christian environment and had read the Bible before, the words suddenly came alive. He felt they conveyed a sense of truth in a very powerful way. Quite soon after this experience he became a Christian.[209]

---

207. Rom 13:13–14.
208. Augustine, *Confessions*. See also Halldorf, *21 kyrkofäder*.
209. Gumbel, *Telling Others*.

13

Personal Evidence

WHAT ABOUT EXTRAORDINARY EVENTS that seem to lack natural explanations, or the changed lives of persons we know of well that became Christians? In this chapter we consider these types of experiences. It is often considered as the strongest type of evidence in favor of Christianity, and therefore we put it last.

Evidence 23: Testimonies. It is well known among psychiatrists and medical doctors that very often religious belief in general and Christian belief in particular is beneficial for human health. For instance, the former Professor of psychiatry Andrew Sims (1938-) cites a major meta-analysis of the American Journal of Human Health on epidemiological studies of the effects of religious belief:

> In the majority of studies, religious involvement is correlated with well-being, happiness and life satisfaction; hope and optimism; purpose and meaning in life; higher self-esteem; better adaptation to bereavement; greater social support and less loneliness; lower rates of depression and faster recovery from depression; lower rates of suicide and fewer positive attitudes towards suicide; less anxiety; less psychosis and fewer psychotic tendencies; lower rates of alcohol and drug use and abuse; less delinquency and criminal activity; greater marital stability and satisfaction... We concluded that for the vast majority of people the apparent benefits of devout religious belief and practice probably outweigh the risks.[1]

---

1. Sims, *Is Faith Delution?*, 100. See also Habermas, "Plight of the New Atheism"; Pearcey, *Total Truth*, 59–60; Lennox, *Gunning for God*, chapter 2 and references therein

This doesn't mean that Christianity is a free ticket to an easy and apparently successful life without complications. It can sometimes rather be the opposite, especially in countries where religious freedom is either absent or at least severely restricted. But recent research indicates that persons who find their life meaningful and regard their work as a special *calling* from God are more likely to be productive in the long run compared to those that are motivated either by reward of success or have a fatalistic point of view, with limited possibilities to influence the outcome of their work. Indeed, persons who feel they are unconditionally loved by God—who has given them responsibility in terms of a calling and natural or spiritual gifts to accomplish it—are more likely not only to endure various types of difficulties and obstacles but also to find creative ways to circumvent them.[2]

The history of the church is full of testimonies of people who claim their lives changed after coming to Christ. The question is whether this is a spiritual reality or if Christians are deluded persons that live on a myth. Many would regard not only their stories but also the visible changes in their lives as very strong *arguments from testimonies* or *arguments from religious experience* in favor of a supernatural explanation.[3] Perhaps the most common reason for people to become Christians is the impact of a relative or close friend who previously came to faith. When noticing the changed priorities and fruits of the Holy Spirit[4] in their friend's life, they find no natural explanations. The more *reliable* the friend is and the more his behavior has changed, the stronger is the evidence.

The testimonies of Christians with a tough background tend to be particularly strong, since their changed way of living is so obvious and their gratitude to God so large. Jesus explained this to Simon the Pharisee when a woman with reputation as a great sinner anointed him with perfume as a token of great love and gratefulness:

> "Therefore, I tell you, her many sins have been forgiven—as her great love has shown. But whoever has been forgiven little loves little." Then Jesus said to her, "Your sins are forgiven."[5]

---

for more details about the emotional and mental advantages of faith.

2. For some recent research results in this direction, see Supphellen, "Økonomiske effekter" and Leijon, "Lutheranism or Secularism" and references therein. See also evidence 4 for a related discussion about creativity and culture.

3. For a comprehensive discussion on religious experience, see Kwan, "Argument from Religious Experience" and references therein.

4. Gal 5:22–26.

5. Luke 7:36–50.

A Christian with deep faith often shows great integrity and he is not easily controlled by the opinion of others. This fits well with the biblical view that the love of God removes fear.[6]

In the Bible we find many testimonies of people whose lives changed after an encounter with Jesus. In chapter 1 of this book we mentioned Paul. He was once a persecutor of the first Christians, but after conversion he became one of the most successful missionaries in the history of the church.[7] Jesus once met a Samaritan woman at Jacob's well at Sychar. Her life had not been easy and she had a bad reputation. She was convinced that Jesus was the Messiah when he spoke prophetically about her five previous husbands and that her spouse was not her husband. Then she gave such a strong testimony in her home town about the conversation with Jesus that several others came to faith.[8] Zacchaeus was a wealthy chief tax collector with a bad reputation of cheating others. One single encounter with Jesus completely changed his priorities. He promised to give half of his possessions to the poor and to pay back four times the amount he had stolen.[9]

The history of the church is full of witnesses of other people whose lives changed completely after becoming Christians. The well-known book *The Cross and the Switchblade* tells the story of a pastor, David Wilkerson (1931–2011), and his work among New York criminal gangs in the 1950s.[10] One of the most feared gangsters, Nicky Cruz (1938–), converted and became a world evangelist.[11] Tass Saada (1951–) was one of Yassir Arafat's most feared snipers in PLO. He was driven by hatred, but after turning to Christ he started to love the Jews he once hated. Today he is a major spokesman for reconciliation between Jews and Palestinians in the Middle East. He believes that the only lasting way to peace is for Jews and Palestinians to give their lives to Jesus.[12]

---

6. 1 John 4:16–18. It may seem as a contradiction that obedience to God gives a person freedom. But from the Christian point of view each one of us is controlled by something that is either good or bad for our long-term well-being (see figure 4.6). Recall the discussion in willingness attitude 1 of chapter 7, and the illustration of figure 14.1, that the perceived reward of not only believing in but also following God increases after becoming a Christian.

7. Acts 9:1–30.

8. John 4:1–42.

9. Luke 19:1–9.

10. Wilkerson, *Cross and the Switchblade*.

11. Cruz and Harris, *Lonely but Never Alone*.

12. Saada and Merrill, *Once an Arafat Man*.

Evidence 24: Miracles and prophecy. We have already argued that the *existence* of miracles does not contradict natural science, since miraculous events are exceptions of the laws of nature.[13] Here we will argue for miracles as *evidence* of Christianity given that they happen and are experienced by people. This is known as the *argument from miracles*.[14]

A miracle or a claimed divine message is first of all not necessarily from God.[15] It has to be tested if it accords with the Bible and glorifies God. But if someone experiences a miracle from God there is possibly no stronger evidence for Christianity, almost like a direct encounter with him. It very often leads to a decision for Christ and usually it has a big impact on the person for the rest of his life.[16]

In the gospels we read about several individuals that came to faith after witnessing a miracle of Jesus. When Jesus healed an official's son the whole family started to believe,[17] and so did a blind man after getting his sight back.[18] When Jesus fed 5,000 people many of them acknowledged him as Messiah and they wanted to make him their king.[19] And many Jews believed after having seen Jesus raising Lazarus from the dead.[20] All four gospels are full of similar details from Jesus' ministry.

The greatest miracle of all is Jesus' resurrection from the tomb. The apostle Thomas's encounter with the risen Jesus made him believe that his teacher was also his savior. The experience of the resurrection was also very important for the other apostles in order to keep their faith and for the early church to spread. Paul's revelation of Jesus on his way from Jerusalem to Damascus converted him from a persecutor of Christians to a follower of Christ.[21] In the First Letter to the Corinthian Church he mentions of followers that Jesus revealed himself to after he had risen from death and before the ascension.[22]

---

13. See evidence 11.

14. See for instance Swinburne, *Existence of God*, chapter 12; McGrew and McGrew, *Argument of Miracles* and references therein.

15. Exod 7:8–13; Jer 23:9–40; Matt 24:24; Mark 13:22; 2 Thess 2:9–12; Rev 13:15.

16. Heb 2:4. The miracle may either happen to oneself or to others. Bovens uses a probabilistic argument to compare the evidentiary force of these two types of miracles (referred to as the St. Paul and Beatist protocols). Bovens, "Does It Matter?"

17. John 4:53.

18. John 9.

19. John 6:14–15.

20. John 11:45.

21. Acts 9:1–19.

22. 1 Cor 15:4–8.

The ministry of the first apostles was also accompanied by miracles that made people believe. A crippled man was healed at the Beautiful Gate in Jerusalem when Peter and John ministered, and the same day a large number of persons came to faith.[23] When Philip preached the Word in Samaria paralytics and cripples were healed, and evil spirits came out of many with shrieks. People reacted with joy and a large number of them became believers.[24] Paul and Barnabas's ministry to the proconsul of Cyprus was opposed by Elymas the magician during their first missionary journey. He was made blind for some time after a harsh reprimand of Paul, and the proconsul became a Christian.[25]

The history of the church is full events that have been interpreted as miracles, especially during times of oppression. This is in fact one of the major reasons why Christianity grew.[26] A well-known event is Constantine's vision in A.D. 312, just before the decisive battle outside Rome in the fight for the emperorship. Together with the soldiers of his army they had a vision in the sky of a bright cross with the inscription, "In this sign you will have victory." This made Constantine accept Christianity as the religion of choice, not only during the battle but also later as an emperor.

New Testament scholar Craig Keener (1960–) has written a very comprehensive and well-researched account of miracle claims throughout the history of the church.[27] Many of the contemporary miracles are well documented and the number of recent claims is particularly large in Asia, Africa, and South America—continents where churches have grown rapidly. These extraordinary events occur among Christians from many denominations, but especially within Pentecostal and charismatic churches. And they are very often preceded by prayer.

Miracle claims are seldom reported in media though and are very often unknown to people.[28] Is it possibly so that David Hume's and others' critique of miracles[29] and our rational, secularized Western thinking have influenced us a lot? This becomes an obstacle for witnessing supernatural events, since a childlike faith in God makes us pray and expect him to do what seems impossible. Indeed, when Jesus ministered in his home town Nazareth he was greatly surprised by their lack of faith and he could do very

---

23. Acts 3, 4:4.
24. Acts 8:4–13.
25. Acts 13:4–12.
26. See evidence 6.
27. Keener, *Miracles*.
28. Recall the discussion in evidence 3 on biased views of Christianity.
29. See evidence 11.

few miracles.[30] This doesn't mean that Christian miracle claims and reason are in conflict, and most Christians regard the work of medical doctors and prayer as complementary. Luke—the travel companion of Paul—was a medical doctor[31] who authored one of the gospels and the book of Acts, both of which are full of reported miracles. The prophet Daniel was another intellectual from the Old Testament who was very open-minded about supernatural events.[32] In fact, the Bible urges us not only to use our heart but *also* our God-given mind and intellect to seek him:

> The Pharisees got together. One of them, an expert in the law, tested him with this question: "Teacher, which is the greatest commandment in the Law?" Jesus replied: "Love the Lord your God with all your heart and with all your soul and with all your mind." This is the first and greatest commandment.[33]

But Scripture also warns us and regards it as unwise to use our minds to oppose God. Such an attitude easily leads to arrogance and pride, and ultimately to disappointment.[34]

An experienced miracle can have just the opposite effect for someone with a negative view of Christianity. The miracle is then either suppressed or it leads to frustration and anger. This happened to the some of the religious leaders in Jerusalem. They were in fact determined to kill Jesus after receiving reports that Lazarus had been raised from death.[35]

Many people report experiences of *supernatural coincidences*. While these do not violate any laws of nature, they are still so overwhelming that they often lead the person to Christ. This includes manifestations of many of the gifts of the Holy Spirit.[36] A person might be told precise details about his past or future through a *prophecy*. But this may also happen during a dream, vision, or revelation. If the prophetic message turns out to be correct, it is regarded as a strong evidence for Christianity. A *message of knowledge* may also contain very penetrating details about the secret

---

30. Mark 6:1–6.
31. Col 4:14.
32. Dan 1.
33. Matt 22:34–38.
34. Recall the argument in evidence 10 that Christianity and reason are not in conflict, and in evidence 4 that God may help our creative thinking. In several Bible verses we are urged to seek God with our intellect, for instance 1 Cor 1:20–29 and Prov 3:1–8, whereas Ezek 28 warns us to use reason for our own purposes.
35. John 11:45–53.
36. See evidence 6.

thoughts of a person or his life situation. The apostle Paul writes[37] that often this has a dramatic effect, in particular for someone who is not a Christian. He might fall down and worship God, realizing that he is indeed real.[38]

---

37. 1 Cor 14:23-24.

38. In statistical language, an experienced coincidence is part of an observational study (cf. evidence 11), not a designed experiment with random sampling of data. Statisticians and psychologists are often careful about drawing conclusions from such coincidences. They typically want to seek natural explanations: First, hidden natural causes, much related to the "God of the gaps" discussion in evidence 10 and 15. Second, unlikely things happen quite frequently by chance if the number of possibilities is large enough, as illustrated by so-called birthday problems. Third, because of our psychological makeup we tend to notice and remember things we are more sensitive to, and this gives a kind of information bias (cf. chapter 14). See Diaconis and Mosteller, *Methods for Studying Coincidences* and references therein. It is indeed wise to take such possible explanations into account, and the Bible teaches us to carefully weigh and test prophetic messages (1 Cor 14:29; 1 Thess 5:20-22; 1 John 4:1). However, a perceived supernatural coincidence is often of such an order of magnitude that any attempt to explain it naturally would still leave us convinced of having witnessed something supernatural. And even if a natural explanation of a coincidence is *possible*, this does not disprove that God planned it anyway.

PART III

Crossing the Line

14

Changed Life Situation

In previous chapters we mentioned various reasons for not becoming a Christian. Perhaps we don't want to give up what we have in life or we are too occupied with it. Some of us are hostile to God, or we may want to postpone the decision because of fear of taking such a big step without enough evidence.[1] In this chapter we will address how our priorities may change when something happens in life.

Perhaps the major reason for postponing the decision about Christianity is a belief that future will give us more time. Sooner or later we hope to start thinking about the big questions in life. But very often this is not the case. We actually tend to cheat ourselves—and even more, according to the Bible we have a tendency of opposing God and desiring to control our own lives so that we gradually drift away from him. This is a consequence of the fall of man, and sometimes a dramatically changed life situation or trial is the only way for us to take a new course and let God work in our lives. God recognizes when we are drifting away along the wrong track, and since he loves us he tries to change our priorities. C. S. Lewis once wrote that

> God whispers to us in our pleasures, speaks in our conscience, but shouts in our pains: it is his megaphone to rouse a deaf world.[2]

This is not to say that God causes all our trials in life, only that he allows some of them to happen for a greater purpose. He may even use a trial in our fallen world that is against his own will once it has occurred.[3] God

---

1. See chapters 4 and 7.
2. Lewis, *Problem of Pain*, 91.
3. See for instance evidence 17.

never tempts us to sin[4] but for our own best he may allow trials to happen in order for us to reprioritize our lives. In the Hebrew Letter we read:

> My son, do not make light of the Lord's discipline, and do not lose heart when he rebukes you, because the Lord disciplines the one he loves, and he chastens everyone he accepts as his son. Endure hardship as discipline; God is treating you as his children. For what children are not disciplined by their father? If you are not disciplined—and everyone undergoes discipline–then you are not legitimate, not true sons and daughters at all.[5]

Although these verses were written to a group of Christians, they actually apply to all grown-up humans in order for them to come to God in the first place. So even though God primarily wants us to be happy and enjoy life, he has an eternal perspective, whereas we tend to be more narrow minded. But since he has given us the ability to make willing choices he never forces us come to him. A trial or changed life situation may threaten our very foundations, such as a serious disease, the death of a beloved one, a divorce, a sudden unemployment or a financial bankruptcy. Sometimes after a middle age crisis we start to question the meaning of all, even though our life seems perfect from the outside.

Many people can testify about difficult periods in life, which in retrospect they are grateful to have experienced—not the trials themselves but, rather the changed priorities that either led them to Christ or, if they were Christians already, the strengthened faith that came out of the trial. But when we face hard times in life our reaction is crucial.[6] If we approach God there is much hope. If not, our deep wounds will not be healed and instead we easily get bitter. The Bible urges us to build our lives on the solid rock, Jesus Christ,[7] which is absolutely reliable no matter what storms in life we encounter. Scripture also promises that God is particularly close during times of sorrow,[8] and he never allows for any temptations beyond our limits:

> No temptation has overtaken you except what is common to mankind. And God is faithful; he will not let you be tempted beyond what you can bear. But when you are tempted, he will also provide a way out so that you can endure it.[9]

4. Jas 1:13.
5. Heb 12:5–8; see also Heb 12:9–13 and Deut 8:1–5.
6. In 2 Cor 7:8–11 Paul distinguishes between godly sorrow, which brings repentance, and worldly sorrow, which causes death.
7. Matt 7:24–29.
8. Ps 34:19–20.
9. 1 Cor 10:13.

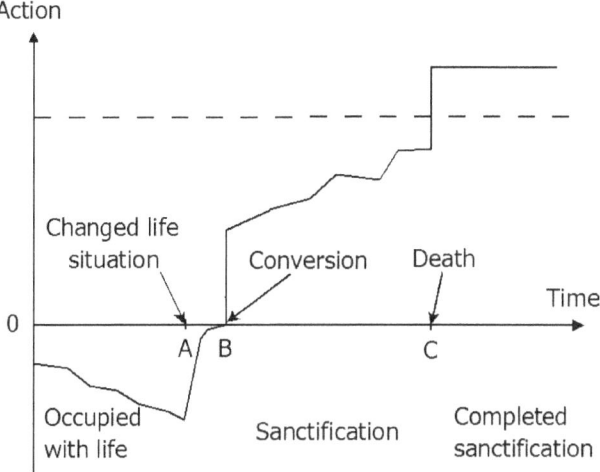

Figure 14.1: Our understanding of God and how it evolves over time. This shows the example of an adult with a changed life situation (A), conversion (B), and death (C) as major events. Action is interpreted as our willingness to act and become a Christian *before* conversion, and our retrospective approval of the decision after conversion. This degree of approval can also be interpreted as our certainty about the decision. The radical increase of Action after conversion represents the effect of the Holy Spirit, who makes us believe by heart and change the priorities of our will in favor of Christianity. After conversion the process of sanctification starts. It is finalized after death when our soul is made perfect in the presence of God.[10] The dashed line indicates that after death we have full certainty about and joy from our Christian faith.[11]

Figure 14.1 illustrates how our response to Christianity may evolve over time,[12] with a changed life situation (A), conversion (B), and death (C) as moments in time when our understanding of God radically changes. The way in which our view of Christianity changes after the life crisis varies, but six major responses are:

a. *Increasing Strength of Evidence by re-evaluation.* We have argued that evaluation of evidence is very subjective. It varies not only between persons but also during different periods of our life, in particular when

---

10. 1 Cor 13:12; Heb 12:23; Rev 21:27.
11. See also Grudem, *Systematic Theology*, chapter 38.
12. One may generalize the mathematical model of the Aposteriori Wager so that our evidence, willingness assignment, and life situation evolve jointly over time, using so-called Markov processes. This is somewhat related to Markovian decision theory. See for instance Ross, *Applied Probability Models* and Puterman, *Markov Decision Processes*.

a life crisis makes us re-evaluate the evidence we already have. We may suddenly recognize the beautiful design in nature, perhaps a previous testimony of a Christian friend is made alive, or we recollect a strong experience many years ago that might have been God.

b. *Increasing Strength of Evidence by gathering new experience.* We may suddenly want to find out whether Christianity is true or not. We start gathering more facts and experiences in order to check if our evidence for Christianity may change. Since it is not only our *evaluation* but also our *acquirement* of evidence that is subjective, the Holy Spirit may lead us in this process. In philosophy, the tendency for people to gather evidence that confirms with existing beliefs, whether true or not, is called *information bias*. We argue here that a changed life situation may drastically change the way we gather and interpret information concerning Christianity. Information bias is then either created or removed, depending on our perspective. Once we have opened up our heart for Christianity as a possible truth, God may lead us to read the Bible or some other Christian book. He may also arrange a meeting with some Christian that can testify about his faith, or he may even confront us with miraculous events.

c. *Increasing Strength of Will.* When our priorities in life change, so does the willingness attitude. There are several types of responses to the gospel that lead to a negative attitude towards Christianity.[13] If this attitude remains, added positive evidence for Christianity will not be enough for us to become Christians. Instead, the willingness assignment of the reward table *has to be changed.* It may happen for instance that when a person loses his job he is no longer too busy with life, and this may lead him to Christ.

d. *Increasing Strength of Evidence and Strength of Will.* This is the reaction of a person who re-evaluates or gathers new evidence (a or b) *and* changes his attitude (c) in favor of Christianity.

e. *Increased Strength of Evidence but decreased Strength of Will.* Suppose someone is exposed to undisputable evidence for the truthfulness of the Bible. In order to avoid becoming a Christian he has to compensate this new evidence by acquiring a more negative attitude towards Christianity.

f. *Decreased Strength of Will.* This is the opposite of c. A life crisis could make a person angry with God, therefore he turns away from the Lord rather than the opposite.

13. See willingness attitudes 6–11 of chapter 7.

These six responses are depicted in figure 14.2. It can be seen that the first four (a–d) lead to conversion, whereas the other two (e–f) do not. Below we will illustrate a–d with five persons from the Bible and the history of the church. They all encountered a radical change in their lives that drew them to God.

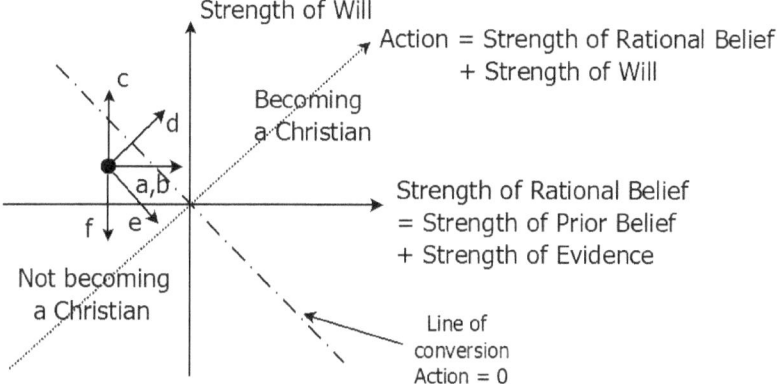

Figure 14.2: Illustration of how a changed life situation may lead a person (represented by the dot) to Christian faith or not. Strength of Evidence increases as one gathers new life experience in favor of Christianity (b) or when old experience is re-evaluated (a). It is also possible that Strength of Will increases (c) or that Strength of Evidence as well as Strength of Will increase (d). Although the changed life situation may involve indisputable new evidence in favor of Christianity. if the person reacts negatively he will not convert, since the increased Strength of Evidence is compensated by a decreased Strength of Will (e), or the Strength of Will alone may decrease (f), for instance when a life crisis makes a person angry with God.

Response 1: King Solomon. Solomon succeeded his father David as king of Israel. He was given extraordinary wisdom by God and in his early years he led Israel in a godly way. He organized the building of the temple in Jerusalem, which he dedicated to the Lord in a humble prayer. But later in life he was trapped by his own wisdom. Eager to build political alliances with other nations, he opposed the law of Israel by taking wives from these countries. He also allowed and introduced foreign religious practices, which eventually led to a divided kingdom after his death.[14]

14. 1 Kgs 1–11.

Solomon had actually been too busy with life,[15] very much driven by search for wisdom and desire. For others it may be a career, money, or some kind of hobby that keeps us busy. Whatever it is, if our motivation is not to serve God our occupation will ultimately betray us and leave us disillusioned.[16] This actually happened to Solomon—as an old man who summarized his life, in retrospect his perceptions of it shifted. He realized that gathering wisdom is not a goal by itself and ultimately it has no meaning. It is rather like chasing a wind:

> I, the Teacher, was king over Israel in Jerusalem. I applied my mind to study and to explore by wisdom all that is done under the heavens. What a heavy burden God has laid on mankind! I have seen all the things that are done under the sun; all of them are meaningless, a chasing after the wind.[17]

This new insight and his desire for meaning and purpose in life made Solomon change his attitude, that is, his will to seek God.[18] At the end of his life his conclusion was:

> Now all has been heard; here is the conclusion of the matter:
> Fear God and keep his commandments, for this is the duty of all mankind.[19]

It is also possible that a prophetic message—where God told Solomon that his disobedience would cause a divided kingdom after death—was a painful kind of new evidence that made Solomon change his priorities.[20]

Although Solomon's life is from the Old Testament it still applies very well to a decision for Christ. The reason is that even before Jesus' incarnation people were called to believe in God, follow him, and get blessed and saved by their faith in him, so that the redemptive work of Christ also applies in retrospect.[21]

---

15. See willingness attitude 7.
16. Matt 6:19–21; Luke 16:9; 16:13.
17. Eccl 1:12–14.
18. See willingness attitude 3.
19. Eccl 12:13.
20. 1 Kgs 11:9–13.
21. For righteousness and eternal life in the Old Testament, see Dan 12:2; Ps 23:6; Rom 3:25–26, 4:1–13; and Grudem, *Systematic Theology*, 821. Other Old Testament witnesses of afterlife are Enoch (Gen 5:24; Heb 11:5) and Elijah (2 Kgs 2:11). They were both taken up to heaven before they died.

Response 2: Manasseh. Manasseh was the king of Judah during 697–42 B.C.[22] He grew up with all the best possibilities to get to know the Lord. His father, Hezekiah, was one of the godliest kings of Judah and during his regime the nation was spiritually restored. The famous prophet Isaiah was sort of a court chaplain of Jerusalem at that time. During the first 11 years as king Manasseh reigned the country together with Hezekiah, and he had great opportunities to learn from his father.

Yet it seems that Manasseh turned his ways against God very early in life. A period of spiritual decline started when he came to power, and Manasseh is remembered as one of the worst kings in the history of Israel. Canaanite Baal altars were rebuilt and he encouraged worship of stars. He practiced witchcraft, consulted mediums, and had altars built in the temple of Jerusalem—the most sacred place for the Jews. He even sacrificed one of his own sons to Canaanite gods. The Lord tried to warn Manasseh through his prophets but he did not listen. Tradition tells that Isaiah was killed during Manasseh's regime. Finally God punished Judah by sending an Assyrian army. Manasseh was captured and brought to Babylon.

The most surprising and wonderful part of Manasseh's story is that in prison he sincerely humbled himself and asked God for forgiveness. The fact that Manasseh was forgiven is one of the finest Old Testament examples of God's grace. Manasseh was brought back to Jerusalem and regained the throne. For the remaining (short) period of his life he started to restore the nation spiritually, knowing that the God of Israel was the only god.

Manasseh's life story beautifully illustrates that even a person who is hostile to God[23] may change his willingness attitude. God always wants to forgive as soon as we come to him.

Response 3: Nebuchadnezzar. Nebuchadnezzar was the sovereign king of Babylonia, the leading world power around the turn of the seventh and sixth centuries B.C.[24] He made Judah a vassal state of Babylonia, and after three attacks on Jerusalem the city was completely destroyed. After the first attack in 609 a group of Israelites was deported to Babylonia. The most gifted of them were educated to serve in the king's palace—among them Daniel, Hananiah, Mishael, and Azariah.

Nebuchadnezzar was to some extent a wise ruler, letting the captured countries retain some of their local culture and religion. But his power also

22. 2 Kgs 21:1–18; 2 Chr 33:1–20.
23. See willingness attitude 11.
24. Dan 1–4.

made him proud and sometimes very cruel. The freedom of his subjects was conditioned on their complete loyalty to Babylon and sometimes it was even required of them to worship Nebuchadnezzar as a god. Still, Daniel and his friends had a big impact on Nebuchadnezzar. God had given Daniel prophetic gifts—he was able to reveal and explain a dream Nebuchadnezzar had about the current and coming kingdoms on Earth, which all the magicians at the king's palace failed to recall and interpret. When Hananiah, Mishael, and Azariah refused to worship a statue of the king they survived after being thrown into a fiery furnace. These miracles made Nebuchadnezzar acknowledge that the God of Israel was very powerful.

Although Nebuchadnezzar gained some faith in God his pride remained. God was still one of many gods for him, not anyone he was prepared to commit his own life to. One night the king had a dream, the meaning of which God revealed to Daniel. God was going to drive the king away from his people and force him to live among the wild animals, eating grass like cattle and being drenched with the dew of heaven. Then, after seven years, he would regain his sanity and understand that God is the ruler of all the Earth. The dream was fulfilled one year later after God had given Nebuchadnezzar some time to repent and commit to him. When Nebuchadnezzar had spent seven years in the wilderness and regained his power, he praised and glorified God and publicly acknowledged him as eternal and the most high God. This powerful message was distributed in a letter all over his kingdom.

Nebuchadnezzar was initially not prepared to commit himself to God, not because of lacking faith but since the cost was too high. Nebuchadnezzar's willingness attitude was primarily not caused by fear of other people's opinions (since he was sovereign) or hostility to God (he acknowledged miracles as the work of Israel's God) but rather by his own pride. But God knew his way to Nebuchadnezzar's heart. The seven years in wilderness was new evidence—a painful kind of miracle that Nebuchadnezzar had to endure. His evidence in favor of God was quite strong already, but the miracle increased it even more. But the main reason why Nebuchadnezzar surrendered to God was that he humbled himself and changed his previous very negative willingness assignment[25] to one that favored belief in God.

Response 4: Paul. Saul was a strict Jew who lived as a Pharisee and tried to follow the will of God. But he did not understand the gospel as a fulfillment of Old Testament prophecies, and instead he was one of the leading persecutors of the first generation of Christians. He was then radically converted

---

25. See willingness attitude 6 and 10 (in particular).

to one of the most influential missionaries in the history of the church, after experiencing Jesus on his way from Jerusalem to Damascus.[26] Near the end of his life he wrote about this in a letter to his disciple Timothy:

> Even though I was once a blasphemer and a persecutor and a violent man, I was shown mercy because I acted in ignorance and unbelief. The grace of our Lord was poured out on me abundantly, along with the faith and love that are in Christ Jesus.[27]

It is obvious that Paul's miraculous experience radically increased the strength of his evidence. But probably it also made him re-evaluate his willingness attitude. His understanding of the Old Testament had been incomplete. Before his conversion he did not realize that Messiah was not only a king, but also a suffering lamb on the cross.[28] After the encounter with Jesus on the Damascus road his attitude changed,[29] to the extent that he became a Christian.

Response 5: Leo Tolstoy. Leo Tolstoy (1828–1910) was a Russian writer and novelist. He grew up in a Christian environment but at the age of 18 he abandoned his faith. His adult life was very successful and seemingly happy. Tolstoy's writing made him famous and books like *War and Peace* and *Anna Karenina* are considered classics. He also became very rich and had a family with a loving wife and 13 children. Yet he underwent a crisis and started to question the meaning of life. This is vividly described in *Confession*, a book he wrote in 1879:

> But five years ago something very strange began to happen to me. At first I began having moments of bewilderment, when my life would come to a halt, as if I did not know how to live or what to do; I would lose my presence of mind and fall into a state of depression. But this passed, and I continued to live as before. Then the moments of bewilderness recurred more frequently, and they always took the same form. Whenever my life would come to a halt, the question would arise: Why? And what next? . . . At first I thought these were pointless and irrelevant questions. I thought that the answers to them were well known and that if I should ever want to resolve them, it would not be

---

26. See chapter 1, evidence 23–24; Acts 9:1–18; 26:4–18; and 1 Tim 1:12–17.
27. 1 Tim 1:13–14.
28. This corresponds to willingness attitude 9.
29. Paul's new view of Christianity was similar to willingness attitude 5.

too hard for me; it was just that I could not be bothered with it now, but if I should take it upon myself, then I would find the answers. But the questions began to come up more and more frequently, and their demands to be answered became more and more urgent. And like points concentrated into one spot, these questions without answers came together to form a single black stain. . . . I did not want to discover truth anymore because I had guessed what it was. The truth was that life is meaningless.[30]

In the midst of his despair, Tolstoy noticed that most other people did not bother to ask the big questions—"Where do I come from?," "Who am I?," "Where am I heading?," and "What is the meaning of life?" He looked for answers in science and philosophy but there were none to find. Then he was deeply touched by many of the rural people who lived a very simple life, in particular the monks of the cave monastery of Kiev. They had found a meaning through belief in Jesus Christ. This finally convinced Tolstoy to return to his Christian faith.

Leo Tolstoy's life story and response is similar to that of Solomon. They had both been very successful, but also too busy with life.[31] The life crisis made Tolstoy change his willingness attitude, and the personal testimony of the rural people was a new strong evidence for Christianity.

---

30. Tolstoy, *Confession*, chapter 5.
31. See willingness attitude 7.

15

Conclusions

It is time to summarize. I hope you have found the wager model helpful for understanding more about the decision to become a Christian. Although I have argued that Christianity is rational, it is not possible with our mind alone to prove it is true. The evidence for Christianity is more like pointers that indicate its truthfulness. The only way of getting full assurance is to take a leap in faith and enter a personal relationship with God. Indeed, the Bible honestly describes the message of the cross as foolishness to those that don't believe:

> For the message of the cross is foolishness to those who are perishing, but to us who are being saved it is the power of God. For it is written: "I will destroy the wisdom of the wise; the intelligence of the intelligent I will frustrate." Where is the wise person? Where is the teacher of the law? Where is the philosopher of this age? Has not God made foolish the wisdom of the world? For since in the wisdom of God the world through its wisdom did not know him, God was pleased through the foolishness of what was preached to save those who believe. Jews demand signs and Greeks look for wisdom, but we preach Christ crucified: a stumbling block to Jews and foolishness to Gentiles, but to those whom God has called, both Jews and Greeks, Christ the power of God and the wisdom of God. For the foolishness of God is wiser than human wisdom, and the weakness of God is stronger than human strength.[1]

---

1. 1 Cor 1:18–25, Luke 10:21, Matt 11:25–26.

This is not to say that Christianity is irrational, only that part of the Christian message has to be understood and received by faith when we get filled with the Holy Spirit of God.² In the Gospel of John, Jesus says:

> I am the way and the truth and the life. No one comes to the Father except through me.³

Two other verses from the Gospel of John summarize the message of the whole Bible:

> For God so loved the world that he gave his one and only Son, that whoever believes in him shall not perish but have eternal life. For God did not send his Son into the world to condemn the world, but to save the world through him.⁴

If the message of the gospel hasn't touched you, you may stop reading here. If it has, perhaps your willingness attitude has changed or you have re-evaluated evidence in favor of Christianity. As a Christian I believe it is God that invites you to be part of his family. The way to become a Christian was described in sections 2.1 and 3.1. It is so simple that a small child can understand it and yet so full of wisdom that even the best-trained theologian cannot fully grasp it. If you want to become a Christian, you simply talk to Jesus as a friend and ask him to come into your life. The following prayer might help you:

> God, I realize that I have not lived my life the way you intended it, and by doing so I have sinned against you. I am truly repentant of my sins, I ask for your forgiveness, and I sincerely believe that you sent your Son Jesus Christ to Earth to die on Calvary as payment for my sins. I also believe that Jesus resurrected from death and that I will spend eternity with you after death. Jesus, from this moment I make you the Lord of my life and I will do my best to follow you.

If you sincerely prayed this prayer you are made righteous in the eyes of God and have become a child of his family, regardless of whether you experienced anything or not during the prayer. The Bible itself promises you this:

> That if you confess with your mouth, "Jesus is Lord," and believe in your heart that God raised him from the dead, you will be

---

2. 1 Cor 2:6–15.
3. John 14:6.
4. John 3:16–17.

saved. For it is with your heart that you believe and are justified, and it is with your mouth that you confess and are saved.[5]

I then congratulate your decision, and I assure you a very exciting life—discovering the plan that God has had for you since you were born. There is no guarantee that the rest of your life will be simple, but you will surely find it meaningful. In order to grow in your newly found faith I recommend you pray and read the Bible regularly and join a local church. Tell your family and friends. People will gradually see the changes in your life as the fruits of the Spirit become visible.

---

5. Rom 10:9–10.

APPENDICES

The Aposteriori Wager was introduced in chapters 1 and 4. In these appendices we give a more formal definition in terms of Bayesian decision theory, with numerical illustrations. Other approaches to decision theory will be mentioned as well.

Appendix A

Bayesian Decision Theory

RECALL FROM SECTION 1.3 that the task of the waging person is to choose between Christianity (C) and Non-Christianity (N). In order to quantify this mathematically we will use the concept of probability that was introduced in sections 1.3 and 4.2. A probaility of an event A is denoted by P(A). In particular, we regard Christianity and Non-Christianity as two mutually exclusive hypotheses with subjective apriori probabilities P(C) and P(N)=1-P(C). These are numbers between zero and 1 that reflect our degree of belief in Christianity and Non-Christianity before taking any evidence into account. We define

$$\text{Strength of Prior Belief} = \log \frac{P(C)}{P(N)} \qquad (A.1)$$

as the (tenth) logarithm of the prior odds of Christianity versus Non-Christianity. It is positive when Christianity is apriori more likely than Non-Christianity and negative when Non-Christianity is more likely apriori. For instance, Strength of Prior Belief=2 means that we believe Christianity to be 100 times more likely than Non-Christianity apriori. It corresponds to probabilities 100/101 for Christianity and 1/101 for Non-Christianity.

We also need the so called conditional probability P(A|B), which is the probability that A holds, given condition B. In order to illustrate this concept, let E refer to all *evidence* we encounter in life that is of relevance for the decision to become a Christian. We define P(E|C) as a probability that reflects how likely we believe this evidence is *given* that Christianity is true. In the same way, P(E|N) quantifies how likely we believe E to be given that Christianity is not true. To quantify whether evidence favors Christianity or not we introduce

$$\text{Strength of Evidence} = \log \frac{P(E|C)}{P(E|N)}. \tag{A.2}$$

It is referred to as the (tenth) logarithm of the likelihood ratio for E when testing Christianity against Non-Christianity. For instance, Strength of Evidence = 3 means that our evidence is regarded as 1,000 times more likely if Christianity is true compared to when it is not. We want to find out how likely our belief in Christianity and Non-Christianity is *given* evidence E. This is expressed through aposteriori probabilities P(C|E) and P(N|E), which, according to Bayes' Rule, can be rewritten as

$$P(C|E) = \frac{P(C)P(E|C)}{P(E)} \quad \text{and} \quad P(N|E) = \frac{P(N)P(E|N)}{P(E)}. \tag{A.3}$$

The number P(C|E) is analogous to the aposteriori probability for the existence of God used by Stephen Unwin[1] and Richard Swinburne.[2] However, we will use a logarithmic scale in order to compare how likely Christianity and Non-Christianity are given evidence, and introduce

$$\text{Strength of Rational Belief} = \log \frac{P(C|E)}{P(N|E)}. \tag{A.4}$$

It is the (tenth) logarithm of the posterior odds of Christianity versus Non-Christianity. Inserting A.3 into A.4, it follows that

Strength of Rational Belief=Strength of Prior Belief+Strength of Evidence.

This last equation is essentially Bayes' Theorem expressed on a logarithmic scale.

---

1. Unwin, *Probability of God*.
2. Swinburne, *Existence of God*.

Appendix B

Reward Table and Strength of Will

Table B.1: Reward table for decision between Christianity (C) and Non-Christianity (N).

Each combination of truth and decision is assigned a separate reward value.

	Decision=N	Decision=C
Truth=N	RDN	WDC
Truth=C	WDN	RDC

IN THIS APPENDIX WE will define one single number—Strength of Will. It summarizes our willingness to become a Christian, based on the rewards that we assign as entries of the table in figure 1.4 of chapter 1. Our starting point is to abbreviate the four possible rewards of this figure, as shown in table B.1. These numbers are either positive or negative, where a negative reward corresponds to a cost. For instance, if Christianity is true the two possibilities are RDC, the reward of rightly deciding for Christianity, and WDN, the reward of wrongly deciding for Non-Christianity. This gives a reward difference of RDC−WDN, which quantifies how much larger the reward of becoming a Christian is when Christianity is true. Similarly, if Christianity is false the reward difference RDN−WDC quantifies how much larger the reward of rightly deciding for Non-Christianity is compared to the reward of wrongly deciding for Christianity. To summarize, both of these reward differences give the increased reward for making the right (=true) decision compared to making the wrong (=false) one.

Once the reward table has been created, if both reward differences are positive we define

$$\text{Strength of Will} = \log \frac{\text{RDC} - \text{WDN}}{\text{RDN} - \text{WDC}} \qquad (B.1)$$

It is a single number that summarizes our willingness attitude towards Christianity by comparing the reward differences when Christianity is true and false in relative terms, on a logarithmic scale. Our willingness assignment favors Christianity when Strength of Will is positive, since then the reward difference is larger when Christianity is true compared to when it is false. Non-Christianity is favored when the Strength of Will is negative, since then our reward difference is larger when Christianity is false. For instance, Strength of Will=3 means that the increased reward of making the right decision is 1,000 times larger when Christianity is true compared to when it is false.

In order to make Strength of Will well defined also when only one reward difference is positive, we let Strength of Will equal infinity if the reward difference is zero or negative when Non-Christianity is true, but positive when Christianity is true. Analogously, we let Strength of Will equal negative infinity when the reward difference is zero or negative when Christianity is true, but positive when Non-Christianity is true.

Appendix C

The Bayesian Decision Rule

IN THIS APPENDIX WE will define the decision rule of the Aposteriori Wager. For this we need to combine the concepts that were introduced in appendices A and B. That is, we will show that the Expectation rule implies a decision as illustrated in figure 4.5 of chapter 4. As a first step, we notice that the Expected Reward for Christianity is

$$\text{ERC} = P(N|E)\text{WDC} + P(C|E)\text{RDC}, \tag{C.1}$$

whereas the Expected Reward for Non-Christianity is

$$\text{ERN} = P(N|E)\text{RDN} + P(C|E)\text{WDN}. \tag{C.2}$$

Both of these expected rewards combine the prior belief, evidence, and willingness assignment. The Expectation rule picks the alternative with largest expected reward:

$$\begin{aligned} \text{ERC} > \text{ERN} &\implies \text{Decision} = C, \\ \text{ERC} < \text{ERN} &\implies \text{Decision} = N. \end{aligned} \tag{C.3}$$

Inserting the formulas of Bayes' Theorem in A.3 into C.1, we find that

$$\text{ERC} = \frac{P(N)P(E|N)\text{WDC} + P(C)P(E|C)\text{RDC}}{P(E)}. \tag{C.4}$$

A similar calculation for the expected reward of Non-Christianity yields

$$\text{ERN} = \frac{P(N)P(E|N)\text{RDN} + P(C)P(E|C)\text{WDN}}{P(E)}. \tag{C.5}$$

As the next step we apply the Expectation rule in C.3, with the two expected rewards ERC and ERN as calculated in C.4 and C.5. After some calculations one notices that according to C.3, a choice for Christianity is mathematically equivalent to

$$P(C)P(E|C)(RDC - WDN) > P(N)P(E|N)(RDN - WDC). \quad (C.6)$$

Dividing both sides of this equation by the expression on its right hand side, taking tenth logarithms, and using definitions A.1, A.2, and B.1, it is seen that C.6 is equivalent to a choice for Christianity when

Action = Strength of Prior Belief + Strength of Evidence + Strength of Will > 0. (C.7)

In the first identity we used the definition of Action from figure 4.5. Since we have shown that ERC is greater than ERN whenever C.7 holds, this proves that the decision rule

$$\begin{aligned} \text{Action} > 0 &\Rightarrow \text{Decision} = C, \\ \text{Action} < 0 &\Rightarrow \text{Decision} = N \end{aligned} \quad (C.8)$$

is equivalent to rule C.3, which bases the decision on maximal expected reward. From A.1, A.2, and B.1 we notice that

$$\text{Action} = \log \frac{P(C)P(E|C)(RDC - WDN)}{P(N)P(E|N)(RDN - WDC)} \quad (C.9)$$

can be expressed directly in terms of probabilities and rewards. We will show that there is another way of interpreting Action that perhaps is more transparent. To start with, we may add or subtract the same number to both rewards of any row of a willingness table without affecting the final decision. As noted by Lara Buchak[1] this follows from C.3, since any of those two operations will change the two expected rewards ERC and ERN by the same amount (because of C.1 and C.2). Since we may also multiply all entries of the willingness table by the same number without changing the final decision, it follows that table B.1 is equivalent to table C.1. In the latter table the rewards for Non-Christianity have been put to zero, and in particular ERN equals zero, whereas RDR is the reward difference ratio that appears in B.1 and C.9. This implies that Christianity is chosen when

$$\text{ERC} = P(C|E) \frac{RDC - WDN}{RDN - WDC} - P(N|E) > 0. \quad (C.10)$$

---

1. Buchak, "Instrumental Rationality" and "Can It Be Rational to Have Faith?"

We deduce from C.9, C.10, and Bayes' Rule A.3 that Action equals the logarithm of the ratio of the two terms of the right-hand side of C.10, i.e.,

$$\text{Action} = \log \frac{P(C|E)(RDC - WDN)}{P(N|E)(RDN - WDC)}. \tag{C.11}$$

In words, Action is the logarithm of the ratio of the two reward differences that tell how much the reward increases by choosing the true alternative, if this truth is Christianity or Non-Christianity, weighted by the aposteriori probabilities of these two alternatives.

Table C.1: Standardized reward table for decision between Christianity and Non-Christianity.

Compared to table B.1 the rewards of N have been normalized to zero and the reward for C when N is true to −1. The Expectation rule generates the same decision for tables B.1 and C.1.

	Decision=N	Decision=C
Truth=N	0	−1
Truth=C	0	RDC

Appendix D

Many Alternatives

WE HAVE SO FAR not been very specific about what to include in Non-Christianity (N). In chapters 2–3 we simplified and included only naturalism, whereas in sections 4.5.3 and 5.1 we allowed for several philosophies of life. Formally, we may write the latter more general approach as

$$N = \{N_1, \ldots, N_m\},$$

where N_i is philosophy of life number i among the alternatives to Christianity. For instance, we may have m=5 such alternatives and put

$$N = \{\text{Naturalism, Judaism, Islam, Hinduism, Buddhism}\}.$$

It turns out that the definitions of Strength of Prior Belief, Strength of Evidence, and Strength of Rational Belief in appendix A remain valid when N contains more than one philosophy of life, provided that we use

$$\begin{aligned} P(N) &= P(N_1) + \cdots + P(N_m) \\ P(E|N) &= P(E|N_1)P(N_1|N) + \cdots + P(E|N_m)P(N_m|N) \end{aligned} \quad \text{(D.1)}$$

in formulas A.1, A.2, and A.4. In the first row of D.1 we expressed the apriori probability of Non-Christianity $P(N)$ as a sum of the apriori probabilities that all philosophies of life consistent with Non-Christianity are true. In the second row we introduced the conditional (apriori) probability $P(N_i|N)=P(N_i)/P(N)$ that philosophy of life i is true given that Christianity is not true, and $P(E|N_i)$, the probability of evidence E given that philosophy of life i is true.

It is reasonable to assume that the reward of rightly deciding against Christianity RDN_i and the reward of wrongly deciding in favor of

Christianity WDC_i both depend on which alternative philosophy of life N_i is true. It turns out that the derivation of the decision rule C.7 in appendix C remains valid under these assumptions, provided that we define the overall rewards of rightly deciding against or wrongly deciding in favor of Christianity, as

$$\begin{aligned} RDN &= RDN_1 P(N_1|N,E) + \cdots + RDN_m P(N_m|N,E), \\ WDC &= WDC_1 P(N_1|N,E) + \cdots + WDC_m P(N_m|N,E) \end{aligned} \quad (D.2)$$

respectively, where

$$P(N_i|N,E) = \frac{P(N_i)P(E|N_i)}{P(N)P(E|N)}$$

is the conditional aposteriori probability that philosophy of life i is true, given evidence E and the assumption N that Christianity is not true. We can interpret RDN as the expected reward of rightly choosing Non-Christianity given evidence and the assumption that Christianity is not true, and WDC as the expected reward of wrongly choosing Christianity given evidence and the assumption that Christianity is not true.

In order to prove that C.7 remains valid we rewrite the expected rewards C.4 and C.5 for Christianity and Non-Christianity as

$$ERC = \frac{P(C)P(E|C)RDC + \sum_{i=1}^{m} P(N_i)P(E|N_i)WDC_i}{P(E)}$$

and

$$ERN = \frac{P(C)P(E|C)WDN + \sum_{i=1}^{m} P(N_i)P(E|N_i)RDN_i}{P(E)}$$

respectively, where the sigma symbol is used as short notation for summation over different terms A_i when the index i ranges from 1 to m ($A_1 + \ldots + A_m$). After some calculations one notices that ERC>ERN is mathematically equivalent to

$$\begin{aligned} P(C)P(E|C)(RDC - WDN) &> \sum_{i=1}^{m} P(N_i)P(E|N_i)(RDN_i - WDC_i) \\ &= P(N)P(E|N) \sum_{i=1}^{m} P(N_i|N,E)(RDN_i - WDC_i) \quad (D.3) \\ &= P(N)P(E|N)(RDN - WDC), \end{aligned}$$

where in the last step we invoked the definitions of RDN and WDC in D.2. Since the left- and right-hand sides of D.3 are identical to those of C.6, we proceed as before to deduce that Christianity is chosen, according to the Expectation Rule ERC>ERN, when Action in C.7 becomes positive.

On the other hand, suppose we want to make a final decision between all m+1 philosophies of life; Christianity on one hand and m alternatives on the other. The decision table must then be expanded so that it consists of m+1 rows, depending on which alternative is true, and m+1 columns, depending on which philosophy of life is decided.[1]

---

1. Bartha, *Many Gods, Many Wagers*.

Appendix E

Accumulation of Evidence

ASSUME THAT EVIDENCE E consists of n units denoted as $E_1, \ldots E_n$. This may be for instance the n=24 pieces of evidence presented in chapters 9–13, or a subset of them. If these units are *independent*, we obtain the probability of evidence if Christianity is true, $P(E|C)$, as well as the probability of evidence if Christianity is not true, $P(E|N)$, by multiplying the probabilities for the individual units of evidence. That is,

$$P(E|C) = P(E_1|C) \cdot \ldots \cdot P(E_n|C),$$
$$P(E|N) = P(E_1|N) \cdot \ldots \cdot P(E_n|N). \quad (E.1)$$

By taking logarithms of the two equations in E.1 and inserting them into the definition of Strength of Evidence in A.2, we find that

$$\text{Strength of Evidence} = \text{Evidence}_1 + \cdots + \text{Evidence}_n, \quad (E.2)$$

where

$$\text{Evidence}_i = \log \frac{P(E_i|C)}{P(E_i|N)}$$

is short notation for Strength of Evidence$_i$, the strength of the i:th unit of evidence. The addition E.2 of evidence is used by Stephen Unwin for calculating the subjective probability that God exists.[1]

The independence assumption E.1 is crucial for having Evidence$_i$ from various units of experience added in E.2.[2] It is more likely though that some

---

1. Unwin, *Probability of God*.

2. This is usually referred to as a naive Bayes assumption in Bayesian statistics. See for instance Hand and Yu, *Idiot's Bayes*.

units of evidence are correlated. For instance, our attitudes towards the Bible and Israel are probably related, as well as our views on design, a first cause, and whether natural science strengthens the credibility of Christianity or not.

Independence between various units of evidence is also lost, for instance, if Non-Christianity (N) consists of several different philosophies of life (N_j). The reason is that even if the units of evidence would be independent conditionally on each single N_j they are not so conditionally on N, as in the lower part of E.1. For instance, Muslims will probably have similar views on issues related to natural theology (design, origin of morality, consciousness . . .), whereas an atheist tends to evaluate such evidence in a different way.

We can resolve the problem of correlated pieces of evidence $E_1, \ldots E_n$ by assuming that they enter *sequentially* into the decision process. It can be shown then that the definition of Strength of Evidence in A.2 can be rewritten as a sum

$$\text{Strength of Evidence} = (\Delta \text{Evidence})_1 + \cdots + (\Delta \text{Evidence})_n,$$

where

$$(\Delta \text{Evidence})_i = \log \frac{P(E_i | E_{i-1}, \ldots, E_1, C)}{P(E_i | E_{i-1}, \ldots, E_1, N)} \qquad (E.3)$$

is the *additional* strength of E_i as an argument of Christianity in favor of Non-Christianity, *given* the previous pieces $E_1, \ldots E_{i-1}$ of evidence, that is, how much E_i increases Strength of Evidence (using the delta symbol to denote such a change). Richard Swinburne[3] refers to an argument E_i (derived from the evidence connected to E_i) as a good C-inductive argument if the right hand side of E.3 is positive. Such an argument makes the conclusion C that Christianity is true more probable, given all previous evidence $E_1, \ldots E_{i-1}$. Equivalently, E_i is said to *confirm* the Christianity hypothesis C if the right hand side of E.3 is positive, given background knowledge $E_1, \ldots E_{i-1}$.

We have defined the aposteriori probabilities $P(C|E)$ and $P(N|E)$ of Christianity and Non-Christianity as subjective probabilities. Swinburne argues that such an approach may fail to have conditional probabilities updated according to Bayes' Theorem, since our evidence might be reinterpreted over time.[4] Although this is true, we will show that the problem can at least be quantified by introducing *hidden variables*.

---

3. Swinburne, *Existence of God*, chapters 1 and 14; *Epistemic Justification*, chapter 4.
4. Swinburne, *Epistemic Justification*, additional note J.

ACCUMULATION OF EVIDENCE 263

Recall that, from a Christian point of view, although Strength of Evidence is part of Strength of Rational Belief it is to some extent influenced by the spiritual world. Such influences may act as hidden variables, creating various sorts of dependencies. For instance, a negative spiritual influence will most likely affect not only the willingness table, but also attitudes towards evidence from the Bible, personal witnesses, and seemingly miraculous events. Moreover, hidden variables will affect the way evidence is interpreted over time. Suppose for instance there are n=2 units of evidence $E=(E_1, E_2)$ available to a person, with E_1 arriving first and then E_2. We introduce the hidden variables

$$X_1, X_2 \in \{-1, 0, 1\},$$

where X_i quantifies spiritual influence or awareness at the time when evidence E_i was collected, with -1 corresponding to influence that from a Christian perspective is negative, zero denoting a neutral influence, and 1 a positive influence. We assume that beliefs are consistent with the calculus of probabilities when the spiritual awareness history X_1, X_2 is taken into account. After new evidence E_2 has arrived, the old evidence E_1 is also *reinterpreted* with X_2 instead of X_1. It follows that the changed Strength of Evidence is

$$(\Delta \text{Evidence})_2 = \log \frac{P(E|X_2, C)}{P(E|X_2, N)} - \log \frac{P(E_1|X_1, C)}{P(E_1|X_1, N)}.$$

Now rewrite the probabilities of evidence when E_2 has arrived under Christianity and Non-Christianity assumptions as products

$$P(E|X_2, C) = P(E_2|E_1, X_2, C) \cdot \frac{P(E_1|X_2, C)}{P(E_1|X_1, C)} \cdot P(E_1|X_1, C),$$

$$P(E|X_2, N) = P(E_2|E_1, X_2, N) \cdot \frac{P(E_1|X_2, N)}{P(E_1|X_1, N)} \cdot P(E_1|X_1, N)$$

of three terms. Combining the last three displayed equations, we find that the changed Strength of Evidence between time points 1 and 2 can be rewritten as a sum

$$(\Delta \text{Evidence})_2 = \log \frac{P(E_2|E_1, X_2, C)}{P(E_2|E_1, X_2, N)} + \log \frac{P(E_1|X_2, C)/P(E_1|X_1, C)}{P(E_1|X_2, N)/P(E_1|X_1, N)} \quad (E.4)$$

of two terms, the first of which quantifies the strength of E_2 in favor of Christianity in light of previous evidence E_1 and the new spiritual awareness variable X_2, and the second term quantifies the extent to which *reevaluation* of old evidence E_1 favors Christianity when X_1 changes to X_2.

In chapter 14 we discussed how a changed life situation affects a person, as illustrated in figure 14.2. Response a) is a consequence of reevaluating old evidence, the second term on the right hand side of E.4, whereas response b) is the effect of taking new evidence E_2 into account, the first term on the right hand side of E.4.

Appendix F

A Numerical Example

W‍E WILL ILLUSTRATE HOW to calculate expected rewards and decisions for two persons, Adam and Ben. They have the same willingness table of figure 1.4 in chapter 1, and both of them have equal apriori probabilities 0.5 for Christianity and Non-Christianity.

Adam regards evidence as equally likely whether Christianity or Non-Christianity is true, that is, $P(E|N)=P(E|C)$. Formula A.3 of appendix A implies that his aposteriori probability for Christianity is

$$P(C|E) = \frac{0.5P(E|C)}{0.5P(E|C) + 0.5P(E|N)} = \frac{0.5P(E|C)}{0.5P(E|C) + 0.5P(E|C)} = 0.5,$$

the same as the aposteriori probability $P(N|E)=0.5$ for Non-Christianity. Adam therefore gives Christianity and Non-Christianity equals odds, 1 to 1, based on his prior belief *and* evidence.

As a next step we combine the C column of Adam's willingness table with his aposteriori probabilities for Christianity and Non-Christianity. From this and formula C.1 it follows that Adam's expected reward for choosing Christianity is

$$ERC = 0.5(-1) + 0.5 \cdot 5 = 2.$$

In the same way, we deduce from formula C.2 and the N column of Adam's willingness assignment that his expected reward for Non-Christianity is

$$ERN = 0.5 \cdot 0 + 0.5(-5) = -2.5.$$

Since Christianity has the highest expected reward, Adam decides to become a Christian.

Ben, on the other hand, regards evidence as making it 19 times more likely that Non-Christianity is true compared to Christianity being true, that is, $P(E|N)=19P(E|C)$. This leads to an aposteriori probability

$$P(C|E) = \frac{0.5P(E|C)}{0.5P(E|C) + 0.5P(E|N)} = \frac{0.5P(E|C)}{0.5P(E|C) + 0.5 \cdot 19P(E|C)} = 0.05$$

for Christianity that is 19 times smaller than the aposteriori probability $P(N|E)=0.95$ for Non-Christianity. This means that Ben has odds 19 to 1 in favor of Non-Christianity based on prior belief and evidence. It follows from the C column of Ben's willingness assignment and formula C.1 that Ben's expected reward for Christianity is

$$ERC = 0.95(-1) + 0.05 \cdot 5 = -0.7.$$

Analogously, the N column of Ben's willingness assignment and formula C.2 implies that his expected reward for Non-Christianity is

$$ERN = 0.95 \cdot 0 + 0.05(-5) = -0.25.$$

Since Non-Christianity gets the highest expected reward, Ben does not become a Christian.

Table F.1: Expected rewards for Adam and Ben

Adam and Ben have the same reward table (figure 1.4) but different odds for Christianity (C) and Non-Christianity (N). Adam gives both alternatives equal odds, but Ben favors N by odds 19 to 1. Adam and Ben's decisions (those with largest expected rewards) are C and N respectively.

Truth	Adam			Ben		
	Probability	Reward		Probability	Reward	
		N	C		N	C
N	0.5	0	−1	0.95	0	−1
C	0.5	−5	5	0.05	−5	5
Exp reward		−2.5	2		−0.25	−0.7

Adam's and Ben's reward calculations are summarized in table F.1. We can also use the theory of appendices A and B, and the graphical representation of the Aposteriori Wager from figure 4.5 of section 4.3 to illustrate the different responses of Adam and Ben to Christianity: It follows from A.4 that

$$\text{Strength of Rational Belief} = \log\frac{0.5}{0.5} = 0$$

for Adam, whereas

$$\text{Strength of Rational Belief} = \log\frac{0.05}{0.95} = -1.28$$

for Ben. On the other hand, since Adam and Ben use the same reward table, it follows from B.1 that both of them have a

$$\text{Strength of Will} = \log\frac{5-(-5)}{0-(-1)} = \log 10 = 1.$$

It is shown in figure F.1 that Adam and Ben indeed end up on different sides of the line of conversion in a plot of Strength of Will versus Strength of Rational Belief.

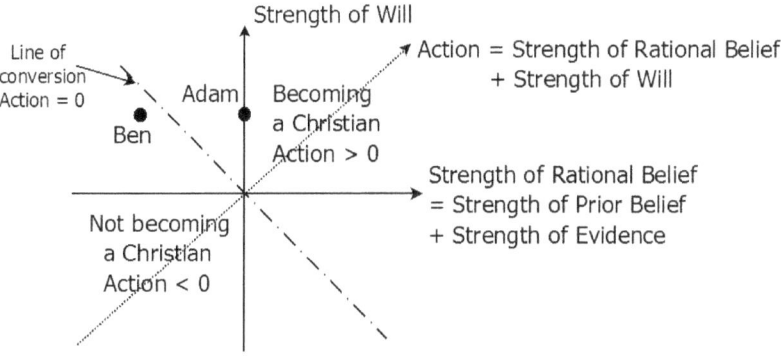

Figure F.1: Illustration of where Adam and Ben are located in a plot of Strength of Will versus Strength of Rational Belief.

Appendix G

Approaches Other than Bayesian Decision Theory

WE HAVE USED CONCEPTS from Bayesian decision theory in this book in order to describe the Aposteriori Wager. In this appendix we will briefly discuss its relation to other methods.

First, evidential decision theory[1] is based on maximizing expected rewards in a way that is essentially equivalent to the Canonical Wager, of which the Aposteriori Wager is a special case.

Second, choice modeling also attempts to describe the decision of an individual—typically a consumer's choice.[2] This is achieved by maximizing a random utility rather than an expected one, as in the Canonical Wager. If instead the Wager has a Maximax decision rule, the two approaches are more similar.[3] But there are still fundamental differences: Whereas the consumer is free to choose between outcomes, the waging person is not, since the outcome of a decision depends on the truth. In addition, choice modeling aims to figure out the probabilities by which a randomly chosen consumer (viewed as a member of a large population) will make different kinds of decisions, whereas the Wager helps a person to make a decision.

Third, the mathematical theory of games is somewhat related to decision theory.[4] However, it deals with situations where each player's actions

   1. Gibbard and Harper, *Counterfactuals*.
   2. Train, *Discrete Choice Methods*.
   3. The Maximax decision rule is based on maximizing the maximal reward of each alternative. See for instance chapter 1 of Jordan, *Pascal's Wager* for a definition of this and other decision rules.
   4. Luce and Raiffa, *Games and Decisions*, and Osborne and Rubinstein, *Course in Game Theory*.

are dependent on the choices of others. It is therefore less relevant for the decision to become a Christian, which is individual—something between each person and God—even though others may influence the decision to some extent.

Bibliography

Adams, Robert. "Kierkegaard's Arguments against Objective Reasoning in Religion." *The Monist* 60:2 (1976) 228–43.
Aikman, David. *Jesus in Beijing: How Christianity Is Transforming China and Changing the Global Balance of Power.* Regnery, 2003.
Albert, Max. "Bayesian Rationality and Decision Making: A Critical Review." *Analyse & Kritik* 25 (2003) 101–17.
Alexander, Denis. *Creation or Evolution: Do We Have to Choose?* Oxford: Monarch, 2008.
Almkvist, Sven. *Framtiden förutsagd: Om Daniel-drömtydaren.* Uppsala: Relevant Media, 2013.
Allen Jr., John L. *The Global War on Christians: Dispatches from the Front Lines of Anti-Christian Persecution.* New York: Crown, 2013.
Anselm, Saint. "Proslogium." In *Saint Anselm: Basic Writings*, translated by Sidney N. Deane. La Salle, IL: Open Court, 1968.
Aronsson, Torbjörn. *Guds eld över Sverige: Svensk väckelsehistoria efter 1945.* 2nd ed. Uppsala: Livets Ords förlag, 2005
Arp, Halton. *Seeing Red: Red Shifts, Cosmology and Academic Science.* Montreal: Apeiron, 1997.
Atkins, Peter. "Will Science Ever Fail?" *New Scientist* (August 8 1992) 32–35.
Atzmon, Gil, et al. "Abraham's Children in the Genome Era: Major Jewish Diaspora Populations Comprise Distinct Genetic Clusters with Shared Middle East Ancestry." *American Journal of Human Genetics* 86 (2010) 850–59.
Augustine, Saint. *The Confessions of St. Augustine.* Translated by Rex Warner. New Kensington, PA: Whitaker House, 1996.
———. *The Literal Meaning of Genesis.* Translated and annotated by John Hammond Taylor, vol. 1–2. New York: Newman, 1982.
Baier, Dirk. "The Influence of Religiosity on Violent Behavior of Adolescents: A Comparison of Christian and Muslim Religiosity." *Journal of Interpersonal Violence* 29:2 (2014) 102–27.
Baker, Ray. *En brännande fråga: Nytt ljus på det yttersta mörkret.* Stockholm: Svenska Evangeliska Alliansen, 2011.

———. "Vår Gud är en förtärande eld: Den bibliska grunden för konditionalism." *Theofilos* 6:1 (2014) 4–19.
Barna Group. "Atheists and Agnostics Take Aim at Christians." Research Releases in Faith and Christianity. Ventura, CA: Barna Group, June 2007. https://barna.org/barna-update/faith-spirituality/102-atheists-and-agnostics-take-aim-at-christians#.V5M_V-TrocA.
Barnes, Luke A. "The Fine-Tuning of the Universe for Intelligent Life." arXiv:1112.4647v1 [physics.hist-ph], December 20, 2011.
Bartha, Paul. "Many Gods, Many Wagers: Pascal's Wager Meets the Replicator Dynamics." In *Probability in the Philosophy of Religion*, edited by Jake Chandler and Victoria S. Harrison, 187–206. Oxford: Oxford University Press, 2012.
Bauckham, Richard. *Jesus and the Eye Witnesses: The Gospels as Eyewitness Testimony*. Grands Rapids: Eerdmans, 2006.
Bayes, Thomas. "An Essay towards Solving a Problem in the Doctrine of Chances." *Philosophical Transactions of the Royal Society of London* 53 (1763) 370–418.
Behar, Doron M., et al. "The Genome-Wide Structure of the Jewish People." *Nature* 466:8 (2010) 238–43.
———. "The Matrilineal Ancestry of Ashkenazi Jewry: Portrait of Recent Founder Event." *American Journal of Human Genetics* 78 (2006) 487–97.
Behe, Michael J. *Darwin's Black Box: The Biochemical Challenge to Evolution*. New York: Free Press, 1999.
Bennett, Dennis J. *Nine O'Clock in the Morning*. Logos, 1971.
Benzmüller, Christoph, and Bruno Woltzenlogel Paleo. "Formalization, Mechanization and Automation of Gödel's Proof of God's Existence." arXiv.org, September 2013. http://arxiv.org/pdf/1308.4526v4.pdf.
Berger, James O. *Statistical Decision Theory and Bayesian Analysis*. 2nd ed. New York: Springer Series in Statistics, 1985.
Bevere, John. *Extraordinary. The Life You are Meant to Live*. Colorado: WaterBrook, 2009.
Bielefeldt, Heiner, et al. "The Global Charter of Conscience. A Global Covenant Concerning Faiths and Freedom of Conscience." Charterofconscience.org, 2012. http://charterofconscience.org.
Bovens, Luc. "Does It Matter Whether a Miracle-Like Event Happens to Oneself Rather than to Someone Else?" In *Probability in the Philosophy of Religion*, edited by Jake Chandler and Victoria S. Harrison, 64–78. Oxford: Oxford University Press, 2012.
Boyarin, Daniel. *The Jewish Gospels: The Story of the Jewish Christ*. New York: New Press, 2012.
Bradley, James. "An Augustinian Perspective on the Philosophy of Mathematics." *Journal of the ACMS*, 2007. https://acmsonline.org/2007-journal/.
Bradley, James, and Russell Howell. *Mathematics Through the Eyes of Faith*. New York: HarperCollins, 2011.
Bray, Steven M., et al. "Signatures of Founder Effects, Admixture, and Selection in the Ashkenazi Jewish Population." *Proceedings of the National Academy of Sciences of the USA* 107:37 (2010) 16222–27.
Buchak, Lara. "Can It Be Rational to Have Faith?" In *Probability in the Philosophy of Religion*, edited by Jake Chandler and Victoria S. Harrison, 225–46. Oxford: Oxford University Press, 2012.

———. "Instrumental Rationality, Epistemic Rationality and Evidence-Gathering." *Philosophical Perspectives* 24 (2010) 85–120.
Burge, Gary M., et al. *The New Testament in Antiquity*. Grand Rapids: Zondervan, 2009.
Burpo, Todd. *Heaven Is for Real: A Little Boy's Astounding Story of His Trip to Heaven and Back*. Written with L. Vincent. Nashville: HIFR Ministries, 2010.
Carlsson, Mark. "Guds gömdhet." In *Gud och hans kritiker, en antologi om nyateismen*, edited by Mats Selander, 75–91. Stockholm: Credoakademin, 2012.
Carmeli, Moshe. *Cosmological Relativity*. Singapore: World Scientific, 2006.
Chalmers, Alan F. *What Is This Thing Called Science?* 3rd ed. St Lucia, Australia: University of Queensland Press, 1994.
Chandler, Jake, and Victoria S. Harrison. "Probability in the Philosophy of Religion." In *Probability in the Philosophy of Religion*, edited by Jake Chandler and Victoria S. Harrison, 1–22. Oxford: Oxford University Press, 2012.
Chen, Ming-Hui, et al., eds. *Frontiers of Statistical Decision Making and Bayesian Analysis*. In Honour of James O. Berger. New York: Springer, 2010.
Chignell, Andrew. "The Ethics of Belief." In *Stanford Encyclopedia of Philosophy*, 2016. https://plato.stanford.edu/entries/ethics-belief/.
Clifford, William K. "The Ethics of Belief." In *Lectures and Essays*, edited by L. Stephen and F. Pollock, 163–205. London: Maximillian, 1879.
Clouser, Roy. *Knowing with the Heart: Religious Experience and Belief in God*. Downers Grove, IL: InterVarsity, 1999.
Cochran, Gregory, et al. "Natural History of Ashkenazi Intelligence." *Journal of Biosocial Science* 38:5 (2006) 659–93.
Coles, Robert. *The Spiritual Life of Children*. Boston: Houghton Mifflin, 1991.
Collins, Francis. *The Language of God*. New York: Free Press, 2006.
Collins, Robin. "The Teleological Argument: An Exploration of the Fine-Tuning of the Universe." In *The Blackwell Companion to Natural Theology*, edited by William L. Craig and J. P. Moreland, 202–81. Chichester, UK: Wiley-Blackwell, 2012.
Conway Morris, Simon. *Life's Solution: Inevitable Humans in a Lonely Universe*. Cambridge: Cambridge University Press, 2003.
Copan, Paul. *Is God a Moral Monster?* Grand Rapids: Baker, 2011.
Courgeau, Daniel. *Probability and Social Science: Methodological Relationships between the Two Approaches*. Dordrecht: Springer, 2012.
Cowan, Louise, and Os Guinness, eds. *Invitation to the Classics: A Guide to the Books You've Always Wanted to Read*. Grand Rapids: Baker, 1998.
Craig, William L. *No Easy Answers: Finding Hope in Doubt, Failure and Unanswered Prayers*. Chicago, IL: Moody, 1990.
———. *The Only Wise God: The Compatibility of Divine Foreknowledge and Human Freedom*. Eugene, OR: Wipf and Stock, 2000.
———. *Reasonable Faith, Christian Truth and Apologetics*. 3rd ed. Wheaton, IL: Crossway, 2008.
Craig, William L., and James D. Sinclair. "The *Kalam* Cosmological Argument." In *The Blackwell Companion to Natural Theology*, edited by William L. Craig and J. P. Moreland, 101–201. Chichester, UK: Wiley-Blackwell, 2012.
Cruz, Nicky, and Madelene Harris. *Lonely but Never Alone*. Grand Rapids: Zondervan, 1981.
Daeschler, Edward B., et al. "A Devonian Tetrapod-Like Fish and the Evolution of the Tetrapod Body Plan." *Nature* 440:7085 (2006) 757–63.

Darwin, Charles. "Letter to William Graham, Down," July 3 1881. Darwin Correspondence Project, letter 13230. https://www.darwinproject.ac.uk/letter/DCP-LETT-13230.xml.

Davies, Paul. "A Brief History of the Multiverse." *New York Times*, August 12 2003, http://www.nytimes.com/2003/04/12/opinion/a-brief-history-of-the-multiverse.html.

Dawkins, Richard. *The Blind Watchmaker*. London: Penguin, 1986.

———. *The God Delusion*. London: Bantam, 2006.

Dennett, Daniel C. *Darwin's Dangerous Idea*. New York: Simon and Schuster, 1995.

DeWitt, David. "What About the DNA Similarity between Human and Chimp DNA?" In *New Answers Book 3: Over 35 Questions on Creation/Evolution and the Bible*, edited by Ken Ham, 99–108. Green Forest, AZ: Master, 2009.

Diaconis, Perci, and Frederick Mosteller. "Methods for Studying Coincidences." *Journal of the American Statistical Association* 84:408 (1989) 853–61.

Diderot, Denis. "Additions to the Philosophical Thoughts." In *Philosophical Thoughts and Other Texts*, translated by Kirk Watson. Audiobook, 2014.

Dodd, Charles H. *The Founder of Christianity*. New York: Macmillan, 1971.

Dostoyevsky, Fyodor M. *The Brothers Karamazov*. Translated by Richard Pevear and Larissa Volhokonsky. New York: North Point, 1990.

Doyle, Tom. *Killing Christians: Living the Faith Where It's Not Safe to Believe*. Nashville: W Publishing, 2015.

D'Souza, Dinesh. *What's So Great about Christianity?* Washington, DC: Regnery, 2007.

Edsinger, Olof. *Krigen i gamla testamentet*. Stockholm: CredoAkademin, 2007.

ENCODE Project. "Encyclopedia of DNA Elements." National Human Genome Research Institute. https://www.genome.gov/10005107/.

Engel, James F. and H. Wilbert Norton. *What's Gone Wrong With the Harvest? A Communication Strategy for the Church and World Evangelism*. Grand Rapids: Zondervan, 1975.

Erasmus, Desiderius. *Education of a Christian Prince*. Translated by Lester K. Born. New York: Octagon, 1963.

Ewert, Per. *Vem tänder stjärnorna?* Vellinge, Sweden: Authentic Media Nordic, 2008.

Ewert, Winston. "Digital Irreducible Complexity: A Survey of Irreducible Complexity in Computer Simulations." *BIO-Complexity* 2014:1 (2014) 1–10.

Ewert, Winston, et al. "Active Information in Metabiology." *BIO-Complexity* 2013:4 (2013) 1–10.

Farmer, Mark A., and Andrea Habura. "Using Protistan Examples to Dispel the Myths of Intelligent Design." *Journal of Eukaryotic Microbiology* 57:1 (2010) 3–10.

Feinberg, Paul D. "Cumulative Case Apologetics." In *Five Views on Apologetics*, edited by Steven B Cowan, 148–72. Grand Rapids: Zondervan, 2000.

Feyerabend, Paul. *Against Method*. London: Humanities, 1975.

Flew, Antony. *There Is a God: How the World's Most Notorious Atheist Changed His Mind*. With contributions from Roy Abraham Varghese. New York: HarperCollins, 2007.

Furuhagen, Hans. *Bibeln och arkeologerna*. Stockholm: Natur och Kultur, 2010.

Gärdeborn, Anders. *Intelligent skapelsetro: En naturvetare läser Första Mosebok*. Extended 2nd ed. Vendelsö: XP Media, 2009.

Garrison, David. *A Wind in the House of Islam: How God Is Drawing Muslims Around the World to Faith in Jesus Christ*. Monument, CO: WIGTake, 2014.

Gauger, Ann, et al. *Science and Human Origins.* Seattle, WA: Discovery Institute Press, 2012.

Gauger, Ann, et al. "Genetic Evidence for Human Uniqueness." In *A Scientific, Theological, and Philosophical Critique of Theistic Evolution*, edited by J. P. Moreland et al., chapter 15. Wheaton, IL: Crossway, 2017.

Geertsema, Jan C. "A Christian View of the Foundations of Statistics." *Perspectives on Science and Christian Faith* 39:3 (1987) 158–64.

Geisler, Norman L. *Systematic Theology.* Vol. 1. Minneapolis: Bethany House, 2002.

Geisler, Norman L., and Thomas Howe. *The Big Book of Bible Difficulties: Clear and Concise Answers from Genesis to Revelation.* Grand Rapids: Baker, 1992.

Gibbard, Allan, and Willam L. Harper. "Counterfactuals and Two Kinds of Expected Utility." In *Ifs: Conditionals, Beliefs, Decision, Chance, and Time*, edited by W. L. Harper et al., 153–90. Dordrecht, Holland: D. Reidel, 1981.

Gitt, Werner. *In the Beginning Was Information: A Scientist Explains the Incredible Design in Nature.* Green Forest, AZ: Master, 2005.

Glueck, Nelson. *Rivers in the Desert: A History of the Negev.* New York: Farrar, Strauss and Cudahy, 1959.

Gonzalez, Guillermo, and Jay Richards. *The Privileged Planet: How Our Place in the Cosmos Is Designed for Discovery.* Washington, DC: Regnery, 2004.

Good, I. J. "On the Principle of Total Evidence." *British Journal of the Philosophy of Science* 17:4 (1967) 319–21.

Gordon, Bruce L. "The Rise of Naturalism and Its Problematic Role in Science and Culture." In *The Nature of Nature*, edited by Bruce L. Gordon and William A. Dembski, 3–61. Wilmington, DE: ISI, 2011.

Gould, Stephen Jay. *Rock of Ages: Science and Religion in the Fullness of Life.* New York: Ballantine, 1999.

Grant, Hugh G. *Scientific Method in Brief.* New York: Cambridge University Press, 2012.

Green, Stefan. "Dödahavsrullarna." *Theofilos* 3:2 (2011) 14–23.

Grim, Melissa, et al. "BUSINESS: A Powerful Source for Interfaith Understanding and Peace." United Nations Global Compact, 2014. http://religiousfreedomandbusiness.org/business-a-powerful-force-for-supporting-interfaith-understanding-and-peace.

Groothuis, Douglas R. *Christian Apologetics.* Downers Grove, IL: InterVarsity, 2011.

———. *On Pascal.* Wadsworth Philosophy Series. Florence, KY: Thompson Learning, 2003.

———. *Unmasking the New Age.* Downers Grove, IL: InterVarsity, 1986.

Grudem, Wayne. *Systematic Theology: An Introduction to Biblical Doctrine.* Grand Rapids: Zondervan, 2000.

Gumbel, Nicky. *Questions of Life.* Eastbourne, UK: Kingsway, 2003.

———. *Telling Others.* Eastbourne, UK: Kingsway, 1997.

Gustavsson, Stefan. "Är Gud ett ondskefullt monster?" In *Gud och hans kritiker, en antologi om nyateismen*, edited by Mats Selander, 115–41. Stockholm: Credoakademin, 2012.

———. *Kristen på goda grunder.* Stockholm: Cordia, 1997.

Habermas, Gary R. "Atheism and Evil: A Fatal Dilemma." In *Why Believe? God Exists!*, edited by T. L. Miethe and Gary R. Habermas, chapter 20. Joplin, MO: College Press, 1993.

———. "Paradigm Shift: A Challenge to Naturalism." Faculty Publications and Presentations at DigitalCommons@LibertyUniversity, School of Religion, paper 8. Lynchburg, VA: Liberty University, 1989.

———. "The Plight of the New Atheism: A Critique." *Journal of the Evangelical Theological Society* 51:4 (2008) 813–27.

———. "The Resurrection of Jesus' Timeline." In *Contending with Christianity's Critics*, 113–25. Nashville: Broadman and Holman, 2009.

Habermas, Gary R., and Michael R. Licona. *The Case of the Resurrection of Jesus*. Grand Rapids: Kregel, 2004.

Hacking, Ian. *The Emergence of Probability: A Philosophical Study of Early Ideas about Probability Induction and Statistical Inference*. 2nd ed. New York: Cambridge University Press, 2006.

———. "The Logic of Pascal's Wager." *American Philosophical Quarterly* 9:2 (1972) 186–91.

Haeckel, Ernst. *The Evolution of Man*. Project Gutenberg ebook 8700, 2005.

Hahn, Ulrike, and Mike Oaksford. "The Rationality of Informal Argumentation: A Bayesian Approach to Reasoning Fallacies." *Psychological Review* 114:3 (2007) 704–32.

Hájek, Alan. "Blaise and Bayes." In *Probability in the Philosophy of Religion*, edited by Jake Chandler and Victoria S. Harrison, 167–86. Oxford: Oxford University Press, 2012.

———. "Pascal's Wager." In *Stanford Encyclopedia of Philosophy*, 2008.

Halldorf, Peter. *21 kyrkofäder: Historien om hur kristendomen formades*. Örebro: Cordia, 2000

Halvorsen, Hans. "A Probability Problem in the Fine Tuning Argument." Archive for Preprints in Philosophy of Science, 2014. http://philsci-archive.pitt.edu/11004/1/fine-tuning-anon.pdf.

Hammer, Michael F. et al. "Extended Y Chromosome Haplotypes Resolve Multiple and Unique Lineages of the Jewish Priesthood." *Human Genetics* 126 (2009) 707–17.

Hamming, Richard W. "The Unreasonable Effectiveness of Mathematics." *American Mathematical Monthly* 87:2 (1980) 81–90.

Hand, David J., and Keming Yu. "Idiot's Bayes—Not So Stupid after All?" *International Statistical Review* 69:3 (2001) 385–99.

Hardy, Godfrey H. *A Mathematician's Apology*. Cambridge: Cambridge University Press, 1940.

Harrigan, Nicholas, and Robert W. Spekkens. "Einstein, Incompletness, and the Epistemic View of Quantum States." *Foundations of Physics* 40 (2010) 125–57.

Harris, Sam. *Letter to a Christian Nation*. New York: Knopf, 2006.

Hartnett, John. "Aberration of Startlight and the One-Way Speed of Light." Bible Science Forum, November 2015. https://bibliescienceforum.com/2015/11/12/aberration-of-starlight-and-the-one-way-speed-of-light/.

———. "Does My Use of Carmeli's Cosmology Provide a Valid Solution to the Startlight-Travel-Time Problem?" Bible Science Forum, November 2016. https://bibliescienceforum.com/2016/11/19/my-use-of-carmelis-cosmology-a-valid-solution/.

———. *Starlight, Time and the New Physics*. Atlanta: Creation, 2007.

Hawking, Stephen, and Leonard Mlodinow. *The Grand Design*. New York: Bantam, 2010.

Hazen, Robert M., et al. "Functional Information and the Emergence of Biocomplexity." *Proceedings of the National Academy of Sciences of the USA* 104 (2007) 8574–81.
Hempel, Carl G. *Philosophy of Natural Science*. Upper Saddle River, NJ: Prentice-Hall, 1966.
Henne, Peter, et al. "Trends in Global Restrictions on Religion." Pew Research Center, June 23 2016. http://www.pewforum.org/2016/06/23/trends-in-global-restrictions-on-religion/.
Hick, John H. *An Interpretation of Religion*. New Haven, CT: Yale University Press, 1989.
Hill, Andrew, and John H. Walton. *A Survey of the Old Testament*. 3rd ed. Grand Rapids: Zondervan, 2009.
Hill, Jonathan. *The History of Christianity*. Oxford: Lion Hudson, 2007.
———. *What Has Christianity Ever Done for Us?* Oxford: Lion Hudson, 2005.
Hitchens, Cristopher. *God Is Not Great: How Religion Poisons Everything*. New York: Twelve (Warner), 2007.
Högås, Markus. "The grand design-Stephen Hawkings kosmologiska kamp med Gud." *Theofilos* 6:1 (2014) 98–115.
Hössjer, Ola. "The Aposteriori Wager: Pascal Meets Bayes." *Theofilos* 5:2 (2013) 13–32.
Hössjer, Ola, et al. "An Alternative Population Genetics Model." In *A Scientific, Theological, and Philosophical Critique of Theistic Evolution*, edited by J. P. Moreland et al., chapter 16. Wheaton, IL: Crossway, 2017.
Howell, Russell W. "The Matter of Mathematics." *Perspectives on Science and Christian Faith* 62:2 (2015) 75–88.
Howson, Colin, and Peter Urbach. *Scientific Reasoning. The Bayesian Approach*. Peru, IL: Open Court, 2006.
Huber, Franz, and Christoph Schmidt-Petri, eds. *Degrees of Belief*. Springer, 2009.
Hume, David. *Enquiry Concerning Human Understanding*. Prepared by Jonathan Bennett. Some Texts from Early Modern Philosophy. 2007. http://www.earlymoderntexts.com/authors/hume.
Humphreys, D. Russell. *Starlight and Time*. Green Forest, AZ: Master, 1994.
Huxley, Julian. *Evolution: The Modern Synthesis*. Cambridge, MA: MIT Press, 1942.
Ibstedt, Nils. *Uppenbarelseboken, kommentarer-tolkningar-studier*. Värnamo: Semnos förlag, 2013.
Ilan, Tal. *Lexicon of Jewish Names in Late Antiquity. Part 1: Palestine 330 BCE–200 CE*. Text and Studies in Ancient Judaism 91. Tubingen: Mohr-Siebeck, 2002.
Internet Evangelism Day. "Gray's the Color of Life: Understanding the Gray Matrix." http://www.internetevangelismday.com/gray-matrix.php.
Ipsos Global @dvisory. "Questions on Supreme Being, Reincarnation, and Evolution." Ipsos, October 2010. http://www.ipsos-na.com/download/pr.aspx?id=10669.
———. "Is Religion a Force for Good in the World?" Ipsos poll, November 26, 2010. http://www.ipsos-na.com/download/pr.aspx?id= 10209.
James, William. *The Will to Believe and Other Essays in Population Philosophy*. Cambridge, MA: Harvard University Press, 1979.
Jansen, Vincent A. A. "On Kin and Group Selection, and the Haystack Model." In *The Mathematics of Darwin's Legacy*, edited by Fabio A. C. C. Chalub and José F. Rodrigues, 139–58. Basel: Birkhäuser Springer, 2011.
Jaynes, Edwin T. *Probability Theory: The Logic of Science*. Cambridge: Cambridge University Press, 2003.

Jeanson, Nathaniel T., and Jason Lisle. "On the Origin of Eukaryotic Species' Genotypic and Phenotypic Diversity: Genetic Clocks, Population Growth Curves and Comparative Nuclear Genome Analyses Suggest Created Heterozygosity in Combination with Natural Processes as a Major Mechanism." *Answers Research Journal* 9 (2016) 81-122.

Johnson, Donald E. *Probability's Nature and Nature's Probability: A Call to Scientific Integrity*. Charleston, SC: Booksurge, 2009.

———. *Programming of Life*. Sylacauga, AL: Big Mac, 2010.

Johnson, Todd M., and Kenneth R. Ross, eds. *Atlas of Global Christianity*. Edinburgh: Edinburgh University Press, 2009.

Johnson, Todd M., et al. "Christianity 2010: A View from the New Atlas of Global Christianity." *International Bulletin of Missionary Research* 34:1 (2010) 29-36.

———. "Christianity 2011: Martyrs and the Resurgence of Religion." *International Bulletin of Missionary Research* 35:1 (2011) 28-29.

Jones, Mark H., et al. *An Introduction to Galaxies and Cosmology*. Cambridge, UK: Cambridge University Press, 2015.

Jonsson, Ulf. *Med tanke på Gud: En introduktion till religionsfilosofin*. 2nd ed. Skellefteå: Artos Norma, 2008.

Jordan, Jeff. *Pascal's Wager: Pragmatic Arguments and Belief in God*. Oxford: Clarendon, 2006.

Joshua Project. "Bringing Definition to an Unfinished Task." https://joshuaproject.net/people_groups/statistics.

Kauffman, Stuart A. *The Origins of Order: Self-Organisation and Selection in Evolution*. Oxford: Oxford University Press, 1993.

Keener, Craig S. *Miracles: The Credibility of the New Testament Accounts*. Grand Rapids: Baker Academic, 2011.

Kelley, Dean M. *Why Conservative Churches Are Growing: A Study of Sociology of Religion*. Updated ed. New York: Harper and Row, 1977.

Kelly, Thomas. "Epistemic Rationality as Instrumental Rationality: A Critique." *Philosophy and Phenomenological Research* 66:3 (2003) 612-40.

Keyes, Dick. "Sentimentality . . . and It Costs." *International Newsletter of L'Abri Fellowship*, November 2009.

Keynes, John Maynard. *A Treatise on Probability*. London: Macmillan, 1921.

Kierkegaard, Søren, A. *Concluding Unscientific Postscript*. Translated by D. F. Swenson. Princeton, NJ: Princeton University Press, 1941.

Kimura, Mooto. *Neutral Theory of Molecular Evolution*. New York: Cambridge University Press, 1983.

Kitchen, Kevin A. *On the Reliability of the Old Testament*. Grand Rapids: Eerdmans, 2003.

Korb, Kevin. "Bayesian Informal Logic and Fallacies." *Informal Logic* 23:2 (2003) 41-70.

Kozulic, Branko, and Matti Leisola. "Have Scientists Already Been Able to Surpass the Capabilities of Evolution?" viXra archive of e-prints in Science and Mathematics, 2015. http://vixra.org/abs/1504.0130.

Kremarik, Akiane, and Foreli Kremarik. *Akiane: Her Life, Her Art, Her Poetry*. Nashville: W Publishing, 2004.

Kuhn, Thomas. *The Structure of Scientific Revolutions*. 50th anniversary ed. Introductory essay by Ian Hacking. Chicago, IL: University of Chicago Press, 2012.

Kwan, Kai-man. "The Argument from Religious Experience." In *The Blackwell Companion to Natural Theology*, edited by William L. Craig and J. P. Moreland, 498–552. Chichester, UK: Wiley-Blackwell, 2012.

Landgren, Per. "The Aristotelian Concept of History: Theory of History in Renaissance Europe and Sweden." PhD diss., University of Gothenburg, 2008.

———. "Makt eller rätt, två tydliga linjer i idéhistorien i väst." *Kristdemokraten* (September 26) 2013.

———. "Tro och vetenskap: Krig, fred eller vad?" *Theofilos* 2:3 (2010) 16–32.

Laplace, Pierre-Simon. *Philosophical Essay on Probabilities*. New York: Dover, 1951.

Lausanne Movement. "The Cape Town Commitment." January 2011. https://www.lausanne.org/content/ctc/ctcommitment.

Leijon, Kjell Olof. "Lutheranism or Secularism." *Theofilos* 5:2 (2013) 4–12.

Lennox, John. *God and Stephen Hawking: Whose Design Is It Anyway?* Oxford: Lion Hudson, 2011.

———. *God's Undertaker: Has Science Buried God?* Oxford: Lion Hudson, 2009.

———. *Gunning for God: Why the New Atheists Are Missing the Target*. Oxford: Lion Hudson, 2011.

———. *The Seven Days that Divide the World: The Beginning According to Genesis and Science*. Grand Rapids: Zondervan, 2011.

Lewis, C.S. *The Case for Christianity*. Nashville: Broadman and Holman, 2000.

———. *Mere Christianity*. London: William Collins, 1944.

———. *Miracles*. Rev. ed. London: Collins/Fontana, 1960.

———. *The Problem of Pain*. New York: Macmillan, 1944.

———. *Surprised by Joy: The Shape of My Early Life*. Orlando, FL: Harcourt, 1955.

———. *The Weight of Glory*. New York: HarperCollins, 1949.

Lewontin, Richard. "Billions and Billions of Demons." Review of *The Demon-Haunted World: Science as a Candle in the Dark* by Carl Sagan. *New York Review* 31 (January 9, 1997). http://www.nybooks.com/articles/1997/01/09/billions-and-billions-of-demons/.

Li, Heng, and Richard Durbin. "Inference of Human Population History from Individual Whole-Genome Sequences." *Nature* 475 (2011) 493–96.

Luce, Robert D., and Howard Raiffa. *Games and Decisions: Introduction and Critical Survey*. New York: Wiley, 1957.

Luskin, Casey. "Missing Transitions: Human Origins and the Fossil Record." In *A Scientific, Theological, and Philosophical Critique of Theistic Evolution*, edited by J. P. Moreland et al., chapter 14. Wheaton, IL: Crossway, 2017.

Machiavelli, Niccolò. *The Prince*. Translated by W. K. Marriott. Project Gutenberg Ebook 1232, 2006.

Marks II, Robert J., et al. *Introduction to Evolutionary Informatics*. Hackensack, NJ: World Scientific, 2017.

Martin, Luther H., and Eugene Bach. *Back to the Jerusalem of the East: The Underground House Church of North Korea*. Blountsville, AL: Back to Jerusalem, 2011.

McCormack, Ian. *A Glimpse of Eternity*. As told by Jenny Sharkey. New Zealand: Arun, 2008.

McGrew, Timothy, and Lydia McGrew. "The Argument from Miracles: A Cumulative Case for the Resurrection of Jesus of Nazareth." In *The Blackwell Companion to Natural Theology*, edited by William L. Craig and J. P. Moreland, 498–552. Chichester, UK: Wiley-Blackwell, 2012.

McIntosh, Andy C. *Genesis for Today: The Relevance of the Creation/Evolution Debate to Today's Society.* 4th ed. Leominster: Day One, 2010.

———. "Information and Entropy—Top-Down or Bottom-Up Development in Living Systems?" *International Journal of Design and Nature and Ecodynamics* 4:4 (2009) 051 95.

Melhus, Kåre. "The Discipline of Journalism: Reflections from a Christian Perspective." *Theofilos* 8:2 (2016) 231–45.

Mellars, Paul. "Going East: New Genetic and Archaeological Perspectives on the Modern Human Colonization of Eurasia." *Science* 313 (2006) 796–800.

Mellor, D. Hugh. "God and Probability." *Religious Studies* 5 (1969) 223–34.

Meyer, Stephen, C. *Darwin's Doubt: The Explosive Origin of Animal Life and the Case for Intelligent Design.* New York: HarperCollins, 2013.

———. *The Signature of the Cell.* New York: HarperCollins, 2009.

Milliam, John. "The Genesis Genealogies: Are They Complete?" Evidence for God from Science, 2010. http://www.godandscience.org/youngearth/genesis_genealogies.html.

Molén, Mats. *Vårt ursprung?: Om universums, jordens och livets uppkomst samt historia.* 4th ed. Haninge: XP Media, 2000.

Möller, Lennart. *The Exodus Case. New Discoveries of the Historical Exodus.* Extended 3rd ed. Copenhagen: Scandinavia, 2008.

Moore, Kevin. *Untrumpable: How Betting against Theism Is a Foolish Bet. What Pascal Should Have Said.* Krestwood, KY: Meta House, 2014.

Moreland, J.P. "The Argument from Consciousness." In *The Blackwell Companion to Natural Theology*, edited by William L. Craig and J. P. Moreland, 282–343. Chichester, UK: Wiley-Blackwell, 2012.

———. *Love Your God with All Your Mind.* Colorado Springs, CO: Navpress, 1997.

Moreland, J. P., and William L. Craig. *Philosophical Foundations for a Christian Worldview.* Downers Grove, IL: InterVarsity, 2003.

Morris, Thomas V. *Making Sense of It All: Pascal and the Meaning of Life.* Grand Rapids: Eerdmans, 1992.

Nagel, Thomas. *Mind and Cosmos: Why the Materialist Neo-Darwinian Conception of Nature Is Almost Certainly False.* Oxford: Oxford University Press, 2012.

Needham, Joseph. *The Grand Titration: Science and Society in East and West.* London: Allen and Unwin, 1969.

Neumann, John von, and Oskar Morgenstern. *Theory of Games and Economic Behavior.* Princeton, NJ: Princeton University Press, 1944.

Neyman, Jerzy. "Frequentist Probability and Frequentist Statistics." *Synthese* 36 (1977) 97–131.

Nevin, Norman C., ed. *Should Christians Embrace Evolution?: Biblical and Scientific Responses.* Nottingham: InterVarsity, 2009.

Noble, Denis. "Physiology Is Rocking the Foundations of Evolutionary Biology." *Experimental Physiology* 98:8 (2013) 1235–43.

Nordström, Ruth. "De mänskliga rättigheternas grund: Om rättspositivism och naturrätt i ett postmodernt samhälle." *Theofilos* 5:1 (2013) 70–78.

Oliviera e Silva, Tomás. "Goldbach Conjecture Verification." December 2015. http://www.ieeta.pt/~tos/goldbach.html.

Open Doors. "World Watch List." https://www.opendoorsusa.org/christian-persecution/world-watch-list/.

Osborne, Martin, and Ariel Rubinstein. *A Course in Game Theory*. Cambridge MA: MIT Press, 1994.
Ottosen, Espen. "The Need for a Comprehensive Revelation: A Christological Solution to J. L. Schellenberg's Hiddenness of God Argument." *Theofilos* 8:2 (2016) 171–84.
Paley, William. *Natural Theology; or, Evidences of the Existence and Attributes of the Deity*. 12th ed. London: J. Faulder, 1809.
Pascal, Blaise. *Pensées*. Translated by A. J. Krailsheimer. Rev. ed. London: Penguin, 1995.
———. *Pensées*. Edited by J. Hagerson et al. Introduction by T. S. Elliot. Project Gutenberg ebook, 2006.
Pearcey, Nancy. *Total Truth: Liberating Christianity from Its Cultural Captivity*. First trade paper ed. Wheaton, IL: Crossway, 2008.
Pearcey, Nancy, and Charles B. Thaxton. *The Soul of Science: Christian Faith and Natural Philosophy*. Wheaton, IL: Crossway, 1994.
Pearl, Judea. *Causality: Models, Reasoning and Inference*. New York: Cambridge University Press, 2000.
Perszyk, Ken, ed. *Molinism: The Contemporary Debate*. Oxford: Oxford University Press, 2011.
Phillips, Dewi Z. *Death and Immortality*. London: Macmillan, 1970.
Pierce, Larry, and Ken Ham. "Are There Gaps in the Genesis Genealogies?" In *The New Answers Book 2*, edited by Ken Ham, 53–62. Green Forest, AR: Master Books, 2008.
Plantinga, Alvin. *The Nature of Necessity*. Oxford: Clarendon, 1974.
———. *Warrant and Proper Function*. Oxford: Oxford University Press, 1993.
———. *Warranted Christian Belief*. Oxford: Oxford University Press, 2000.
———. *Where the Conflict Really Lies: Science, Religion and Naturalism*. Oxford: Oxford University Press, 2011.
Plessis, David du. *A Man Called Mr. Pentecost*. Alachua, FL: Bridge-Logos, 1977.
Plotnitsky, Arkady. *Epistemology and Probability: Bohr, Heisenberg, Schrödinger, and the Nature of Quantum-Theoretical Thinking*. New York: Springer, 2010.
Polyani, Michael. "Life's Irreducible Structure." *Science* 160 (1968) 1308–12.
Popper, Karl. *Conjectures and Refutations: The Growth of Scientific Knowledge*. London: Routledge and Kegan Paul, 1963.
Posner, Sarah. "Kosher Jesus: Messianic Jews in the Holy Land." *The Atlantic*, November 29, 2012.
Puterman, Martin L. *Markov Decision Processes*. New York: Wiley, 1994.
Reichmann, Sven. *Judarna: Det nya förbundets folk*. 2nd ed. Mölndal: Sven Reichmann och Uttrycket, 1995.
Renard, Krister. "Dateringsmetoder." http://www.gluefox.com/skap/skev/dat/dat.shtm.
Rosenbaum, Paul R. *Design of Observational Studies*. New York: Springer, 2010.
Ross, Sheldon M. *Applied Probability Models with Optimization Applications*. New York: Dover, 1970.
Rota, Michael. *Taking Pascal's Wager: Faith, Evidence, and the Abundant Life*. Downers Grove, IL: InterVarsity, 2016.
Rubin, Donald. B., et al. *Bayesian Data Analysis*. 2nd ed. Boca Raton, FL: Chapman and Hall/CRC, 2003.
Ruiz-Orera, Jorge, et al. "Origins of *de Novo* Genes in Human and Chimpanzee." *PLoS Genetics* 11:12 (2015) e1005721.

Ruse, Michael, and Edward O. Wilson. "The Evolution of Ethics." In *Religion and the Natural Sciences*, edited by J.E. Huchingson, 310–11. Orlando, FL: Harcourt Brace, 1993.

Russell, Bertrand. "Is There a God?" In *Collected Papers of Bertrand Russell*, vol. 11, *Last Philosophical Testament 1943–1968*, edited by John G. Slater and Peter Köllner, 542–48. London: Routledge, 1997.

———. *Why I Am Not a Christian, and Other Essays on Religion and Related Subjects.* Edited by Paul Edwards. New York: Touchstone, 1957.

Saada, Tass, and Dean Merrill. *Once an Arafat Man: The True Story of a How a PLO Sniper Found a New Life.* Basel: Brunnen, 2008.

Sahlberg, Carl-Erik. *Missionens historia genom 2000 år.* Örebro: Libris, 2008.

Sanford, John C. *Genetic Entropy and the Mystery of the Genome.* 3rd ed. Waterloo, NY: FMS, 2008.

Sanford John, C., and Robert Carter. "In Light of Genetics . . . Adam, Eve and the Creation/Fall." *Christian Apologetics Journal* 12:2 (2008) 51–98.

Savage, Leonard J. *The Foundations of Statistics.* New York: Wiley, 1954.

Sayer, George. *Jack: A Life of C.S. Lewis.* Wheaton, IL: Crossway, 1988.

Schaefer, Henry F. *Science and Christianity: Conflict or Coherence?* Athens, GA: University of Georgia Printing Department, 2003.

Scharfstein, Sol. *Understanding Jewish History.* 2 vols. Hoboken, NJ: Ktav, 1997.

Schellenberg, John L. *Divine Hiddenness and Human Reason.* Ithaca, NY: Cornell University Press, 2006.

Searle, John R. "Contemporary Philosophy in the Unites States." In *The Blackwell Companion to Philosophy*, edited by Nicholas Bunnin and E. P. Tsui-James, 1–22. 2nd ed. Malden, MA: Blackwell, 2003.

Selander, Mats. "Gud och bevisbördan." In *Gud och hans kritiker, en antologi om nyateismen*, edited by Mats Selander, 59–74 . Stockholm: Credoakademin, 2012.

———. "Richard Dawkins moralsyn." In *Gud och hans kritiker, en antologi om nyateismen*, edited by Mats Selander, 92–114 . Stockholm: Credoakademin, 2012.

———. *Utan Jesus ingen mobil i fickan: Om hur kristen tro lade grunden för modern vetenskap.* Stockholm: Credoakademin, 2017.

———. "Vetenskap och tro." Credoakademin, 2007. http://www.credoakademin.nu/index.php/articles/article/vetenskap_och_tro/.

Shapiro, James A. *Evolution: A View from the 21st Century.* Upper Saddle River, NJ: Pearson Education, 2011.

Sims, Andrew. *Is Faith Delution?: Why Religion Is Food for Your Health.* London: Continuum, 2009.

Sire, James W. *Why Should Anyone Believe Anything at All?* Downers Grove, IL: InterVarsity, 1994.

Skorecki, Karl, et al. "Y Chromosomes of Jewish Priests." *Nature* 385 (1997) 32.

Smith, John Maynard. *Evolution and the Theory of Games.* Cambridge: Cambridge University Press, 1982.

Springer, Rebecca. *Within Heaven's Gates.* New Kensington, PA: Whitaker House, 1984.

Stark, Rodney. *The Triumph of Christianity: How the Jesus Movement Became the World's Largest Religion.* New York: HarperCollins, 2012.

Stenumgaard, Peter. *Vetenskap och tro.* Handen, Stockholm: XP Media, 2008.

———. *Vetenskapens illusioner.* Handen, Stockholm: XP Media, 2011.

Stigler, Stephen. *The History of Statistics: The Measurement of Uncertainty before 1900.* Cambridge, MA: Harvard University Press, 1986.
Strand, Robert. *Angels at My Door.* Mobile, AL: Evergreen, 2003.
Strobel, Lee. *The Case for Christ: A Journalist's Personal Investigation of the Evidence for Jesus.* Grand Rapids: Zondervan, 1998.
Stump, Eleonore. "The Problem of Evil: Analytic Philosophy and Narrative." *Theofilos* 5:1 (2013) 4–15.
Suarez, Antoine. "Can We Give Up the Origin of Humanity from a Primal Couple without Giving Up the Teaching of Original Sin and Atonement?" *Science and Christian Belief* 27:1 (2015) 59–83.
Supphellen, Magne. "Økonomiske effekter av religiøse holdninger til arbeid og næringsvirksomhet: Et overblikk og et rammeverk for videre forskning." *Theofilos* 5:2 (2013) 48–61.
Swärd, Stefan. *Efter detta: Om Guds kärlek och rättvisa, himmel och helvete.* Handen, Stockholm: XP Media, 2011.
Swinburne, Richard. "Bayes, God and the Multiverse." In *Probability in the Philosophy of Religion*, edited by Jake Chandler and Victoria S. Harrison, 103–26. Oxford: Oxford University Press, 2012.
———. *Epistemic Justification.* Oxford: Oxford University Press, 2001.
———. *The Existence of God.* 3rd ed. Oxford: Oxford University Press, 2004.
———. *Faith and Reason.* 2nd ed. Oxford: Oxford University Press, 2005.
Taylor, Peter. "Group Theory in Homogeneous Populations." In *The Mathematics of Darwin's Legacy*, edited by Fabio A. C. C. Chalub and José F. Rodrigues, 105–18. Basel: Birkhäuser, 2011.
Tegmark, Max. "The Multiverse Hierarchy." In *Universe or Multiverse?*, edited by B. Carr, 99–127. Cambridge: Cambridge University Press, 2007.
Tenaillon, Olivier, et al. "Tempo and Mode of Genome Evolution in a 50 000-Generation Experiment." *Nature* 536 (2016) 165–70.
Thiselton, Anthony C. *Hermeneutics: An Introduction.* Cambridge, UK: Eerdmans, 2009.
Thomas, Mark G., et al. "Origins of Old Testament Priests." *Nature* 394 (1998) 138–40.
Tolstoy, Leo. *Confessions.* Translated by David Patterson. New York: Norton, 1983.
Tomkins, Jeffrey, and Jerry Bergman. "Genomic Monkey Business—Estimates of Nearly Identical Human-Chimp DNA Similarity Re-Evaluated Using Omitted Data." *Journal of Creation* 26:1 (2012) 94–100.
Train, Kenneth. *Discrete Choice Methods with Simulation.* 2nd ed. Cambridge: Cambridge University Press, 2009.
Unwin, Stephen D. *The Probability of God: A Simple Calculation That Proves the Ultimate Truth.* New York: Crown Forum, 2003.
Vanhoozer, Kevin J. *Is There a Meaning in This Text?: The Bible, the Reader and the Morality of Literary Knowledge.* Grand Rapids: Zondervan, 1998.
Walvoord, John F. *Israel in Prophecy.* Grand Rapids: Zondervan, 1962.
Weber, Max. *The Protestant Ethic and the Spirit of Capitalism.* Translated by Stephen Kalberg. New York: Routledge, 2001.
Wells, Jonathan. *The Myth of Junk DNA.* Seattle, WA: Discovery Institute Press, 2011.
Whitehead, Alfred N., and Bertrand Russell. *Principia Mathematica.* 2nd ed. Cambridge: Cambridge University Press, 1927.

Wigner, Eugene. "The Unreasonable Effectiveness of Mathematics in Natural Sciences." *Communications in Pure and Applied Mathematics* 13:1 (1960) 1–14.

Wilkerson, David. *The Cross and the Switchblade*. Written with John and Elizabeth Sherrill. New York: B. Geiss, 1963.

Williams, Alex, and John Hartnett. *Dismantling the Big Bang*. Green Forest, AR: Master, 2005.

Williams, Peter S. "Apologetics in 3-D: Persuading across Spiritualities with the Apostle Paul." *Theofilos* 4:1 (2012) 3–24.

Wilson, Julian. *Wigglesworth: The Complete Story*. Milon Keynes, UK: Authentic Media, 2002.

Woodberry, Robert D. "The Missionary Roots of Liberal Democracy." *American Political Science Review* 106:2 (2012) 244–74.

Wright, N. T. "Jesus' Resurrection and Christian Origins." In *Passionate Conviction: Contemporary Discourses in Christian Apologetics*, edited by Paul Copan and William L. Craig, 123–37. Nashville: Broadman and Holman, 2002.

Young, Davis A. "The Contemporary Relevance of Augustine's View of Creation." *Perspectives on Science and Christian Faith* 40:1 (1988) 42–45.

Name Index

Aaron, brother of Moses, 217
Abraham, patriarch, 72, 90, 116–17, 192, 198, 198n57, 215n152, 216n153, 222
Adam, first man, 22, 129, 149, 156, 159–60, 165–66, 206, 208–9
Adams, Robert, 41n19
Ahab, Old Testament king, 215
Aikman, David, 112n44, 122n94
Albert, Max, 15n21
Alexander, Denis, 150n49, 157n70
Allen Jr., John L., 224n205
Almkvist, Sven, 221n186
Andrew, apostle, 81
Anselm, archbishop of Canterbury, 48, 49n32, 66
Aquina, Thomas, 50–51, 110, 132
Arafat, Yassir, 228
Aristotle, Greek philosopher and scientist, 110, 142, 156, 168
Aronsson, Torbjörn, 124n100
Arp, Halton, 151–52, 152n51
Artaxerxes I, Persian king, 221
Atkins, Peter, 137, 137n3
Atzmon, Gil, 216n153
Augustine, church father, 140, 140n19, 179, 225, 225n208
Axe, Doug, 164
Azariah, friend of Daniel, 241–42

Bach, Eugene, 7n10, 106n13
Bach, Johann Sebastian, 113
Bacon, Francis, 139
Baier, Dirk, 57n65
Baker, Ray, 212n136, 213n140

Balaam, Old Testament pagan prophet, 197
bar Kokhba, Simon, 114, 117
Barnabas, apostle and travel companion of Paul, 120, 223, 230
Barnes, Luke A., 174, 175n124
Bartha, Paul, 56n59, 57n61, 260n1
Bauckham, Richard, 218n164, 219n166
Bayes, Thomas, 15–16, 15n21
Behar, Doron M., 216n153, 217n158
Behe, Michael J., 163n85, 173, 173n119
Belfour, Sir Arthur, 126
Bennett, Dennis J., 124n100
Bentham, Jeremy, 134
Benzmüller, Cristroph, 67n17
Bergman, Jerry, 165n94
Berger, James O., 15n20, 15n21, 61n5
Bevere, John, 49n34, 114n49
Bezalel, chief artisan of the Tabernacle, 113
Bielefeldt, Heiner, 135n39
Borde, Arvind, 155
Bovens, Luc, 229n16
Boyarin, Daniel, 89n44, 200n67
Bradley, James, 38n13, 179n138, 179n140, 180n141
Bray, Steven M., 216n153
Buchak, Lara, 14n19, 36, 36n5, 36n6, 41, 41n19, 72n5, 256, 256n1
Bunyan, John, 113
Burge, Gary M., 218n161
Burpo, Colton, 127n10
Burpo, Todd, 127n10

285

NAME INDEX

Caiaphas, high priest, 86
Calvin, John, 111, 119
Carlsson, Mark, 202n73
Carmeli, Moshe, 152, 153n55
Carter, Robert, 100n95
Chandler, Jake, 13n17
Chen, Ming-Hui, 15n21
Chignell, Andrew, 44n24
Chrysostom, John, 118
Clifford, William K., 51, 51n43
Clouser, Roy, 40n17, 48n31
Cochran, Gregory, 115n53
Coles, Robert, 63n9
Collins, Francis, 131, 131n24, 157n70
Collins, Robin, 39n15, 170n106
Columbus, Christopher, 34
Constantine, Roman emperor, 122, 133, 230
Conway Morris, Simon, 157, 157n70
Copan, Paul, 111n38, 190, 190n23, 198, 198n59
Copernicus, Nicolaus, 152
Courgeau, Daniel, 13n18
Cowan, Louise, 6n7
Craig, William L., 6n6, 11n14, 18n27, 25n23, 31n18, 44n24, 65n14, 67n18, 67n19, 92n2, 95n8, 128n13, 146n39, 154n59, 154n62, 156n67, 169n105, 179n137, 184n2, 186n9, 188, 188n17, 206n94, 219n168
Crick, Francis, 162
Cruz, Nicky, 228, 228n11

Daeschler, Edward B., 161n82
Daniel, Old Testament prophet, 211, 221, 221n186, 231, 241–42
Darby, John Nelson, 119
Darwin, Charles, 25, 125–26, 125n2, 131, 161–62
David, Old Testament king, 104, 118, 191, 215, 222, 239
Davies, Paul, 175, 175n128
Dawkins, Richard, 25, 25n21, 31, 31n20, 132n27, 172–73, 173n117, 190, 190n21, 197, 206–7, 206n99
Dennett, Daniel C., 25, 25n21

Descartes, René, 141, 180
DeWitt, David, 165n94
Diaconis, Perci, 232n38
Diderot, Denis, 56, 56n59
Diocletian, Roman emperor, 122
Dodd, Charles H., 218n163
Dostoyevsky, Fyodor M., 113, 132, 132n129
Doyle, Tom, 123n95
Draper, John William, 110
D'Souza, Dinesh, 107n19
Durbin, Richard, 158n72

Edsinger, Olof, 190n23
Eldredge, Niles, 164
Elijah, Old Testament prophet, 240n21
Elymas, magician from New Testament, 230
Einstein, Albert, 38n14, 142, 152, 177
Engel, James, 47–48, 47n29, 50
Enoch, ancestor of Abraham, 192, 240n21
Erasmus, Desiderius, 132, 133n31
Esau, son of Isaac, 222
Eve, first woman, 22, 129, 149, 156, 159, 165–66, 206, 208–9
Ewert, Per, 106n14, 219n168
Ewert, Winston, 167n99, 173n121
Ezekiel, Old Testament prophet, 211
Ezra, Old Testament priest, 221

Faraday, Michael, 139
Farmer, Mark A., 161n82
Feinberg, Paul D., 75n10
Fermat, Pierre de, 13, 176
Feyerabend, Paul, 142n25
Fisher, Ronald A., 162
Flew, Antony, 171, 171n110
Furuhagen, Hans, 215n152

Galerius, Roman emperor, 122
Galilei, Galileo, 110, 139, 144, 152, 176, 179
Gallio, proconsul of Achaia, 218–19
Gamaliel I, Jewish rabbi and Pharisee, 123
Gärdeborn, Anders, 153n55
Garrison, David, 123n95

NAME INDEX 287

Gauger, Ann, 163n86, 164, 164n88, 165n93, 165n94
Gauss, Carl Friedrich, 177
Geertsema, Jan C., 142n26
Geisler, Norman L., 21n3, 190n23, 215n146
Gibbard, Allan, 268n1
Gibbons, Edward, 110
Gideon, Old Testament judge, 113
Gitt, Werner, 172, 172n116
Glueck, Nelson, 215, 215n146
Goldbach, Christian, 37–38
Gonzales, Guillermo, 170, 170n107
Good, I.J., 72n5,
Gordon, Bruce L., 110n31
Gould, Stephen Jay, 137, 137n2, 164
Grant, Hugh G., 142n23
Gravelet, Jean Francois, 47
Graunt, John, 176
Gray, Frank, 47n29
Green, Stefan, 218n162
Gregory I, pope, 128
Grim, Melissa, 134n38
Groothuis, Douglas R., xv, 4n3, 6n6, 51n42, 53n48, 57n63, 57n64, 104n2, 106n14, 204n88, 207n104
Grotius, Hugo, 132
Grudem, Wayne, 23n13, 149n46, 184n2, 186n9, 208n110, 237n11, 240n21
Guinness, Os, 6n7, 135
Gumbel, Nicky, 29n12, 47n27, 225, 225n209
Gustavsson, Stefan, 190n23, 219n168
Guth, Alan, 151, 155

Habakkuk, Old Testament prophet, 189
Habermas, Gary R., 107n19, 127n9, 184n1, 218n163, 220, 220n171, 226n1
Habura, Andrea, 161n82
Hacking, Ian, 13n18, 14n19, 78n4
Haeckel, Ernst, 162n84
Hahn, Ulrike, 145n32
Hájek, Alan, 6n6, 14n19, 78n4
Haldane, J.B.S., 126, 162

Halldorf, Peter, 225n208
Halvorsen, Hans, 170n106
Ham, Ken, 149n45, 149n46
Hammer, Michael F., 270n160
Hamming, Richard W., 180, 180n141
Hananiah, friend of Daniel, 241–42
Hand, David J., 261n2
Hardy, Godfrey H., 178, 178n136
Harper, William L., 268n1
Harrigan, Nicholas, 38n14
Harris, Madalene, 228n11
Harris, Sam, 25, 25n21
Harrison, Victoria S., 13n17
Hartnett, John, 149n47, 150n49, 152, 152n53, 153n55, 153n56, 153n57
Hawking, Stephen, 155, 155n63
Hazen, Robert M., 164n88
Hempel, Carl G., 141, 141n21, 143
Henne, Peter, 224n205
Herod 1, client king of Judea, 89
Herzl, Theodor, 114
Hezekiah, Old Testament king, 215, 241
Hick, John H., 104, 104n4
Hilbert, David, 181
Hill, Andrew, 200n67
Hill, Jonathan, 113n45, 121n88
Hitchens, Cristopher, 25, 25n21
Hitler, Adolf, 107
Howe, Thomas, 190n23
Howell, Russell, 38n13, 177n132, 178n135, 179n138, 179n140, 180n141
Howson, Colin, 142n24
Högås, Markus, 155n64, 155n66
Hössjer, Ola, xvin1, 166n95
Hubble, Edwin, 150
Huber, Franz, 15n21
Hume, David, 131–32, 146–47, 147n40, 230
Humphreys, D. Russell, 152, 153n55
Hutton, James, 149
Huxley, Julian, 162, 162n83

Ibstedt, Nils, 223n202
Il-Sung, Kim, 7, 106
Ilan, Tal, 218n164

288 NAME INDEX

Isaac, son of Abraham, 116, 116n57, 215n152, 222
Isaiah, Old Testament prophet, 117, 210, 241
Ishmael, son of Abraham, 116n57

Jacob, son of Isaac, 215n152, 217, 222, 228
James, apostle, 81, 211, 222
James, brother of Jesus, 218n163, 220
James, William, 52, 52n47
Jansen, Vincent A.A., 132n27
Jaynes, Edwin T., 61n5
Jeanson, Nathaniel T., 157n68, 166n95
Jeremiah, Old Testament prophet, 195
Job, man from Old Testament, 187, 192
Joel, Old Testament prophet, 123
John, apostle, 21, 71, 81, 113, 153, 211, 218n162, 222, 230, 246
Johnson, Donald E., 161n81, 161n82, 171n108, 173n121
Johnson, Todd M., 120n78, 124n100, 224n205
Jones, Mark H., 151n50, 154n62
Jong-Il, Kim, 106
Jonsson, Ulf, 11n14
Jordan, Jeff, xvi, 6n6, 14n19, 51n42, 56n59, 57n61, 95, 268n3
Joseph, step father of Jesus, 89
Joseph from Arimathea, 221n181
Josephus, Jewish historian, 218
Joshua, successor of Moses, 113, 116–17, 196–98
Justin Martyr, early church father, 118

Kauffman, Stuart A., 166, 166n98
Keener, Craig S., 146n39, 147n42, 230, 230n27
Kelley, Dean M., 123n97
Kelly, Thomas, 36n5
Kepler, Johannes, 142, 176
Keyes, Dick, 207n101
Keynes, John Maynard, 39n15
Kierkegaard, Søren A., 41, 41n19
Kimura, Mooto, 163n86
Kitchen, Kevin A., 149n45, 215n152
Korb, Kevin, 15n21
Kozulic, Branko, 164n88

Kremarik, Akiane, 78, 78n7
Kremarik, Foreli, 78–79
Kuhn, Thomas,, 143, 143n27
Kuyper, Abraham, 133
Kwan, Kai-man, 227n3

Landgren, Per, 110n31, 110n33, 134n35
Laplace, Pierre-Simon, 15n21
Lazarus, friend of Jesus, 229, 231
Leibnitz, Gottfried, 177n131
Leijon, Kjell Olof, 112n43, 227n2
Leisola, Matti, 164n88
Lemaître, George, 150
Lennox, John, 98n18, 107n20, 131n25, 144n28, 145, 146n36, 147, 147n42, 149n46, 155, 155n64, 157n69, 169n105, 190n23, 208n105, 226n1
Lenski, Richard, 173, 173n120
Leo XIII, pope, 133
Lewis, C.S., 6–7, 7n8, 113, 126, 126n3, 131, 131n23, 147–48, 148n43, 183, 184n1, 188, 194, 194n39, 219, 219n167, 235, 235n2
Lewontin, Richard, 144, 144n30
Li, Heng, 158n72
Licona, Michael R., 218n163, 220, 220n171
Lisle, Jason, 153, 157n68, 166n95
Louis XIV, King of France, 115
Luce, Robert D., 268n4
Luke, author of gospel, 113, 190, 218, 231
Luskin, Casey, 165n92
Luther, Martin, 111, 118
Lyell, Charles, 149

Machiavelli, Niccolò, 134, 134n35
Manasseh, Old Testament king, 196n50, 241
Marcion of Sinope, 190
Mark, author of gospel, 218, 223
Marks II, Robert J., 174n122
Martin, Luther H., 7n10, 106n13
Mary, mother of Jesus, 89
Matthew, apostle, 50, 218
Maxwell, James Clerk, 139

NAME INDEX   289

McCormack, Ian, 24n20
McGrew, Lydia, 220n171, 229n14
McGrew, Timothy, 220n171, 229n14
McIntosh, Andy C., 150n49, 174n122
Melhus, Kåre, 134n37
Melito of Sardes, early church father, 118
Mellars, Paul, 158n72
Mellor, D. Hugh, 60n3
Mendel, Gregor, 162
Merrill, Dean, 228n12
Meyer, Stephen C., 157n69, 161n81, 161n82, 164n90, 166n96, 166n98
Milliam, John, 149n45
Mishael, friend of Daniel, 241–42
Mlodinow, Leonard, 155, 155n63
Molén, Mats, 150n49
Möller, Lennart, 216n152
Moore, Kevin, 79n9
Moreland, J.P., 11n14, 25n23, 34, 34n2, 44n24, 65n14, 92n2, 95n8, 126n5, 127, 127n7
Morgenstern, Oskar, 15n20
Morris, Thomas V., xv, 3, 3n1, 51n42
Moses, leader of exodus, 72, 104, 113, 116, 118, 192–93, 192n32, 197–98, 211, 217, 222–23
Mosteller, Frederick, 232n38

Nagel, Thomas, 126, 126n4
Nebuchadnezzar, Babylonian king, 241–42
Needham, Joseph, 139, 139n15
Neumann, John von, 15n20
Nevin, Norman C., 157n69
Newton, Isaac, 139, 141–42, 144, 176–77, 179
Newton, John, 6
Neyman, Jerzy, 15n21
Nietzsche, Friedrich, 6, 25, 107
Noah, survivor of the flood, 150, 192
Noble, Denis, 166n97
Nordström, Ruth, 132n30

Oaksford, Mike, 145n32
Oholiab, artisan of the Tabernacle, 113
Oliviera e Silva, Tomás, 38n12

Origen, church father, 159
Osborne, Martin, 268n4
Ottosen, Espen, 205n92

Paley, William, 168–69, 168n101, 172–73
Papias, bishop of Hierapolis, 219
Pascal, Blaise, xv–xvi, 4–8, 6n4, 6n5, 8n11, 12–17, 12n16, 14n19, 31, 31n19, 48, 48n31, 50, 50n38, 52–53, 52n46, 53n48, 56–57, 75, 77–78, 78n4, 86–87, 87n34, 97–98, 115, 176, 207, 207n104
Paul, apostle, 4, 21, 34, 64, 68–69, 83–84, 89, 109, 113, 120, 129–30, 159–60, 187, 190–91, 202, 206–7, 209, 218n163, 219–20, 223, 225, 228–32, 229n16, 236n6, 242–43, 243n29
Pearcey, Nancy, 106n14, 110n31, 110n32, 111n40, 136n1, 138n4, 226n1
Pearl, Judea, 17n25
Perszyk, Ken, 186n9
Peter, apostle, 21, 80–82, 89, 122–23, 191, 211, 218n163, 222–23, 230
Philip, evangelist of the early church, 230
Phillips, Dewi Z., 54, 54n55
Pierce, Larry, 149n45, 149n46
Pilate, prefect of Judea, 221
Plantinga, Alvin, 39n15, 67n17, 92n2, 92n3, 95, 95n9, 144n29, 146, 146n37
Plessis, David du, 124n100
Plotnitsky, Arkady, 155n65
Polyani, Michael, 172n114
Popper, Karl, 142, 145, 145n33, 164
Posner, Sarah, 119n73
Price, Richard, 15n21
Ptolemy, Claudius, 110
Puterman, Martin L., 237n12

Rahab, inhabitant of Jericho, 117, 196–97
Raiffa, Howard, 268n4
Rebekah, Isaac's wife, 222
Reichmann, Sven, 115n54

290 NAME INDEX

Renard, Krister, 149n47
Richards, Jay, 170, 170n107
Rosenbaum, Paul R., 148n44
Ross, Kenneth R., 120n78
Ross, Sheldon M., 23) n12
Rota, Michael, xvi, 6n6, 51n42
Rubin, Donald. B., 61n5
Rubinstein, Ariel, 268n4
Ruiz-Orera, Jorge, 163n87
Ruse, Michael, 131, 131n26
Russell, Bertrand, 7, 7n9, 30, 30n17, 53, 54n51, 181
Rutherford, Ernest, 143

Saada, Tass, 228, 228n12
Sahlberg, Carl-Erik, 121n88
Samuel, Old Testament judge, 197–98
Sanford, John C., 164, 164n91, 166n95, 171n108
Sarah, Abraham's wife, 116, 222
Saul, Old Testament king, 118, 197, 215
Savage, Leonard J., 15n21
Sayer, George, 7n8
Schaefer, Henry F., 161n81
Scharfstein, Sol, 115n54
Schellenberg, John L., 202–3, 202n73, 205
Schmidt-Petri, Christoph, 15n21
Searle, John R., 142n24
Selander, Mats, 54n51, 132n27, 139, 139n17
Semler, Johann, 96
Shapiro, James A., 166n97
Silas, travel companion of Paul, 83
Sims, Andrew, 226, 226n1
Sinclair, James D., 67n19, 154n62, 156n67, 179n137
Sire, James W., 34n2
Skorecki, Karl, 217n160
Smith, John Maynard, 132n27
Socrates, Greek philosopher, 171
Solomon, Old Testament king, 113, 117, 211, 216n153, 239–40, 244
Sorley, William, 128
Spekkens, Robert W., 38n14
Spencer, Herbert, 131
Springer, Rebecca, 24n20

Stalin, Joseph, 107
Stark, Rodney, 109, 109n30, 110n31, 121n88, 133n33, 199n64
Stenumgaard, Peter, 110n31, 139n14
Stephen, first Christian martyr, 122
Stigler, Stephen, 15n21
Strand, Robert, 22n7
Strobel, Lee, 84, 84n28
Stump, Eleonore, xvi, xvin2
Suarez, Antoine, 159, 159n75, 159n77
Supphellen, Magne, 227n2
Swärd, Stefan, 213n137
Swinburne, Richard, 13n17, 33n1, 36, 36n9, 39n15, 40, 41n18, 50, 50n37, 50n39, 54n55, 60n3, 61–63, 61n4, 62n7, 67n20, 75n10, 92n2, 93, 93n5, 97n17, 126, 126n5, 128, 128n14, 132n28, 141n21, 176, 176n130, 229n14, 252, 252n2, 262, 262n3, 262n4

Tacitus, Roman historian, 217
Taylor, Peter, 132n27
Tegmark, Max, 175, 175n126
Tenaillon, Olivier, 173n120
Tertullian, church father, 122
Thaxton, Charles B., 110n31, 110n32, 138n3
Thiselton, Anthony C., 96n12, 140n18
Thomas, apostle, 71, 84, 229
Thomas, Mark G., 217n160
Timothy, disciple of Paul, 243
Titus, Roman emperor, 117
Tolkien, J.R.R., 6, 113
Tolstoy, Leo, 243–44, 244n30
Tomkins, Jeffrey, 165n94
Train, Kenneth, 268n2

Unwin, Stephen, 17, 17n24, 36, 36n9, 43, 43n23, 252, 252n1, 261, 261n1
Urbach, Peter, 142n24
Urban II, pope, 109
Ussher, James, 149

Vanhoozer, Kevin J., 96n12, 140n18
Vilenkin, Alexander, 154–55

Voltaire, Francois-Marie Arouet, 110

Walton, John H., 200n67
Walvoord, John F., 115n54
Watson, James, 162
Weber, Max, 111n42
Wells, Jonathan, 171n109
Wesley, John, 112
White, Andrew Dickson, 110
Whitehead, Alfred North, 7, 7n9, 181
Wigglesworth, Smith, 211
Wigner, Eugene, 177, 177n133
Wilberforce, William, 112
Wilkerson, David, 228, 228n10
Williams, Alex, 149n47, 150n49
Williams, Peter S., 35, 35n4
Wilson, Edward O., 131, 131n26
Wilson, Julian, 211n131
Woltzenloger Paleo, Bruno, 67n17
Woodberry, Robert D., 112, 112n43, 194n40
Wright, N.T., 89n45, 127n8
Wright, Sewall, 162

Young, Davis A., 140n19
Yu, Keming, 261n2

Zacchaeus, tax collector, 228
Zechariah, Old Testament prophet, 117
Zedong, Mao, 107

Subject Index

afterlife
    heaven, 21–24, 64n12, 127, 157–58, 187–88, 212–14
    Jewish expectation, 240n21
    naturalistic expectation, 24–26, 30–31
    pagan expectation, 89
    paradise, 24n20, 127
angels,
    creation of, 22, 185–86
    fallen, 214n144
    messengers, 22n7, 158
    protection by, 22n7
    rebellion among, 22n10, 185
apologetics, xv, xvii, 18–19
    cumulative case, 75
    defensive, 18n27
    offensive, 18n27
Aposteriori Wager, concepts of
    Action, 35, 43–44, 43n23, 47–48, 47n29, 50, 57n62, 65n13, 203n79, 237–39, 256–57, 259, 267
    expected reward, 14, 43, 56n61, 255–57, 259, 265–66, 268
    faith math approach, 17, 43, 43n23
    graphical interpretation, 16, 43–44, 239, 266–67
    hidden variables, 262–64
    line of conversion, 16, 44, 47–48, 239, 267
    many alternatives to Christianity, 56n61, 59–63, 60n2, 258–60
    naive Bayes evidence gathering, 74n9, 261n2
    reward assignment. *See* decision.
    reward difference, 253–54, 256–57
    reward difference ratio, 256–57
    sequential evidence gathering, 262–64
    Strength of Evidence, 40, 43–46, 57n62, 65n13, 74, 203n79, 237–39, 251–52, 256, 258, 261–63
    Strength of Prior Belief, 40, 43–46, 57n62, 65n13, 239, 251–52, 256 , 258
    Strength of Rational Belief, 36, 39–40, 39n16, 43–44, 47–48, 48n30, 78n5, 90n50, 252, 258, 263, 266–67
    Strength of Will, 41–47, 47n29, 48n30, 57n62, 65n13, 77, 78n4, 79–80 , 85, 88, 91, 203n79, 238–39, 253–54, 256, 267
    willingness assignment. *See* decision.
argument
    based on epistemic reasons, 51
    C-inductive, 262
    from ignorance, 145
    pragmatic, 51, 78, 97
    truth-dependent pragmatic, 95, 97
    truth-independent pragmatic, 95, 97
belief
    basic, 65, 65n14, 92, 94, 94n6
    by heart, 17, 48–50 , 48n31
    centrality of, 34–35
    content of, 34

belief (*continued*)
  degree of, 14–15, 17, 37, 43n23, 48n30, 251
  non-basic, 94
  prior, xvi, 16–17, 20, 40, 43n23, 45, 57–71, 76, 80–83, 92–94, 255, 265–66
  rational, 16–17, 28, 36, 39–40, 43–44, 46–51, 48n30, 54, 71–72, 77–78, 80–82, 84–85, 90, 93
  strength of, 13, 34–36, 39, 97
belief formation
  doxastic involuntarism, 44n24
  doxastic voluntarism, 44n24
  ethical evidentialism, 55
  evidentialism, 51–53, 71n1
  fideism, 41n19, 52n45, 137
  inductive criteria for, 15n21, 60–61, 93–94, 142, 180n142
Bible
  accurate text of, 218
  apocalyptic message of, 223–24
  archaeological support of, 215
  authorship of, 214, 223
  clarity of, 214–15
  contents of, 20–24, 214–25
  depth of, 214
  double-edged sword, 224–25
  genetic support of, 216–17
  honesty of, 222–23
  messianic prophecies in, 20, 118–19, 199-200, 220–21, 242
  reliability of, 21, 103–4, 139, 214–25
  translation of, 111
Bible, text and copies of
  Chester Beatty Papyri, 218n162
  Dead Sea Scrolls, 218n162, 220
  early New Testament creeds, 218
  John Rylands Papyri, 218n162
  name statistics, 218
biblical and early church periods/events
  Assyrian captivity, 114
  Babylonian captivity, 114, 117, 119, 197, 216, 221
  church council of Carthage, 21
  church council of Hippo, 21
  conquest of Canaan, 116, 197–99
  Creation, 22, 68, 132, 138–39, 149–50, 153, 158–59, 185–87, 186n9, 193–94, 202
  Day of Atonement, 209
  day of Pentecost, 80, 122, 219–20
  exodus from Egypt, 116, 146, 197, 215n152, 223
  fall of man, 22–24, 23n14, 26n27, 27n28, 29, 53, 57, 66, 80, 98, 105–7, 114, 129, 157, 159–60, 172, 185–87, 192, 206–212, 235
  final judgment, 24, 201, 212–14
  flood of Noah, 150, 192
  Israel, Northern Kingdom, 114, 195, 215, 239–40
  Jesus' life. *See* Jesus.
  Judah, Southern Kingdom, 114, 195, 215, 239–41
  missionary journeys of Paul, 4, 83, 89, 120, 219, 223, 228, 230–31, 243
  Patriarchal Age, 116, 192, 198n57, 215n152, 217, 222
  period of the Judges, 195
  Second Temple period, 117
  United Monarchy (Israel), 117–18, 197, 211, 215, 239–40
  Yahweh wars. *See* conquest of Caanan.
biblical hermeneutics, 96n12, 140–41, 140n18
  Bible inspired by humans, 21, 104
  Bible inspired by God, 21, 103, 139–40, 191, 215, 224
  interpretation of book of Revelation, 140, 158, 223–24
biblical places
  Ai, 198
  Antioch, 120
  Assyria, 114, 196, 215, 241
  Athens, 34
  Babylonia, 114, 117, 119, 197, 215–16, 221, 241–42
  Bethlehem, 220
  Calvary, 21, 23–24, 28n1, 29, 69, 86, 210, 221, 246
  Canaan, 116, 197–99, 241

SUBJECT INDEX 295

Corinth, 84–85, 109, 123, 218–19, 229
Cyprus, 120, 230
Damascus, 4, 120, 229, 243
Delphi, 218
Egypt, 89, 116–18, 146, 195–97, 215, 216n152
Galilee, 89, 220
garden of Eden, 22, 157–58
Gibea, 215
Greece, 4, 120
Jericho, 117, 196, 198, 215, 216n152
Jerusalem, 4, 21, 80, 86, 89–90, 109, 114, 117, 120–23, 197, 211, 215, 218n163, 221, 224, 229–31, 239–41, 243
Judea, 89, 120–21
Mount Sinai, 116–17, 192, 209, 211
Nazareth, 20, 230
Nineveh, 196, 215
Patmos, 211
Persia, 221
Philippi, 83
Phoenicia, 120
Red Sea, 146, 196–97
Rome, 111, 120, 230
Samaria, 120–21, 230
Sychar, 228
Ur, 116

chance
  epistemic, 37, 38n14, 141n22
  ontological, 37, 38n14, 141n22
changed life situation, response to Christianity, 17, 203n79, 235–44
  acquisition of new evidence, 17, 238–39, 264
  changed willingness assignment, 17, 238–39
  reevaluation of evidence, 17, 237–39, 264
Christian and other organizations
  Barna Group, 111n39
  Caritas Internationalis, 111
  Christian Aid Mission, 111
  Internet Evangelism Day, 47n29
  Ipsos, 20n1, 105n11
  Joshua Project, 223n200
  Lausanne Movement, 204, 204n85
  Open Doors, 224n205
  Pew Research Center, 224n205
  Religious Freedom & Business Foundation, 134, 134n38
  Samaritan's Purse, 111
  United Nations, 115, 134
Christian faith
  Lutheran view, 50, 97
  Pragmatic view, 50, 97
  Thomist view, 50–51
Christian movements/denominations/churches
  Calvinism/Reformed, xvii, 111, 119, 185
  Catholicism, 5, 110, 124, 132–33
  Charismatic Movement, xvii, 123–24, 124n100, 230
  Evangelicalism, 223n200, 224n205
  Jansenism, 5, 75
  Lutheranism, xvii, 6, 111, 112n43, 227n2
  Methodism, 111
  Pentecostalism, xvii, 123, 123n99, 230.
  Pietism, 111
  Presbyterianism, 15–16. See also Calvinism.
  Protestantism, 111–12, 111n42, 119, 124. See also Calvinism, Charismatic Movement, Evangelicalism, Lutheranism, Methodism, Pentecostalism, Pietism.
  Puritanism, 119. See also Calvinism.
  Yoido Full Gospel Church, South Korea, 124
Christianity
  classical, 17, 17n26, 21–22, 104, 123, 139, 204, 213, 215
  criteria for justifying, 92–99
  gospel of, 4–5, 14, 21, 23–24, 28, 48, 74, 88–89, 98, 113, 121–22, 201, 203–6, 210, 212, 223, 238, 242, 246

Christianity (*continued*)
  liberal form of, 21, 104, 220
  spread of, 119–24
  universality of, 57, 108, 120
  warrant of, 92n3. *See also* criteria for justifying.
Christianity, argument (against)
  burden of proof, 19, 53–54, 54n51
  counter cosmological, 19, 153–56
  destiny of unevangelized, 19, 64n12, 201, 212–13
  from age of universe, 19, 150–53
  from common descent, 96, 156–67
  from de facto objections, 95–98
  from de jure objections, 95–98, 95n9
  from inconsistent revelations, 19, 103
  from parsimony, xvi, 19, 53, 62–63, 174
  from poor design, 172
  from religious wars, 19, 105–7
  from unbelief, 19, 184n3, 202–5, 205n91
  God of the Old Testament, 19, 104, 190–201
  hiddenness of God, xv, 19, 201–6
  misconduct of Christians, 19, 107–110
  no reason, 19, 184
  problem of evil, xvin2, 19, 95, 157, 183–90, 212
  problem of free will, xvii, 19, 38, 185–86, 186n9, 205n91
  problem of hell, 19, 212–14
  reductionism, 172
  universalism/perennialism, 19, 103–4
Christianity, argument (for)
  anthropological, 52–53, 207
  apocalyptic, 19, 119, 223–24
  cosmological, 19, 67–68, 153–56, 156n167, 171
  from absurdity of life without God, 30–31
  from church history, 19, 119–24
  from consciousness, 19, 126
  from democracy and human rights, 19, 111–12, 134–35, 134n37, 194
  from divine honesty of Bible. *See* Bible.
  from effectiveness of mathematics. *See* mathematics.
  from genetic evidence of Jewish ancestry. *See* Jews.
  from impact on culture, 19, 21, 112–14, 120–22, 227
  from Jewish history. *See* Jews.
  from miracles, 52, 57, 96, 146–48, 146n39, 148n44, 203n82, 220n171, 229–32
  from Old Testament prophecies, 19, 52, 96, 116–119, 199–200, 215, 220–21, 223n202, 242
  from reason, 19, 125–26, 126n3, 138, 146, 180
  from reliability of Bible. *See* Bible.
  from religious experience/testimonies, 4–7, 57–58, 127, 226–28, 227n3
  from resurrection of Jesus. *See* Jesus.
  from simplicity, 19, 62–63, 67, 176
  from supernatural coincidences, 231–32, 232n38
  moral. *See* moral values.
  ontological, 19, 67, 67n17
  teleological/design. *See* design.
  transcendental, 19, 67, 138
  will to believe, 19, 52
Christianity versus science
  classification of conflicts, 139–41
  coherence scenario, 137–39
  conflict scenario, 137
  demarcation problem, 137
  Non-Overlapping Magisteria (complementary) scenario, 137, 139
church
  adopted into, 30
  Christ head of, 30, 68
  history of, 119–24
  unity within, 30, 108, 123

SUBJECT INDEX   297

cosmology
    astroparticle physics, 151
    Big Bang. See Standard Model.
    Copernican principle, 152
    cosmic background radiation, 150-52, 175
    dark energy, 151, 153
    dark matter, 151, 153
    eternal inflation, 175
    geocentric, 140, 144, 152
    heliocentric, 110, 144, 152
    Hubble volume, 175
    inflationary theory, 151, 153-55, 175n127
    M-theory, 155, 175, 176n129
    multiverse theory, 26, 175-76
    quantum cosmology, 154
    quantum fluctuation, 154
    Standard Model, 26, 26n24, 150-54, 156, 175, 175n127
    Steady State Model, 151, 156, 156n67
    redshift of light, 150-51, 153
    string theory, 155, 156n67
    young earth cosmology, 152-53, 155-56

dating methods/principles
    cooling of earth, 150
    ice-layer variations, 150
    genetic (molecular clock), 150, 217n158, 217n160
    magnetic field variations, 150
    radiometric, 150
    sedimentary rock layer variations, 150
    sodium level variations of the sea, 150
    telescoping of genealogies, 149, 149n45
    variations of earth's orbit, 150
death
    biological, 127
    clinical, 127
    near-death experience, 24n20, 127, 127n10

decision (maker)
    action of, 9n12, 34-36, 39, 41, 93, 96-97, 237
    alternative of, 8-13, 9n12, 15, 20, 33-34, 56n61, 59-62, 94n7, 255-60
    Christian interpretation of, 17, 33, 45-51
    consequence of, xviii, 8-11, 20, 24, 27n29, 31-32, 56
    Engel's scale for, 47-48, 47n29, 50
    faith required for, 16, 36, 41
    goal of, 9-10, 34, 36, 42, 76-77
    Gray matrix for, 47n29
    informed, 10, 84, 99, 214
    naturalistic interpretation of, 17, 33, 46
    psychological struggle behind, 27, 31, 232n38
    reward assignment of, 9, 12-14, 41, 57-58, 76-91, 78n4, 253-54. See also willingness assignment.
    reward of a consequence of, 9-14, 41, 76-91, 253-54
    reward table of, 11, 65n13, 78n4, 238, 253, 257, 266. See also willingness table.
    spiritual battle behind, 28, 45-47, 63-64, 72
    tacit assumptions of, 10n13
    utility of a consequence of, 9, 57n61, 268. See also reward.
    willingness assignment of, 41-42, 57-58, 76-91, 93, 237n12, 238, 254-55, 265-66
    willingness attitude about, 19, 41, 46, 51, 76-91, 93-94, 238, 246, 254
    willingness table of, 41-43, 76-77, 79-80, 85, 91
decision rule
    Dominance rule, 14n19
    Expectation rule, 14, 14n19, 43n22, 56n61, 255-57, 259, 265-66

decision rule (*continued*)
   Maximax rule, 14n19, 268, 268n3
   Minimax rule, 14n19
   Next Best Thing rule, 14n19, 56n61
   Risk-Weighted Expectation rule, 14n19
   Satisfactory Act rule, 14n19
   Schlesinger's Principle, 57n61
decision theory, xv, 3, 8, 14–15, 15n21, 268
   Bayesian, 15–16, 15n20, 15n21, 61n5, 249, 251–52, 255–57, 268
   choice modeling, 268
   evidential, 268
   Markovian, xvi, 237n12
   relative utility theory, 57n61
design or apparent design mechanisms/features
   bottom-up. *See* reductionism.
   created diversity within kinds, 166–67, 166n95
   created kinds, 156–57
   discoverability, 170
   evolution. *See* evolution.
   fine tuning, 170, 170n106, 174–75
   habitability, 170, 174
   irreducible complexity, 163, 163n85, 173, 173n121, 174n122
   reductionism, 172, 174n122, 181
   second law of thermodynamics, 174, 174n122
   self-organization, 160, 166–67, 172, 174n122
   Shannon entropy, 174n122
   top-down, 174n122
   watchmaker analogy, 168–69, 172–73
   weak anthropic principle, 174
devil/Satan
   accuser, 88
   causing division, 108
   defeated, 28n1
   fallen angle/rebellious, 22, 22n10, 51
   influencing our decisions/causing temptations, 28, 45–46, 72, 88
   leader of evil part of world/enemy of Christians, 22, 199
   manifesting himself as an angle of light, 214n144

Eastern (inspired) religions/philosophies/practices
   Buddhism, 59, 62, 103–4, 106, 183
   Hinduism, 59, 62, 103–4, 106, 183
   Juche cult, 7, 106, 224n205
   mindfulness, 106
   New Age, 106, 106n14
   pantheism, 26, 106
   Taoism, 103
   yoga, 106
epistemic theory
   coherentism, 94
   diachronic, 94
   externalism, 94
   foundationalism, 65, 65n14, 94
   internalism, 94
   synchronic, 94
evidence (formation of)
   accumulation of, 15, 15n21, 41, 61, 74–75, 238, 261–64
   acquisition of new, 41, 53, 71–72, 93, 238
   birthday problem bias of, 232n38
   full, 41n20, 52, 99
   inconclusive, xvi, 51, 97, 145
   information bias of, 232n38, 238
   psychological makeup bias of, 232n38
   reevaluation of, 237–38, 264
   spiritual influence of, 4–6, 28, 40, 45-6, 72, 90n50, 188, 229, 229n16, 242–43, 263–64
   subjective interpretation of, xvi, 40, 45, 72, 75, 92, 145, 205, 237–38
evidence, types of, 17, 73–75, 261–62
   consciousness/morality, 125–35
   historical/cultural, 103–124
   personal, 226–32
   philosophical, 183–90, 201–6
   scientific, 136–82
   theological, 183–225
evil, 19, 22, 26, 95, 106, 113, 129–30, 157, 183–90, 206–8, 212, 224

demons/evil spirits, 51, 188, 230
devil. *See* devil.
  evidential problem of, 186–87
  logical problem of, 95, 184–86, 184n3
  natural, 187
  route to God, 187–89, 235–36
  theodicies for solving problem of, 184
evolutionary mechanism
  created diversity within kinds. *See* design.
  created kinds. *See* design.
  epigenetic, 166–67
  evo-devo, 166
  game theory, 131
  genetic drift, 26, 162, 167
  increased genetic entropy 164–65, 164n91, 174n122
  migration/separation, 157–58, 216
  mutations, 26, 156–57, 162–67, 173, 173n120, 174n122, 217n158
  natural selection, 25–26, 115, 131, 156–57, 162, 164, 167, 173, 174n122
  pleiotropy, 131
  punctuated equilibrium, 164, 166
  self-organization. *See* design.
  selfish gene, 131
  speciation, 162, 164
evolutionary theory
  blind evolution, 26, 26n25, 93, 96, 126, 145–46, 157, 171, 173, 174n122, 180
  chemical evolution, 160
  cultural evolution, 26
  macroevolution (Darwinian evolution), 25, 125, 136, 145, 156–68, 172–74
  microevolution, 156–57, 161n82, 162, 173n120
  neo-Darwinism/modern synthesis, 156, 162, 164, 166
  organic evolution, 160
  particle evolution, 160
  planetary and stellar evolution, 160
  population genetics, 162, 164–66, 166n95, 216–17
  social evolution, 26, 131–32
  theistic evolution, 157–60
Father
  cannot be seen directly, 210–12
  part of Trinity, 21–22, 70
  revealed through Christ, 53, 70, 98, 211–12, 246
  sending Christ, 5, 23, 98, 246
  source of agape love/father of Christians, 66, 70, 187
  united with Christ, 108
fossil record
  abrupt changes of, 161
  Cambrian explosion, 161, 161n82, 163
  transitional forms, 161, 161n82, 164–65
  tribolites, 163
free will
  Arminian interpretation, xvi, 185
  Calvinist/Reformed interpretation, xvi, 185
  determinism, 38
  indeterminism, 38
  Molinism, xvi, 185–86, 186n9
God
  agape love of, 69
  almighty/omnipotent, 22–23, 63, 89, 95, 104, 138, 148, 172, 184, 186, 191, 210, 212
  creative, 114
  Creator, 21–24, 45, 67–68, 89, 104, 148, 169, 172, 182, 191, 195, 214
  disciplines humans, 197, 236
  divine humility of, 191–92
  divine jealousy of, 192
  eternal, 22, 63, 67
  first cause, 63, 67, 146, 153–56, 171
  free, 63, 138
  gentleman, 133, 203
  good/benevolent, 22, 172, 184, 186
  holy, 23, 69, 82, 191, 195, 209–211
  intelligent/rational, 138

God (*continued*)
  loving, 69, 95, 183, 190–91, 202, 210, 212
  omniscient, 63, 110, 184
  personal, xvii, 22, 28, 32, 201–2, 236, 245
  present/immanent, 22, 148, 189, 210, 237
  transcendent, xvii, 67, 138, 185
  Trinity, 21–22, 67, 70, 179, 184–85, 192
  truthful/trustworthy/just and fair, 22, 138–39, 195, 214, 236
  Upholder of Creation, 22, 45, 68, 148
  Yahweh, 194, 198–99
Greek (inspired) philosophies
  Aristotelianism, 110, 110n33, 144, 179
  Epicureanism, 24
  Neoplatonism, 106
  Stoicism, 24

hell, 19, 183, 212–14
  conditionalism, 213
  issuant view of, 213
  traditionalism, 213
  universalism, 212–13
history, modern periods/events
  burning of witches, 108
  Crusades, 107–9, 199
  Dreyfus affair, 114
  Enlightenment, 24–25, 96, 106–7, 110, 136, 180
  Israel, modern state, 115, 117, 119, 223–24
  Middle Ages, 24, 108, 110–11, 114, 139, 179, 199
  Reformation, 111
  Renaissance 24, 110, 179
  scientific revolution, 24, 136, 176
  World War II, 106, 114–15, 122, 131, 134, 188
Holy Spirit
  calls to repentance, to become a Christian, 28, 45–46, 54, 64, 72, 78–84, 203

  comforter, guide and source of inspiration, 21, 29, 208, 238
  creates unity among Christians, 30, 108
  fruits of, 29, 128n12, 227, 247
  gifts of, 29, 123, 123n98, 231, 242
  hurting, 90
  outpouring of, 80, 122
  part of Trinity, 21–22
  prophecy as gift of, 123, 231, 232n38
  renewal of spirit/new birth/ transformed heart through, 24, 29, 47–49, 48n31, 97–98, 105, 118, 130, 133, 237, 246
  reveals Scripture, 140, 224–25
  sanctification through, 29, 108, 237
  speaking in tongues as gift of, 80, 122–23
  source of power, 29, 108, 122, 219
  wisdom as fruit of, 98
  word of wisdom and word of knowledge as gifts of, 123, 231–32

Islam, 56–59, 62–63, 104, 107, 123, 129, 199
  Allah, 104
  jihad, 107, 199
  Mohammad, 57, 199
  Qur'an, 57–58, 104
  Sharia law, 133

Jesus Christ
  accepted by Jews. *See* Jews messianic.
  ascension of, 21, 80, 119, 121–22, 189, 229
  atonement for our sins, Redeemer, 23–24, 69, 80, 86, 88–89, 104, 119, 130, 159, 185, 195, 201, 206–8, 210, 212, 240, 245
  belief in/surrender to, 24, 28–29, 47–48, 58, 71, 78, 80, 84, 88–89, 97–98 , 118, 123, 130, 133, 188, 201, 206, 208, 211, 213, 227–29, 231, 236, 238, 240, 243–44

birth and early life of, 20, 22n7, 89, 118–19, 146–47
children belonging to, 57n62, 64, 64n12, 65n13, 83
Creator (together with Father and Holy Spirit), 67–68
death of, sacrificing himself, 23, 29, 88, 104, 119, 189–90, 200, 204, 207, 209–210, 212, 219–21, 243, 246
defeater of devil, 28n1
disciples/followers of, 21, 24, 71, 81–82, 84, 104, 108–9, 121–23, 138, 219, 222–23, 229
divine qualities of, 104, 219
eternal pre-existence of, 68
existence of, 217–18
God/Son of God, 7, 24, 56, 84, 86, 189, 213, 219–22, 246
Holy Spirit points to, 28, 81, 98
head of church, 30, 68
incarnation/sent by Father, 5, 23, 88–89, 98, 130, 185, 206, 240
intercessor/high preast, 189
Judge, 201
Lamb, 158, 243
Lewis's trilemma, 219
Lord/King/Ruler, 4, 24, 71, 81, 83, 118, 130, 157, 204, 221, 225, 246
love of, 69, 210, 212, 243
made righteous and justified through, 24, 88, 98, 159, 204, 206, 246–47
Messiah/messianic prophecies of, 20–21, 57, 82, 89, 104, 118, 199–200, 214, 220–21, 228–29, 243
ministry of, 21, 64, 69, 71–72, 76, 80–81, 86–87, 89–90, 99, 109, 122, 130, 133, 190–91, 193, 199–200, 214–15, 219, 227, 230–31
miracle worker/power of God, 72, 104, 146, 189, 229, 245
missionary command of, 21, 121

opens up way to the Father, and to sending of the Holy Spirit, 24, 29, 47, 70, 104, 113, 130, 133, 190, 200, 205n92, 211
part of Trinity, 21–22, 184–85
prophet, 56–57, 104, 228
relation with/following, xvii, 5–7, 24, 27n28, 29–32, 69, 79, 84, 105, 107–8, 113, 123, 201, 225, 228, 236, 246
reliably described in the Bible, 218–19
resurrection of, 19, 21, 24, 37, 54, 58, 71, 80, 84–86, 95, 119, 122, 140, 146–47, 200, 204, 207, 209, 219–21, 229, 246
revelation of, 4, 203–6, 211, 228, 243
Savior/life changer/rock, 24, 29, 32, 56, 71, 89, 98, 100, 103–4, 118, 130, 157, 199, 204, 206, 209, 212–14, 221, 227–28, 236, 244, 246–47
second coming of, 24, 24n20, 100, 119, 201, 223–24
sinless, 23, 104, 200, 210
Son of Man, 89n44
Upholder of Creation. *See* God.
the Way and the Truth, 214, 246
the Word/wisdom of God, 67, 245
Jews
anti-Semitism against, 114–15
Ashkenazi, 115, 216–17, 216n153, 216n156, 217n158
Christian Zionism regarding, 119
Cohanim, 217, 217n160
Ethiopian, 216n153
genetic evidence for biblical ancestry of, 216–17
history of, 114–18
Holocaust, 114, 131, 188
Indian, 216n153
Levite, 217n160
Messiah anticipation among, 89, 89n44
messianic, 118–19, 119n73

Jews (*continued*)
  North African, 216n153
  oral traditions of, 218
  Pharisees, 72, 86, 90, 193, 200
  Sadducees, 72
  Sephardi, 216n153
  success of, 114
  Zionist movement among, 114, 119
Judaism
  Mishnah, 104
  Orthodox, 104
  Talmud, 104
  tradition of the elders, 200

legislations/creeds
  Babylonian laws, 192
  Cape Town Commitment, 204, 204n85
  ceremonial laws of Old Testament, 200
  the Global Charter of Conscience, 135
  golden rule, 26n27, 110, 130, 133, 194
  Great Commandment, 231
  Hettite laws, 192
  moral laws of Old Testament, 200
  Mosaic Law, 104–5, 116, 130, 192–95, 199–200, 209
  Nicene Creed, 21
  social laws of Old Testament, 200
  Sumerian laws, 192
  Ten Commandments, 129, 194, 200
  the Two Great Commandments, 69
  Universal Declaration of Human Rights, 134
life
  absurdity of, 30
  meaning/purpose of, xv, 3–4, 30–32, 55, 64, 68–69, 76, 81–82, 87, 137, 207, 226–27, 236, 240, 243–44, 247

man; nature, position or parts of
  body/flesh, 23–25, 23n12, 46, 49, 68, 86, 127, 130, 140, 147, 160, 172, 193, 205, 220
  body-mind problem, 25n23, 125-27
  created in God's image, 22, 24, 53, 57, 105, 107, 111, 114, 138, 179, 191, 195, 208
  dichotomy view, 23, 23n13
  dualism, 126–27, 127n6
  fallen, 53, 57, 106, 129, 206-11
  flesh, 23, 23n14, 28–29, 45–46, 86, 88, 90, 106n15, 128n11, 130, 225
  made righteous/justified. *See* Jesus Christ.
  monism, 127n6
  neuroplasticity, 126
  physicalism, 25
  property dualism/pluralism, 25
  psychosomatic disorders, 126
  soul, 7, 23–25, 23n12, 23n13, 24n20, 25n23, 28n3, 30, 32, 45–46, 49, 54, 80, 90, 105, 125, 127, 205, 213, 224, 231, 237
  spirit, 23–25, 23n13, 24n20, 28–29, 28n3, 32, 45, 49, 64, 80, 84, 88, 90, 105, 113, 130, 205, 224
  split condition, xv, 52-53, 98
  trichotomy view, 22–23, 23n13, 49
man, origin and history of
  common ancestry, 158, 165–67
  first created couple, 22–23, 149, 156–60, 165–67
  Out of Africa hypothesis, 158, 166
  Neolithic Revolution, 158
  retelling story, 159
mathematics
  axioms, 7, 37, 176–77, 181
  beauty of/aesthetic argument for, 178–79, 178n135
  Christian mathematical empiricism, 179
  Christian Platonism, 179
  deductive science, 142, 176
  effectiveness of, 177, 179–80
  future-valued argument for, 177n132
  incompleteness of, 37n11, 172, 181–82
  ontological nominalism, 179

SUBJECT INDEX   303

ontological realism, 179
model selection,
   law of parsimony/Occam's razor,
      xvi, 53, 62, 174
molecular genetics
   amino acid, 160, 163–64, 170–71
   DNA, 19, 143, 150, 156, 160, 162–
      67, 170–72, 216–17, 217n158
   ENCOCE project, 171, 171n109
   epigenetics, 166
   exons, 163, 171n109
   gene expression/gene activity, 157,
      162–63, 165–66, 171
   genes, 131, 157, 162–63, 165–66,
      171, 171n109
   genetic code, 162–63, 171
   genetic similarity among humans,
      165–66
   genetic similarity with chimps, 165
   introns, 163, 171n109
   microtubules, 170
   mitochondria, 170, 217n158
   non-coding DNA, 165, 171–72,
      171n109
   ribosomes, 170
   RNA, 160–61, 164n88, 171n109
   orphan genes, 163, 163n87
   proteins, 143, 160–61, 163–66,
      164n88, 170–72
moral values
   evil. See evil.
   good, 4, 22, 26, 56, 58, 87–88, 106–
      7, 109, 113, 128–32, 138, 153,
      157, 172, 184–86, 191, 193,
      197, 199, 201, 208, 228n6
   moral law, 26, 128–30, 188,
      194n41, 200, 207
   seven deadly sins, 128
   seven virtues, 128
   sin. See sin.

naturalism (or inspired by)
   Amsterdam Declaration, 25
   atheism, 12, 24–25, 30, 79, 107,
      126, 184
   communism, 25
   existentialism, 25, 30
   Human Manifesto III, 25

   humanism, 25–26, 201
   Khmer Rouge, 107
   metaphysical naturalism, 25
   New Atheism, 25, 137, 190
   physicalism. See man.
   property dualism/pluralism. See
      man.
   psychoanalysis, 25
   religious naturalism, 26n26
   secularism, xv, 106–7, 110, 112–13,
      121, 135–36, 157, 167, 212, 230
   Übermensch philosophy, 107

odds. See statistical concepts.
Old Testament interpretation
   cultural snobbery, 194
   explained/revealed/confirmed by
      New Testament, 104, 190–91,
      200–201
   explaining New Testament, 119,
      201
   hiding New Testament, 23, 119,
      214, 220–21, 224
   sentimental view, 207

people groups
   Amalekites, 118, 197–98
   Ammonites, 197
   Canaanites, 197–99, 241
   Edomites, 197
   Kenites, 118
   Midianites, 197–98
   Moabites, 197
   Seljuk Turks, 109
philosophies of life
   agnosticism, 20, 74, 98, 111
   deism, 26
   naturalism. See naturalism.
   postmodernism, 25, 104
   theism, 19, 56, 60, 63, 127, 136,
      138, 174, 176
philosophy, disciplines of
   analytical, xvi, 7
   epistemology, 8, 92
   metaphysics, 67n17
   philosophy of science, 137, 145
prior belief, criteria for choosing
   Bertrand's paradox, 62n6

prior belief (*continued*)
   bridge player's fallacy, 60–61
   inborn conception of a first cause, 66–68
   inborn conception of God, 36, 63–64, 66–67, 80, 92, 105
   inborn desire for meaning and purpose, 64, 66, 68–69, 81
   inborn desire to be loved unconditionally, 64, 66, 69–70, 82
   predictivist theory, 60n3
   principle of indifference, 61–62
   scope, 62, 62n7
   simplicity, xvi, 19, 53, 62–63, 62n7, 67, 88–89, 93, 141–42, 174
   timeless theory, 60n3
probability, 13, 13n18, 36–39
   aposteriori, 15–16, 36–37, 39, 39n16, 43n23, 78n5, 252, 257, 259, 262, 265–66
   apriori, 15, 15n21, 36–37, 58, 60–63 , 60n3, 61n5, 62n7, 65, 65n13, 142n24, 145n34, 251, 258, 265
   epistemic, 38
   frequentist/statistical, 15n21, 39
   historical development of, 13n18
   inductive, 38
   physical, 37
   subjective, 13–14 , 14n19, 15n21, 37–39 , 39n16, 145n34, 251, 261–62

quantum mechanics, 38, 141, 153–56, 175, 177. *See also* cosmology.
   Bell's Theorem, 155n65
   Heisenberg's uncertainty principle, 38
   interpretation of, 38, 38n14

rational belief, formed by
   authorities, 4, 40, 52, 74–75 , 92–93, 238
   deductions, 40, 93–94, 110, 123, 138, 141–42, 171, 177
   dreams/visions, 5, 75, 123, 205, 211, 230–31, 242

   memories, 4, 40, 74, 92, 94, 238
   miracles. *See* Christianity, argument (for).
   perceptions, 40, 65n14, 72, 92, 123, 147, 229–31, 238, 242–43
   revelations. *See* revelation.
   self-evident knowledge, 40, 48n31, 61, 65n14, 79n8, 90n50, 177
   spiritual influence, 40, 45–50, 48n31, 72, 90n50, 237–38, 263–64
   supernatural coincidences, 231–32, 232n38, 240
   testimonies, 4, 19, 40, 74–75 , 89, 92–93, 127, 203, 226–28, 238, 244
rationality
   epistemic, 36
   instrumental, 36
revelation, 19, 24, 26, 25n22, 44, 57, 97, 104, 138n9, 203, 211, 214, 229, 231
   direct, 203, 203n82
   general, 202–3
   special, 203

scientific explanation, 141, 147, 167
   deterministic model, 38–39, 141
   initial conditions, 39, 62, 141, 143–45, 155, 167–68, 170, 170n106, 175
   laws of nature, 24, 26, 62, 129, 130n18, 138–39, 141–44, 146–48, 155, 167–68, 170, 176, 229, 231
   personal agent, 63, 126–27, 143–44, 147–48, 155, 176
   statistical model, 38, 141
scientific theories, tools for and formation of
   change of paradigm/revolutions, 93, 143–44, 151
   falsification, 62, 142, 145, 164, 175
   God of the gaps argument, 140, 145, 145n31, 148, 171, 232n38
   hypothetico-deductive method, 142
   induction, 110, 141–42, 147

SUBJECT INDEX 305

logical positivism, 141–42
methodological naturalism, 25n22, 52n44, 96, 144–45, 167, 176
naturalism of the gaps argument, 145, 145n31, 172
strong methodological naturalism, 144, 144n29, 152, 167
uniformity of experience, 96, 147
uniformity of laws of nature, 147
sin, 5, 22–24, 28, 58, 64, 69–70, 80–81, 85, 88, 90, 113, 128–30, 159, 185–87, 195–96, 199, 206–210, 223, 227, 236, 246
  atonement for. See Jesus Christ.
  consequence of, 22–23, 196, 206–214
  origin of, 22, 22n10, 185–87
society, organization of
  democracy, 19, 111–13, 115, 134n37, 194
  freedom of conscience, 134–35
  freedom of religion, 27, 27n29, 112, 114–15, 133–35, 227
  human rights, 19, 111–15, 132, 134, 194
  independent sovereign spheres, 133
  legal positivism, 134
  natural law, 132–33
  social laws, 132, 200
  theocracy, 133, 194
  value system, 133–34
soteriology
  assurance of salvation, 29, 29n13
  inclusivism, 204
  made righteous/justified. See Jesus Christ.
  moral accountability, 64, 64n12, 185, 199, 212–13
  particularism, 204
  salvation by grace, 24, 29, 58, 88–89, 98, 104, 112, 118, 195, 200
  salvation by works, 58, 104
statistical concepts
  Bayes' Rule/Bayes' Theorem, 15–17, 36, 40, 252, 255, 257, 262
  chance. See chance.

decision theory. See decision theory.
designed experiment, 148n44, 232n38
game theory, 15n20, 131, 268–69, 268n4
likelihood ratio, 251
observational study, 148n44, 232n38
odds, 14, 39n16, 265–66
posterior odds, 252
prior odds, 251
probability. See probability.

theology
  historical critical method for, 96, 146n39
  liberal, 21, 104, 220
  natural, 56, 202, 262
  replacement/supersessionism, 118
  scholastic, 110, 139
  systematic, 21
  voluntarist, 110, 138n11, 139, 179
truth
  coherence theory of, 10n14
  consequence of a decision, 10–12
  correspondence theory of, 10n14, 12n15

Wager, xv–xvi, 12–17, 14n19, 20, 33, 37, 43, 43n22, 51, 54–56, 56n61, 78, 92, 245, 268
  Aposteriori, xvin1, 16–17, 33, 36, 39–46, 58–60, 92, 203n79, 237n12, 249, 255, 266, 268
  Canonical, 14n19, 57n61, 268
  Ecumenical, 56, 60
  Jamesian, 56n61
  Pascal's, xv–xvi, 6, 11, 14n19, 16, 56, 57n61, 59, 78n4, 103
Wager, objections
  Avarice charge/cupidity, 55
  lack of evidential reasons, 51–54
  many gods, 56–58
  prudential reasons, 54–55
  unethical, 55
willingness attitude, of decision maker
  desire for inner peace, 80–81

willingness attitude (*continued*)
    desire for meaning, 81–82
    desire to be loved unconditionally, 82
    doesn't need God, 90
    doesn't want God, 90–91
    neutral, 42–43, 83
    not good enough, 88
    nothing to lose, 78–80
    self-control, 86
    too busy with life, 86–88
    too simple or odd, 88–90
    wanting to know the truth first, 83–85

Scripture Index

Genesis
1   68n21, 138n5, 149n46
1:1–5   153n58
1:1–2   22n6
1:14–19   153, 153n54
1:27   138n8
1:28–30   26n26
1:28   138n12
1:31   22, 22n9, 138n7, 172n113
2:7   158, 158n73
2:21   158, 158n73
2:24   193, 193n36
3:1–7   22n11
3:1   22n10
3:5   129n15
3:14–15   23n17
3:15   207n100
3:17   159, 159n74
3:22   129n15
5:24   240n21
6:13—8:19   150n48
9:6   195n45
12:1–3   116n55
13:14–17   116n56
15:1–20   116n56
15:16   198n57
17:1–18   116n56
17:20–27   116n57
20:1–17   222n187
21:1–6   116n57
26:1–32   222n188
27   222n189

Exodus
2   113n48
2:11–13   222n190
7:8–13   229n15
12:46   221n180
17:8–16   197n55
20–30   116n58
20:3   105n5, 129n16
20:13   195n45
20:18–19   211n128
21:16   193n35
22:21–27   195n43
28–29   217n159
31:1–11   113n47
31:15–17   149n46
33:12–23   211n123
33:20   210n121
34:28–35   211n130
34:29–35   211n123
36:26–27   28n3

Leviticus
1–17   209n114
8–10   209n115
16   209n116
17   210n119
18:20–30   198n56
19:18   194n41
19:34   55n56
23:26–32   209n116
24:22   192, 192n33
25   195n43
25:39   193n35

Numbers
9:12   221n180
25   197n54
31   197n54

SCRIPTURE INDEX

Deuteronomy
2	197n53
6:5	194n41
6:10-19	195n42
6:10-11	198n59
7:7-8	119n75
7:22	198n58
8:1-5	236n5
13:1-4	195n42
15:7-15	193, 193n34
18:15	23n17
18:18-19	118n64
20:5-8	194n38
20:10	194n38
20:16-18	199n61
24:10-22	195n43
30:11-14	129n15
32:16-17	22n10

Joshua
1:1-9	113n48
2:8-11	196-97, 197n51
2:9-13	117n59
3	198n57
6	216n152
6:1-30	215n148
8	216n152
12-13	198n58
23:7	198n58
24:2	192n31

Judges
2:10-13	198n58
3:13	197n55
6:3-7	197n55
6:11—8:21	113n48
6:33	197n55

1 Samuel
10:25-27	215n149
15	197n55
15:1-6	118n63
30	198n58

2 Samuel
7:8-16	23n17
11	222n191
12:23	64n12

1 Kings
1-11	239n14
8:1-11	211n129
10:10-13	216n153
11:9-13	240n20
22	215n151

2 Kings
2:11	240n21
17:7-41	216n154
20:20	215n150
21:1-18	241n22

1 Chronicles
4:43	198n58
17:14	118n65
21:1	22n10

2 Chronicles
7:1-2	211n129
33:1-20	241n22

Ezra
7	221n185

Esther
3:10	198n58

Job
1-42	187n13
1-2	51n40, 88n37
1:7—2:7	22n10
1:8-13	45n25
20:28	149n46

Psalms
8	169n103
14:1-3	72n6
14:1	79, 79n10
16:10	221n182
19	169n103
19:1-7	140, 140n20
20:1	149n46
22:19	221n178
23:6	240n21
32:8	29n11
34:19-20	236n8
34:20	221n180
41:2-3	195n43

73	188n15	18:1–4	221n176
89:35–38	118n68	23:9–40	229n15
103:8–18	191, 191n29	29:10–11	197, 197n52
106:35–37	22n10	31:31–33	195, 195n44
110	118n67	31:35–36	119n74
133	108n26	32:27	119n74
139:1–18	66n16	32:36—33:26	197n52
139:5	189n20	32:38–41	119n72
139:13–16	68, 68n24		

Proverbs

Ezekiel

1–4	98n19	1–2	211n124
3:1–8	231n34	18	196n50
6:16–19	128n11	28	231n34
8–9	98n19	28:12–17	22n10
11:4	149n46	33:11	203n77
11:24–31	195n43	38:8	119n74
29:18	201n71		

Daniel

Ecclesiastes

1:12–14	240, 240n17	1–4	241n24
3:11	66, 66n15	1	231n32
3:18–20	201n71	7:13–14	89n44, 221n183
12:13	240, 240n19	9	223n199
		9:24–27	221n184
Isaiah		10:1–10	211n125
		12	223n199
6:1–8	210, 210n122	12:2	240n21
7:14	220n174		
7:16	64n12	Hosea	
9:1–7	220n175	6:1–2	221n182
9:7	118n67		
10:1–4	195n43	Joel	
11:10–12	119n74	2:12–14	203n77
14:12–15	22n10	2:28–29	123n98
26:9–11	196n49		
43:7	185:5	Amos	
53	23n17, 118n66, 207n100	1–9	195n43
		Jonah	
53:1–12	221n177	1–4	196n48
53:9	221n180	2:1	221n182
53:10	221n183		
55:9	138n10	Micah	
61:8–9	117n60	5:2	220n173
62	197n52	7:9	196n50
		7:18–20	196n50
Jeremiah		Nahum	
10:1–16	105n8	1:13–15	215n147

SCRIPTURE INDEX 311

14:17–25	210n120	1:35–51	82n18
14:66–72	223n194	3:3	29n6
		3:8	29n10
Luke		3:16–18	213n141
1:26–38	220n174	3:16–17	246, 246n4
2	89n40	4	219n168
2:1–21	220n173	4:1–42	228n8
5:1–11	81, 81n17	4:53	229n17
6:22	187n13	6:14–15	229n19
7:36–50	227, 227n5	6:44	28n2
9:28–36	211n126	8:31–59	90n48
9:51–56	222n192	9	187n13, 229n18
10:8–11	27n29	9:41	64n12
10:21	72n3, 245n1	10:7–10	100n24
10:25–37	111n36	10:10–15	201n68
10:27	55n56, 69, 69n25	11:16	84n27
11:9–10	203, 203n78	11:45–53	86n33, 231n35
12:48	72n5	11:45	229n20
13:1–5	187n13	11:46–53	213n138
13:18–21	133n34	12:42–43	86n31
14:15–23	87n35	13:1–17	89n43
14:22–30	213n137	13:35	108n26
14:27–30	76, 76n1	14:6–7	70n31
15:1–10	213n142	14:6	104n3, 204n86, 214n144, 246, 246n3
15:1–7	203n77		
15:11–32	70, 70n30	14:11	72n4
16:9	240n16	15:18–25	32n21
16:13	240n16	15:22–25	72n5
16:24–26	204n87	15:23–25	90n49
16:31	72n7	16:8–10	28n4
17:20–21	133n34	16:9	208n109
18:15–17	64, 64n11	17:3	98, 98n20
19:1–10	219n168	17:5	185n4
19:1–9	228n9	17:21–23	108n26
19:47–48	219n168	17:24	185n4
21:7–24	223n199	18:31–33	218n162
22:14–30	210n120	18:36	199n63
22:54–62	223n194	19:31–33	221n180
23:39–43	204n84	19:34–35	221n179
23:43	24n20	19:35–37	219n169
24:47	121n86	19:36	221n180
		20:24–29	71, 71n2
John			
1:1–4	22n6, 67–68, 68n21	Acts	
1:1–3	153, 153n58	1–2	219n170
1:3	138n6	1:8	121n87
1:12	30n14	1:11	223n197
1:18	70n31, 211, 211n132	2:1–47	120n77

Acts (*continued*)		5:18–19	208n110
2:1–41	80n14	5:20–21	130n19
2:1–40	122n90	6	29n8
2:37–39	80, 80n15	7:8–10	64, 64n12
2:47	122n91	7:14	23n14
3	230n23	7:21–25	130, 130n21
4:4	230n23	7:21	23n14
5:1–11	201n68	8:1–17	29n7, 105n10
5:33–39	123n96	8:3–6	130, 130n22
7:54–60	122n92	8:3	23n14
8	23n15, 120n80, 122n93	8:14–17	30n14
		8:15–16	29n13
8:4–13	230n24	8:19–22	172n113, 187, 187n12
9:1–30	228n7		
9:1–19	4, 4n2, 229n21	9:6–8	118n71
9:1–18	243n26	10:9–14	204, 204n89
9:10–25	120n81	10:9–10	86n32, 246–47, 247n5
11:19–30	120n82		
12:20–23	201n68	11:25–32	119n72
13–14	120n83	12	30n15
13:4–12	230n25	12:4–8	123n98
15:36–20:38	120n84	12:14	89n42
15:36–41	223n195	13:13–14	225, 225n207
16:22–34	83, 83n23	14:17	133n34
17:22–23	34, 34n3		
17:32–33	89n45	1 Corinthians	
18:12–17	219n165	1:18–31	32n21
20:24	78n6	1:18–25	89n41, 245, 245n1
26:4–18	243n26	1:20–29	231n34
28:11–31	120n85	1:23	89n45
		2:6–15	246n2
Romans		2:13–16	90n46
1:18–25	201n71	2:14—3:4	23n13
1:18–23	169n102	9:14–22	105n9
1:20	202, 202n76	10:13	236, 236n9
2:9–20	28n5	10:31	68n23
2:14–16	203n83	11:23–32	210n120
2:14–15	129, 129n15, 129n17	12:4–10	123n98
3:9–10	23n16	13:12	191n25, 237n10
3:21–31	89n39	14	123n98
3:22–25	88, 88n38	14:14	23n13
3:23	28n5	14:23–24	232n37
3:25–26	240n21	14:29	232n38
4:1–13	240n21	15:3–8	218n163
5:12–21	209n112	15:4–8	229n22
5:12–14	23n16	15:13–19	85n29
5:13–14	208n110	15:21–22	209, 209n112
5:17–19	159, 159n76	15:35–58	24n19

15:39	160, 160n78
15:45	160, 160n78

2 Corinthians

2:14–17	199n29
3:7–8	211n130
4:7	108n25
5:1–5	24n19
5:8	24n20
5:10	204n87
7:8–11	236n6
10:3–5	199n63
11:14	214n144

Galatians

1:18–19	218n163
2:15–21	118n69
2:21	212n133
5:16–21	128n11
5:17–21	23n14
5:19–21	106n15
5:22–26	29n9, 128n12, 227n4

Ephesians

1:3–12	23n17
1:9–10	185, 185n7
1:11–12	185n5
2:1–6	69n29
2:8	28n5
2:14–18	199n63
3:17–19	69, 69n28
4:11–13	123n98
4:17–32	107n21
5:17	29n11
6:10–18	45n25, 199n63

Philippians

1:22–24	24n20
3:7–16	78n6
3:10–11	32n22

Colossians

1:9	29n11
1:16–19	68, 68n22
1:16–17	138n6
1:16	22n8
1:26–27	23n17
4:14	231n31

1 Thessalonians

5:20–22	232n38
5:23	23n13

2 Thessalonians

2:1–12	223n199
2:9–12	229n15

1 Timothy

1:12–17	243n26
1:13–14	243, 243n27
1:18–20	108n24
2:4	203n77

2 Timothy

3:1–9	223n201
3:16–17	21n4
3:16	139n16, 191n27

Hebrews

1:3	185n8
2:4	229n16
3:13	90n51
4:4–6	203n83
4:12	23n13, 49:33, 224, 224n206
4:14–16	189, 189n20
8–10	210n118
9:27	204n87
10:15–17	118n70
11:1	47, 47n28
11:3	138n6
11:4	209n117
11:5	240n21
11:6	205, 205n90
12:5–8	236, 236n5
12:9–13	236n5
12:21	211n123
12:23	24n20, 237n10

James

1:13	236n4
2:14–26	69n27
2:19	51, 51n40

1 Peter

1:20	23n17
1:23	29n6
2:4–6	30n16

1 Peter (*continued*)
2:21–25	32n22
3:9	89n42
4:14	187n13
4:15	188n18

2 Peter
1:16–18	211n126
1:20–21	21n4
2	108n24
2:4	21n10
3:8–9	203, 203n77
3:9	55n57
3:15–16	191n28

1 John
3:8–9	109n28
4:1	232n38
4:16–18	228n6

Jude
6	22n10

Revelation
1:9–20	211n127
9:20–21	213n138
11:1–14	224n204
12	119n72
12:7–10	22n10
12:10–13	45n25
13	223n199, 224n203
13:15	229n15
20:10–14	213n139
20:11–15	201n70, 212n134
21:1–7	188n15
21:27	237n10
22:1–3	158, 158n71

www.ingramcontent.com/pod-product-compliance
Lightning Source LLC
Chambersburg PA
CBHW050617300426
44112CB00012B/1540

Habakkuk

1–2	188n15
1:2–4	189, 189n19

Zechariah

3:1–3	88n37
3:1	22n10
8:18–23	117n61
11:12–13	221n176
12	119n72
12:10	221n179
14	223n199

Malachi

3:5	195n43

Matthew

1–2	89n40
1:21	207n100
1:23	220n175
4:7	148n44
4:18–22	81n17
5:11	187n13
5:12–14	108n23
5:17–20	199–200, 200n66
5:17–19	191n26
5:38–48	23n14, 89n42, 199n63
5:38–45	186–87, 187n11
6:19–21	240n16
6:19–20	69n26
7:7–12	203n78
7:7–8	50, 50n35
7:12	26n27, 111, 111n35, 130n20, 194n41
7:15–20	29n9
7:15–18	109, 109n28
7:24–29	236n7
8:14	213n139
11:20–24	72n5
11:25–26	53, 53:49, 245n1
11:28–30	28n2, 80, 80n13
12:38–41	221n182
13:20–21	76n1
13:24–30	214n143
13:44	99, 99n23
13:47–52	214n143
15:1–2	200n67
16:1–4	72n8, 202n76
16:21	24n17
17:1–8	211n126
17:20	50n36
17:22–23	24n17
19:3–8	193–94, 194n37
19:19	55, 55n56
20:1–16	206n95
20:17–19	24n17
20:20–28	222n193
20:25–28	89n42
22:34–38	231, 231n33
22:36–40	69n25
22:37	23n13
22:39	55n56
24:1–22	223n199, 224n204
24:14	223n200
24:24	229n15
24:32–36	223n198
25:1–12	213n137
25:31–46	24n18, 212n134
25:31–40	206n96
26:20–29	210n120
26:69–75	223n194
27:9	221n176
27:15–26	221n177
27:35	221n178
27:57–60	221n181
28:11–15	86n33
28:18–20	27n29, 86n32, 121n86

Mark

1:14–20	81n17
4:1–20	87n36
4:26–32	133, 133n34
6:1–6	231n30
6:6–13	121n89
6:10–11	27n29
6:52–53	218n162
7:1–9	200n67
7:5–14	21n4
9:2–8	211n126
9:14–26	189, 189n18
9:43–48	213n139
12:30	23n13
12:31	55n56
13:22	229n15